THE OXFORD
BOOK OF
CANADIAN
SHORT STORIES
IN ENGLISH

THE OXFORD BOOK OF CANADIAN SHORT STORIES
IN ENGLISH

SELECTED BY
MARGARET ATWOOD & ROBERT WEAVER

TORONTO   OXFORD   NEW YORK
OXFORD UNIVERSITY PRESS
1986

CANADIAN CATALOGUING IN PUBLICATION DATA
Main entry under title:
The Oxford book of Canadian short stories in
English
ISBN 0-19-540565-X

1. Short stories, Canadian (English).*
2. Canadian fiction (English)—19th century.*
3. Canadian fiction (English)—20th century.*
I. Atwood, Margaret, 1939- . II. Weaver,
Robert, 1921- .

PS8319.095 1986   C813'.01'08   C86-094632-0
PR9197.32.095 1986

1 2 3 4 - 9 8 7 6
Printed in Canada by John Deyell Company

Contents

Acknowledgements

EDNA ALFORD. 'Mid-May's Eldest Child' reprinted from *A Sleep Full of Dreams* by Edna Alford with permission of the publisher Oolichan Books.

MARGARET ATWOOD. 'The Sin Eater' from *Bluebeard's Egg* by Margaret Atwood. © 1983, 1986 by O.W. Toad, Ltd. First American edition 1986. Reprinted by permission of The Canadian Publishers, McClelland and Stewart Limited, Toronto, Houghton Mifflin Company, and Jonathan Cape Ltd.

SANDRA BIRDSELL. 'The Wild Plum Tree' is reprinted by permission from *Night Travellers* © Sandra Birdsell, 1982 (Turnstone Press, Winnipeg).

CLARK BLAISE. 'A Class of New Canadians' from *A North American Education* by Clark Blaise. Copyright © 1970 by Clark Blaise. Reprinted by permission of Doubleday & Company, Inc.

GEORGE BOWERING. 'A Short Story' from *A Place to Die* by George Bowering. Used by permission of Oberon Press.

BARRY CALLAGHAN. 'The Black Queen' from *The Black Queen Stories* by Barry Callaghan. Used by permission of Lester & Orpen Dennys Ltd.

MORLEY CALLAGHAN. 'Last Spring They Came Over' from *Morley Callaghan's Stories* © 1959 by Morley Callaghan. Reprinted by permission of Macmillan of Canada, A Division of Canada Publishing Corporation.

AUSTIN C. CLARKE. 'Griff!' from *When Women Rule* by Austin Clarke. Used by permission of The Canadian Publishers, McClelland and Stewart Limited, Toronto and Harold Ober Associates Incorporated.

MATT COHEN. 'The Eiffel Tower In Three Parts' is used by permission of the author.

MARIAN ENGEL. 'Anita's Dance' from *The Tattooed Woman* by Marian Engel. Copyright © The Estate of Marian Engel 1985. Reprinted by permission of Penguin Books Canada Limited.

TIMOTHY FINDLEY. 'Dinner Along the Amazon' from *Dinner Along the Amazon* by Timothy Findley. Copyright © Pebble Productions Inc., 1984. Reprinted by permission of Penguin Books Canada Limited.

MAVIS GALLANT. 'The Ice Wagon Going Down the Street' from *Home Truths* © 1956 by Mavis Gallant. Reprinted by permission of Macmillan of Canada, A Division of Canada Publishing Corporation and Jonathan Cape Ltd. Copyright © 1981 by Mavis Gallant. Reprinted by permission of Random House, Inc.

HUGH GARNER. 'One, Two, Three Little Indians' from *Hugh Garner's Best Stories* Copyright © Hugh Garner. Reprinted by permission of McGraw-Hill Ryerson Limited.

KATHERINE GOVIER. 'Sociology' from *Fables of Brunswick Avenue* by Katherine Govier. Copyright © Katherine Govier 1985. Reprinted by permission of Penguin Books Canada Limited.

JACK HODGINS. 'By the River' from *Spit Delaney's Island* © 1976 by Jack Hodgins. Reprinted by permission of Macmillan of Canada, A Division of Canada Publishing Corporation.

HUGH HOOD. 'Flying a Red Kite' from *Flying a Red Kite* used by permission of the author.

W.P. KINSELLA. 'The Thrill of the Grass' from *The Thrill of the Grass* by W.P. Kinsella. Copyright © W.P. Kinsella 1984. Reprinted by permission of Penguin Books Canada Limited.

MARGARET LAURENCE. 'The Loons' Copyright © 1966 by Margaret Laurence. From *A Bird In the House* by Margaret Laurence. Reprinted by permission of: Alfred A. Knopf Inc.; The Canadian Publishers, McClelland and Stewart Limited, Toronto; and Macmillan Publishers Ltd.

STEPHEN LEACOCK. 'The Marine Excursion of the Knights of Pythias' from *Sunshine Sketches of a Little Town* by Stephen Leacock. Used by permission of The Canadian Publishers, McClelland and Stewart Limited, Toronto.

NORMAN LEVINE. 'We All Begin in a Little Magazine' from *Thin Ice*. Used by permission of the author.

JOYCE MARSHALL. 'The Old Woman' used by permission of the author.

BHARATI MUKHERJEE. 'The Lady From Lucknow' from *Darkness* by Bharati Mukherjee. Copyright © Bharati Mukherjee 1985. Reprinted by permission of Penguin Books Canada Limited.

ALICE MUNRO. 'The Peace of Utrecht' from *Dance of the Happy Shades* by Alice Munro. Reprinted by permission of McGraw-Hill Ryerson Limited and Virginia Barber Literary Agency Inc.

THOMAS RADDALL. 'The Wedding Gift' from *The Wedding Gift* by Thomas Raddall. Used by permission of The Canadian Publishers, McClelland and Stewart Limited, Toronto and the author.

JAMES REANEY. 'The Bully' from *Canadian Short Stories*, edited by Robert Weaver and Helen James, Oxford University Press Canada, 1952, thanks are due to the author.

MORDECAI RICHLER. 'The Summer My Grandmother Was Supposed to Die' from *The Street* by Mordecai Richler. Used by permission of The Canadian Publishers, McClelland and Stewart Limited, Toronto.

CHARLES G.D. ROBERTS. 'Do Seek Their Meat from God' from *Earth's Enigmas* by Charles G.D. Roberts. Used by permission of The Canadian Publishers, McClelland and Stewart Limited, Toronto.

LEON ROOKE. 'The Woman Who Talked to Horses' from *Sing Me No Love Songs I'll Say You No Prayers* by Leon Rooke, copyright © 1984 by Leon Rooke. Published by The Ecco Press in 1984. Reprinted by permission.

SINCLAIR ROSS. 'The Lamp at Noon' from *The Lamp at Noon and Other Stories* by Sinclair Ross. Used by permission of The Canadian Publishers, McClelland and Stewart Limited, Toronto.

JANE RULE. 'Slogans' reprinted from *Inland Passage and other Stories* by Jane Rule, Naiad Press 1985, with permission of the publisher and the author, and Lester & Orpen Dennys Limited.

GLORIA SAWAI. 'The Day I Sat With Jesus on The Sundeck and the Wind Came Up and Blew My Kimono Open and He Saw My Breasts' used by permission of the author.

DUNCAN CAMPBELL SCOTT. 'The Desjardins' from *In the Village of Viger*. Used by permission of John G. Aylen.

RAY SMITH. 'Cape Breton Is the Thought Control Centre of Canada' from *Cape Breton Is the Thought Control Centre of Canada*. Used by permission of the author.

AUDREY THOMAS. 'Kill Day on the Government Wharf' is used by permission of the author.

W.D. VALGARDSON. 'Bloodflowers' is reprinted from *Bloodflowers* by W.D. Valgardson by permission of Oberon Press and W.D. Valgardson.

GUY VANDERHAEGHE. 'Dancing Bear' from *Man Descending* © 1982 by Guy Vander-haeghe. Reprinted by permission of Macmillan of Canada, A Division of Canada Publishing Corporation.

HELEN WEINZWEIG. 'Causation' © Helen Weinzweig from *Small Wonders*. Used by permission of the author and CBC Enterprises/Les Entreprises Radio-Canada.

RUDY WIEBE. 'Where Is the Voice Coming From?' from *Where Is the Voice Coming From?* by Rudy Wiebe. Used by permission of The Canadian Publishers, McClelland and Stewart Limited, Toronto.

ETHEL WILSON. 'From Flores' from *Mrs Golightly and Other Stories* © Ethel Wilson 1961. Reprinted by permission of Macmillan of Canada, A Division of Canada Publishing Corporation.

Introduction

I. BY MARGARET ATWOOD

I read my first Canadian short stories as a child, although I didn't think of them as Canadian. Stephen Leacock was doled out in school as an example of humour, and earlier I had sniffled my way through Sir Charles G.D. Roberts' *Kings In Exile* and Ernest Thompson Seton's *Wild Animals I Have Known*, both of which were filled with stories about the deaths of wild animals and were therefore considered suitable as Christmas presents for small Canadian children of that generation. I will probably always associate boxes of chocolates with trapped wolves.

But the first Canadian short stories I read knowingly were in an anthology called, unmistakably, *Canadian Short Stories*. It was edited by Robert Weaver, which makes our co-editing of this collection both a pleasure and a piece of poetic justice, since it's to him that I owe my first impressions of the literary uses to which snow, dust, the edges of lonely highways, and the denizens of forbidding small towns may be put. That was in 1959, when I was an aspiring writer of nineteen; I immediately composed several stories in which bleakness was well to the fore.

That I should have stumbled across these short stories long before I got my hands on much of anything resembling a Canadian novel was perhaps chance, but it may also have reflected the state of affairs at the time. The novel had flourished earlier, but the publishing of Canadian novels had been blighted by the Depression, the war, and the advent of the foreign-controlled paperback industry. In the late fifties, short stories were more easily publishable—in magazines and through Robert Weaver's CBC radio program *Anthology*—than were novels.

This may be one of the factors that account for the short story's relative popularity, both with writers and with readers, in Anglophone Canada, where it is possible for writers such as Alice Munro and Mavis Gallant to write nothing but short stories and be considered major; nor is a book of short stories excluded, by its genre, from best-seller lists. For whatever reasons, the form has been practised by many writers; Canadian poets have frequently taken a crack at it, and many novelists—though not all—have also done so. This remains true despite the shrivelling of traditional magazine and radio markets and the shift to little-magazine publication. With such abundance, variety, and quality on hand, any editor would find it impossible to make an all-inclusive selection.

In Wales, which is the only other area I know of where the story has such comparative importance, this fact is ascribed to the poverty of the writers: few can live by their writing, so few have the time to complete novels. This may once have been true in Canada, but the short story here has had a different genesis and line of descent. Canada as a territory was 'discovered' at about the same time as was the United States; but with the exception of Québec, Newfoundland, and the Maritimes, the bulk of European settlement came much later, in the nineteenth century rather than the seventeenth; and the nation did not coalesce from its separate colonies until 1867. Under frontier and colonial conditions, poetry was the first literary form to appear in significant quantity and quality, perhaps because it was short, perhaps because it was so popular in the nineteenth century, perhaps because the imagination, confronted by geographical and cultural surroundings alien to it, begins with lyric description. The novel—which, with the exception of the adventure story, requires a social structure within which its characters can live through time—emerged later. The short story, however, preceded it, and it's worth noting that three of the earliest story writers in this collection were primarily poets.

But several forms of short prose narrative were written before people got around to talking about art, and I like to think that the Canadian short story owes something to them, as recent poetry certainly does. These were the explorers' journals, which were naturally episodic, and the later travellers' accounts, such as Anna Jamieson's, and descriptions of the country, such as Susanna Moodie's and Joseph Howe's, which also contain many 'character sketches' and short narrative episodes. The short story in Québec draws from the *fabliau* and from the oral fairy-tale traditions there, and that of English Canada has frequently made use of its own oral forms, the tall tale or yarn, the local—usually scandalous or supernatural—legend, and the joke. The Jamesian psychological study and the Zolaesque slice of life are only two of the Canadian short story's many forebears.

What, if anything, distinguishes a 'Canadian' short story from one of any other kind? Individually considered, probably nothing. There is no essence of Canada that, sprinkled on a piece of prose fiction, will magically transform it. A Canadian short story may or may not be set in the frozen North or trackless wilderness and contain snow, beavers, Mounties, Inuit, or dead animals, but these days the odds are against it; Mounties in particular have become somewhat scarce. Nor is the place of origin of the writer any necessary clue. Twelve per cent of Canada's population was not born there. Several of the writers in this collection first saw the light of day elsewhere; several spent their childhoods here but now live in other countries. The definition of 'Canadian short story', like that of 'Canadian' itself, has a hard core with fuzzy edges. Nor is style an indication: Canadian short-story writers are now as eclectic in their approach as story writers elsewhere in the English-speaking world.

When the Canadian short story is considered not singly but as a body of work, however, a few generalizations can be made. One is the rela- tively large number of woman writers who have, despite adverse social conditions—women were not legally 'persons' in Canada until 1929, for instance—made contributions of a high order to the tradition. Of the writers in this book born before 1930, a third are women; of those born after, almost a half. I don't know the reason for this, though I could speculate about it—the relative literacy of the nineteenth-century women settlers, the fact that in a frontier society the arts tend to be left to the women while men go around chopping trees—but the result, achieved without any editorial arm-twisting, remains. When you count age instead of sex, another telling statistic emerges: of the writers in this book, five- sixths are still alive, half are fifty-five and under, and almost a third are under fifty, which testifies to the remarkable and by now often remarked- upon explosion of talent in the sixties and seventies, an explosion that was not unconnected with a general increase in national consciousness and confidence at that time. In addition, there has been a noteworthy upsurge of writing in the West. Among the writers born before 1930, only three out of seventeen were from west of Ontario. Of those born after 1930, an astonishing twelve out of twenty-one are either from the West or currently living there. One last, sad statistic: in the stories presented here, Indians frequently appear as characters, but none of the stories is by an Indian or Inuit. I hope that this situation will change, as Indian and Inuit writers begin to claim their own territory through writing, as they have in the visual arts.

So much for demographics. What about the stories themselves? Here I'm tempted to abdicate and simply let the reader read, and draw his or her own conclusions; but I will attempt a few suggestions.

Canada shares with all of the New World ex-colonies, and with others such as Australia and New Zealand, the historically recent experience of a collision between a landscape and a language and social history not at first indigenous to it, with each side altering the other. 'The land was ours before we were the land's', Robert Frost intoned, speaking of the American collision; but it's not the sort of statement a Canadian writer would be likely to make. For one thing the land—being vast, northern, and cold—is not as a whole nearly so possessible, imaginatively and otherwise. In relation to Canadian geography, Frost's confidence would appear misplaced. Is the land 'ours' or its own? Are we the land's? Just what do we mean by 'ours', and who anyway are 'we,' multiple as we find ourselves? Just who really lives here, and what do we mean when we say 'living here'? Such questions are not far in the background of such stories as Joyce Marshall's 'The Old Woman' and Margaret Laurence's 'The Loons', and hover between the lines of many another Canadian short story as well. The collision between mind and land continues, as new groups of immigrants arrive and attempt in their turn to describe the double impact.

One of the first orders of business under colonial conditions is what we would call straight speech, the attempt to describe observed reality as it is, and not through imported conventions that may not apply to it. Realism of this kind, then—as in Sinclair Ross's 'The Lamp at Noon' and Hugh Garner's 'One, Two, Three Little Indians'—has been a constant presence in the Canadian story, and it is still alive and well, as witness the work of Edna Alford and Sandra Birdsell, among others.

But in a new colony this sort of realism—local or regional in its application—is not succeeded by more international perspectives, but exists with them simultaneously. English Canadians, not being autochthonous, often have itchy feet. The movement of the imagination across oceans and national boundaries is a constant motif. Often, as in Mavis Gallant's 'The Ice Wagon Going Down The Street', 'here' and 'I' are defined by juxtaposition with 'there' and 'them'.

Realism, however, whether of setting or psyche, has never been the only string on the fiddle. Even Leacock is a surrealist of a kind, or perhaps we might say a non-realist; and with James Reaney's strange story 'The Bully', with Gloria Sawai's extravaganza on the prairie manifestation of Jesus, and with Leon Rooke's talking horses, we are obviously being made to dance to other tunes as well. Some writers have borrowed techniques from non-fictional genres to expand the short story's usual range—see, for instance, Rudy Wiebe's and Ray Smith's transformations of historical method—and several, such as George Bowering and Matt Cohen, have experimented with techniques that draw attention to the artificiality of art.

This brings me to the end of my generalities. A body of work cannot be more than the sum of its parts unless the parts are worthwhile, and although the reader may emerge from this book having gained at least an impression that such an animal as the Canadian short story does indeed exist, my main hope is that she or he will enjoy the individual voices gathered here, and the individual stories they tell. From the evidence, I expect readers will conclude that the short story continues to grow, flourish, mutate, and re-seed itself in English Canada with as much exuberance as the dandelion—once also a transplant and now prolific as . . . well, as short stories. In my role as co-editor I could wish that there weren't so many of them; but as a reader I'm glad that there are.

II. BY ROBERT WEAVER

When I began working for the radio service of the Canadian Broadcasting Corporation in 1948 one of my first assignments was to edit a series of readings called 'Canadian Short Stories'. It was a weekly 15-minute program, which meant that the stories we broadcast all had to be about 2,000 words long, and the writers were paid $35 for their work. This was a modest enough beginning to what would become, to my own surprise, almost a life's work. In a year or so we managed to increase the fee for short stories to $50. Writers always need money and we, alas, had little enough to offer them. But writers also need to be published, to be read in the magazines, to have their voices heard. We sent begging letters across the country, not only to writers but also to other editors and to book publishers, saying that there was a market at the CBC, and manuscripts began to find their way to us. From time to time we were also able to schedule longer stories on 'CBC Wednesday Night', CBC Radio's prestige series of documentaries, dramas, and musical programs.

By 1952 we had broadcast enough good stories that I was able—with Helen James, who worked with me on several literary programs—to put together an anthology of stories that had received their first publication as broadcasts on the CBC. This book, *Canadian Short Stories* (1952), was the beginning of my long association with Oxford Canada. I can't help but take pleasure in noting that among the stories Margaret Atwood and I chose for this new collection, three were in that first anthology: Joyce Marshall's 'The Old Woman', Hugh Garner's 'One, Two, Three Little Indians', and James Reaney's 'The Bully'.

It was my good fortune that my early years as an editor and broadcaster coincided with the growth of Canadian writing during the 1950s. It has been pointed out—by me, among others—that through all of the 1950s only a handful of writers in Canada were able to have a book of their own stories published, whereas by the 1970s and 1980s more short-fiction collections than this would routinely appear in every publishing season. It could also be a grindingly slow process establishing one's credentials as a writer of fiction in Canada in the 1950s. Alice Munro was a young writer at the beginning of the decade, and in the years that followed her stories were published in *The Montrealer, The Tamarack Review, The Canadian Forum, Chatelaine*, and were broadcast on 'Anthology', the successor at the CBC to the 'Canadian Short Stories' program. But she had to wait more than fifteen years before her first collection of stories, *Dance of the Happy Shades* (1968), appeared. This long apprenticeship stood her in good stead as a writer, but it was a frustration that no one approaching her calibre encountered in the 1970s and 1980s.

Nevertheless the period following 1948 was in many respects a fine and hopeful time for writers and editors. In the 1950s Ethel Wilson—a marvellous older writer, a true late-bloomer—was presiding in Vancouver. Young writers as different as Mordecai Richler, Brian Moore, Hugh Hood, and Norman Levine had made their appearance. Mavis Gallant was contributing stories to *The New Yorker* and her first collection was published in 1956. Margaret Laurence began to publish her African stories in Canadian and American magazines. The CBC was still a relatively small and informal place to work, and public broadcasting, in Canada and other countries, was still thought to be important by its critics as well as by its supporters. *The Tamarack Review* was founded in Toronto in 1956 and survived for twenty-five years. (William Toye, my editor at Oxford, and I were two of the magazine's founding editors.) The Canada Council was established in 1957 and soon began to change the face of writing and publishing across the country. And as if to crown the decade, *Morley Callaghan's Stories* was published in 1959: a big, retrospective collection of more than 50 stories that had first appeared in the expatriate 'little magazines' in Europe in the 1920s, and in the 1930s in such American periodicals as *The New Yorker, Scribner's*, and *Esquire*.

Today the position of the short story in Canadian writing is unassailable. There is a network of 'little magazines' across the country, and while there is some irony in the title of Norman Levine's short story in this book, 'We All Begin in a Little Magazine', most young fiction writers still begin there. Book publishers now compete for the opportunity to publish short-story collections. Most of the stories in this book were written in the last thirty-five years, when I had the privilege of knowing and working with many of the writers represented, and observing the growth of some remarkable talents. The richness of this period is apparent in the stories Margaret Atwood and I have chosen. But *The Oxford Book of Canadian Short Stories in English* has been compiled as a historical anthology—the writing covers more than 100 years, beginning when Canada scarcely had a literature in English. Here you will encounter both the familiar and the unfamiliar—forty-one stories in all—and it's our hope that the book's readers will find much to enjoy among renewed acquaintances and new discoveries.

ISABELLA VALANCY CRAWFORD

1850-1887

Extradited

'Oh, Sam! back so soon? Well, I'm glad.'

She had her arms round his neck. She curved serpent-wise in his clasp to get her eyes on his eye.

'How's mammy?' she asked, in a slight panic, 'not worse, is she?'

'Better,' returned Sam; he pushed her away mechanically, and glanced round the rude room with its touches of refinement: the stop organ against the wall of unplastered logs, the primitive hearth, its floor of hewn planks.

'Oh yes! Baby!' she exclaimed, 'you missed him; he's asleep on our bed; I'll fetch him.'

He caught her apron string, still staring round the apartment.

'Where's Joe, Bess? I don't see him round.'

Bessie crimsoned petulantly.

'You can think of the hired man first before me and Baby!'

'Baby's a sort of fixed fact. A hired man, ain't,' said Sam, slowly. 'Mebbe Joe's at the barn!'

'Maybe he is, and maybe he isn't,' retorted Bessie sharply. 'I didn't marry Samuel O'Dwyer to have a hired man set before me and my child, and I won't stand it—so there!'

'You needn't to,' said Sam, smiling. He was an Irish Canadian; a rich smack of brogue adorned his tongue; a kindly graciousness of eye made a plain face almost captivating, while the proud and melancholy Celtic fire and intentness of his glance gave dignity to his expression. The lips were curved in a humorous smile, but round them were deeply graven heroic and Spartan lines.

'Sure, darlin', isn't it you an' the boy are the pulses of my heart?' he said, smiling. 'Sure Joe can wait. I was sort of wonderin' at not seein' him—that's all. Say, I'll unhitch the horses. They've done fifteen miles o' mud holes an' corduroy since noon, an' then we'll have supper. I

1

could 'most eat my boots, so hurry up, woman darlin', or maybe it's the boy I'll be aitin', or the bit of a dog your daddy sent to him. Hear the baste howlin' like a banshee out yonder.'

'It's one of Cricket's last year's pups,' cried Bessie, running to the waggon. 'Wonder Father spared him; he thinks a sight of her pups. My! ain't he a beauty; won't baby just love him!'

She carried the yelping youngster into the house, while Sam took the horses to the barn, a primitive edifice of rough logs, standing in a bleak chaos of burned stumps, for 'O'Dwyer's Clearing' was but two years old, and had the rage of its clearing fires on it yet. The uncouth eaves were fine crimson on one side, from the sunset; on the other a delicate, spiritual silver, from the moon hanging above the cedar swamp; the rude doors stood open; a vigorous purple haze, shot with heavy bars of crimson light, filled the interior; a 'Whip-Poor-Will' chanted from a distant tree, like a muezzin from a minaret; the tired horses whinnied at a whiff of fresh clover, and rubbed noses in sedate congratulation. Sam looked at the ground a moment, reflectively, and then shouted:

'Hullo, Joe!'

'Hullo, Sam!'

By this time Sam was stooping over the waggon-tongue, his rugged face in the shadow, too intent on straps and buckles to glance up.

'Back all right, you see, Joe,' he remarked. 'How's things gettin' along?'

'Sublimely,' said Joe, coming to his assistance. 'I got the south corner cut—we've only to draw it tomorrow.'

'I never seen the beat of you at hard work,' remarked Sam. 'A slight young chap like you, too. It's just the spirit of you! But you mustn't outdo the strength that is in you for all that. I'm no slavedriver; I don't want your heart's blood. Sure, I've had your sweat two long years—an' the place shows it—it's had your sense an' sinews, so it had. I'll never forget it to you, Joe.'

Joe's tanned, nervous face was shaded by the flap of his limp straw hat. He looked piercingly at Sam, as the released horses walked decorously into the barn.

'Go to your supper, Sam,' he said. 'I'll bed them. I venture to say you're pretty sharp-set; go in.'

'I'll lend a hand first,' returned Sam. He followed the other into the barn.

'It's got dark in here suddenly,' remarked Joe. 'I'll get the lantern.'

'Don't,' said Sam, slowly. 'There's something to be spoke about betwixt you an' me, Joe, an' I'd as lieve say it in the dark; let the lantern be—I'd as lieve say it in the dark.'

'A thousand dollars!'

Bessie rose on her elbow and looked at her sleeping husband. Slumber brought the iron to the surface instead of melting it, and his face became sterner and more resolute in its repose. Its owner was not a man to be trifled with, she admitted as she gazed, and watching him she shivered slightly in the mournful moonlight. Many of her exceedingly respectable virtues were composed mainly of two or three minor vices: her conjugal love was a compound of vanity and jealousy; her maternal affection an agreement of rapacity and animal instinct. In giving her a child, nature had developed the she eagle in her breast. She was full of impotent, unrecognized impulses to prey on all things in her child's behalf. By training and habit she was honest, but her mind was becoming active with the ingenuity of self-cheatry. She held a quiet contempt for her husband, the unlearned man who had won the pretty schoolmistress; and, hedged in by the prim fence of routine knowledge and imperfect education, she despised the large crude movements of the untrained intellect, and the primitive power of the strong and lofty soul. He muttered uneasily as she slipped out of bed. The electric chill of the moonlight did not affect her spirit—she was not vulnerable to these hints and petitions of nature. She crept carefully into the great rude room, which was hall, parlor, and kitchen. The back log, which never died out, smouldered on the hearth. A block of moonlight fell like a slab of marble on the floor of loose planks which rattled faintly under her firm, bare foot. The wooden benches, the coarse table, the log walls, started through the gloom like bleak sentinels of the great Army of Privation. She looked at them without disgust, as she stole to the corner where her organ stood. She sang a silent little hymn of self-laudation.

'Some women would spend it on fine fallals for their backs or houses,' she thought. 'I won't. I'll bank every cent of it for baby. Money doubles in ten years. A thousand dollars will grow nicely in twenty—or I'll get Daddy to loan it out on farm mortgages. I guess Sam will stare twenty years hence when he finds how rich I've got to be. I'm glad I know my duty as a parent—Sam would never see things as I do—and a thousand dollars is a sight of money.'

She groped on the organ for her paper portefolio, an elegant trifle Joe had sent to the city for, to delicately grace her last birthday; its scent of violets guided her. She took from it a paper and pencil, and standing in the moonlight scribbled a few lines. She dotted her 'i's' and crossed her 't's' with particularity, and was finnickin in her nice folding of the written sheet. Her cool cheeks kept their steady pink; her round eyes their untroubled calm; her chin bridled a little with spiritual pride, as she cautiously opened the outer door.

'It's my clear duty as a parent and a citizen,' she thought, with self-approval, 'the thousand dollars would not tempt me if my duty were not so plainly set before me; and the money will be in good hands. I'm not one to spend it in vain show. Money's a great evil to a weak and worldly mind, but I'm not one for vain show.'

She looked up at the sky from under the morning glories Joe had thoughtfully planted to make cool shadows for her rocker in the porch.

'It will rain to-morrow. So I'll not wash till Friday; I wonder will that pink print Sam fetched home turn out a fast colour; I'll make it up for Baby; he'll look too cunning for anything in it, with those coral sleeve links Joe gave him. I hope he won't cry, and wake Sam before I get back.'

He did not. As she had left him she found him on her return, a little snowy ball, curled up against his father's massive shoulder, the beautiful, black, baby head, thrust against the starting sinews of the man's bare and massive throat. When choice was possible Baby scrambled into the aura of the father—not of the mother. Sam stirred, started, and yawned.

'What's up, Bess?' he asked sleepily.

'I went to the well to draw fresh water,' she replied, folding her shawl neatly on the back of a chair. 'I was wakeful and thirsty—the night is so hot.'

'Guess that consarned pup worried you with his howlen',' he said. 'I don't hear him now—hope he won't get out of the barn—but that ain't probable—Joe shut him in, right enough; you should have sent me to the well, girl darlin', so you should.'

Bessie picked out a burr which she felt in the fringes of her shawl, and said nothing. She was strictly truthful, so far as the letter of truth went; she had gone to the well and had drawn a bucket of cool water from that shaft of solid shadow. What else she had accomplished she decidedly had no intention of confiding to Sam. She slipped into bed, took the baby on her arm, and kissed his pouting lips.

'God bless the darling,' she said with her pretty smile.

'Amen,' said Sam earnestly. 'God come betwixt every man's child an' harm.' Bessie dosed off placidly, the child on her arm. Sam lay staring at the moonlight, listening, thinking, and grandly sorrowing.

There was the unceasing sound of someone tossing feverishly on a creaking bedstead, the eternal sound of heavy sighs resolutely smothered.

'He ain't sleepin' well, ain't Joe,' thought Sam. 'Not even though he knows Bessie an' me is his friends, true as the day. Guess he ain't sleepin' at all, poor chap!'

'The consarned pup is gone,' remarked Sam, disgustedly, as he came in to breakfast. 'Guess he scrambled up to the hay gap and jumped out. Too bad!'

'He's safe enough,' said Joe. 'He probably ran for home. You will find him at your father's on your next visit, Mrs O'Dwyer. Dogs have the "homing" instinct as well as pigeons.'

'Yes, I guess he went back to pa,' said Bessie. Her colour rose, her eyes flashed. 'Do put baby down, Joe,' she said sharply, 'I don't want— that is, you are mussing his clean frock.'

Joe looked keenly at her.

'I understand,' he said, gently. He placed the child tenderly on the rude lounge, which yet was pretty like all Bessie's belongings, and walked to the open door.

'I think I'll straighten things a bit at the landing,' he said. 'Piner's booms burst yesterday and before the drive reaches here it's as well to see to the boats—those river drivers help themselves to canoes wherever they come across them.'

'Just as you say, Joe,' said Sam, gravely. 'I've never known your head or your heart at fault yet.'

Joe gave a long, wistful look of gratitude, and went out. He did not glance at Bessie, nor she at him.

'Bess, woman,' said Sam, 'what ails you at Joe?'

'You know well enough,' she said placidly. 'He's free to stay here; I don't deny he's working well; though that was his duty, and he was paid for it, but he shan't touch my child again. No parent who understood her duty would permit it; I know mine, I'm thankful to say.'

Her small rancors and spites were the 'Judas' doors' through which she most frequently betrayed herself. She had always faintly disliked Joe, before whom her shabby little school routine, her small affectations of intellectual superiority had shrivelled into siccous leaves. She would assert herself now against Sam's dearly-loved friend, she thought, jealously and with an approving conscience, and it was her plain duty to tear him out of that large and constant heart, she was pleased to feel.

Sam's face changed, in a breath, to a passionate pallor of skin; a proud and piercing gloom of anger darkened his blue eyes to black; he looked at her in wonder.

'What's all this, woman?' he demanded, slowly. 'But it's never your heart that's said it! Him that gave the sweat of his body and the work of his mind to help me make this home for you! Him that's saved my life more nor once at risk of his own young days! Him that's as close to my heart as my own brother! Tut, woman! It's never you would press the thorn in the breast of him into his heart's core. I won't demane myself with leavin' the thought to you, Bessie O'Dwyer!'

He struck his fist on the table; he stared levelly at her, defying her to lower herself in his eyes.

She smoothly repaired her error.

'I spoke in a hurry,' she said, lifting the baby's palm, and covering Sam's lips with its daintiness. 'I feel hurt he had so little confidence in me. I wish him well; you know that.'

Sam smiled under the fluttering of the child's palm upon his lips; he gave a sigh of relief. 'Be kind to him, Bessie darlin',' he said, 'Shure our own boy is born—but he isn't dead yet: the Lord stand betwixt the child an' harm! An' there is no tellin' when he, too, may need the kind word and the tender heart. Shure I'm sorry I took you up in arnest just now.'

'I spoke in a pet,' said Bessie gently. 'I remember, of course, all we owe to Joe—how could I forget it?'

'Forgettin's about the aisiest job in life,' said Sam, rising. 'Guess I'll help Joe at the landin'; he's downhearted, an' I won't lave him alone to his throuble.'

Bessie looked after him disapprovingly.

'Trouble indeed! I thought Sam had clearer ideas on such points. The notion of confounding trouble with rightdown sin and wickedness! Well, it's a good thing I know my duty. I wonder if Pa has any mortgage in his mind ready for that money? It must be a first mortgage; I won't risk any other—I know my responsibility as a mother better than that.'

'Why, man alive!'

Sam was astonished; for the first time in his experience of Joe, the latter was idle. He sat on a fallen tree, looking vacantly into the strong current below him.

'I'm floored, Sam,' he answered, without looking up, 'I've no grit left in me—not a grain.'

'Then it's the first time since I've known you,' said Sam, regarding him with wistful gravity. 'Don't let the sorrow master you, Joe.'

'You call it sorrow, Sam?'

'That's the blessed an' holy name for it now,' said Sam, with his lofty, simple seriousness, 'what ever it may have been afore. Hearten up, Joe! Shure you're as safe at O'Dwyer's Clearin', as if you were hid unther a hill. Rouse your heart, man alive! What's to fear?'

'Not much to fear, but a great deal to feel,' said Joe. 'Am I not stripped of my cloak to you—that's bitter.'

'The only differ is that I'm dead sure now of what I suspicioned right along,' said Sam. 'It's not in reason that a schollard an' a gentleman should bury himself on O'Dwyer's Clearin' for morenor two years, unless to sconce shame an' danger. Rouse your sowl, Joe! don't I owe half of all I have to your arm an' your larnin'? When this danger blows past I'll divide with you, an' you can make a fresh start in some sthrange counthry. South Americay's a grond place, they tell me; shure, I'll take Bessie an' the boy an' go with you. I've no kin nor kith of my own, an' next to her an' the child it is yourself is in the core of my heart. Kape the sorrow, Joe; it's the pardon of God on you, but lave the shame an' the fear go; you'll do the world's wonder yet, boy.'

Joe was about three-and-twenty, Sam in middle age. He placed his massive hand on the other's bare and throbbing head, and both looked silently at the dark and rapid river: Joe with a faint pulse of hope in his bruised and broken soul.

'Piner's logs'll get here about to-morrow,' said Sam at last, 'shure it's Bessie'll be in the twitteration, watchin' the hens an' geese from them mauraudtherin river drivers. I wish the pup hadn't got away; it's a good watch dog his mother is, an' likely he'd show her blood in him—the villain that he was to run away with himself, like that, but liberty's a swate toothful, so it is, to man or brute.'

The following day, Bessie having finished her ironing and baking with triumphant exactness, stood looking from the lovely vines of the porch, down the wild farm road. She was crystal-clean and fresh, and the child in her arms was like a damask rose in his turkey-red frock and white bib. A model young matron was Mrs O'Dwyer and looked it to the fine point of perfection, Sam thought, as he glanced back at her, pride and tenderness in his eyes. She was not looking after his retreating figure, but eagerly down the farm road, and, it seemed to Sam, she was listening intently. 'Mebbe she thinks the shouting of them river drivers is folks comin' up the road,' he thought, as he turned the clump of cedar bushes by the landing, and found Joe at work, patching a bark canoe. As usual he was labouring fiercely as men rush in battle, the sweat on his brow, his teeth set, his eyes fixed. Sam smiled reprovingly.

'Shure, it's all smashed up; you'll have her, Joe, again she's mended,' he remarked, 'more power to your elbow; but take it easy, man! You'll wear out soon enough.'

'I must work like the devil, or think,' said Joe, feverishly. 'Some day, Sam, I'll tell you all the treasures of life I threw from me, then you'll understand.'

'When a man understands by the road of the heart, where's the good of larnin' by the road of the ears?' said Sam, with the tenderest compassion;

'but I'll listen when it's your will to tell, never fear. Hark, now! don't I hear them rollickin' divvils of pike pole men shoutin' beyant the bend there?'

'Yes; Piner's logs must be pretty close,' answered Joe, looking up the river.

'They'll come down the rapids in style,' said Sam, throwing a chip on the current, 'the sthrame's swift as a swallow and strong as a giant with the rains.'

They worked in silence for a while, then Joe began to whistle softly. Sam smiled.

'That's right, Joe,' he said, 'there's nothing so bad that it mightn't be worse—there's hope ahead for you yet, never fear.'

A glimmer of some old joyous spirit sparkled in the young man's melancholy eyes, to fade instantly. 'It's past all that, dear old friend,' he said. As he spoke he glanced towards the cedar scrub between them and the house.

'Here comes Mrs O'Dwyer with the boy,' he said, 'and Sam, there are three men, strangers, with her.'

'Shanty bosses come to buy farm stuff,' said Sam. He turned on Joe with an air of sudden mastery.

'Away with you down the bank,' he said, 'Into the bush with you, an' don't come out until you hear me fire five shots in a string. Away with you!'

'Too late, Sam,' said the other, 'they have seen me.'

'What's all this, Bessie?'

Bessie wiped the baby's wet lips with her apron.

'These gentlemen asked to see you, Sam. I guess they want some farm stuff off us for Piner's Camp. So I brought them along.'

She looked placidly at her husband; the baby sprang in her arms eager to get to his friend Joe, whose red flannel shirt he found very attractive.

'Potatoes or flour?' asked Sam curtly, turning on the strangers.

'Well, it ain't neither,' said one of them—he laid his hand on Joe's wrist. 'It's this young gentleman we're after; he robbed his employer two years' back, and he's wanted back by Uncle Sam. That's about the size of it.'

There was nothing brutal in his look or speech; he knew he was not dealing with a hardened criminal: he even felt compassion for the wretched quarry he had in his talons.

'He's in Canada—on British soil; I dare you to touch him!' said Sam fiercely.

'We have his extradition papers right enough,' said one of the other detectives. 'Don't be so foolish as to resist the law, Mr O'Dwyer.'

'He shan't for me,' said Joe, quietly. He stood motionless while the detective snapped one manacle of the handcuffs on his wrist; the steel glittered like a band of fire in the sun.

The child leaped strongly in Bessie's arms, crowing with delight at the pretty brightness. She was a little off her guard, somewhat faint as she watched the deathly shame on the young man's face which had never turned on her or hers but with tenderness and goodwill. Her brain reeled a little, her hands felt weak.

Suddenly there was a shriek, a flash of red, a soft plunge in the water. Joe threw his arms open, dashing aside the detectives like straws.

'Don't hold me—let me save him!' he cried.

Sam could not swim; he stood on the bank holding Bessie, who screamed and struggled in convulsions of fright as she saw her child drowning. Joe rose in the current, fighting his way superbly towards the little red bundle whirling before him. One of the detectives covered him with a revolver.

'Try to escape and I'll shoot,' he called out, 'understand?'

Joe smiled. Escape to the opposite shore and leave Sam's child to drown? No; he had no idea of it. It was a terrible fight between the man and the river—and the man subdued it unto him. He turned back to shore, the child in his teeth, both arms—one with the shining hand-cuff on it—beating the hostile current with fine, steady strokes.

Another moment and he would be safe on shore, a captive and ashamed.

He spurned the yellow fringes of the current; he felt ground under his feet; he half rose to step on the bank. Then there rose a bewildering cry from Sam and the men watching him; he turned and saw his danger

With one sublime effort he flung the child on the bank, and then with the force of a battering ram the first of Piner's logs crashed upon him. It reared against him like a living thing instinct with rage, and wallowing monster-like led its barky hordes down the rushing stream, rolling triumphantly over a bruised and shattered pigmy of creation, a man.

'Extradited, by ginger,' said one of the detectives, as the groaning logs rolled compactly together over the spot where Joe had gone down.

Before the men departed, Bessie, with the baby on her arm, in a nice clean frock, found opportunity to ask one of them a momentous question. 'Do you think, he being dead, that I shall get any of the reward promised for his arrest? Only for me sending that note to Pa tied round the pup's neck, you would never have found him away back here, you know.'

'I guess not,' replied the detective eyeing her thoughtfully. 'You're a smart woman, you are, but you won't get no reward all the same; pity, ain't it?'

'It's a shame,' she said, bursting into a passion of tears. 'It don't seem that there's any reward for doing one's duty; oh, it's a down-right shame.'

'Best keep all this tol'ble shady from that man of yours,' said the detective, meditatively. 'He ain't got no idee of dooty to speak of, he ain't, and seein' he was powerful fond of that poor, brave, young chap as saved that remarkably fine infant in your arms, he might cut up rough. Some folks ain't got no notion of dooty, they ain't. You best keep dark, ma'am, on the inspiritin' subject of havin' done your dooty an' lost a thousand dollars reward.'

And Bessie followed his advice very carefully indeed, though she always had the private luxury of regarding herself as an unrewarded and unrecognized heroine of duty.

SUSIE FRANCES HARRISON

1859–1935

The Idyl of the Island

There lies mid-way between parallels 48 and 49 of latitude, and degrees 89 and 90 of longitude, in the northern hemisphere of the New World, serenely anchored on an ever-rippling and excited surface, an exquisitely lovely island. No tropical wonder of palm-treed stateliness, or hot tangle of gaudy bird and glowing creeper, can compare with it; no other northern isle, cool and green and refreshing to the eye like itself, can surpass it. It is not a large island. It is about half-a-mile long and quarter of a mile broad. It is an irregular oval in shape, and has two distinct and different sides. On the west side its grey limestone rises to the height of twenty feet straight out of the water. On the east side there occurs a gradual shelving of a sumach-fringed shore, that mingles finally with the ever-rippling water. For the waters in this northern country are never still. They are perpetually bubbling up and boiling over; seething and fuming and frothing and foaming and yet remaining so cool and clear that a quick fancy would discover thousands of banished fountains under that agitated and impatient surface. Both ends of the island are as much alike as its sides are dissimilar. They taper off almost to a distinct bladepoint of rock, in which a mere doll's flagstaff of a pine-tree grows; then comes a small detached rock, with a small evergreen on it, then a still smaller rock, with a tuft of grass, then a line of partially submerged stones, and so out to the deep yet ever-bubbling water. This island might seem just the size for two, and there were two on it on a certain July morning at five o'clock. One of these was a lady who lay at full length and fast asleep upon a most unique couch. These northern islands are in many places completely covered with a variety of yellowish-green moss, varying from a couple of inches to a foot and a half in thickness; and yielding to the pressure of the foot or the body as comfortably as a feather bed, if not more so, being elastic in nature. A large square of this had been cut up from some other part of the island and placed on the already moss-grown and cushioned ground, serving as a mattress, while

11

two smaller pieces served as pillows. A sumach tree at the head of the improvised couch gave the necessary shade to the face of the sleeper, while a wild grapevine, after having run over and encircled with its moist green every stone and stem on the island, fulfilled its longing at length in a tumultuous possession of the sumach making a massive yet aerial patched green curtain or canopy to the fantastic bed, and ending seemingly in two tiny transparent spirals curling up to the sky.

If there were a fault in the structure it was that it was too clever, too well thought out, too rectangular, too much in fact like a bed. But it told certainly of a skilful pair of hands and of a beautiful mind and the union of art with nature perfectly suited the charms—contradictory yet consistent—of the occupant. For being anything but a beautiful woman she was still far from a plain one, which though no original mode of putting it does convey the actual impression she made upon a gentleman in a small boat who rowing past this island at the hour of five o'clock in the morning was so much struck with this curious sight, quite visible from the water below, that he was rude enough to stand up that he might see better. The lady was dressed in some dark blue stuff that evidently covered her all over and fitted tightly where it could be seen. A small linen collar, worn all night and therefore shorn of its usual freshness was round her neck, and she was tucked up from the waist under a Scotch woollen rug. Her hair, of a peculiar red-brown, was allowed to hang about her and was lovely; her mouth sad; her nose, rather too prominent; her complexion natural and healthy, but marred by freckles and moles, not many of either but undeniably scattered over the countenance. All told but her eyes which, if they proved to match with her hair, would atone for these other shortcomings. The gentleman sat down again and reflected.

'How still it is!' he said under his breath. 'Absolutely not a thing stirring. This is the time when the fish bite. I ought to be fishing I suppose. Going to be warm by-and-bye.'

It was indeed almost absolutely silent. The sun climbed higher but the lady slept on, and the gentleman gazed as if fascinated. The only sound that broke the beautiful early morning silence was the occasional weird laugh of the loon. It came twice and then a third time. The sleeper stirred.

'If that thing out there cries again she will wake,' said the gentleman to himself. 'I must be off before that happens. But I *should* like to see her eyes. What a pretty picture it is!' Once more the loon gave its maniacal laugh and the lady started, sat bolt upright and wide awake. Her admirer had not time to retreat but he took his oars up and confronted her manfully. It was an awkward moment. He apologized. The lady listened very politely. Then she smiled.

'Most of the islands in this lake are owned by private people,' she said, 'who use them during the summer months for the purpose of camping out upon them. I should advise you, if you row about much here, to keep to the open water, unless you wish to be seriously handled by the fathers and mothers of families.'

'Thank you very much,' returned the gentleman, standing up in his boat, 'I assure you I intended no rudeness, but I have never seen so charming a summer couch before, and I was really fascinated by the —ah,—the picture you made. May I ask what you mean by 'camping out'? Is it always done in this fashion?'

The lady stared. 'Have *you* never camped out?'

'Never in my life,' said the gentleman. 'I am an Englishman, staying at the hotel near the point for a day or two. I came out to see something of the country.'

'Then you should at least have camped out for a week or so. That is a genuine Canadian experience,' said the lady with a frankness which completely restored the equanimity of the Englishman.

'But how do you live?' he went on in a puzzled manner that caused the lady with the red-brown hair, still all hanging about her, much amusement.

'O, capitally! Upon fish and eggs, and gooseberry tarts, and home-made bread and French coffee. Just what you would get in town, and much better than you get at the hotel.'

'O, that would be easy!' the gentleman groaned. 'I eat my meals in a pitch-dark room, in deadly fear and horror of the regiments of flies that swarm in and settle on everything the minute one raises the green paper blinds.'

The lady nodded. 'I know. We tried it for two or three seasons, but we could not endure it; the whole thing, whitewash and all, is so trying, isn't it? So we bought this lovely island and bring our tent here and live *so* comfortably.' The gentleman did not reply at once. He was thinking that it was his place to say 'Good morning,' and go, although he would much have liked to remain a little longer. He hazarded the remark:

'Now, for instance, what are you going to breakfast on presently?'

The lady laughed lightly and shook her red-brown hair.

'First of all I have to make a fire.'

'Oh!'

'But that is not so very difficult.'

'How do you do it?'

'Would you like to know?'

'Very much indeed. I should like to see, if I may.'

The lady reflected a moment. 'I suppose you may, but if you do, you ought to help me, don't you think?' The gentleman was much amused and greatly interested.

'Ah but you see, it is you I want to see make it. I am very useless you know at that sort of thing, still, if you will allow me, I will try my best. Am I to come ashore?'

'Certainly, if you are to be of any use.'

The lady jumped lightly off the pretty couch of moss and wound her plentiful hair round her head with one turn of her arm. Her dress was creased but well-fitting, her figure not plump enough for beauty but decidedly youthful. She watched her new friend moor his boat and ascend with one or two strides of his long legs up the side of the cliff that was not so steep. He took off his hat.

'I am at your service,' he said with a profound bow. The lady made him another, during which all her long hair fell about her again, at which they both laughed.

'What do we do first?' said he.

'O we find a lot of sticks and pieces of bark, mostly birch bark, and anything else that will burn—you may have to fell a tree while you are about it—and I'll show you how to place them properly between two walls of stones, put a match to them and there is our fire. Will you come with me?'

He assented of course, and they were soon busy in the interior of the little wood that grew up towards the centre of the island. I must digress here to say that the gentleman's name was Amherst. He was known to the world in latter life as Admiral Amherst, and he was a great friend of mine. When he related this story to me, he was very particular in describing the island as I have done—indeed he carried a little chart about with him of it which he had made from memory, and he told me besides that he never forgot the peculiar beauty of that same little tract of wood. The early hour, the delicious morning air, the great moss-grown and brown decaying tree trunks, the white, clammy, ghostly, flower or fungus of the Indian Pipe at his feet the masses of ferns, the elastic ground he trod upon, and the singular circumstance that he was alone in this exquisite spot with a woman he had never seen until five minutes previously, all combined to make an ineffaceable impression upon his mind. The lady showed herself proficient in the art of building a fire and attended by Amherst soon had a fine flame rising up from between the fortifications evidently piled by stronger hands than her own.

'What do we do now?' asked Amherst. 'I should suggest—a kettle.'

'Of course, that is the next step. If I give it to you, you might run and fill it, eh?'

'Delighted!' and away went Amherst. When he returned the lady was not to be seen. The place was shorn of its beauty, but he waited discreetly and patiently, putting the kettle on to boil in the meanwhile.

'It's very singular,' said he, 'how I came to be here. I wonder who are with her in her party; no one else appears to be up or about. That striped red and white thing is the tent, I see, over there. Ah! that's where she has gone, and now she beckons me! Oh! I'll go, but I don't want to meet the rest of them!'

But when he reached the tent, it was quite empty, save for rugs and wraps, boxes, etc., and the lady was laughingly holding out a loaf of bread in one hand and a paper package in the other.

'You will stay and breakfast with me?' 'What will you give me?' said Amherst, smiling. 'I can only give you eggs, boiled in the kettle, coffee and bread and butter. The fish haven't come in yet.'

'What can be nicer than eggs—especially when boiled in the kettle, that is, if you make the coffee first.'

'Certainly I do.'

'And it is really French coffee?'

'Really. Café des Gourmets, you know; we—I always use it—do not like any other.'

Amherst was fast falling in love. He told me that at this point his mind was quite made up that if it were possible he would remain in the neighbourhood a few days at least, in order to see more of this charming girl. She seemed to him to be about twenty-six or seven, and so frank, simple, and graceful, one could not have resisted liking her. Her hair and eyes were identical in colour and both were beautiful; her expression was arch and some of her gestures almost childish, but a certain dignity appeared at times and sat well upon her. Her hands were destitute of rings as Amherst soon discovered, and were fine and small though brown. While she made the coffee, Amherst threw himself down on the wonderful moss, the like of which he had never seen before and looked out over the water. An unmistakeable constraint had taken the place of the unaffected hilarity of the first ten minutes. A reaction had set in. Amherst could of course only answer to me in telling this for himself, but he divined at the time a change in his companion's manner as well.

'I hope you like your eggs,' she said presently.

'They are very nice, indeed, thank you,' rejoined Amherst.

'And I have made your coffee as you like it?'

'Perfectly, thank you. But you—you are not eating anything! Why is that?'

As he asked the question he turned quickly around, in order to rise that he might help her with the ponderous kettle that she was about lifting off the camp-fire, when a long strand of her hair again escaping from its coil blew directly across his face. Amherst uttered a radiant 'Oh!' and taking it to his lips forgot himself so far as to press kiss after kiss upon it. The lady stood as if transfixed and did not move, even when Amherst actually swept all her hair down over one arm and turning her face to his, pressed one long long kiss on her forehead.

The moment he had done this his senses returned and he stepped back in indignation with himself. But his companion was still apparently transfixed. Amherst looked at her in dismay. She did not seem to see him and had grown very pale. He touched her gently on the arm but she did not show that she felt the touch. He retreated a few paces and stood by himself, overcome with shame and contrition. What had he done? How should he ever atone for such an unwarrantable action? Had it been the outcome of any ordinary flirtation, he would have felt no such scruples, but the encounter, though short, had been one of singular idyllic charm until he had by his own rash act spoilt it. A few minutes passed thus in self contemplation appeared like an eternity. He must speak.

'If you would allow me—'

But the lady put out her left hand in deprecation as it were and he got no further. The silence was unendurable. Amherst took a step or two forward and perceived great tears rolling down her cheeks.

'Oh!' he began desperately, 'won't you allow me to say a word to tell you how very, very sorry I am, how grieved I am and always shall be? I never—I give you my word of honour—I never do those sort of things, have never done such a thing before! But I can't tell what it was, the place is so beautiful, and when all that lovely hair came sweeping past my face, I could not help doing as I did, it was so electrical! Any man would have done the same. I know that sounds like a miserable, cowardly excuse, but it is true, perfectly true.' The lady seemed to struggle to appear calm and with a great effort she turned her face towards Amherst.

'I know one man,' she said, in a voice choked with sobs, 'who would not have done it.'

Amherst started. 'I am sorrier than ever, believe me. I might have known you were engaged, or had a lover—one so charming'—

'It is not that,' said the lady. 'I am married.' She was still struggling with her emotion.

Amherst recoiled. He was torn with conflicting thoughts. What if he had been seen giving that involuntary salute? He might have ruined her peace for ever. Who would believe in the truth of any possible explanation?

'I will leave you at once,' he said stiffly; 'there is nothing more to be said.'

'Oh! you will reproach me now!' said his companion, wiping her eyes as the tears came afresh.

'I will try not to,' said Amherst; 'but you could so easily have told me; I do not think it was—quite—fair.' Yet he could not be altogether angry with the partner of his thoughtlessness, nor could he be entirely cold. Her beautiful eyes, her despairing attitude would haunt him he knew for many a day. She had ceased weeping and stood quietly awaiting his departure. Amherst felt all the force of a strong and novel passion sweep along his frame as he looked at her. Was she happy, was she a loved and loving wife? Somehow the conviction forced itself upon him that she was not. Yet he could not ask her, it must remain her secret.

Amherst looked at his watch. It aroused her.

'What is the time?' she said lifting her head for the first time since he had kissed her.

'Ten minutes past six,' Amherst replied.

'You must go,' she said, with an effort at self-control. 'I shall have much to do presently.'

He cast one look about and approached her.

'Will you forgive me'—he began in a tone of repression, then with another mighty and involuntary movement he caught her hands and pressed them to his breast. 'My God,' he exclaimed, 'how I should have loved you!'

A moment after he flung her hands away and strode down the cliff, unfastened his boat and rowed away in the direction of the hotel as fast as he could. Rounding a sharp rock that hid what lay beyond it, he nearly succeeded in overturning another boat like his own, in which sat a gentleman of middle age, stout and pleasant and mild of countenance. The bottom of the boat was full of fish. Amherst made an incoherent apology, to which the gentleman answered with a good-natured laugh, insisting that the fault was his own. He would have liked to enter into conversation with Amherst, but my friend was only anxious to escape from the place altogether and forget his recent adventure in the hurry of departure from the hotel. Three days after he embarked at Quebec for England, and never revisited Canada. But he never married and never forgot the woman whom he always asserted he might have truly and passionately loved. He was about twenty-eight when that happened and perfectly heart-whole. Why—I used to say to him, why did you not learn her name and that of her husband? Perhaps she is a widow now, perhaps you made as great an impression upon her mind and affections as she did upon yours.

But my friend Admiral Amherst, as the world knew him, was a strange, irrational creature in many ways, and none of these ideas would he ever entertain. That the comfortable gentleman in the boat was her husband he never doubted; more it was impossible to divine. But the cool northern isle, with its dark fringe of pines; its wonderful moss, its fragrant and dewy ferns, its graceful sumachs, just putting on their scarlet-lipped leaves, the morning stillness broken only by the faint unearthly cry of the melancholy loon, the spar-dyked cliffs of limestone, and the fantastic couch, with its too lovely occupant, never faded from his memory and remained to the last as realities which indeed they have become likewise to me, through the intensity with which they were described to me.

CHARLES G.D. ROBERTS
1860-1943

Do Seek Their Meat from God

One side of the ravine was in darkness. The darkness was soft and rich, suggesting thick foliage. Along the crest of the slope tree-tops came into view—great pines and hemlocks of the ancient unviolated forest—revealed against the orange disk of a full moon just rising. The low rays slanting through the moveless tops lit strangely the upper portion of the opposite steep—the western wall of the ravine, barren, unlike its fellow, bossed with great rocky projections and harsh with stunted junipers. Out of the sluggish dark that lay along the ravine as in a trough rose the brawl of a swollen, obstructed stream.

Out of a shadowy hollow behind a long white rock, on the lower edge of that part of the steep which lay in the moonlight, came softly a great panther. In common daylight his coat would have shown a warm fulvous hue, but in the elvish decolorizing rays of that half-hidden moon he seemed to wear a sort of spectral gray. He lifted his smooth round head to gaze on the increasing flame, which presently he greeted with a shrill cry. That terrible cry, at once plaintive and menacing, with an undertone like the fierce protestations of a saw beneath the file, was a summons to his mate, telling her that the hour had come when they should seek their prey. From the lair behind the rock, where the cubs were being suckled by their dam, came no immediate answer. Only a pair of crows, that had their nest in a giant fir-tree across the gulf, woke up and croaked harshly their indignation. These three summers past they had built in the same spot, and had been nightly awakened to vent the same rasping complaints.

The panther walked restlessly up and down, half a score of paces each way, along the edge of the shadow, keeping his wide-open green eyes upon the rising light. His short, muscular tail twitched impatiently, but he made no sound. Soon the breadth of confused brightness had spread itself farther down the steep, disclosing the foot of the white rock, and the bones and antlers of a deer which had been dragged thither and devoured.

By this time the cubs had made their meal, and their dam was ready for such enterprise as must be accomplished ere her own hunger, now grown savage, could hope to be assuaged. She glided supplely forth into the glimmer, raised her head, and screamed at the moon in a voice as terrible as her mate's. Again the crows stirred, croaking harshly; and the two beasts, noiselessly mounting the steep, stole into the shadows of the forest that clothed the high plateau.

The panthers were fierce with hunger. These two days past their hunting had been wellnigh fruitless. What scant prey they had slain had for the most part been devoured by the female; for had she not those small blind cubs at home to nourish, who soon must suffer at any lack of hers? The settlements of late had been making great inroads on the world of ancient forest, driving before them the deer and smaller game. Hence the sharp hunger of the panther parents, and hence it came that on this night they hunted together. They purposed to steal upon the settlements in their sleep, and take tribute of the enemies' flocks. Through the dark of the thick woods, here and there pierced by the moonlight, they moved swiftly and silently. Now and again a dry twig would snap beneath the discreet and padded footfalls. Now and again, as they rustled some low tree, a pewee or a nuthatch would give a startled chirp. For an hour the noiseless journeying continued, and ever and anon the two gray, sinuous shapes would come for a moment into the view of the now well-risen moon. Suddenly there fell upon their ears, far off and faint, but clearly defined against the vast stillness of the Northern forest, a sound which made those stealthy hunters pause and lift their heads. It was the voice of a child crying—crying long and loud, hopelessly, as if there were no one by to comfort it. The panthers turned aside from their former course and glided toward the sound. They were not yet come to the outskirts of the settlement, but they knew of a solitary cabin lying in the thick of the woods a mile and more from the nearest neighbour. Thither they bent their way, fired with fierce hope. Soon would they break their bitter fast.

Up to noon of the previous day the lonely cabin had been occupied. Then its owner, a shiftless fellow, who spent his days for the most part at the corner tavern three miles distant, had suddenly grown disgusted with a land wherein one must work to live, and had betaken himself with his seven-year-old boy to seek some more indolent clime. During the long lonely days when his father was away at the tavern the little boy had been wont to visit the house of the next neighbour, to play with a child of some five summers, who had no other playmate. The next neighbour was a prosperous pioneer, being master of a substantial frame-house in the midst of a large and well-tilled clearing. At times, though rarely, because it was forbidden, the younger child would make his way by a rough wood road to visit his poor little disreputable playmate. At length it had appeared that the five-year-old was learning unsavoury language from the elder boy, who rarely had an opportunity of hearing speech more desirable. To the bitter grief of both children, the companionship had at length been stopped by unalterable decree of the master of the frame-house.

Hence it had come to pass that the little boy was unaware of his comrade's departure. Yielding at last to an eager longing for that comrade, he had stolen away late in the afternoon, traversed with endless misgivings the lonely stretch of wood road, and reached the cabin, only to find it empty. The door, on its leathern hinges, swung idly open. The one room had been stripped of its few poor furnishings. After looking in the rickety shed, whence darted two wild and hawklike chickens, the child had seated himself on the hacked threshold, and sobbed passionately with a grief that he did not fully comprehend. Then seeing the shadows lengthen across the tiny clearing, he had grown afraid to start for home. As the dusk gathered, he had crept trembling into the cabin, whose door would not stay shut. When it grew quite dark, he crouched in the inmost corner of the room, desperate with fear and loneliness, and lifted up his voice piteously. From time to time his lamentations would be choked by sobs or he would grow breathless, and in the terrifying silence would listen hard to hear if anyone or anything were coming. Then again would the shrill childish wailings arise, startling the unexpectant night and piercing the forest depths, even to the ears of those great beasts which had set forth to seek their meat from God.

The lonely cabin stood some distance, perhaps a quarter of a mile, back from the highway connecting the settlements. Along this main road a man was plodding wearily. All day he had been walking, and now as he neared home his steps began to quicken with anticipation of rest. Over his shoulder projected a double-barrelled fowling-piece, from which was slung a bundle of such necessities as he had purchased in town that morning. It was the prosperous settler, the master of the frame-house. His mare being with foal, he had chosen to make the tedious journey on foot.

The settler passed the mouth of the wood road leading to the cabin. He had gone perhaps a furlong beyond, when his ears were startled by the sound of a child crying in the woods. He stopped, lowered his burden to the road, and stood straining ears and eyes in the direction of the sound. It was just at this time that the two panthers also stopped and lifted their heads to listen. Their ears were keener than those of the man, and the sound had reached them at a greater distance.

Presently the settler realized whence the cries were coming. He called to mind the cabin, but he did not know the cabin's owner had departed. He cherished a hearty contempt for the drunken squatter; and on the drunken squatter's child he looked with small favour, especially as a playmate for his own boy. Nevertheless, he hesitated before resuming his journey.

'Poor little devil!' he muttered, half in wrath. 'I reckon his precious father's drunk down at "the Corners"', and him crying for loneliness!' Then he reshouldered his burden and strode on doggedly.

But louder, shriller, more hopeless and more appealing, arose the childish voice, and the settler paused again, irresolute and with deepening indignation. In his fancy he saw the steaming supper his wife would have awaiting him. He loathed the thought of retracing his steps, and then stumbling a quarter of a mile through the stumps and bog of the wood road. He was foot-sore as well as hungry, and he cursed the vagabond squatter with serious emphasis; but in that wailing was a terror which would not let him go on. He thought of his own little one left in such a position, and straightway his heart melted. He turned, dropped his bundle behind some bushes, grasped his gun, and made speed back for the cabin.

'Who knows,' he said to himself, 'but that drunken idiot has left his youngster without a bite to eat in the whole miserable shanty? Or maybe he's locked out, and the poor little beggar's half scared to death. Sounds as if he was scared'; and at this thought the settler quickened his pace.

As the hungry panthers drew near the cabin and the cries of the lonely child grew clearer, they hastened their steps, and their eyes opened to a wider circle, flaming with a greener fire. It would be thoughtless superstition to say the beasts were cruel. They were simply keen with hunger and alive with the eager passion of the chase. They were not ferocious with any anticipation of battle, for they knew the voice was the voice of a child, and something in the voice told them the child was solitary. Theirs was no hideous or unnatural rage, as it is the custom to describe it. They were but seeking with the strength, the cunning, the deadly swiftness given them to that end, the food convenient for them. On their success in accomplishing that for which nature had so exquisitely designed them depended not only their own but the lives of their blind and helpless young, now whimpering in the cave on the slope of the moonlit ravine. They crept through a wet alder thicket, bounded lightly over the ragged brush fence, and paused to reconnoitre on the edge of the clearing in the full glare of the moon. At the same moment the settler emerged from the darkness of the wood-road on the opposite side of the clearing. He saw the two great beasts, heads down and snouts thrust forward, gliding toward the open cabin door.

For a few moments the child had been silent. Now his voice rose again in pitiful appeal, a very ecstasy of loneliness and terror. There was a note in the cry that shook the settler's soul. He had a vision of his own boy, at home with his mother, safeguarded from even the thought of peril. And here was this little one left to the wild beasts! 'Thank God! Thank God I came!' murmured the settler, as he dropped on one knee to take a sure aim. There was a loud report (not like the sharp crack of a rifle), and the female panther, shot through the loins, fell in a heap, snarling furiously and striking with her forepaws.

The male walked around her in fierce and anxious amazement. As the smoke lifted he discerned the settler kneeling for a second shot. With a high screech of fury, the lithe brute sprang upon his enemy, taking a bullet full in his chest without seeming to know he was hit. Ere the man could slip in another cartridge the beast was upon him, bearing him to the ground and fixing keen fangs in his shoulder. Without a word, the man set his strong fingers desperately into the brute's throat, wrenched himself partly free, and was struggling to rise when the panther's body collapsed upon him all at once, a dead weight which he easily flung aside. The bullet had done its work just in time.

Quivering from the swift and dreadful contest, bleeding profusely from his mangled shoulder, the settler stepped up to the cabin door and peered in. He heard sobs in the darkness,

'Don't be scared, sonny,' he said in a reassuring voice. 'I'm going to take you home along with me. Poor little lad, I'll look after you if folks that ought to don't.'

Out of the dark corner came a shout of delight, in a voice which made the settler's heart stand still. 'Daddy, daddy,' it said, 'I knew you'd come. I was so frightened when it got dark!' And a little figure launched itself into the settler's arms and clung to him trembling. The man sat down on the threshold and strained the child to his breast. He remembered how near he had been to disregarding the far-off cries, and great beads of sweat broke out upon his forehead.

Not many weeks afterwards the settler was following the fresh trail of a bear which had killed his sheep. The trail led him at last along the slope of a deep ravine, from whose bottom came the brawl of a swollen and obstructed stream. In the ravine he found a shallow cave, behind a great white rock. The cave was plainly a wild beast's lair, and he entered circumspectly. There were bones scattered about, and on some dry herbage in the deepest corner of the den he found the dead bodies, now rapidly decaying, of two small panther cubs.

DUNCAN CAMPBELL SCOTT

1862–1947

The Desjardins

Just at the foot of the hill, where the bridge crossed the Blanche, stood one of the oldest houses in Viger. It was built of massive timbers. The roof curved and projected beyond the eaves, forming the top of a narrow veranda. The whole house was painted a dazzling white except the window-frames, which were green. There was a low stone fence between the road and the garden, where a few simple flowers grew. Beyond the fence was a row of Lombardy poplars, some of which had commenced to die out. On the opposite side of the road was a marshy field, where by day the marsh marigolds shone, and by night, the fireflies. There were places in this field where you could thrust down a long pole and not touch bottom. In the fall a few muskrats built a house there, in remembrance of the time when it was a favourite wintering-ground. In the spring the Blanche came up and flowed over it. Beyond that again the hill curved round, with a scarped, yellowish slope.

In this house lived Adèle Desjardin with her two brothers, Charles and Philippe. Their father was dead, and when he died there was hardly a person in the whole parish who was sorry. They could remember him as a tall, dark, forbidding-looking man, with long arms out of all proportion to his body. He had inherited his fine farm from his father, and had added to and improved it. He had always been prosperous, and was considered the wealthiest man in the parish. He was inhospitable, and became more taciturn and morose after his wife died. His pride was excessive and kept him from associating with his neighbours, although he was in no way above them. Very little was known about his manner of life, and there was a mystery about his father's death. For some time the old man had not been seen about the place, when one day he came from the city, dead and in his coffin, which was thought strange. This gave rise to all sorts of rumour and gossip; but the generally accredited story was that there was insanity in the family and that he had died crazy.

However cold Isidore Desjardin was to his neighbours, no one could

have charged him with being unkind or harsh with his children, and as
they grew up he gave them all the advantages which it was possible for
them to have. Adèle went for a year to the Convent of the Sacré Coeur in
the city, and could play tunes on the piano when she came back; so that
she had to have a piano of her own, which was the first one ever heard in
Viger. She was a slight, angular girl, with a dark thin face and black hair
and eyes. She looked like her father and took after him in many ways.
Charles, the elder son, was like his grandfather, tall and muscular, with a
fine head and a handsome face. He was studious and read a great deal,
and was always talking to the curé about studying the law. Philippe did
not care about books; his father could never keep him at school. He was
short and thick-set and had merry eyes set deep in his head. 'Someone
must learn to look after things,' he said, and when his father died he took
sole charge of everything.

If the Desjardins were unsociable with others, they were happy among
themselves. Almost every evening during the winter, when the work was
done, they would light up the front room with candles, and Adèle would
play on the piano and sing. Charles would pace to and fro behind her,
and Philippe would thrust his feet far under the stove that projected from
the next room through the partition, and fall fast asleep. Her songs were
mostly old French songs, and she could sing 'Partant pour la Syrie' and
'La Marseillaise'. This last was a favourite with Charles; he could not
sing himself, but he accompanied the music by making wild movements
with his arms, tramping heavily up and down before the piano, and
shouting out so loudly as to wake Philippe. 'Aux armes, citoyens!' On
fine summer evenings Philippe and Adèle would walk up and down the
road watching the marsh fireflies and pausing on the bridge to hear the
fish jump in the pool and the deep, vibrant croak of the distant frogs. It
was not always Philippe who walked there with Adèle; he sometimes sat
on the veranda and watched her walk with someone else. He would have
waking dreams, as he smoked, that the two figures moving before him
were himself and someone into whose eyes he was looking.

At last it came to be reality for him, and then he could not sit quietly
and watch the lovers; he would let his pipe go out and stride impatiently
up and down the veranda. And on Sunday afternoons he would harness
his horse, dress himself carefully, and drive off with short laughs and
twinklings of the eyes and wavings of the hands. They were evidently
planning the future and it seemed a distance of vague happiness.

Charles kept on his wonted way. If they talked in the parlour, they
could hear him stirring upstairs; if they strolled in the road, they could
see his light in the window. Philippe humoured his studious habits. He

only worked in the mornings; in the afternoons he read, history principally. His favourite study was the *Life of Napoleon Bonaparte*, which seemed to absorb him completely. He was growing more retired and preoccupied every day—lost in deep reveries, swallowed of ambitious dreams.

It had been a somewhat longer day than usual in the harvest field, and it was late when the last meal was ready. Philippe, as he called Charles from the foot of the stair, could hear him walking up and down, seemingly reading out loud, and when he received no response to his demand he went up the stairs. Pushing open the door, he saw his brother striding up and down the room with his hands clasped behind him and his head bent muttering to himself.

'Charles!' He seemed to collect himself and looked up. 'Come down to supper!' They went downstairs together. Adèle and Philippe kept up a conversation throughout the meal, but Charles hardly spoke. Suddenly he pushed his plate away and stood upright to his full height; a look of calm, severe dignity came over his face.

'I!' said he. 'I am the Great Napoleon!'

'Charles!' cried Adèle. 'What is the matter?'

'The prosperity of the nation depends upon the execution of my plans. Go!' said he, dismissing some imaginary person with an imperious gesture.

They sat as if stunned, and between them stood this majestic figure with outstretched hand. Then Charles turned away and commenced to pace the room.

'It has come!' sobbed Adèle as she sank on her knees beside the table.

'There is only one thing to do,' said Philippe after some hours of silence. 'It is hard, but there is only one thing to do.' The room was perfectly dark. He stood in the window where he had seen the light die out of the sky, and now in the marshy field he saw the fireflies gleam. He knew that Adèle was in the dark somewhere beside him, for he could hear her breathe. 'We must cut ourselves off; we must be the last of our race.' In those words, which in after years were often on his lips, he seemed to find some comfort, and he continued to repeat them to himself.

Charles lay in bed in a sort of stupor for three days. On Sunday morning he rose. The church bells were ringing. He met Philippe in the hall.

'Is this Sunday?' he asked.

'Yes.'

'Come here!' They went into the front room.

'This is Sunday, you say. The last thing I remember was you telling me to go in—that was Wednesday. What has happened?' Philippe dropped his head in his hands.

'Tell me, Philippe, what has happened?'

'I cannot.'

'I must know, Philippe. Where have I been?'

'On Wednesday night,' said he, as if the words were choking him, 'you said, "I am the great Napoloen!" Then you said something about the nation and you have not spoken since.'

Charles dropped on his knees beside the table against which Philippe was leaning. He hid his face in his arms. Philippe, reaching across, thrust his fingers into his brother's brown hair. The warm grasp came as an answer to all Charles's unasked questions; he knew that, whatever might happen, his brother would guard him.

For a month or two he lay wavering between two worlds; but when he saw the first snow and lost sight of the brown earth, he at once commenced to order supplies, to write dispatches, and to make preparations for the gigantic expedition which was to end in the overthrow of the Emperor of all the Russias. And the snow continues to bring him this activity. During the summer he is engaged, with no very definite operations, in the field, but when winter comes he always prepares for the invasion of Russia. With the exception of certain days of dejection and trouble, which Adèle calls the Waterloo days, in the summer he is triumphant with perpetual victory. On a little bare hill about a mile from the house from which you can get an extensive view of the sloping country, he watches the movements of the enemy. The blasts at the distant quarries sound in his ears like the roar of guns. Beside him the old grey horse that Philippe has set apart for his service crops the grass or stands for hours patiently. Down in the shallow valley the Blanche runs, glistening; the mowers sway and bend; on the horizon shafts of smoke rise, little clouds break away from the masses and drop their quiet shadows on the fields. And through his glass Charles watches the moving shadows, the shafts of smoke, and the swaying mowers, watches the distant hills fringed with beech-groves. He dispatches his aides-de-camp with important orders, or rides down the slope to oversee the fording of the Blanche. Half-frightened village boys hide in the long grass to hear him go muttering by. In the autumn he comes sadly up out of the valley leading his horse, the rein through his arm and his hands in his coatsleeves. The sleet dashes against him, and the wind rushes and screams around him as he ascends the little knoll. But whatever the weather, Philippe waits in the road for him and helps him dismount. There is something heroic in his short figure.

'Sire, my brother!' he says, 'Sire, let us go in!'

'Is the King of Rome better?'

'Yes.'

'And the Empress?'

'She is well.'

Only once has a gleam of light pierced these mists. It was in the year when, as Adèle said, he had had two Waterloos and had taken to his bed in consequence. One evening Adèle brought him a bowl of gruel. He stared like a child awakened from sleep when she carried in the lamp. She approached the bed and he started up.

'Adèle!' he said hoarsely, and pulling her face down, kissed her lips. For a moment she had hope. But with the next week came winter, and he commenced his annual preparations for the invasion of Russia.

STEPHEN LEACOCK

1869-1944

The Marine Excursion of the Knights of Pythias

HALF PAST six on a July morning! The *Mariposa Belle* is at the wharf, decked in flags, with steam up ready to start.

Excursion day!

Half-past six on a July morning, and Lake Wissanotti lying in the sun as calm as glass. The opal colours of the morning light are shot from the surface of the water.

Out on the lake the last thin threads of the mist are clearing away like flecks of cotton wool

The long call of the loon echoes over the lake. The air is cool and fresh. There is in it all the new life of the land of the silent pine and the moving waters. Lake Wissanotti in the morning sunlight! Don't talk to me of the Italian lakes, or the Tyrol or the Swiss Alps. Take them away. Move them somewhere else. I don't want them.

Excursion Day, at half-past six of a summer morning! With the boat all decked in flags and all the people in Mariposa on the wharf, and the band in peaked caps with big cornets tied to their bodies ready to play at any minute! I say! Don't tell me about the Carnival of Venice and the Delhi Durbar. Don't! I wouldn't look at them. I'd shut my eyes! For light and colour give me every time an excursion out of Mariposa down the lake to the Indian's Island out of sight in the morning mist. Talk of your Papal Zouaves and your Buckingham Palace Guard! I want to see the Mariposa band in uniform and the Mariposa Knights of Pythias with their aprons and their insignia and their picnic baskets and their five-cent cigars!

Half-past six in the morning, and all the crowd on the wharf and the boat due to leave in half an hour. Notice it!—in half an hour. Already she's whistled twice (at six, and at six fifteen), and at any minute now, Christie Johnson will step into the pilot house and pull the string for the warning whistle that the boat will leave in half an hour. So keep ready.

Don't think of running back to Smith's Hotel for the sandwiches. Don't be fool enough to try to go up to the Greek Store, next to Netley's, and buy fruit. You'll be left behind for sure if you do. Never mind the sandwiches and the fruit! Anyway, here comes Mr Smith himself with a huge basket of provender that would feed a factory. There must be sandwiches in that. I think I can hear them clinking. And behind Mr Smith is the German waiter from the caff with another basket—indubitably lager beer; and behind him, the bartender of the hotel, carrying nothing, as far as one can see. But of course if you know Mariposa you will understand that why he looks so nonchalant and empty-handed is because he has two bottles of rye whisky under his linen duster. You know, I think, the peculiar walk of a man with two bottles of whisky in the inside pockets of a linen coat. In Mariposa, you see, to bring beer to an excursion is quite in keeping with public opinion. But, whisky—well, one has to be a little careful.

Do I say that Mr Smith is here? Why, everybody's here. There's Hussell the editor of the *Newspacket*, wearing a blue ribbon on his coat, for the Mariposa Knights of Pythias are, by their constitution, dedicated to temperance; and there's Henry Mullins, the manager of the Exchange Bank, also a Knight of Pythias, with a small flask of Pogram's Special in his hip pocket as a sort of amendment to the constitution. And there's Dean Drone, the Chaplain of the Order, with a fishing-rod (you never saw such green bass as lie among the rocks at Indian's Island), and with a trolling line in case of maskinonge, and a landing-net in case of pickerel, and with his eldest daughter, Lilian Drone, in case of young men. There never was such a fisherman as the Rev. Rupert Drone.

Perhaps I ought to explain that when I speak of the excursion as being of the Knights of Pythias, the thing must not be understood in any narrow sense. In Mariposa practically everybody belongs to the Knights of Pythias just as they do to everything else. That's the great thing about the town and that's what makes it so different from the city. Everybody is in everything.

You should see them on the seventeenth of March, for example, when everybody wears a green ribbon and they're all laughing and glad—you know what the Celtic nature is—and talking about Home Rule.

On St Andrew's Day every man in town wears a thistle and shakes hands with everybody else, and you see the fine old Scotch honesty beaming out of their eyes.

And on St George's Day!—well, there's no heartiness like the good old English spirit, after all; why shouldn't a man feel glad that he's an Englishman?

Then on the Fourth of July there are stars and stripes flying over half the stores in town, and suddenly all the men are seen to smoke cigars, and to know all about Roosevelt and Bryan and the Philippine Islands. Then you learn for the first time that Jeff Thorpe's people came from Massachusetts and that his uncle fought at Bunker Hill (it must have been Bunker Hill—anyway Jefferson will swear it was in Dakota all right enough); and you find that George Duff has a married sister in Rochester and that her husband is all right; in fact, George was down there as recently as eight years ago. Oh, it's the most American town imaginable is Mariposa—on the fourth of July.

But wait, just wait, if you feel anxious about the solidity of the British connexion, till the twelfth of the month, when everybody is wearing an orange streamer in his coat and the Orangemen (every man in town) walk in the big procession. Allegiance! Well, perhaps you remember the address they gave to the Prince of Wales on the platform of the Mariposa station as he went through on his tour to the west. I think that pretty well settled that question.

So you will easily understand that of course everybody belongs to the Knights of Pythias and the Masons and Oddfellows, just as they all belong to the Snow Shoe Club and the Girls' Friendly Society.

And meanwhile the whistle of the steamer has blown again for a quarter to seven—loud and long this time, for any one not here now is late for certain, unless he should happen to come down in the last fifteen minutes.

What a crowd upon the wharf and how they pile onto the steamer! It's a wonder that the boat can hold them all. But that's just the marvellous thing about the *Mariposa Belle*.

I don't know—I have never known—where the steamers like the *Mariposa Belle* come from. Whether they are built by Harland and Wolff of Belfast, or whether, on the other hand, they are not built by Harland and Wolff of Belfast, is more than one would like to say offhand.

The *Mariposa Belle* always seems to me to have some of those strange properties that distinguish Mariposa itself. I mean, her size seems to vary so. If you see her there in the winter, frozen in the ice beside the wharf with a snowdrift against the windows of the pilot house, she looks a pathetic little thing the size of a butternut. But in the summer time, especially after you've been in Mariposa for a month or two, and have paddled alongside of her in a canoe, she gets larger and taller, and with a great sweep of black sides, till you see no difference between the *Mariposa Belle* and the *Lusitania*. Each one is a big steamer and that's all you can say.

Nor do her measurements help you much. She draws about eighteen inches forward, and more than that—at least half an inch more, astern, and when she's loaded down with an excursion crowd she draws a good two inches more. And above the water—why, look at all the decks on her! There's the deck you walk onto, from the wharf, all shut in, with windows along it, and the after cabin with the long table, and above that the deck with all the chairs piled upon it, and the deck in front where the band stand round in a circle, and the pilot house is higher than that, and above the pilot house is the board with the gold name and the flag pole and the steel ropes and the flags; and fixed in somewhere on the different levels is the lunch counter where they sell the sandwiches, and the engine room, and down below the deck level, beneath the water line, is the place where the crew sleep. What with steps and stairs and passages and piles of cordwood for the engine—oh, no, I guess Harland and Wolff didn't build her. They couldn't have.

Yet even with a huge boat like the *Mariposa Belle*, it would be impossible for her to carry all of the crowd that you see in the boat and on the wharf. In reality, the crowd is made up of two classes—all of the people in Mariposa who are going on the excursion and all those who are not. Some come for the one reason and some for the other.

The two tellers of the Exchange Bank are both there standing side by side. But one of them—the one with the cameo pin and the long face like a horse—is going, and the other—with the other cameo pin and the face like another horse—is not. In the same way, Hussell of the *Newspacket* is going, but his brother, beside him, isn't. Lilian Drone is going, but her sister can't; and so on all through the crowd.

And to think that things should look like that on the morning of a steamboat accident.

How strange life is!

To think of all these people so eager and anxious to catch the steamer, and some of them running to catch it, and so fearful that they might miss it—the morning of a steamboat accident. And the captain blowing his whistle, and warning them so severely that he would leave them behind— leave them out of the accident! And everybody crowding so eagerly to be in the accident.

Perhaps life is like that all through.

Strangest of all to think, in a case like this, of the people who were left behind, or in some way or other prevented from going, and always afterwards told of how they had escaped being on board the *Mariposa Belle* that day!

Some of the instances were certainly extraordinary.

Nivens, the lawyer, escaped from being there merely by the fact that he was away in the city.

Towers, the tailor, only escaped owing to the fact that, not intending to go on the excursion he had stayed in bed till eight o'clock and so had not gone. He narrated afterwards that waking up that morning at half-past five, he had thought of the excursion and for some unaccountable reason had felt glad that he was not going.

The case of Yodel, the auctioneer, was even more inscrutable. He had been to the Oddfellows' excursion on the train the week before and to the Conservative picnic the week before that, and had decided not to go on this trip. In fact, he had not the least intention of going. He narrated afterwards how the night before someone had stopped him on the corner of Nippewa and Tecumseh Streets (he indicated the very spot) and asked: 'Are you going to take in the excursion tomorrow?' and he had said, just as simply as he was talking when narrating it: 'No.' And ten minutes after that, at the corner of Dalhousie and Brock Streets (he offered to lead a party of verification to the precise place) somebody else had stopped him and asked: 'Well, are you going on the steamer trip tomorrow?' Again he had answered: 'No', apparently almost in the same tone as before.

He said afterwards that when he heard the rumour of the accident it seemed like the finger of Providence, and he fell on his knees in thankfulness.

There was the similar case of Morison (I mean the one in Glover's hardware store that married one of the Thompsons). He said afterwards that he had read so much in the papers about accidents lately—mining accidents, and aeroplanes and gasoline—that he had grown nervous. The night before his wife had asked him at supper: 'Are you going on the excursion?' He had answered: 'No, I don't think I feel like it,' and had added: 'Perhaps your mother might like to go.' And the next evening just at dusk, when the news ran through the town, he said the first thought that flashed through his head was: 'Mrs Thompson's on that boat.'

He told this right as I say it—without the least doubt or confusion. He never for a moment imagined she was on the *Lusitania* or the *Olympic* or any other boat. He knew she was on this one. He said you could have knocked him down where he stood. But no one had. Not even when he got half-way down—on his knees, and it would have been easier still to knock him down or kick him. People do miss a lot of chances.

Still, as I say, neither Yodel nor Morison nor anyone thought about there being an accident until just after sundown when they—

Well, have you ever heard the long booming whistle of a steamboat two miles out on the lake in the dusk, and while you listen and count and wonder, seen the crimson rockets going up against the sky and then heard the fire bell ringing right there beside you in the town, and seen the people running to the town wharf?

That's what the people of Mariposa saw and felt that summer evening as they watched the Mackinaw lifeboat go plunging out into the lake with seven sweeps to a side and the foam clear to the gunwale with the lifting stroke of fourteen men!

But, dear me, I am afraid that this is no way to tell a story. I suppose the true art would have been to have said nothing about the accident till it happened. But when you write about Mariposa, or hear of it, if you know the place, it's all so vivid and real that a thing like the contrast between the excursion crowd in the morning and the scene at night leaps into your mind and you must think of it.

But never mind about the accident—let us turn back again to the morning.

The boat was due to leave at seven. There was no doubt about the hour—not only seven, but seven sharp. The notice in the *Newspacket* said: 'The boat will leave sharp at seven'; and the advertising posters on the telegraph poles on Missinaba Street that began, 'Ho, for Indian's Island!' ended up with the words: 'Boat leaves at seven sharp.' There was a big notice on the wharf that said: 'Boat leaves sharp on time.'

So at seven, right on the hour, the whistle blew loud and long, and then at seven-fifteen three short peremptory blasts, and at seven-thirty one quick angry call—just one—and very soon after that they cast off the last of the ropes and the *Mariposa Belle* sailed off in her cloud of flags, and the band of the Knights of Pythias, timing it to a nicety, broke into the 'Maple Leaf for Ever!'

I suppose that all excursions when they start are much the same. Anyway, on the *Mariposa Belle* everybody went running up and down all over the boat with deck chairs and camp stools and baskets, and found places, splendid places to sit, and then got scared that there might be better ones and chased off again. People hunted for places out of the sun and when they got them swore that they weren't going to freeze to please anybody; and the people in the sun said that they hadn't paid fifty cents to get roasted. Others said that they hadn't paid fifty cents to get covered with cinders, and there were still others who hadn't paid fifty cents to get shaken to death with the propeller.

Still, it was all right presently. The people seemed to get sorted out into the places on the boat where they belonged. The women, the older ones, all gravitated into the cabin on the lower deck and by getting round the table with needlework, and with all the windows shut, they soon had it, as they said themselves, just like being at home.

All the young boys and the toughs and the men in the band got down on the lower deck forward, where the boat was dirtiest and where the anchor was and the coils of rope.

And upstairs on the after deck there were Lilian Drone and Miss Lawson, the high-school teacher, with a book of German poetry—Gothey I think it was—and the bank teller and the younger men.

In the centre, standing beside the rail, were Dean Drone and Dr. Gallagher, looking through binocular glasses at the shore.

Up in front on the little deck forward of the pilot house was a group of the older men, Mullins and Duff and Mr Smith in a deck chair, and beside him Mr Golgotha Gingham, the undertaker of Mariposa, on a stool. It was part of Mr Gingham's principles to take in an outing of this sort, a business matter, more or less—for you never know what may happen at these water parties. At any rate, he was there in a neat suit of black, not, of course, his heavier or professional suit, but a soft clinging effect as of burnt paper that combined gaiety and decorum to a nicety.

'Yes,' said Mr Gingham, waving his black glove in a general way towards the shore, 'I know the lake well, very well. I've been pretty much all over it in my time.'

'Canoeing?' asked somebody.

'No,' said Mr Gingham, 'not in a canoe.' There seemed a peculiar and quiet meaning in his tone.

'Sailing, I suppose,' said somebody else.

'No,' said Mr Gingham. 'I don't understand it.'

'I never knowed that you went onto the water at all, Gol,' said Mr Smith, breaking in.

'Ah, not now,' explained Mr Gingham; 'it was years ago, the first summer I came to Mariposa. I was on the water practically all day. Nothing like it to give a man an appetite and keep him in shape.'

'Was you camping?' asked Mr Smith.

'We camped at night,' assented the undertaker, 'but we put in practically the whole day on the water. You see we were after a party that had come up here from the city on his vacation and gone out in a sailing canoe. We were dragging. We were up every morning at sunrise, lit a fire on the beach and cooked breakfast, and then we'd light our pipes and be off with the net for a whole day. It's a great life,' concluded Mr Gingham wistfully.

'Did you get him?' asked two or three together.

There was a pause before Mr Gingham answered.

'We did,' he said—'down in the reeds past Horseshoe Point. But it was no use. He turned blue on me right away.'

After which Mr Gingham fell into such a deep reverie that the boat had steamed another half-mile down the lake before anybody broke the silence again.

Talk of this sort—and after all what more suitable for a day on the water?—beguiled the way.

Down the lake, mile by mile over the calm water, steamed the *Mariposa Belle*. They passed Poplar Point where the high sand-banks are with all the swallows' nests in them, and Dean Drone and Dr Gallagher looked at them alternately through the binocular glasses, and it was wonderful how plainly one could see the swallows and the banks and the shrubs—just as plainly as with the naked eye.

And a little farther down they passed the Shingle Beach, and Dr Gallagher, who knew Canadian history, said to Dean Drone that it was strange to think that Champlain had landed there with his French explorers three hundred years ago; and Dean Drone, who didn't know Canadian history, said it was stranger still to think that the hand of the Almighty had piled up the hills and rocks long before that; and Dr Gallagher said it was wonderful how the French had found their way through such a pathless wilderness; and Dean Drone said that it was wonderful also to think that the Almighty had placed even the smallest shrub in its appointed place. Dr Gallagher said it filled him with admiration. Dean Drone said it filled him with awe. Dr Gallagher said he'd been full of it ever since he was a boy; and Dean Drone said so had he.

Then a little farther, as the *Mariposa Belle* steamed on down the lake, they passed the Old Indian Portage where the great grey rocks are; and Dr Gallagher drew Dean Drone's attention to the place where the narrow canoe track wound up from the shore to the woods, and Dean Drone said he could see it perfectly well without the glasses.

Dr Gallagher said that it was just here that a party of five hundred French had made their way with all their baggage and accoutrements across the rocks of the divide and down to the Great Bay. And Dean Drone said that it reminded him of Xenophon leading his ten thousand Greeks over the hill passes of Armenia down to the sea. Dr Gallagher said that he had often wished he could have seen and spoken to Champlain, and Dean Drone said how much he regretted to have never known Xenophon.

And then after that they fell to talking of relics and traces of the past, and Dr Gallagher said that if Dean Drone would come round to his house some night he would show him some Indian arrow heads that he had dug up in his garden. And Dean Drone said that if Dr Gallagher would come round to the rectory any afternoon he would show him a map of Xerxes' invasion of Greece. Only he must come some time between the Infant Class and the Mothers' Auxiliary.

So presently they both knew that they were blocked out of one another's houses for some time to come, and Dr Gallagher walked forward and told Mr Smith, who had never studied Greek, about Champlain crossing the rock divide.

Mr Smith turned his head and looked at the divide for half a second and then said he had crossed a worse one up north back of the Wahnipitae and that the flies were Hades—and then went on playing freezeout poker with the two juniors in Duff's bank.

So Dr Gallagher realized that that's always the way when you try to tell people things, and that as far as gratitude and appreciation goes one might as well never read books or travel anywhere or do anything.

In fact, it was at this very moment that he made up his mind to give the arrows to the Mariposa Mechanics' Institute—they afterwards became, as you know, the Gallagher Collection. But, for the time being, the doctor was sick of them and wandered off round the boat and watched Henry Mullins showing George Duff how to make a John Collins without lemons, and finally went and sat down among the Mariposa band and wished that he hadn't come.

So the boat steamed on and the sun rose higher and higher, and the freshness of the morning changed into the full glare of noon, and they went on to where the lake began to narrow in at its foot, just where the Indian's Island is—all grass and trees and with a log wharf running into the water. Below it the Lower Ossawippi runs out of the lake, and quite near are the rapids, and you can see down among the trees the red brick of the power house and hear the roar of the leaping water.

The Indian's Island itself is all covered with trees and tangled vines, and the water about it is so still that it's all reflected double and looks the same either way up. Then when the steamer's whistle blows as it comes into the wharf, you hear it echo among the trees of the island, and reverberate back from the shores of the lake.

The scene is all so quiet and still and unbroken, that Miss Cleghorn—the sallow girl in the telephone exchange, that I spoke of—said she'd like to be buried there. But all the people were so busy getting their baskets and gathering up their things that no one had time to attend to it.

I mustn't even try to describe the landing and the boat crunching against the wooden wharf and all the people running to the same side of the deck and Christie Johnson calling out to the crowd to keep to the starboard and nobody being able to find it. Everyone who has been on a Mariposa excursion knows all about that.

Nor can I describe the day itself and the picnic under the trees. There were speeches afterwards, and Judge Pepperleigh gave such offence by bringing in Conservative politics that a man called Patriotus Canadiensis wrote and asked for some of the invaluable space of the *Mariposa Times-Herald* and exposed it.

I should say that there were races too, on the grass on the open side of the island, graded mostly according to ages—races for boys under thirteen and girls over nineteen and all that sort of thing. Sports are generally conducted on that plan in Mariposa. It is realized that a woman of sixty has an unfair advantage over a mere child.

Dean Drone managed the races and decided the ages and gave out the prizes; the Wesleyan minister helped, and he and the young student, who was relieving in the Presbyterian Church, held the string at the winning point.

They had to get mostly clergymen for the races because all the men had wandered off, somehow, to where they were drinking lager beer out of two kegs stuck on pine logs among the trees.

But if you've ever been on a Mariposa excursion you know all about these details anyway.

So the day wore on and presently the sun came through the trees on a slant and the steamer whistle blew with a great puff of white steam and all the people came straggling down to the wharf and pretty soon the *Mariposa Belle* had floated out onto the lake again and headed for the town, twenty miles away.

I suppose you have often noticed the contrast there is between an excursion on its way out in the morning and what it looks like on the way home.

In the morning everybody is so restless and animated and moves to and fro all over the boat and asks questions. But coming home, as the afternoon gets later and later and the sun sinks beyond the hills, all the people seem to get so still and quiet and drowsy.

So it was with the people on the *Mariposa Belle*. They sat there on the benches and the deck chairs in little clusters, and listened to the regular beat of the propeller and almost dozed off asleep as they sat. Then when the sun set and the dusk drew on, it grew almost dark on the deck and so still that you could hardly tell there was anyone on board.

And if you had looked at the steamer from the shore or from one of the islands, you'd have seen the row of lights from the cabin windows shining on the water and the red glare of the burning hemlock from the funnel, and you'd have heard the soft thud of the propeller miles away over the lake.

Now and then, too, you could have heard them singing on the steamer— the voices of the girls and the men blended into unison by the distance, rising and falling in long-drawn melody: *O—Can-a-da—O—Can-a-da.*'

You may talk as you will about the intoning choirs of your European cathedrals, but the sound of '*O Can-a-da*', borne across the waters of a silent lake at evening is good enough for those of us who know Mariposa.

I think that it was just as they were singing like this: '*O—Can-a-da*', that word went round that the boat was sinking.

If you have ever been in any sudden emergency on the water, you will understand the strange psychology of it—the way in which what is happening seems to become known all in a moment without a word being said. The news is transmitted from one to the other by some mysterious process.

At any rate, on the *Mariposa Belle* first one and then the other heard that the steamer was sinking. As far as I could ever learn the first of it was that George Duff, the bank manager, came very quietly to Dr Gallagher and asked him if he thought that the boat was sinking. The doctor said no, that he had thought so earlier in the day but that he didn't now think that she was.

After that Duff, according to his own account, had said to Macartney, the lawyer, that the boat was sinking, and Macartney said that he doubted it very much.

Then somebody came to Judge Pepperleigh and woke him up and said that there was six inches of water in the steamer and that she was sinking. And Pepperleigh said it was perfect scandal and passed the news on to his wife and she said that they had no business to allow it and that if the steamer sank that was the last excursion she'd go on.

So the news went all round the boat and everywhere the people gathered in groups and talked about it in the angry and excited way that people have when a steamer is sinking on one of the lakes like Lake Wissanotti.

Dean Drone, of course, and some others were quieter about it, and said that one must make allowances and that naturally there were two sides to everything. But most of them wouldn't listen to reason at all. I think, perhaps, that some of them were frightened. You see the last time but one that the steamer had sunk, there had been a man drowned and it made them nervous.

What? Hadn't I explained about the depth of Lake Wissanotti? I had taken it for granted that you knew; and in any case parts of it are deep enough, though I don't suppose in this stretch of it from the big reed beds up to within a mile of the town wharf, you could find six feet of water in it if you tried. Oh, pshaw! I was not talking about a steamer sinking in the ocean and carrying down its screaming crowds of people into the hideous depths of green water. Oh, dear me, no! That kind of thing never happens on Lake Wissanotti.

But what does happen is that the *Mariposa Belle* sinks every now and then, and sticks there on the bottom till they get things straightened up.

On the lakes round Mariposa, if a person arrives late anywhere and explains that the steamer sank everybody understands the situation.

You see when Harland and Wolff built the *Mariposa Belle*, they left some cracks in between the timbers that you fill up with cotton waste every Sunday. If this is not attended to, the boat sinks. In fact, it is part of the law of the province that all the steamers like the *Mariposa Belle* must be properly corked—I think that is the word—every season. There are inspectors who visit all the hotels in the province to see that it is done.

So you can imagine now that I've explained it a little straighter, the indignation of the people when they knew that the boat had come uncorked and that they might be stuck out there on a shoal or a mud-bank half the night.

I don't say either that there wasn't any danger; anyway, it doesn't feel very safe when you realize that the boat is settling down with every hundred yards that she goes, and you look over the side and see only the black water in the gathering night.

Safe! I'm not sure now that I come to think of it that it isn't worse than sinking in the Atlantic. After all, in the Atlantic there is wireless telegraphy, and a lot of trained sailors and stewards. But out on Lake Wissanotti—far out, so that you can only just see the lights of the town away off to the south—when the propeller comes to a stop—and you can hear the hiss of steam as they start to rake out the engine fires to prevent an explosion—and when you turn from the red glare that comes from the furnace doors as they open them, to the black dark that is gathering over the lake—and there's a night wind beginning to run among the rushes—and you see the men going forward to the roof of the pilot house to send up the rockets to rouse the town—safe? Safe yourself, if you like; as for me, let me once get back into Mariposa again, under the night shadow of the maple trees, and this shall be the last, last time I'll go on Lake Wissanotti.

Safe! Oh, yes! Isn't it strange how safe other people's adventures seem after they happen. But you'd have been scared, too, if you'd been there just before the steamer sank, and seen them bringing up all the women onto the top deck.

I don't see how some of the people took it so calmly; how Mr Smith, for instance, could have gone on smoking and telling how he'd had a steamer 'sink on him' on Lake Nipissing and a still bigger one, a side-wheeler, sink on him in Lake Abbitibbi.

Then, quite suddenly, with a quiver, down she went. You could feel the boat sink, sink—down, down—would it never get to the bottom? The water came flush up to the lower deck, and then—thank heaven—the sinking stopped and there was the *Mariposa Belle* safe and tight on a reed bank.

Really, it made one positively laugh! It seemed so queer and, anyway, if a man has a sort of natural courage, danger makes him laugh. Danger? pshaw! fiddlesticks! everybody scouted the idea. Why, it is just the little things like this that give zest to a day on the water.

Within half a minute they were all running round looking for sand-wiches and cracking jokes and talking of making coffee over the remains of the engine fires.

I don't need to tell at length how it all happened after that.

I suppose the people on the *Mariposa Belle* would have had to settle down there all night or till help came from the town, but some of the men who had gone forward and were peering out into the dark said that it couldn't be more than a mile across the water to Miller's Point. You could almost see it over there to the left—some of them, I think, said 'off on the port bow', because you know when you get mixed up in these marine disasters, you soon catch the atmosphere of the thing.

So pretty soon they had the davits swung out over the side and were lowering the old lifeboat from the top deck into the water.

There were men leaning out over the rail of the *Mariposa Belle* with lanterns that threw the light as they let her down, and the glare fell on the water and the reeds. But when they got the boat lowered, it looked such a frail, clumsy thing as one saw it from the rail above, that the cry was raised: 'Women and children first!' For what was the sense, if it should turn out that the boat wouldn't even hold women and children, of trying to jam a lot of heavy men into it?

So they put in mostly women and children and the boat pushed out into the darkness so freighted down it would hardly float.

In the bow of it was the Presbyterian student who was relieving the minister, and he called out that they were in the hands of Providence. But he was crouched and ready to spring out of them at the first moment.

So the boat went and was lost in the darkness except for the lantern in the bow that you could see bobbing on the water. Then presently it came back and they sent another load, till pretty soon the decks began to thin out and everybody got impatient to be gone.

It was about the time that the third boatload put off that Mr Smith took a bet with Mullins for twenty-five dollars, that he'd be home in Mariposa before the people in the boats had walked round the shore.

No one knew just what he meant, but pretty soon they saw Mr Smith disappear down below into the lowest part of the steamer with a mallet in one hand and a big bundle of marline in the other.

They might have wondered more about it, but it was just at this time that they heard the shouts from the rescue boat—the big Mackinaw lifeboat—that had put out from the town with fourteen men at the sweeps when they saw the first rockets go up.

I suppose there is always something inspiring about a rescue at sea, or on the water.

After all, the bravery of the lifeboat man is the true bravery—expended to save life, not to destroy it.

Certainly they told for months after of how the rescue boat came out to the *Mariposa Belle*.

I suppose that when they put her in the water the lifeboat touched it for the first time since the old Macdonald Government placed her on Lake Wissanotti.

Anyway, the water poured in at every seam. But not for a moment—even with two miles of water between them and the steamer—did the rowers pause for that.

By the time they were halfway there the water was almost up to the thwarts, but they drove her on. Panting and exhausted (for mind you, if you haven't been in a fool boat like that for years, rowing takes it out of you), the rowers stuck to their task. They threw the ballast over and chucked into the water the heavy cork jackets and lifebelts that encumbered their movements. There was no thought of turning back. They were nearer to the steamer than the shore.

'Hang to it, boys,' called the crowd from the steamer's deck, and hang they did.

They were almost exhausted when they got them; men leaning from the steamer threw them ropes and one by one every man was hauled aboard just as the lifeboat sank under their feet.

Saved! by heaven, saved by one of the smartest pieces of rescue work ever seen on the lake.

There's no use describing it; you need to see rescue work of this kind by lifeboats to understand it.

Nor were the lifeboat crew the only ones that distinguished themselves.

Boat after boat and canoe after canoe had put out from Mariposa to the help of the steamer. They got them all.

Pupkin, the other bank teller, with a face like a horse, who hadn't gone on the excursion—as soon as he knew that the boat was signalling for help and that Miss Lawson was sending up rockets—rushed for a row boat, grabbed an oar (two would have hampered him), and paddled madly out into the lake. He struck right out into the dark with the crazy skiff almost sinking beneath his feet. But they got him. They rescued him. They watched him, almost dead with exhaustion, make his way to the steamer, where he was hauled up with ropes. Saved! Saved!

They might have gone on that way half the night, picking up the rescuers, only, at the very moment when the tenth load of people left for the shore—just as suddenly and saucily as you please, up came the *Mariposa Belle* from the mud bottom and floated.

FLOATED?

Why, of course she did. If you take a hundred and fifty people off a steamer that has sunk, and if you get a man as shrewd as Mr Smith to plug the timber seams with mallet and marline, and if you turn ten bandsmen of the Mariposa band onto your hand pump on the bow of the lower decks—float? why, what else can she do?

Then, if you stuff in hemlock into the embers of the fire that you were raking out, till it hums and crackles under the boiler, it won't be long before you hear the propeller thud—thudding at the stern again, and before the long roar of the steam whistle echoes over to the town.

And so the *Mariposa Belle*, with all steam up again and with the long train of sparks careering from the funnel, is heading for the town.

But no Christie Johnson at the wheel in the pilot house this time.

'Smith! Get Smith!' is the cry.

Can he take her in? Well, now! Ask a man who has had steamers sink on him in half the lakes from Temiscaming to the Bay, if he can take her in? Ask a man who has run a York boat down the rapids of the Moose when the ice is moving, if he can grip the steering wheel of the *Mariposa Belle*? So there she steams safe and sound to the town wharf!

Look at the lights and the crowd! If only the federal census taker could count us now! Hear them calling and shouting back and forward from the deck to the shore! Listen! There is the rattle of the shore ropes as they get them ready, and there's the Mariposa band—actually forming in a circle on the upper deck just as she docks, and the leader with his baton—one—two—ready now—

'O CAN-A-DA!'

ETHEL WILSON
1888–1980

From Flores

Up at Flores Island, Captain Findlay Crabbe readied his fishboat the *Effie Cee* for the journey home and set out in good spirits while the weather was fair. But even by the time he saw the red shirt flapping like mad from the rocky point just north of the Indian's place the wind had freshened. Nevertheless Fin Crabbe told the big man at the wheel to turn into shore because there must be some trouble there and that Indian family was pretty isolated. As the man at the wheel turned the nose of the boat towards the shore, the skipper listened to the radio. The weather report was good, and so he went out on the small deck well satisfied and stood there with his hands on his hips, looking at the shore where the red flag was.

The third man on the fishboat was just a young fellow. Up at Flores Island he had come down to the float with his gear all stowed in a duffel bag and asked the skipper to take him down to Port Alberni. He was an anxious kid, tall, dark, and thin-faced. He said he'd pay money for the ride and he spoke of bad news which with a young man sounds like parents or a girl and with an older young man sounds like a wife or children or a girl. Fin Crabbe said shortly that the boy could come, although the little *Effie Cee* was not geared for passengers. He didn't need to pay.

Captain Crabbe was small. He had come as an undersized boy to the west coast of Vancouver Island and there he had stayed. He had been fairish and was now bald. His eyes were sad like a little bloodhound's eyes and pink under, but he was not sad. He was a contented man and rejoiced always to be joined again with his wife and his gangling son and daughter. Mrs Crabbe's name was Effie but she was called Mrs Crabbe or Mom and her name had come to be used only for the *Effie Cee* which was by this time more Effie than Mrs Crabbe was. 'I'm taking home an Indian basket for Mrs Crabbe,' the skipper might say. 'Mrs Crabbe sure is an authority on Indian baskets.' Fin Crabbe was his name up and down the coast but at home he was the Captain or Pop, and so Mrs Crabbe would say, 'The Captain plans to be home for Christmas. The Captain's a great family man. I said to him "Pop, if you're not home for Christmas, I'll . . . !" ' Thus they daily elevated each other in esteem and loved each other with simple mutual gratification. In bed no names were needed by Mrs Crabbe and the Captain. (When they shall be dead, as they will be, what will avail this happy self-satisfaction. But now they are not dead, and the Captain's wife as often before awaits the Captain who is on his way down the coast from Flores Island, coming home for Christmas.)

Fin Crabbe had planned for some time to reach Port Alberni early in Christmas week and that suited Ed, the big crewman, too. Ed was not a family man although he had a wife somewhere; but what strong upspringing black curly hair he had and what gambling eyes. He was powerful, not to be governed, and a heller when he drank. He was quick to laugh, quick to hit out, quick to take a girl, quick to leave her, a difficult wilful volatile enjoying man of poor judgement, but he got along all right with little Fin Crabbe. He did not want to spend Christmas in Flores Island when there was so much doing in Alberni and Port Alberni.

Captain Crabbe's family lived in Alberni proper, which to the dweller in a city seems like a fairly raw small town at the end of a long arm through the forest to nowhere, and to the dweller up the coast or in the Queen Charlottes seems like a small city with every comfort, every luxury, motor cars speeding in and out by the long road that leads through the forest to the fine Island Highway, lighted streets, plumbing, beer parlours, a hospital, churches, schools, lumber mills, wharves. It lives for and on trees and salt water. Behind it is a huge hinterland of giant forests. Before it lies the long tortuous salt-water arm of the open sea.

Captain Crabbe, as the bow of the *Effie Cee* turned towards the pine-clad but desolate and rocky shore, cutting across the tricky undulations of the ocean, again gave his habitual look at the sky, north and west. The sky was overclouded but so it usually is in these parts at this time of year. Since these rocky shores are not protected as are the rocky shores of the British Columbia mainland by the long stretches of sweet liveable gulf islands and by the high barrier of mountainous Vancouver Island itself, the west coast of the island lies naked to the Pacific Ocean, which rolls in all the way from Asia and breaks upon the reefs and rocks and hard sands, and the continuous brewing of weather up in an air cauldron in the north seethes and spills over and rushes out of the Gulf of Alaska, often moderating before it reaches lower latitudes; but sometimes it roars down and attacks like all hell. The fishboat and tugboat men know this weather well and govern themselves accordingly. Next morning, perhaps the ocean smiles like a dissolute angel. The fishboat and tugboat men know that, too, and are not deceived. So that although Fin Crabbe knew all this as well as he knew his own thumb, he did not hesitate to turn the *Effie Cee* towards the shore when he saw the red shirt flapping at the end of the rock point but he had no intention of stopping there nor of spending any time at all unless his judgement warranted it, for on this trip his mind was closely set to home.

The turning aside of the fishboat in her journey irked the young passenger very much. Since the weather report on the radio was fairly good and anyway he was used to poor weather, he felt no concern about that. But here was delay and how much of it. He did not know how often he had read the letter, which he again took out of his pocket, not looking at big Ed nor at little Captain Crabbe but frowning at the letter and at some memory. He was possessed entirely, usurped, by impatience for contact, by letter, by wire or—best of all—by speech and sight and touch with the writer of this letter. Now that he had started on the journey towards her, now that he had started, now that he was on his way, his confusion seemed to clear. He read again in the letter: 'Dear Jason I am very unhappy I dont know I should tell you Ive thought and thought before I wrote you and then what kind of a letter because I could say awful things and say you must come to Vancouver right away and marry me or believe me I could just cry and cry or I could write and say plain to you O Jason do I beseech you think if we couldnt get married right away. I could say I love you and I do.'

The young man folded the letter again. He looked with distaste at the red flag that signified an Indian's trouble and his own delay and his mind ran backwards again. The letter had found him at last and only two days ago. He had left the camp and had crossed to Flores and there an old man with a beard had told him that Fin Crabbe was all set to go to Alberni the next morning, and he had enquired for Captain Crabbe. As he had walked up and down the float pushing time forward, sometimes a violence of joy rose in him and surprised him. This was succeeded by a real fear that something would happen to prevent the fishboat from leaving, would prevent them reaching Alberni very soon, while all the time Josie did not even know whether he had received the letter. Many feelings were induced in him by what Josie had written, and now he thought ceaselessly about her to whom, only three days before, he had barely given a thought. He unfolded the letter again.

'I gess I dont know too much about love like in the pictures but I do love you Jason and I wouldnt ever ever be a person who would throw this up at you. I dont sleep very good and some nights I threton to myself to kill myself and tho I am awful scared of that maybe that would be better and easiest for us all and the next night I say no. Lots of girls go through with this but what do they do with the Baby and no real home for it and then I am bafled again and the time is going.'

Jason, looking out to the ocean but not seeing it, was aware of a different Josie. If a person had told me, he thought, that I'd want to get married and that I'd be crazy for this baby I'd say they were crazy, I'd say they were nuts, and impatience against delay surged over him again. The boat neared the mouth of the bay.

'One thing I do know I couldnt go back to the prairies with the Baby,' (no, that's right, you couldn't go back) 'so where would the Baby and me go. Mother would let me feel it every day even if she didnt mean to tho she would take us but Father no never. Then I think its the best thing for the Baby I should drown myself its quite easy in Vancouver its not like the prairies I do mean that.'

The skipper was talking back and forth to the crewman at the wheel and the *Effie Cee* slowed down. There were beams of sunshine that came and went.

'I cant believe its me and I do pitty any poor girl but not begging you Jason because you must decide for yourself. Some people would pay no attention to this letter but I kind of feel youre not like some people but O please Jason get me a word soon and then I can know what. Josie.'

From the pages arose the helpless and lonely anguish of little Josie and this anguish entered and consumed him too and it was all part of one storm of anxiety and anger that she was alone and she so quiet, and not her fault (he said), and impatience rose within him to reach a place where he could say to her Don't you worry kid, I'm coming! He thought with surprise Maybe I'm a real bad guy and I never knew it, maybe we're all bad and we don't know it. He read once more: 'I am bafled again and the time is going . . . I do love you Jason.' He put his head in his hands with dumb anger that she should be driven to this, but as soon as he reached a telephone in Alberni everything would be all right. As he suddenly looked up he thought he would go mad at this turning off course for any sick guy, or any kid who'd been crazy enough to break an arm. In his frustration and impatience there was an infusion of being a hero and rushing to save someone. Some hero, he said very sourly to himself, some hero.

The *Effie Cee* slowed to a stop and a black volley of cormorants, disturbed, flew away in a dark line. There was an Indian and an Indian woman and a little boy in a rowboat almost alongside the fishboat. The little boy was half lying down in an uncomfortable way and two rough sticks were tied to his leg. Three smaller children stood solemnly on the rocky shore looking at the two boats. Then they turned to play in a clumsy ceremonial fashion among the barnacled rocks. They did not laugh as they played.

Jason put the letter in his pocket and stood up. The rowboat jiggled on the water and Captain Crabbe was bending down and talking to the Indian. He listened and talked and explained. The Indian's voice was slow and muffled, but not much talk was needed. Anyone could see. 'Okay,' said the skipper and then he straightened himself and turned to look at Ed and Jason as much as to say . . . and Jason said, 'Better I got into the rowboat and helped him lift the kid up,' and the skipper said 'Okay.'

All this time the woman did not say anything. She kept her hands wrapped in her stuff dress and looked away or at the child. Jason slipped over the side and the rowboat at once became overcrowded, which made it difficult for him and the Indian to lift the child up carefully without hurting him and without separating the boats. The Indian child made no sound and no expression appeared on his face so no one knew how much pain he suffered or whether he suffered at all. His eyes were brown and without meaning like the dusky opaque eyes of a fawn. The Indian spoke to his wife and she reached out her hands and held on to the fishboat so that the two craft would not be parted. Jason and the father succeeded in slipping their arms—'This way,' said Jason, 'see? do it this way'—under the child and raised him gradually up to where Ed and the skipper were kneeling. Everyone leaned too much to one side of the rowboat and Jason tried to steady it so that they would not fall with the child into the sea. All this time the woman had not spoken but had accepted whatever other people did as if she had no rights in the matter. When the child was safely on board, Jason sprang onto the deck and at once, at once, the *Effie Cee* turned and tore away with a white bone of spume in her mouth and a white wake of foam behind, leaving the Indians in the rowboat and the children on the shore looking after her.

'Best lay him on the floor, he'd maybe roll off of the bunk,' said Fin Crabbe when they had lifted the child inside. 'Mustn't let you get cold, Sonny,' he said, and took down a coat that swung from a hook. The child regarded him in silence and with fear in his heart. One two another white man taking him to some place he did not know.

'Make supper Ed, and I'll take the wheel,' said the skipper. The boat went faster ahead, rising and plunging as there was now a small sea running.

What'd I better do, thought Fin Crabbe and did not consult the crewman who hadn't much judgement. There were good reasons for going on
through and trying to make Alberni late in the night or in early morning.
That would surprise Mrs Crabbe and she would be pleased, and the
young fella seemed desperate to get to Alberni on account of this bad
news; but here was this boy he'd taken aboard and the sooner they got
him into hospital the better. I think it's his hip (he thought), I could turn
back to Tofino but it'd be dark then and would he be any better off
landing him in the dark and likely no doctor. Anyway I can make Ucluelet
easy and spend the night. I don't like to take no chances but all in all I
think we'll go on. And they went on.

Evening came and black night. It was winter cold outside and Jason
crowded into the wheelhouse and looked out at the dark. The coming of
night brought him nearer the telephone, so near he could all but touch it,
but he could not touch it.

The *Effie Cee* could not make much speed now and ploughed slowly
for hours never ending, it seemed to Jason, through water that had
become stormy and in the dark she followed a sideways course so that
she could cut a little across the waves that were now high and deep. Ed
had the wheel and Captain Crabbe stood beside him. The storm increased.
The boat's nose plunged into the waves and rose with the waves and the
water streamed over. There was a wallowing, a sideways wallowing.
The little fishboat became a world of noise and motion, a plunging, a
rising, a plunging again. Jason wedged the child against the base of the
bunk. The child cried out, and vomited with seasickness and fear. 'Now
now,' said Jason, patting him. 'Try the radio again,' said Captain Crabbe.

Jason fiddled with the radio. 'Can't seem to get anything,' he said.

'Let me,' said the skipper.

'Bust,' he said.

But now the storm rapidly accelerated and the waves, innocent and
savage as tigers, leaped at the *Effie Cee* and the oncoming rollers struck
broadside and continuously. The little boy made sounds like an animal
and Jason, in whom for the first time fear of what might come had struck
down all elation and expectation, took the child's hand and held it. The
little plunging boat was now the whole world and fate to Jason and to Fin
Crabbe and to the Indian boy but not to Ed who had no fear. Perhaps
because he had no love he had no fear. Standing over the wheel and
peering into the dark, he seemed like a great black bull and it was to
Jason as though he filled the cabin.

Ed turned the boat's nose towards shore to get away from the broadside of the waves. Fin Crabbe shouted at him to be heard above the

storm. The boat had been shipping water and Jason, crouching beside the shaking child in a wash of water heard the words 'Ucluelet' and 'lighthouse' and 'rocks' but Ed would not listen. The skipper went on shouting at him and then he seized the wheel. He pushed the big man with all his strength, turning the wheel to starboard. Jason and the Indian child saw the big man and the little man fighting in the small space, in the din of the ocean, the howl of the wind, for possession of the wheel. As quick as a cat Ed drew off and hit the older man a great blow. Fin Crabbe crumpled and fell. He lay in the wash of water at Ed's feet and Ed had his way, so the fishboat drove inshore, hurled by the waves onto the reefs, or onto the hard sand, or onto the place that Ed knew that he knew, whichever the dark should disclose, but not to the open sea. Captain Crabbe tried to raise himself and Jason crawled over towards him.

The skipper could not stand in the pitching boat. He looked up at Ed who was his executioner, the avenger of all that he had ever done, driving on against death for sure.

The thought of the abandonment of Josie (for now a belief was formed terribly in him that she was to be abandoned) pierced Jason through and through and then in the immediate danger the thought of Josie was no longer real but fled away on the wind and water, and there was nothing but fear. Without knowing what he did, he seized and held the child. Never could a man feel greater despair than Jason in the walnut shell of a reeling boat soon to be cracked between land and water. Ed, bent over the wheel, knowing everything, knowing just where they were, but not knowing, looked only forward into the blackness and drove on. The sea poured into the boat and at the same minute the lights went out and they were no longer together. Then the *Effie Cee* rose on a great wave, was hurled upwards and downwards, struck the barnacled reef, and split, and the following seas washed over.

A few days later the newspapers stated that in the recent storm on the west coast of Vancouver Island the fishboat *Effie Cee* was missing with two men aboard. These men were Findlay Crabbe aged fifty-six and Edward Morgan aged thirty-five, both of Alberni. Planes were continuing the search.

A day or two afterwards the newspapers stated that it was thought that there might have been a third man aboard the *Effie Cee*. He was identified as Jason Black aged twenty-two, employed as a logger up the coast near Flores Island.

On the second morning after the wreck of the *Effie Cee* the skies were a cold blue and the ocean lay sparkling and lazy beneath the sun. Up the

Alberni Canal the sea and air were chilly and brilliant but still. Mrs Crabbe spent the day waiting on the wharf in the cold sunshine. She stood or walked or sat, accompanied by two friends or by the gangling son and daughter, and next day it was the same, and the next. People said to her, 'But he didn't set a day? When did he *say* he'd be back?'

'He never said what day,' she said. 'The Captain couldn't ever say what day. He just said the beginning of the week, maybe Monday was what he said.' She said 'he said, he said, he said' because it seemed to establish him as living. People had to stop asking because they could not bear to speak to Mrs Crabbe standing and waiting on the busy wharf, paying the exorbitant price of love. They wished she would not wait there because it made them uncomfortable and unhappy to see her.

Because Josie did not read the papers, she did not know that Jason was dead. Days had passed and continued to pass. Distraught, alone, deprived of hope and faith (two sovereign remedies) and without the consolation of love, she took secretly and with terror what she deemed to be the appropriate path.

The Indian, who had fully trusted the man who took his son away, heard nothing more. He waited until steady fine weather came and then took his family in his small boat to Tofino. From there he made his way to Alberni. Here he walked slowly up and down the docks and at last asked someone where the hospital was; but at the hospital no one seemed to know anything about his only son.

MORLEY CALLAGHAN

b.1903

Last Spring They Came Over

Alfred Bowles came to Canada from England and got a job on a Toronto paper. He was a young fellow with clear, blue eyes and heavy pimples on the lower part of his face, the son of a Baptist minister whose family was too large for his salary. He got thirty dollars a week on the paper and said it was surprisingly good screw to start. For five a week he got an attic room in a brick house painted brown on Mutual Street. He ate his meals in a quick-lunch near the office. He bought a cane and a light-gray fedora.

He wasn't a good reporter but was inoffensive and obliging. After he had been working two weeks the fellows took it for granted he would be fired in a little while and were nice to him, liking the way the most trifling occurrences surprised him. He was happy to carry his cane on his arm and wear the fedora at a jaunty angle, quite the reporter. He liked to explain that he was doing well. He wrote home about it.

When they put him doing night police he felt important, phoning the fire department, hospitals, and police stations, trying to be efficient. He was getting along all right. It was disappointing when after a week the assistant city editor, Mr H. J. Brownson, warned him to phone his home if anything important happened, and he would have another man cover it. But Bowles got to like hearing the weary, irritable voice of the assistant city editor called from his bed at three o'clock in the morning. He liked to politely call Mr Brownson as often and as late as possible, thinking it a bit of good fun.

Alfred wrote long letters to his brother and to his father, the Baptist minister, using a typewriter, carefully tapping the keys, occasionally laughing to himself. In a month's time he had written six letters describing the long city room, the fat belly of the city editor, and the bad words the night editor used when speaking of the Orangemen.

The night editor took a fancy to him because of the astounding puerility of his political opinions. Alfred was always willing to talk pompously of the British Empire policing the world and about all Catholics being aliens, and the future of Ireland and Canada resting with the Orangemen. He flung his arms wide and talked in the hoarse voice of a bad actor, but no one would have thought of taking him seriously. He was merely having a dandy time. The night editor liked him because he was such a nice boy.

Then Alfred's brother came out from the Old Country, and got a job on the same paper. Some of the men started talking about cheap cockney labourers crowding the good guys out of the jobs, but Harry Bowles was frankly glad to get the thirty a week. It never occurred to him that he had a funny idea of good money. With his first pay he bought a derby hat, a pair of spats, and a cane, but even though his face was clear and had a good colour he never looked as nice as his younger brother because his heavy nose curved up at the end. The landlady on Mutual Street moved a double bed into Alfred's room and Harry slept with his brother.

The days passed with many good times together. At first it was awkward that Alfred should be working at night and his brother in the day-time, but Harry was pleased to come down to the office every night at eleven and they went down the street to the hotel that didn't bother about Prohibition. They drank a few glasses of good beer. It became a kind of rite that had to be performed carefully. Harry would put his left foot and Alfred his right foot on the rail and leaning an elbow on the bar they would slowly survey the zigzag line of frothing glasses the length of the long bar. Men jostled them for a place at the foot-rail.

And Alfred said: 'Well, a bit of luck.'

Harry grinning and raising his glass said: 'Righto.'

'It's the stuff that heals.'

'Down she goes.'

'It helps the night along.'

'Fill them up again.'

'Toodleoo.'

Then they would walk out of the crowded bar-room, vaguely pleased with themselves. Walking slowly and erectly along the street they talked with assurance, a mutual respect for each other's opinion making it merely an exchange of information. They talked of the Englishman in Canada, comparing his lot with that of the Englishman in South Africa and India. They had never travelled but to ask what they knew of strange lands would have made one feel uncomfortable; it was better to take it for granted that the Bowles boys knew all about the ends of the earth and had judged them carefully, for in their eyes was the light of far-away places. Once in a while, after walking a block or two, one of the brothers would say he would damn well like to see India and the other would say it would be simply topping.

After work and on Sundays they took a look at the places they had heard about in the city. One Sunday they got up in good time and took the boat to Niagara. Their father had written asking if they had seen the Falls and would they send some souvenirs. That day they had as nice a time as a man would want to have. Standing near the pipe-rail a little way from the hotel that overlooks the Falls they watched the water-line just before the drop, smooth as a long strip of bevelled glass, and Harry compared it favourably with a cataract in the Himalayas and a giant waterfall in Africa, just above the Congo. They took a car along the gorge and getting off near the whirlpool, picked out a little hollow near a big rock at the top of the embankment where the grass was lush and green. They stretched themselves out with hats tilted over their eyes for sunshades. The river whirled below. They talked about the funny ways of Mr Brownson and his short fat legs and about the crazy women who fainted at the lifted hand of the faith healer who was in the city for the week. They liked the distant rumble of the Falls. They agreed to try and save a lot of money and go west to the Pacific in a year's time. They never mentioned trying to get a raise in pay.

Afterwards they each wrote home about the trip, sending the souvenirs.

Neither one was doing well on the paper. Harry wasn't much good because he hated writing the plain copy and it was hard for him to be strictly accurate. He liked telling a good tale but it never occurred to him that he was deliberately lying. He imagined a thing and straightway felt it to be true. But it never occurred to Alfred to depart from the truth. He was accurate but lazy, never knowing when he was really working. He was taken off night police and for two weeks helped a man do courts at the City Hall. He got to know the boys at the press gallery, who smiled at his naïve sincerity and thought him a decent chap, without making up their minds about him. Every noonhour Harry came to the press gallery and the brothers, sitting at typewriters, wrote long letters all about the country and the people, anything interesting, and after exchanging letters, tilted back in their swivel chairs, laughing out loud. Heaven only knows who got the letters in the long run. Neither one when in the press gallery seemed to write anything for the paper.

Some of the men tried kidding Alfred, teasing him about women, asking if he found the girls in this country to his liking; but he seemed to enjoy it more than they did. Seriously he explained that he had never met a girl in this country, but they looked very nice. Once Alfred and Bun Brophy, a red-headed fellow with a sharp tongue who did City Hall for the paper, were alone in the gallery. Brophy had in his hands a big picture of five girls in masquerade costumes. Without explaining that he loved one of the girls Brophy asked Bowles which of the lot was the prettiest.

'You want me to settle that,' said Alfred, grinning and waving his pipe. He very deliberately selected a demure little girl with a shy smile.

Brophy was disappointed. 'Don't you think this one is pretty?'—a colourful, bold-looking girl.

'Well, she's all right in her way, but she's too vivacious. I'll take this one. I like them kittenish,' Alfred said.

Brophy wanted to start an argument but Alfred said it was neither here nor there. He really didn't like women.

'You mean to say you never step out?' Brophy said.

'I've never seemed to mix with them,' he said, adding that the whole business didn't matter because he liked boys much better.

The men in the press room heard about it and some suggested nasty things to Alfred. It was hard to tease him when he wouldn't be serious. Sometimes they asked if he took Harry out walking in the evenings. Brophy called them the heavy lovers. The brothers didn't mind because they thought the fellows were having a little fun.

In the fall Harry was fired. The editor in a nice note said that he was satisfied Mr H. W. Bowles could not adapt himself to their methods. But everybody wondered why he hadn't been fired sooner. He was no good on the paper.

The brothers smiled, shrugged their shoulders and went on living together. Alfred still had his job. Every noon-hour in the City Hall press room they were together, writing letters.

Time passed and the weather got cold. Alfred's heavy coat came from the Old Country and he gave his vest and a thin sweater to Harry, who had only a light spring coat. As the weather got colder Harry buttoned his coat higher up on his throat and even though he looked cold he was neat as a pin with his derby and cane.

Then Alfred lost his job. The editor, disgusted, called him a fool. For the first time since coming over last spring he felt hurt, something inside him was hurt and he told his brother about it, wanting to know why people acted in such a way. He said he had been doing night police. On the way over to No. 1 station very late Thursday night he had met two men from other papers. They told him about a big fire earlier in the evening just about the time when Alfred was accustomed to going to the hotel to have a drink with his brother. They were willing to give all the details and Alfred thankfully shook hands with them and hurried back to the office to write the story. Next morning the assistant city editor phoned Alfred and asked how it was the morning papers missed the story. Alfred tried to explain but Mr Brownson said he was a damn fool for not phoning the police and making sure instead of trying to make the paper look like a pack of fools printing a fake story. The fellows who had kidded him said that too. Alfred kept asking his brother why the fellows had to do it. He seemed to be losing a good feeling for people.

Still the brothers appeared at noontime in the press room. They didn't write so many letters. They were agreeable, cheerful, on good terms with everybody. Bun Brophy every day asked how they were doing and they felt at home there. Harry would stand for a while watching the checker game always in progress, knowing that if he stood staring intently at the black and red squares, watching every deliberate move, he would be asked to sit in when it was necessary that one of the players make the rounds in the hall. Once Brophy gave Harry his place and walked over to the window where Alfred stood watching the fleet of automobiles arranged in a square in the courtyard. The police wagon with a load of drunks was backing toward the cells.

'Say, Alfie, I often wonder how you guys manage,' he said.

'Oh, first rate.'

'Well, you ought to be in a bad way by now.'

'Oh no, we have solved the problem,' said Alfred in a grand way, grinning, as if talking about the British Empire.

He was eager to tell how they did it. There was a store in their block where a package of tobacco could be got for five cents; they did their own cooking and were able to live on five dollars a week.

'What about coming over and having tea with us sometimes?' Alfred said. He was decidedly on his uppers but he asked Brophy to visit them and have tea.

Brophy, abashed, suggested the three of them go over to the café and have a little toast. Harry talked volubly on the way over and while having coffee. He was really a better talker than his brother. They sat in an arm-chair lunch, gripped the handles of their thick mugs, and talked about religion. The brothers were sons of a Baptist minister but never thought of going to church. It seemed that Brophy had travelled a lot during war-time and afterward in Asia Minor and India. He was telling about a great golden temple of the Sikhs at Amritsar and Harry listened carefully, asking many questions. Then they talked about newspapers until Harry started talking about the East, slowly feeling his way. All of a sudden he told about standing on a height of land near Amritsar, looking down at a temple. It couldn't have been so but he would have it that Brophy and he had seen the same temple and he described the country in the words Brophy had used. When he talked that way you actually believed that he had seen the temple.

Alfred liked listening to his brother but he said finally: 'Religion is a funny business. I tell you it's a funny business.' And for the time being no one would have thought of talking seriously about religion. Alfred had a casual way of making a cherished belief or opinion seem unimportant, a way of dismissing even the bright yarns of his brother.

After that afternoon in the café Brophy never saw Harry. Alfred came often to the City Hall but never mentioned his brother. Someone said maybe Harry had a job but Alfred laughed and said no such luck in this country, explaining casually that Harry had a bit of a cold and was resting up. In the passing days Alfred came only once in a while to the City Hall, writing his letter without enthusiasm.

The press men would have tried to help the brothers if they had heard Harry was sick. They were entirely ignorant of the matter. On a Friday afternoon at three-thirty Alfred came into the gallery and, smiling apologetically, told Brophy that his brother was dead; the funeral was to be in three-quarters of an hour; would he mind coming? It was pneumonia, he added. Brophy, looking hard at Alfred, put on his hat and coat and they went out.

It was a poor funeral. The hearse went on before along the way to the Anglican cemetery that overlooks the ravine. One old cab followed behind. There had been a heavy fall of snow in the morning, and the slush of the pavement was thick. Alfred and Brophy sat in the old cab, silent. Alfred was leaning forward, his chin resting on his hands, the cane acting as a support, and the heavy pimples stood out on the lower part of his white face. Brophy was uncomfortable and chilly but he mopped his shining forehead with a big handkerchief. The window was open and the air was cold and damp.

Alfred politely asked how Mrs Brophy was doing. Then he asked about Mr Brownson.

'Oh, he's fine,' Brophy said. He wanted to close the window but it would have been necessary to move Alfred so he sat huddled in the corner, shivering.

Alfred asked suddenly if funerals didn't leave a bad taste in the mouth and Brophy, surprised, started talking absently about that golden temple of the Sikhs in India. Alfred appeared interested until they got to the cemetery. He said suddenly he would have to take a look at the temple one fine day.

They buried Harry Bowles in a grave in the paupers' section on a slippery slope of the hill. The earth was hard and chunky and it thumped down on the coffin case. It snowed a little near the end.

On the way along the narrow, slippery foot-path up the hill Alfred thanked Brophy for being thoughtful enough to come to the funeral. There was little to say. They shook hands and went different ways.

After a day or two Alfred again appeared in the press room. He watched the checker game, congratulated the winner and then wrote home. The men were sympathetic and said it was too bad about his brother. And he smiled cheerfully and said they were good fellows. In a little while he seemed to have convinced them that nothing important had really happened.

His last cent must have gone to the undertaker, for he was particular about paying bills, but he seemed to get along all right. Occasionally he did a little work for the paper, a story from a night assignment when the editor thought the staff was being overworked.

One afternoon at two-thirty in the press gallery Brophy saw the last of Alfred, who was sucking his pipe, his feet up on a desk, wanting to be amused. Brophy asked if anything had turned up. In a playful, resigned tone, his eye on the big clock, Alfred said he had until three to join the Air Force. They wouldn't take him, he said, unless he let them know by three.

Brophy said, 'How will you like that?'

'I don't fancy it.'

'But you're going through.'

'Well, I'm not sure. Something else may come along.' It was a quarter to three and he was sitting there waiting for a job to turn up before three.

No one saw him after that, but he didn't join the Air Force. Someone in the gallery said that wherever he went he probably wrote home as soon as he got there.

THOMAS H. RADDALL

b. 1903

The Wedding Gift

Nova Scotia, in 1794. Winter. Snow on the ground. Two feet of it in the woods, less by the shore, except in drifts against Port Marriott's barns and fences; but enough to set sleigh bells ringing through the town, enough to require a multitude of paths and burrows from doors to streets, to carpet the wharves and the decks of the shipping, and to trim the ships' yards with tippets of ermine. Enough to require fires roaring in the town's chimneys, and blue wood smoke hanging low over the roof tops in the still December air. Enough to squeal under foot in the trodden places and to muffle the step everywhere else. Enough for the hunters, whose snowshoes now could overtake the floundering moose and caribou. Even enough for the always-complaining loggers, whose ox sleds now could haul their cut from every part of the woods. But not enough, not nearly enough snow for Miss Kezia Barnes, who was going to Bristol Creek to marry Mr Hathaway.

Kezia did not want to marry Mr Hathaway. Indeed she had told Mr and Mrs Barclay in a tearful voice that she didn't want to marry anybody. But Mr Barclay had taken snuff and said 'Ha! Humph!' in the severe tone he used when he was displeased; and Mrs Barclay had sniffed and said it was a very good match for her, and revolved the cold blue eyes in her fat moon face, and said Kezia must not be a little fool.

There were two ways of going to Bristol Creek. One was by sea, in one of the fishing sloops. But the preacher objected to that. He was a pallid young man lately sent out from England by Lady Huntingdon's Connexion, and seasick five weeks on the way. He held Mr Barclay in some awe, for Mr Barclay had the best pew in the meetinghouse and was the chief pillar of godliness in Port Marriott. But young Mr Mears was firm on this point. He would go by road, he said, or not at all. Mr Barclay had retorted 'Ha! Humph!' The road was twenty miles of horse path through the woods, now deep in snow. Also the path began at Harper's Farm on the far side of the harbour, and Harper had but one horse.

'I shall walk,' declared the preacher calmly, 'and the young woman can ride.'

Kezia had prayed for snow, storms of snow, to bury the trail and keep anyone from crossing the cape to Bristol Creek. But now they were setting out from Harper's Farm, with Harper's big brown horse, and all Kezia's prayers had gone for naught. Like any anxious lover, busy Mr Hathaway had sent Black Sam overland on foot to find out what delayed his wedding, and now Sam's day-old tracks marked for Kezia the road to marriage.

She was a meek little thing, as became an orphan brought up as house-help in the Barclay home; but now she looked at the preacher and saw how young and helpless he looked so far from his native Yorkshire, and how ill-clad for this bitter trans-Atlantic weather, and she spoke up.

'You'd better take my shawl, sir. I don't need it. I've got Miss Julia's old riding cloak. And we'll go ride-and-tie.'

'Ride and what?' murmured Mr Mears.

'I'll ride a mile or so, then I'll get down and tie the horse to a tree and walk on. When you come up to the horse, you mount and ride a mile or so, passing me on the way, and you tie him and walk on. Like that. Ride-and-tie, ride-and-tie. The horse gets a rest between.'

Young Mr Mears nodded and took the proffered shawl absently. It was a black thing that matched his sober broadcloth coat and smallclothes, his black woollen stockings and his round black hat. At Mr Barclay's suggestion he had borrowed a pair of moose-hide moccasins for the journey. As he walked a prayer-book in his coat-skirts bumped the back of his legs.

At the top of the ridge above Harper's pasture, where the narrow path led off through gloomy hemlock woods, Kezia paused for a last look back across the harbour. In the morning sunlight the white roofs of the little lonely town resembled a tidal wave flung up by the sea and frozen as it broke against the dark pine forest to the west. Kezia sighed, and young Mr Mears was surprised to see tears in her eyes.

She rode off ahead. The saddle was a man's, of course, awkward to ride modestly, woman-fashion. As soon as she was out of the preacher's sight she rucked her skirts and slid a leg over to the other stirrup. That was better. There was a pleasant sensation of freedom about it, too. For a moment she forgot that she was going to Bristol Creek, in finery second-hand from the Barclay girls, in a new linen shift and drawers that she had sewn herself in the light of the kitchen candles, in white cotton stockings and a bonnet and shoes from Mr Barclay's store, to marry Mr Hathaway.

The Barclays had done well for her from the time when, a skinny weeping creature of fourteen, she was taken into the Barclay household and, as Mrs Barclay so often said, 'treated more like one of my own than a bond-girl from the poorhouse.' She had first choice of the clothing cast off by Miss Julia and Miss Clara. She was permitted to sit in the same room, and learn what she could, when the schoolmaster came to give private lessons to the Barclay girls. She waited on table, of course, and helped in the kitchen, and made beds, and dusted and scrubbed. But then she had been taught to spin and to sew and to knit. And she was permitted, indeed encouraged, to sit with the Barclays in the meetinghouse, at the convenient end of the pew, where she could worship the Barclays' God and assist with the Barclay wraps at the beginning and end of the service. And now, to complete her rewards, she had been granted the hand of a rejected Barclay suitor.

Mr Hathaway was Barclay's agent at Bristol Creek, where he sold rum and gunpowder and corn meal and such things to the fishermen and hunters, and bought split cod—fresh, pickled or dry—and ran a small sawmill, and cut and shipped firewood by schooner to Port Marriott, and managed a farm, all for a salary of fifty pounds, Halifax currency, per year. Hathaway was a most capable fellow, Mr Barclay often acknowledged. But when after fifteen capable years he came seeking a wife, and cast a sheep's eye first at Miss Julia, and then at Miss Clara, Mrs Barclay observed with a sniff that Hathaway was looking a bit high.

So he was. The older daughter of Port Marriott's most prosperous merchant was even then receiving polite attentions from Mr Gamage, the new collector of customs, and a connection of the Halifax Gamages, as Mrs Barclay was fond of pointing out. And Miss Clara was going to Halifax in the spring to learn the gentle art of playing the pianoforte, and incidentally to display her charms to the naval and military young gentlemen who thronged the Halifax drawingrooms. The dear girls laughed behind their hands whenever long solemn Mr Hathaway came to town aboard one of the Barclay vessels and called at the big house under the elms. Mrs Barclay bridled at Hathaway's presumption, but shrewd Mr Barclay narrowed his little black eyes and took snuff and said 'Ha! Humph!'

It was plain to Mr Barclay that an emergency had arisen. Hathaway was a good man—in his place; and Hathaway must be kept content there, to go on making profit for Mr Barclay at a cost of only £50 a year. 'Twas a pity Hathaway couldn't satisfy himself with one of the fishermen's girls at the Creek, but there 'twas. If Hathaway had set his mind on a town miss, then a town miss he must have; but she must be the right kind, the sort who would content herself and Hathaway at Bristol Creek and not go nagging the man to remove and try his capabilities elsewhere.

At once Mr Barclay thought of Kezia—dear little Kezzie. A colourless little creature but quiet and well-mannered and pious, and only twenty-two.

Mr Hathaway was nearly forty and far from handsome, and he had a rather cold, seeking way about him—useful in business of course—that rubbed women the wrong way. Privately Mr Barclay thought Hathaway lucky to get Kezia. But it was a nice match for the girl, better than anything she could have expected. He impressed that upon her and introduced the suitor from Bristol Creek. Mr Hathaway spent two or three evenings courting Kezia in the kitchen—Kezia in a quite good gown of Miss Clara's, gazing out at the November moon on the snow, murmuring now and again in the tones of someone in a rather dismal trance, while the kitchen help listened behind one door and the Barclay girls giggled behind another.

The decision, reached mainly by the Barclays, was that Mr Hathaway should come to Port Marriott aboard the packet schooner on December twenty-third, to be married in the Barclay parlour and then take his bride home for Christmas. But an unforeseen circumstance had changed all this. The circumstance was a ship, 'from Mogador in Barbary' as Mr Barclay wrote afterwards in the salvage claim, driven off her course by gales and wrecked at the very entrance to Bristol Creek. She was a valuable wreck, laden with such queer things as goatskins in pickle, almonds, wormseed, pomegranate skins and gum arabic, and capable Mr Hathaway had lost no time in salvage for the benefit of his employer.

As a result he could not come to Port Marriott for a wedding or anything else. A storm might blow up at any time and demolish this fat prize. He dispatched a note by Black Sam, urging Mr Barclay to send Kezia and the preacher by return. It was not the orthodox note of an impatient sweetheart, but it said that he had moved into his new house by the Creek and found it 'extream empty lacking a woman', and it suggested delicately that while his days were full, the nights were dull.

Kezia was no judge of distance. She rode for what she considered a reasonable time and then slid off and tied the brown horse to a maple tree beside the path. She had brought a couple of lamp wicks to tie about her shoes, to keep them from coming off in the snow, and she set out afoot in the big splayed tracks of Black Sam. The soft snow came almost to her knees in places and she lifted her skirts high. The path was no wider than the span of a man's arms, cut out with axes years before. She stumbled over a concealed stump from time to time, and the huckleberry bushes dragged at her cloak, but the effort warmed her. It had been cold, sitting on the horse with the wind blowing up her legs.

After a time the preacher overtook her, riding awkwardly and holding the reins in a nervous grip. The stirrups were too short for his long black-stockinged legs. He called out cheerfully as he passed, 'Are you all right, Miss?' She nodded, standing aside with her back to a tree. When he disappeared ahead, with a last flutter of black shawl tassels in the wind, she picked up her skirts and went on. The path climbed and dropped monotonously over a succession of wooded ridges. Here and there in a hollow she heard water running, and the creak of frosty poles underfoot, and knew she was crossing a small stream, and once the trail ran across a wide swamp on half-rotten corduroy, wind-swept and bare of snow.

She found the horse tethered clumsily not far ahead, and the tracks of the preacher going on. She had to lead the horse to a stump so she could mount, and when she passed Mr Mears again she called out, 'Please, sir, next time leave the horse by a stump or a rock so I can get on.' In his quaint old-country accent he murmured, 'I'm very sorry,' and gazed down at the snow. She forgot she was riding astride until she had passed him, and then she flushed, and gave the indignant horse a cut of the switch. Next time she remembered and swung her right leg back where it should be, and tucked the skirts modestly about her ankles; but young Mr Mears looked down at the snow anyway, and after that she did not trouble to shift when she overtook him.

The ridges became steeper, and the streams roared under the ice and snow in the swales. They emerged upon the high tableland between Port Marriott and Bristol Creek, a gusty wilderness of young hardwood scrub struggling up amongst the gray snags of an old forest fire, and now that they were out of the gloomy softwoods they could see a stretch of sky. It was blue-grey and forbidding, and the wind whistling up from the invisible sea felt raw on the cheek. At their next meeting Kezia said, 'It's going to snow.'

She had no knowledge of the trail but she guessed that they were not much more than half way across the cape. On this high barren the track was no longer straight and clear, it meandered amongst the meagre hardwood clumps where the path-makers had not bothered to cut, and only Black Sam's footprints really marked it for her unaccustomed eyes. The preacher nodded vaguely at her remark. The woods, like everything else about his chosen mission field, were new and very interesting, and he could not understand the alarm in her voice. He looked confidently at Black Sam's tracks.

Kezia tied the horse farther on and began her spell of walking. Her shoes were solid things, the kind of shoes Mr Barclay invoiced as 'a

Common Strong sort, for women, Five Shillings'; but the snow worked into them and melted and saturated the leather. Her feet were numb every time she slid down from the horse and it took several minutes of stumbling through the snow to bring back an aching warmth. Beneath her arm she clutched the small bundle which contained all she had in the world—two flannel nightgowns, a shift of linen, three pairs of stout wool stockings—and of course Mr Barclay's wedding gift for Mr Hathaway.

Now as she plunged along she felt the first sting of snow on her face and, looking up, saw the stuff borne on the wind in small hard pellets that fell amongst the bare hardwoods and set up a whisper everywhere. When Mr Mears rode up to her the snow was thick in their faces, like flung salt.

'It's a nor-easter!' she cried up to him. She knew the meaning of snow from the sea. She had been born in a fishing village down the coast.

'Yes,' mumbled the preacher, and drew a fold of the shawl about his face. He disappeared. She struggled on, gasping, and after what seemed a tremendous journey came upon him standing alone and bewildered, looking off somewhere to the right.

'The horse!' he shouted, 'I got off him, and before I could fasten the reins some snow fell off a branch—startled him, you know—and he ran off, over that way.' He gestured with a mittened hand. 'I must fetch him back,' he added confusedly.

'No!' Kezia cried. 'Don't you try. You'd only get lost. So would I. Oh, dear! This is awful. We'll have to go on, the best we can.'

He was doubtful. The horse tracks looked very plain. But Kezia was looking at Black Sam's tracks, and tugging his arm. He gave in, and they struggled along for half an hour or so. Then the last trace of the old footprints vanished.

'What shall we do now?' the preacher asked, astonished.

'I don't know,' whispered Kezia, and leaned against a dead pine stub in an attitude of weariness and indifference that dismayed him.

'We must keep moving, my dear, mustn't we? I mean, we can't stay here.'

'Can't stay here,' she echoed.

'Down there—a hollow, I think. I see some hemlock trees, or are they pines?—I'm never quite sure. Shelter, anyway.'

'Shelter,' muttered Kezia.

He took her by the hand and like a pair of lost children they dragged their steps into the deep snow of the hollow. The trees were tall spruces, a thick bunch in a ravine, where they had escaped the old fire. A stream thundered amongst them somewhere. There was no wind in this place, only the fine snow whirling thickly down between the trees like a sediment from the storm overhead.

'Look!' cried Mr Mears. A hut loomed out of the whiteness before them, a small structure of moss-chinked logs with a roof of poles and birch-bark. It had an abandoned look. Long streamers of moss hung out between the logs. On the roof shreds of birch-bark wavered gently in the drifting snow. The door stood half open and a thin drift of snow lay along the split-pole floor. Instinctively Kezia went to the stone hearth. There were old ashes sodden with rain down the chimney and now frozen to a cake.

'Have you got flint and steel?' she asked. She saw in his eyes something dazed and forlorn. He shook his head, and she was filled with a sudden anger, not so much at him as at Mr Barclay and that—that Hathaway, and all the rest of menkind. They ruled the world and made such a sorry mess of it. In a small fury she began to rummage about the hut.

There was a crude bed of poles and brushwood by the fireplace—brushwood so old that only a few brown needles clung to the twigs. A rough bench whittled from a pine log, with round birch sticks for legs. A broken earthenware pot in a corner. In another some ash-wood frames such as trappers used for stretching skins. Nothing else. The single window was covered with a stretched moose-bladder, cracked and dry-rotten, but it still let in some daylight while keeping out the snow.

She scooped up the snow from the floor with her mittened hands, throwing it outside, and closed the door carefully, dropping the bar into place, as if she could shut out and bar the cold in such a fashion. The air inside was frigid. Their breath hung visible in the dim light from the window. Young Mr Mears dropped on his wet knees and began to pray in a loud voice. His face was pinched with cold and his teeth rattled as he prayed. He was a pitiable object.

'Prayers won't keep you warm,' said Kezia crossly.

He looked up, amazed at the change in her. She had seemed such a meek little thing. Kezia was surprised at herself, and surprisingly she went on, 'You'd far better take off those wet moccasins and stockings and shake the snow out of your clothes.' She set the example, vigorously shaking out her skirts and Miss Julia's cloak, and she turned her small back on him and took off her own shoes and stockings, and pulled on dry stockings from her bundle. She threw him a pair.

'Put those on.'

He looked at them and at his large feet, hopelessly.

'I'm afraid they wouldn't go on.'

She tossed him one of her flannel nightgowns. 'Then take off your stockings and wrap your feet and legs in that.'

He obeyed, in an embarrassed silence. She rolled her eyes upward, for his modesty's sake, and saw a bundle on one of the low rafters—the late owner's bedding, stowed away from mice. She stood on the bench and pulled down three bearskins, marred with bullet holes. A rank and musty smell arose in the cold. She considered the find gravely.

'You take them,' Mr Mears said gallantly. 'I shall be quite all right.'

'You'll be dead by morning, and so shall I,' she answered vigorously, 'if you don't do what I say. We've got to roll up in these.'

'Together?' he cried in horror.

'Of course! To keep each other warm. It's the only way.'

She spread the skins on the floor, hair uppermost, one overlapping another, and dragged the flustered young man down beside her, clutched him in her arms, and rolled with him, over, and over again, so that they became a single shapeless heap in the corner farthest from the draft between door and chimney.

'Put your arms around me,' commanded the new Kezia, and he obeyed.

'Now,' she said, 'you can pray. God helps those that help themselves.'

He prayed aloud for a long time, and privately called upon heaven to witness the purity of his thoughts in this strange and shocking situation. He said 'Amen' at last; and 'Amen', echoed Kezia, piously.

They lay silent a long time, breathing on each other's necks and hearing their own hearts—poor Mr Mears' fluttering in an agitated way, Kezia's as steady as a clock. A delicious warmth crept over them. They relaxed in each other's arms. Outside, the storm hissed in the spruce tops and set up an occasional cold moan in the cracked clay chimney. The down-swirling snow brushed softly against the bladder pane.

'I'm warm now,' murmured Kezia. 'Are you?'

'Yes. How long must we stay here like this?'

'Till the storm's over, of course. Tomorrow, probably. Nor'easters usually blow themselves out in a day and a night, 'specially when they come up sharp, like this one. Are you hungry?'

'No.'

'Abigail—that's the black cook at Barclay's—gave me bread and cheese in a handkerchief. I've got it in my bundle. Mr Barclay thought we ought to reach Bristol Creek by supper time, but Nabby said I must have a bite to eat on the road. She's a good kind thing, old Nabby. Sure you're not hungry?'

'Quite. I feel somewhat fatigued but not hungry.'

'Then we'll eat the bread and cheese for breakfast. Have you got a watch?'

'No, I'm sorry. They cost such a lot of money. In Lady Huntingdon's Connexion we—'

'Oh well, it doesn't matter. It must be about four o'clock—the light's getting dim. Of course, the dark comes very quick in a snowstorm.'

'Dark,' echoed young Mr Mears drowsily. Kezia's hair, washed last night for the wedding journey, smelled pleasant so close to his face. It reminded him of something. He went to sleep dreaming of his mother, with his face snug in the curve of Kezia's neck and shoulder, and smiling, and muttering words that Kezia could not catch. After a time she kissed his cheek. It seemed a very natural thing to do.

Soon she was dozing herself, and dreaming, too; but her dreams were full of forbidding faces—Mr Barclay's, Mrs Barclay's, Mr Hathaway's; especially Mr Hathaway's. Out of a confused darkness Mr Hathaway's hard acquisitive gaze searched her shrinking flesh like a cold wind. Then she was shuddering by the kitchen fire at Barclay's, accepting Mr Hathaway's courtship and wishing she was dead. In the midst of that sickening wooing she wakened sharply.

It was quite dark in the hut. Mr Mears was breathing quietly against her throat. But there was a sound of heavy steps outside, muffled in the snow and somehow felt rather than heard. She shook the young man and he wakened with a start, clutching her convulsively.

'Sh-h-h!' she warned. 'Something's moving outside.' She felt him stiffen.

'Bears?' he whispered.

Silly! thought Kezia. People from the old country could think of nothing but bears in the woods. Besides, bears holed up in winter. A caribou, perhaps. More likely a moose. Caribou moved inland before this, to the wide mossy bogs up the river, away from the coastal storms. Again the sound.

'There!' hissed the preacher. Their hearts beat rapidly together.

'The door—you fastened it, didn't you?'

'Yes,' she said. Suddenly she knew.

'Unroll, quick!' she cried . . .'No, not this way—your way.'

They unrolled, ludicrously, and the girl scrambled up and ran across the floor in her stockinged feet, and fumbled with the rotten door-bar. Mr Mears attempted to follow but he tripped over the nightgown still wound about his feet, and fell with a crash. He was up again in a moment, catching up the clumsy wooden bench for a weapon, his bare feet slapping on the icy floor. He tried to shoulder her aside, crying 'Stand back! Leave it to me!' and waving the bench uncertainly in the darkness.

She laughed excitedly. 'Silly!' she said. 'It's the horse.' She flung the door open. In the queer ghostly murk of a night filled with snow they beheld a large dark shape. The shape whinnied softly and thrust a long face into the doorway. Mr Mears dropped the bench, astonished.

'He got over his fright and followed us here somehow,' Kezia said, and laughed again. She put her arms about the snowy head and laid her face against it.

'Good horse! Oh, good, good horse!'

'What are you going to do?' the preacher murmured over her shoulder. After the warmth of their nest in the furs they were shivering in this icy atmosphere.

'Bring him in, of course. We can't leave him out in the storm.' She caught the bridle and urged the horse inside with expert clucking sounds. The animal hesitated, but fear of the storm and a desire for shelter and company decided him. In he came, tramping ponderously on the split-pole floor. The preacher closed and barred the door.

'And now?' he asked.

'Back to the furs. Quick! It's awful cold.'

Rolled in the furs once more, their arms went about each other instinctively, and the young man's face found the comfortable nook against Kezia's soft throat. But sleep was difficult after that. The horse whinnied gently from time to time, and stamped about the floor. The decayed poles crackled dangerously under his hoofs whenever he moved, and Kezia trembled, thinking he might break through and frighten himself, and flounder about till he tumbled the crazy hut about their heads. She called out to him 'Steady, boy! Steady!'

It was a long night. The pole floor made its irregularities felt through the thickness of fur; and because there seemed nowhere to put their arms but about each other the flesh became cramped, and spread its protest along the bones. They were stiff and sore when the first light of morning stained the window. They unrolled and stood up thankfully, and tramped up and down the floor, threshing their arms in an effort to fight off the gripping cold. Kezia undid her bundle in a corner and brought forth Nabby's bread and cheese, and they ate it sitting together on the edge of the brushwood bed with the skins about their shoulders. Outside the snow had ceased.

'We must set off at once,' the preacher said. 'Mr Hathaway will be anxious.'

Kezia was silent. She did not move, and he looked at her curiously. She appeared very fresh, considering the hardships of the previous day and the night. He passed a hand over his cheeks and thought how unclean he must appear in her eyes, with this stubble on his pale face.

'Mr Hathaway—' he began again.

'I'm not going to Mr Hathaway,' Kezia said quietly.

'But—the wedding!'

'There'll be no wedding. I don't want to marry Mr Hathaway. 'Twas Mr Hathaway's idea, and Mr and Mrs Barclay's. They wanted me to marry him.'

'What will the Barclays say, my dear?'

She shrugged. 'I've been their bond-girl ever since I was fourteen, but I'm not a slave like poor black Nabby, to be handed over, body and soul, whenever it suits.'

'Your soul belongs to God,' said Mr Mears devoutly.

'And my body belongs to me.'

He was a little shocked at this outspokenness but he said gently, 'Of course. To give oneself in marriage without true affection would be an offense in the sight of heaven. But what will Mr Hathaway say?'

''Well, to begin with, he'll ask where I spent the night, and I'll have to tell the truth. I'll have to say I bundled with you in a hut in the woods.'

'Bundled?'

'A custom the people brought with them from Connecticut when they came to settle in Nova Scotia. Poor folk still do it. Sweethearts, I mean. It saves fire and candles when you're courting on a winter evening. It's harmless—they keep their clothes on, you see, like you and me—but Mr Barclay and the other Methody people are terrible set against it. Mr Barclay got old Mr Mings—he's the Methody preacher that died last year—to make a sermon against it. Mr Mings said bundling was an invention of the devil.'

'Then if you go back to Mr Barclay—'

'He'll ask me the same question and I'll have to give him the same answer. I couldn't tell a lie, could I?' She turned a pair of round blue eyes and met his embarrassed gaze.

'No! No, you mustn't lie. Whatever shall we do?' he murmured in a dazed voice. Again she was silent, looking modestly down her small nose.

'It's so very strange,' he floundered. 'This country—there are so many things I don't know, so many things to learn. You—I—we shall have to tell the truth, of course. Doubtless I can find a place in the Lord's service somewhere else, but what about you, poor girl?'

'I heard say the people at Scrod Harbour want a preacher.'

'But—the tale would follow me, wouldn't it, my dear? This—er—bundling with a young woman?'

''Twouldn't matter if the young woman was your wife.'

'Eh?' His mouth fell open. He was like an astonished child, for all his preacher's clothes and the new beard on his jaws.

'I'm a good girl,' Kezia said, inspecting her foot. 'I can read and write, and know all the tunes in the psalter. And—and you need someone to look after you.'

He considered the truth of that. Then he murmured uncertainly, 'We'd be very poor, my dear. The Connexion gives some support, but of course—'

'I've always been poor,' Kezia said. She sat very still but her cold fingers writhed in her lap.

He did something then that made her want to cry. He took hold of her hands and bowed his head and kissed them.

'It's strange—I don't even know your name, my dear.'

'It's Kezia—Kezia Barnes.'

He said quietly 'You're a brave girl, Kezia Barnes, and I shall try to be a good husband to you. Shall we go?'

'Hadn't you better kiss me, first?' Kezia said faintly.

He put his lips awkwardly to hers; and then, as if the taste of her clean mouth itself provided strength and purpose, he kissed her again, and firmly. She threw her arms about his neck.

'Oh, Mr Mears!'

How little he knew about everything! He hadn't even known enough to wear two or three pairs of stockings inside those roomy moccasins, nor to carry a pair of dry ones. Yesterday's wet stockings were lying like sticks on the frosty floor. She showed him how to knead the hard-frozen moccasins into softness, and while he worked at the stiff leather she tore up one of her wedding bed-shirts and wound the flannel strips about his legs and feet. It looked very queer when she had finished, and they both laughed.

They were chilled to the bone when they set off, Kezia on the horse and the preacher walking ahead, holding the reins. When they regained the slope where they had lost the path, Kezia said, 'The sun rises some-where between east and southeast, this time of year. Keep it on your left shoulder a while. That will take us back towards Port Marriott.'

When they came to the green timber she told him to shift the sun to his left eye.

'Have you changed your mind?' he asked cheerfully. The exercise had warmed him.

'No, but the sun moves across the sky.'

'Ah! What a wise little head it is!'

They came over a ridge of mixed hemlock and hardwood and looked upon a long swale full of bare hackmatacks.

'Look!' the girl cried. The white slot of the axe path showed clearly in the trees at the foot of the swale, and again where it entered the dark mass of the pines beyond.

'Praise the Lord!' said Mr Mears.

When at last they stood in the trail, Kezia slid down from the horse.

'No!' Mr Mears protested.

'Ride-and-tie,' she said firmly. 'That's the way we came, and that's the way we'll go. Besides, I want to get warm.'

He climbed up clumsily and smiled down at her.

'What shall we do when we get to Port Marriott, my dear?'

'Get the New Light preacher to marry us, and catch the packet for Scrod Harbour.'

He nodded and gave a pull at his broad hat brim. She thought of everything. A splendid helpmeet for the world's wilderness. He saw it all very humbly now as a dispensation of Providence.

Kezia watched him out of sight. Then, swiftly, she undid her bundle and took out the thing that had lain there (and on her conscience) through the night—the tinderbox—Mr Barclay's wedding gift to Mr Hathaway. She flung it into the woods and walked on, skirts lifted, in the track of the horse, humming a psalm tune to the silent trees and the snow.

SINCLAIR ROSS

b. 1908

The Lamp at Noon

A little before noon she lit the lamp. Demented wind fled keening past the house: a wail through the eaves that died every minute or two. Three days now without respite it had held. The dust was thickening to an impenetrable fog.

She lit the lamp, then for a long time stood at the window motionless. In dim, fitful outline the stable and oat granary still were visible; beyond, obscuring fields and landmarks, the lower of dust clouds made the farmyard seem an isolated acre, poised aloft above a sombre void. At each blast of wind it shook, as it to topple and spin hurtling with the dust-reel into space.

From the window she went to the door, opening it a little, and peering toward the stable again. He was not coming yet. As she watched there was a sudden rift overhead, and for a moment through the tattered clouds the sun raced like a wizened orange. It shed a soft, diffused light, dim and yellow as if it were the light from the lamp reaching out through the open door.

She closed the door, and going to the stove tried the potatoes with a fork. Her eyes all the while were fixed and wide with a curious immobility. It was the window. Standing at it, she had let her forehead press against the pane until the eyes were strained apart and rigid. Wide like that they had looked out of the deepening ruin of the storm. Now she could not close them.

The baby started to cry. He was lying in a homemade crib over which she had arranged a tent of muslin. Careful not to disturb the folds of it, she knelt and tried to still him, whispering huskily in a singsong voice that he must hush and go to sleep again. She would have liked to rock him, to feel the comfort of his little body in her arms, but a fear obsessed her that in the dust-filled air he might contract pneumonia. There was dust sifting everywhere. Her own throat was parched with it. The table had been set less than ten minutes, and already a film was gathering on

73

the dishes. The little cry continued, and with wincing, frightened lips she glanced around as if to find a corner where the air was less oppressive. But while the lips winced the eyes maintained their wide, immobile stare. 'Sleep,' she whispered again. 'It's too soon for you to be hungry. Daddy's coming for his dinner.'

He seemed a long time. Even the clock, still a few minutes off noon, could not dispel a foreboding sense that he was longer than he should be. She went to the door again—and then recoiled slowly to stand white and breathless in the middle of the room. She mustn't. He would only despise her if she ran to the stable looking for him. There was too much grim endurance in his nature ever to let him understand the fear and weakness of a woman. She must stay quiet and wait. Nothing was wrong. At noon he would come—and perhaps after dinner stay with her awhile.

Yesterday, and again at breakfast this morning, they had quarrelled bitterly. She wanted him now, the assurance of his strength and nearness, but he would stand aloof, wary, remembering the words she had flung at him in her anger, unable to understand it was only the dust and wind that had driven her.

Tense, she fixed her eyes upon the clock, listening. There were two winds: the wind in flight, and the wind that pursued. The one sought refuge in the eaves, whimpering, in fear; the other assailed it there, and shook the eaves apart to make it flee again. Once as she listened this first wind sprang inside the room, distraught like a bird that has felt the graze of talons on its wing; while furious the other wind shook the walls, and thudded tumbleweeds against the window till its quarry glanced away again in fright. But only to return—to return and quake among the feeble eaves, as if in all this dust-mad wilderness it knew no other sanctuary.

Then Paul came. At his step she hurried to the stove, intent upon the pots and frying-pan. 'The worst wind yet,' he ventured, hanging up his cap and smock. 'I had to light the lantern in the tool shed, too.'

They looked at each other, then away. She wanted to go to him, to feel his arms supporting her, to cry a little just that he might soothe her, but because his presence made the menace of the wind seem less, she gripped herself and thought, 'I'm in the right. I won't give in. For his sake, too, I won't.'

He washed, hurriedly, so that a few dark welts of dust remained to indent upon his face a haggard strength. It was all she could see as she wiped the dishes and set the food before him: the strength, the grimness, the young Paul growing old and hard, buckled against a desert even grimmer than his will. 'Hungry?' she asked, touched to a twinge of pity she had not intended. 'There's dust in everything. It keeps coming faster than I can clean it up.'

He nodded. 'Tonight, though, you'll see it go down. This is the third day.'

She looked at him in silence a moment, and then as if to herself muttered broodingly, 'Until the next time. Until it starts again.'

There was a dark resentment in her voice now that boded another quarrel. He waited, his eyes on her dubiously as she mashed a potato with her fork. The lamp between them threw strong lights and shadows on their faces. Dust and drought, earth that betrayed alike his labour and his faith, to him the struggle had given sternness, an impassive courage. Beneath the whip of sand his youth had been effaced. Youth, zest, exuberance—there remained only a harsh and clenched virility that yet became him, that seemed at the cost of more engaging qualities to be fulfilment of his inmost and essential nature. Whereas to her the same debts and poverty had brought a plaintive indignation, a nervous dread of what was still to come. The eyes were hollowed, the lips pinched dry and colourless. It was the face of a woman that had aged without maturing, that had loved the little vanities of life, and lost them wistfully.

'I'm afraid, Paul,' she said suddenly. 'I can't stand it any longer. He cries all the time. You will go, Paul—say you will. We aren't living here—not really living '

The pleading in her voice now, after its shrill bitterness yesterday, made him think that this was only another way to persuade him. He answered evenly, 'I told you this morning, Ellen; we keep on right where we are. At least I do. It's yourself you're thinking about, not the baby.'

This morning such an accusation would have stung her to rage; now, her voice swift and panting, she pressed on, 'Listen, Paul—I'm thinking of all of us—you, too. Look at the sky—what's happening. Are you blind? Thistles and tumbleweeds—it's a desert. You won't have a straw this fall. You won't be able to feed a cow or a chicken. Please, Paul, say we'll go away—'

'Go where?' His voice as he answered was still remote and even, inflexibly in unison with the narrowed eyes and the great hunch of muscle-knotted shoulder. 'Even as a desert it's better than sweeping out your father's store and running his errands. That's all I've got ahead of me if I do what you want.'

'And here—' she faltered. 'What's ahead of you here? At least we'll get enough to eat and wear when you're sweeping out his store. Look at it—look at it, you fool. Desert—the lamp lit at noon—'

'You'll see it come back. There's good wheat in it yet.'

'But in the meantime—year after year—can't you understand, Paul? We'll never get them back—'

He put down his knife and fork and leaned toward her across the table. 'I can't go, Ellen. Living off your people—charity—stop and think of it. This is where I belong. I can't do anything else.'

'Charity!' she repeated him, letting her voice rise in derision. 'And this—you call this independence! Borrowed money you can't even pay the interest on, seed from the government—grocery bills—doctor bills—'

'We'll have crops again,' he persisted. 'Good crops—the land will come back. It's worth waiting for.'

'And while we're waiting, Paul!' It was not anger now, but a kind of sob. 'Think of me—and him. It's not fair. We have our lives, too, to live.'

'And you think that going home to your family—taking your husband with you—'

'I don't care—anything would be better than this. Look at the air he's breathing. He cries all the time. For his sake, Paul. What's ahead of him here, even if you do get crops?'

He clenched his lips a minute, then, with his eyes hard and contemptuous, struck back, 'As much as in town, growing up a pauper. You're the one who wants to go, it's not for his sake. You think that in town you'd have a better time—not so much work—more clothes—'

'Maybe—' She dropped her head defencelessly. 'I'm young still. I like pretty things.'

There was silence now—a deep fastness of it enclosed by rushing wind and creaking walls. It seemed the yellow lamplight cast a hush upon them. Through the haze of dusty air the walls receded, dimmed, and came again. At last she raised her head and said listlessly, 'Go on—your dinner's getting cold. Don't sit and stare at me. I've said it all.'

The spent quietness in her voice was even harder to endure than her anger. It reproached him, against his will insisted that he see and understand her lot. To justify himself he tried, 'I was a poor man when you married me. You said you didn't mind. Farming's never been easy, and never will be.'

'I wouldn't mind the work or the skimping if there was something to look forward to. It's the hopelessness—going on—watching the land blow away.'

'The land's all right,' he repeated. 'The dry years won't last forever.'

'But it's not just dry years, Paul!' The little sob in her voice gave way suddenly to a ring of exasperation. 'Will you never see? It's the land itself—the soil. You've plowed and harrowed until there's not a root or fibre left to hold it down. That's why the soil drifts—that's why in a year or two there'll be nothing left but the bare clay. If in the first place you farmers had taken care of your land—if you hadn't been so greedy for wheat every year—'

She had taught school before she married him, and of late in her anger there had been a kind of disdain, an attitude almost of condescension, as if she no longer looked upon the farmers as her equals. He sat still, his eyes fixed on the yellow lamp flame, and seeming to know her words had hurt him, she went on softly, 'I want to help you, Paul. That's why I won't sit quiet while you go on wasting your life. You're only thirty— you owe it to yourself as well as me.'

He sat staring at the lamp without answering, his mouth sullen. It seemed indifference now, as if he were ignoring her, and stung to anger again she cried, 'Do you ever think what my life is? Two rooms to live in—once a month to town, and nothing to spend when I get there. I'm still young—I wasn't brought up this way.'

'You're a farmer's wife now. It doesn't matter what you used to be, or how you were brought up. You get enough to eat and wear. Just now that's all I can do. I'm not to blame that we've been dried out five years.'

'Enough to eat!' she laughed back shrilly. 'Enough salt pork—enough potatoes and eggs And look—' Springing to the middle of the room she thrust out a foot for him to see the scuffed old slipper. 'When they're completely gone I suppose you'll tell me I can go barefoot—that I'm a farmer's wife—that it's not your fault we're dried out—'

'And what about these?' He pushed his chair away from the table now to let her see what he was wearing. 'Cowhide—hard as boards—but my feet are so calloused I don't feel them any more.'

Then he stood up, ashamed of having tried to match her hardships with his own. But frightened now as he reached for his smock she pressed close to him. 'Don't go yet. I brood and worry when I'm left alone. Please, Paul—you can't work on the land anyway.'

'And keep on like this? You start before I'm through the door. Week in and week out—I've troubles enough of my own.'

'Paul—please stay—' The eyes were glazed now, distended a little as if with the intensity of her dread and pleading. 'We won't quarrel any more. Hear it! I can't work—I just stand still and listen—'

The eyes frightened him, but responding to a kind of instinct that he must withstand her, that it was his self-respect and manhood against the fretful weakness of a woman, he answered unfeelingly, 'In here safe and quiet—you don't know how well off you are. If you were out in it—fighting it—swallowing it—'

'Sometimes, Paul, I wish I was. I'm so caged—if I could only break away and run. See—I stand like this all day. I can't relax. My throat's so tight it aches—'

With a jerk he freed his smock from her clutch. 'If I say we'll only keep on all afternoon. Wait till tomorrow—we'll talk things over when the wind goes down.'

Then without meeting her eyes again he swung outside, and doubled low against the buffets of the wind, fought his way slowly toward the stable. There was a deep hollow calm within, a vast darkness engulfed beneath the tides of moaning wind. He stood breathless a moment, hushed almost to a stupor by the sudden extinction of the storm and the stillness that enfolded him. It was a long, far-reaching stillness. The first dim stalls and rafters led the way into cavern-like obscurity, into vaults and recesses that extended far beyond the stable walls. Nor in these first quiet moments did he forbid the illusion, the sense of release from a harsh, familiar world into one of peace and darkness. The contentious mood that his stand against Ellen had roused him to, his tenacity and clenched despair before the ravages of wind, it was ebbing now, losing itself in the cover of darkness. Ellen and the wheat seemed remote, unimportant. At a whinny from the bay mare, Bess, he went forward and into her stall. She seemed grateful for his presence, and thrust her nose deep between his arm and body. They stood a long time motionless, comforting and assuring each other.

For soon again the first deep sense of quiet and peace was shrunken to the battered shelter of the stable. Instead of release or escape from the assaulting wind, the walls were but a feeble stand against it. They creaked and sawed as if the fingers of a giant were tightening to collapse them; the empty loft sustained a pipelike cry that rose and fell but never ended. He saw the dust-black sky again, and his fields blown smooth with drifted soil.

But always, even while listening to the storm outside, he could feel the tense and apprehensive stillness of the stable. There was not a hoof that clumped or shifted, not a rub of halter against manger. And yet, though it had been a strange stable, he would have known, despite the darkness, that every stall was filled. They, too, were all listening.

From Bess he went to the big grey gelding, Prince. Prince was twenty years old, with rib-grooved sides, and high, protruding hipbones. Paul ran his hand over the ribs, and felt a sudden shame, a sting of fear that Ellen might be right in what she said. For wasn't it true—nine years a farmer now on his own land, and still he couldn't even feed his horses? What, then, could he hope to do for his wife and son?

There was much he planned. And so vivid was the future of his planning, so real and constant, that often the actual present was but half felt, but half endured. Its difficulties were lessened by a confidence in what lay beyond them. A new house—land for the boy—land and still more land—or education, whatever he might want.

But all the time was he only a blind and stubborn fool? Was Ellen right? Was he trampling on her life, and throwing away his own? The five years since he married her, were they to go on repeating themselves, five, ten, twenty, until all the brave future he looked forward to was but a stark and futile past?

She looked forward to no future. She had no faith or dream with which to make the dust and the poverty less real. He understood suddenly. He saw her face again as only a few minutes ago it had begged him not to leave her. The darkness round him now was as a slate on which her lonely terror limned itself. He went from Prince to the other horses, combing their manes and forelocks with his fingers, but always it was her face before him, its staring eyes and twisted suffering. 'See Paul—I stand like this all day. I just stand still—My throat's so tight it aches—'

And always the wind, the creak of walls, the wild lipless wailing through the loft. Until at last as he stood there, staring into the livid face before him, it seemed that this scream of wind was a cry from her parched and frantic lips. He knew it couldn't be, he knew that she was safe within the house, but still the wind persisted in a woman's cry. The cry of a woman with eyes like those that watched him through the dark. Eyes that were mad now—lips that even as they cried still pleaded, 'See Paul—I stand like this all day. I just stand still—so caged! If I could only run!'

He saw her running, pulled and driven headlong by the wind, but when at last he returned to the house, compelled by his anxiety, she was walking quietly back and forth with the baby in her arms. Careful, despite his concern, not to reveal a fear or weakness that she might think capitulation to her wishes, he watched a moment through the window, and then went off to the tool shed to mend harness. All afternoon he stitched and riveted. It was easier with the lantern lit and his hands occupied. There was a wind whining high past the tool shed too, but it was only wind. He remembered the arguments with which Ellen had tried to persuade him away from the farm, and one by one he defeated them. There would be rain again—next year or the next. Maybe in his ignorance he had farmed his land the wrong way, seeding wheat every year, working the soil till it was lifeless dust—but he would do better now. He would plant clover and alfalfa, breed cattle, acre by acre and year by year restore to his land its fibre and fertility. That was something to work for, a way to prove himself. It was ruthless wind, blackening the sky with his earth, but it was not his master. Out of his land it had made a wilderness. He now, out of the wilderness, would make a farm and home again.

Tonight he must talk with Ellen. Patiently, when the wind was down, and they were both quiet again. It was she who had told him to grow fibrous crops, who had called him an ignorant fool because he kept on with summer fallow and wheat. Now she might be gratified to find him acknowledging her wisdom. Perhaps she would begin to feel the power and steadfastness of the land, to take a pride in it, to understand that he was not a fool, but working for her future and their son's.

And already the wind was slackening. At four o'clock he could sense a lull. At five, straining his eyes from the tool shed doorway, he could make out a neighbour's buildings half a mile away. It was over—three days of blight and havoc like a scourge—three days so bitter and so long that for a moment he stood still, unseeing, his senses idle with a numbness of relief.

But only for a moment. Suddenly he emerged from the numbness; suddenly the fields before him struck his eyes to comprehension. They lay black, naked. Beaten and mounded smooth with dust as if a sea in gentle swell had turned to stone. And though he had tried to prepare himself for such a scene, though he had known since yesterday that not a blade would last the storm, still now, before the utter waste confronting him, he sickened and stood cold. Suddenly like the fields he was naked. Everything that had sheathed him a little from the realities of existence: vision and purpose, faith in the land, in the future, in himself—it was all rent now, stripped away. 'Desert,' he heard her voice begin to sob. 'Desert, you fool—the lamp lit at noon!'

In the stable again, measuring out their feed to the horses, he wondered what he would say to her tonight. For so deep were his instincts of loyalty to the land that still, even with the images of his betrayal stark upon his mind, his concern was how to withstand her, how to go on again and justify himself. It had not occurred to him yet that he might or should abandon the land. He had lived with it too long. Rather was his impulse still to defend it—as a man defends against the scorn of strangers even his most worthless kin.

He fed his horses, then waited. She too would be waiting, ready to cry at him, 'Look now—that crop that was to feed and clothe us! And you'll still keep on! You'll still say "Next year—there'll be rain next year"!'

But she was gone when he reached the house. The door was open, the lamp blown out, the crib empty. The dishes from their meal at noon were still on the table. She had perhaps begun to sweep, for the broom was lying in the middle of the floor. He tried to call, but a terror clamped upon his throat. In the wan, returning light it seemed that even the deserted kitchen was straining to whisper what it had seen. The tatters of the storm still whimpered through the eaves, and in their moaning told the desolation of the miles they had traversed. On tiptoe at last he crossed to the adjoining room; then at the threshold, without even a glance inside to satisfy himself that she was really gone, he wheeled again and plunged outside.

He ran a long time—distraught and headlong as a few hours ago he had seemed to watch her run—around the farmyard, a little distance into the pasture, back again blindly to the house to see whether she had returned—and then at a stumble down the road for help.

They joined him in the search, rode away for others, spread calling across the fields in the direction she might have been carried by the wind—but nearly two hours later it was himself who came upon her. Crouched down against a drift of sand as if for shelter, her hair in matted strands around her neck and face, the child clasped tightly in her arms.

The child was quite cold. It had been her arms, perhaps, too frantic to protect him, or the smother of dust upon his throat and lungs. 'Hold him,' she said as he knelt beside her. 'So—with his face away from the wind. Hold him until I tidy my hair.'

Her eyes were still wide in an immobile stare, but with her lips she smiled at him. For a long time he knelt transfixed, trying to speak to her, touching fearfully with his fingertips the dust-grimed cheeks and eyelids of the child. At last she said, 'I'll take him again. Such clumsy hands—you don't know how to hold a baby yet. See how his head falls forward on your arm.'

Yet it all seemed familiar—a confirmation of what he had known since noon. He gave her the child, then, gathering them up in his arms, struggled to his feet, and turned toward home.

It was evening now. Across the fields a few spent clouds of dust still shook and fled. Beyond, as if through smoke, the sunset smouldered like a distant fire.

He walked with a long dull stride, his eyes before him, heedless of her weight. Once he glanced down and with her eyes she still was smiling. 'Such strong arms, Paul—and I was so tired just carrying him. . . .'

He tried to answer, but it seemed that now the dusk was drawn apart in breathless waiting, a finger on its lips until they passed. 'You were right, Paul. . . .' Her voice came whispering, as if she too could feel the hush. 'You said tonight we'd see the storm go down. So still now, and a red sky—it means tomorrow will be fine.'

HUGH GARNER
1913–1979

One-Two-Three Little Indians

After they had eaten, Big Tom pushed the cracked and dirty supper things to the back of the table and took the baby from its high chair carefully, so as not to spill the flotsam of bread crumbs and boiled potatoes from the chair to the floor.

He undressed the youngster, talking to it in the old dialect, trying to awaken its interest. All evening it had been listless and fretful by turns, but now it seemed to be soothed by the story of Po-chee-ah, and the Lynx, although it was too young to understand him as his voice slid awkwardly through the ageless folk-tale of his people.

For long minutes after the baby was asleep he talked on, letting the victorious words fill the small cabin so that they shut out the sounds of the Northern Ontario night: the buzz of mosquitoes, the far-off bark of a dog, the noise of the cars and transport trucks passing on the gravelled road.

The melodious hum of his voice was like a strong soporific, lulling him with the return of half-forgotten memories, strengthening him with the knowledge that once his people had been strong and brave, men with a nation of their own, encompassing a million miles of teeming forest, lake and tamarack swamp.

When he halted his monologue to place the baby in the big brass bed in the corner the sudden silence was loud in his ears, and he cringed a bit as the present suddenly caught up with the past.

He covered the baby with a corner of the church-donated patchwork quilt, and lit the kerosene lamp that stood on the mirrorless dressing table beside the stove. Taking a broom from a corner he swept the mealtime debris across the doorsill.

This done, he stood and watched the headlights of the cars run along the trees bordering the road, like a small boy's stick along a picket fence. From the direction of the trailer camp a hundred yards away came the sound of a car engine being gunned, and the halting note-tumbles of a clarinet from a tourist's radio. The soft summer smell of spruce needles and wood smoke blended with the evening dampness of the earth, and felt good in his nostrils, so that he filled his worn lungs until he began to cough. He spat the resinous phlegm into the weed-filled yard.

It had been this summer smell, and the feeling of freedom it gave, which had brought him back to the woods after three years in the mines during the war. But only part of him had come back, for the mining towns and the big money had done more than etch his lungs with silica: they had also brought him pain and distrust, and a wife who had learned to live in gaudy imitation of the boomtown life.

When his coughing attack subsided he peered along the path, hoping to catch a glimpse of his wife Mary returning from her work at the trailer camp. He was becoming worried about the baby, and her presence, while it might not make the baby well, would mean that there was someone else to share his fears. He could see nothing but the still blackness of the trees, their shadows interwoven in a sombre pattern across the mottled ground.

He re-entered the cabin and began washing the dishes, stopping once or twice to cover the moving form of the sleeping baby. He wondered if he could have transmitted his own wasting sickness to the lungs of his son. He stood for long minutes at the side of the bed, staring, trying to diagnose the child's restlessness into something other than what he feared.

His wife came in and placed some things on the table. He picked up a can of pork-and-beans she had bought and weighed it in the palm of his hand. 'The baby seems pretty sick,' he said.

She crossed the room, and looked at the sleeping child 'I guess it's his teeth.'

He placed the pork-and-beans on the table again and walked over to his chair beside the empty stove. As he sat down he noticed for the first time that his wife was beginning to show her pregnancy. Her squat form had sunk lower, and almost filled the shapeless dress she wore. Her brown ankles were puffed above the broken-down heels of the dirty silver dancing pumps she was wearing.

'Is the trailer camp full?' he asked.

'Nearly. Two more Americans came about half an hour ago.'

'Was Billy Woodhen around?'

'I didn't see him, only Elsie,' she answered. 'A woman promised me a dress tomorrow if I scrub out her trailer.'

'Yeh.' He saw the happiness rise over her like a colour as she mentioned this. She was much younger than he was — twenty-two years against his thirty-nine — and her dark face had a fullness that is common to many Indian women. She was no longer pretty, and as he watched her he thought that wherever they went the squalor of their existence seemed to follow them.

'It's a silk dress,' Mary said, as though the repeated mention of it brought it nearer.

'A silk dress is no damn good around here. You should get some overalls,' he said, angered by her lack of shame in accepting the cast-off garments of the trailer women.

She seemed not to notice his anger. 'It'll do for the dances next winter.'

'A lot of dancing you'll do,' he said pointing to her swollen body. 'You'd better learn to stay around here and take care of the kid.'

She busied herself over the stove, lighting it with newspapers and kindling. 'I'm going to have some fun. You should have married a grandmother.'

He filled the kettle with water from an open pail near the door. The baby began to cough, and the mother turned it on its side in the bed. 'As soon as I draw my money from Cooper I'm going to get him some cough syrup from the store,' she said.

'It won't do any good. We should take him to the doctor in town tomorrow.'

'I can't. I've got to stay here and work.'

He knew the folly of trying to reason with her. She had her heart set on earning the silk dress the woman had promised.

After they had drunk their tea he blew out the light, and they took off some of their clothes and climbed over the baby into the bed. Long after his wife had fallen asleep he lay in the darkness listening to a ground moth beating its futile wings against the glass of the window.

They were awakened in the morning by the twittering of a small colony of tree sparrows who were feasting on the kitchen sweepings of the night before. Mary got up and went outside, returning a few minutes later carrying a handful of birch and poplar stovewood.

He waited until the beans were in the pan before rising and pulling on his pants. He stood in the doorway scratching his head and absorbing the sunlight through his bare feet upon the step.

The baby awoke while they were eating their breakfast.

'He don't look good,' Big Tom said as he dipped some brown sauce from his plate with a hunk of bread.

'He'll be all right later,' his wife insisted. She poured some crusted tinned milk from a tin into a cup and mixed it with water from the kettle.

Big Tom splashed his hands and face with cold water, and dried himself on a soiled shirt that lay over the back of a chair. 'When you going to the camp, this morning?'

'This afternoon,' Mary answered.

'I'll be back by then.'

He took up a small pile of woven baskets from a corner and hung the handles over his arm. From the warming shelf of the stove he pulled a bedraggled band of cloth, into which a large goose feather had been sewn. Carrying this in his hand he went outside and strode down the path toward the highway.

He ignored the chattering sauciness of a squirrel that hurtled up the green ladder of a tree beside him. Above the small noises of the woods could be heard the roar of a transport truck braking its way down the hill from the burnt-out sapling covered ridge to the north. The truck passed him as he reached the road, and he waved a desultory greeting to the driver, who answered with a short blare of the horn.

Placing the baskets in a pile on the shoulder of the road he adjusted the corduroy band on his head so that the feather stuck up at the rear. He knew that by so doing he became a part of the local colour, 'a real Indian with a feather'n everything,' and also that he sold more baskets while wearing it. In the time he had been living along the highway he had learned to give them what they expected.

The trailer residents were not yet awake, so he sat down on the wooden walk leading to the shower room, his baskets resting on the ground in a half circle behind him.

After a few minutes a small boy descended from the door of a trailer and stood staring at him. Then he leaned back inside the doorway and pointed in Big Tom's direction. In a moment a man's hand parted the heavy curtains on the window and a bed-mussed unshaven face stared out. The small boy climbed back inside.

A little later two women approached on the duckboard walk, one attired in a pair of buttock-pinching brown slacks, and the other wearing a blue chenille dressing gown. They circled him warily and entered the shower room. From inside came the buzz of whispered conversation and the louder noises of running water.

During the rest of the morning several people approached and stared at Big Tom and the baskets. He sold two small ones to an elderly woman. She seemed surprised when she asked him what tribe he belonged to, and instead of answering in a monosyllable he said, 'I belong to the Algonquins, Ma'am.' He also got rid of one of his big forty-five cent baskets to the mother of the small boy who had been the first one up earlier in the day.

A man took a series of photographs of him with an expensive-looking camera, pacing off the distance and being very careful in setting his lens openings and shutter speeds.

'I wish he'd look into the camera,' the man said loudly to a couple standing nearby, as if he were talking about an animal in a cage.

'You can't get any good picshus around here. Harold tried to get one of the five Dionney kids, but they wouldn't let him. The way they keep them quints hid you'd think they was made of china or somep'n,' a woman standing by said.

She glanced at her companion for confirmation.

'They want you to *buy* their picshus,' the man said. 'We was disappointed in 'em. They used to look cute before, when they was small, but now they're just five plain-looking kids.'

'Yeah. My Gawd, you'd never believe how homely they got, would you, Harold? An' everything's pure robbery in Callander. You know, Old Man Dionney's minting money up there. Runs his own soovenir stand.'

'That's durin' the day, when he's got time,' her husband said.

The man with the camera, and the woman, laughed.

After lunch Big Tom watched Cooper prepare for his trip to North Bay. 'Is there anybody going fishing, Mr Cooper?' he asked.

The man took the radiator cap off the old truck he was inspecting, and peered inside.

'Mr Cooper!'

'Hey?' Cooper turned and looked at the Indian standing behind him, hands in pockets, his manner shy and deferential. He showed a vague irritation as though he sensed the overtone of servility in the Indian's attitude.

'Anybody going fishing?' Big Tom asked again.

'Seems to me Mr Staynor said he'd like to go,' Cooper answered. His voice was kind, with the amused kindness of a man talking to a child.

The big Indian remained standing where he was, saying nothing. His old second-hand army trousers drooped around his lean loins, and his plaid shirt was open at the throat, showing a grey high-water mark of dirt where his face washing began and ended.

'What's the matter?' Cooper asked. 'You seem pretty anxious to go today.'

'My kid's sick. I want to make enough to take him to the doctor.'

Cooper walked around the truck and opened one of the doors, rattling the handle in his hand as if it was stuck. 'You should stay home with it. Make it some pine-sap syrup. No need to worry, it's as healthy as a bear cub.'

Mrs Cooper came out of the house and eased her bulk into the truck cab. 'Where's Mary?' she asked.

'Up at the shack,' answered Big Tom.

'Tell her to scrub the washrooms before she does anything else. Mrs Anderson, in that trailer over there, wants her to do her floors.' She pointed across the lot to a large blue and white trailer parked behind a Buick.

'I'll tell her,' he answered.

The Coopers drove between the whitewashed stones marking the entrance to the camp, and swung up the highway, leaving behind them a small cloud of dust from the pulverized gravel of the road.

Big Tom fetched Mary and the baby from the shack. He gave his wife Mrs Cooper's instructions, and she transferred the baby from her arms to his. The child was feverish, its breath noisy and fast.

'Keep him warm,' she said. 'He's been worse since we got up. I think he's got a touch of the' flu.'

Big Tom placed his hand inside the old blanket and felt the baby's cheek. It was dry and burning to his palm. He adjusted the baby's small weight in his arm and walked across the camp and down the narrow path to the shore of the lake where the boats were moored.

A man sitting in the sternsheets of a new-painted skiff looked up and smiled at his approach. 'You coming out with me, Tom?' he asked.

The Indian nodded.

'Are you bringing the papoose along?'

Big Tom winced at the word 'papoose', but he answered, 'He won't bother us. The wife is working this afternoon.'

'O.K. I thought maybe we'd go over to the other side of the lake today and try to get some of them big fellows at the creek mouth. Like to try?'

'Sure,' the Indian answered, placing the baby along the wide seat in the stern, and unshipping the oars.

He rowed silently for the best part of an hour, the sun beating through his shirt causing the sweat to trickle coldly down his back. At times his efforts at the oars caused a constriction in his chest, and he coughed and spat into the water.

When they reached the mouth of the creek across the lake, he let the oars drag and leaned over to look at the baby. It was sleeping restlessly, its lips slightly blue and its breath laboured and harsh. Mr Staynor was busy with his lines and tackle in the bow of the boat.

Tom picked the child up and felt its little body for sweat.

The baby's skin was bone dry. He picked up the bailing can from the boat bottom and dipped it over the side. With the tips of his fingers he brushed some of the cold water across the baby's forehead. The child woke up, looked at the strange surroundings, and smiled up at him. He gave it a drink of water from the can. Feeling reassured now he placed the baby on the seat and went forward to help the man with his gear.

Mr Staynor fished for a half hour or so, catching some small fish and a large black bass, which writhed in the bottom of the boat. Big Tom watched its gills gasping its death throes, and noted the similarity between the struggles of the fish and those of the baby lying on the seat in the blanket.

He became frightened again after a time, and he turned to the man in the bow and said, 'We'll have to go pretty soon. I'm afraid my kid's pretty sick.'

'Eh! We've hardly started,' the man answered. 'Don't worry, there's not much wrong with the papoose.'

Big Tom lifted the child from the seat and cradled it in his arms. He opened the blanket, and shading the baby's face, allowed the warm sun to shine on its chest. He thought, if I could only get him to sweat; everything would be all right then.

He waited again as long as he dared, noting the blueness creeping over the baby's lips, before he placed the child again on the seat and addressed the man in the bow. 'I'm going back now. You'd better pull in your line.'

The man turned and felt his way along the boat. He stood over the Indian and parted the folds of the blanket, looking at the baby. 'My God, he is sick, Tom! You'd better get him to a doctor right away!' He stepped across the writhing fish to the bow and began pulling in the line. Then he busied himself with his tackle, stealing glances now and again at the Indian and the baby.

Big Tom turned the boat around, and with long straight pulls on the oars headed back across the lake. The man took the child in his arms and blew cooling drafts of air against its fevered face.

As soon as they reached the jetty below the tourist camp, Tom tied the boat's painter to a stump and took the child from the other man's arms.

Mr Staynor handed him the fee for a full afternoon's work. 'I'm sorry the youngster is sick, Tom,' he said. 'Don't play around. Get him up to the doctor in town right away. We'll try her again tomorrow afternoon.'

Big Tom thanked him. Then, carrying the baby and unmindful of the grasping hands of the undergrowth, he climbed the path through the trees. On reaching the parked cars and trailers he headed in the direction of the large blue and white one where his wife would be working.

When he knocked, the door opened and a woman said, 'Yes?' He recognized her as the one who had been standing nearby in the morning while his picture was being taken.

'Is my wife here?' he asked.

'Your wife. Oh, I know who you mean. No, she's gone. She went down the road in a car a few minutes ago.'

The camp was almost empty, most of the tourists having gone to the small bathing beach farther down the lake. A car full of bathers was pulling away to go down to the beach. Big Tom hurried over and held up his hand until it stopped. 'Could you drive me to the doctor in town?' he asked. 'My baby seems pretty sick.'

There was a turning of heads within the car. A woman in the back seat began talking about the weather. The driver said, 'I'll see what I can do, Chief, after I take the girls to the beach.'

Big Tom sat down at the side of the driveway to wait. After a precious half hour had gone by and they did not return, he got to his feet and started up the highway in the direction of town.

His long legs pounded on the loose gravel of the road, his anger and terror giving strength to his stride. He noticed that the passengers in the few cars he met were pointing at him and laughing, and suddenly he realized that he was still wearing the feather in the band around his head. He reached up, pulled it off, and threw it in the ditch.

When a car or truck came up from behind him he would step off the road and raise his hand to beg a ride. After several passed without pausing he stopped this useless time-wasting gesture and strode ahead, impervious to the noise of their horns as they approached him.

Now and again he placed his hand on the baby's face as he plodded along, reassuring himself that it was still alive. It had been hours since it had cried or shown any other signs of consciousness.

Once, he stepped off the road at a small bridge over a stream, and making a crude cup with his hands, tried to get the baby to drink. He succeeded only in making it cough, harshly, so that its tiny face became livid with its efforts to breathe.

It was impossible that the baby should die. Babies did not die like this, in their father's arms, on a highway than ran fifteen miles north through a small town, where there was a doctor and all the life-saving devices to prevent their deaths.

The sun fell low behind the trees and the swarms of black flies and mosquitoes began their nightly forage. He waved his hand above the fevered face of the baby, keeping them off, while at the same time trying to waft a little air into the child's tortured lungs.

But suddenly, with feelings as black as hell itself, he knew that the baby was dying. He had seen too much of it not to know now, that the child was in an advanced stage of pneumonia. He stumbled along as fast as he could, his eyes devouring the darkening face of his son, while the hot tears ran from the corners of his eyes.

With nightfall he knew that it was too late. He looked up at the sky where the first stars were being drawn in silver on a burnished copper plate, and he cursed them, and cursed what made them possible.

To the north-west the clouds were piling up in preparation for a summer storm. Reluctantly he turned and headed back down the road in the direction he had come.

It was almost midnight before he felt his way along the path through the trees to his shack. It was hard to see anything in the teeming rain, and he let the water run from his shoulders in an unheeded stream, soaking the sodden bundle he still carried in his arms.

When he reached the shanty he opened the door and fell inside. He placed the body of his son on the bed in the corner. Then, groping around the newspaper-lined walls, he found some matches in a pocket of his mackinaw and lit the lamp. With a glance around the room he knew that his wife had not yet returned, so he placed the lamp on the table under the window and headed out again into the rain.

At the trailer camp he sat down on the rail fence near the entrance to wait. Some lights shone from the small windows of the trailers and from Cooper's house across the road. The illuminated sign said: COOPER'S TRAILER CAMP—Hot And Cold Running Water, Rest Rooms. FISHING AND BOATING — INDIAN GUIDES.

One by one, as he waited, the lights went out, until only the sign lit up a small area at the gate. He saw the car's headlights first, about a hundred yards down the road. When it pulled to a stop he heard some giggling, and Mary and another Indian girl, Elsie Woodhen, staggered out into the rain.

A man's voice shouted through the door, 'See you again, sweetheart. Don't forget next Saturday night.' The voice belonged to one of the French-Canadians who worked at a creosote camp across the lake.

Another male voice shouted, 'Wahoo!'

The girls clung to each other, laughing drunkenly, as the car pulled away.

They were not aware of Big Tom's approach until he grasped his wife by the hair and pulled her backwards to the ground. Elsie Woodhen screamed, and ran away in the direction of the Cooper house. Big Tom bent down as if he was going to strike at Mary's face with his fist. Then he changed his mind and let her go.

She stared into his eyes and saw what was there. Crawling to her feet and sobbing hysterically she left one of her silver shoes in the mud and limped along towards the shack.

Big Tom followed behind, all the anguish and frustration drained from him, so that there was nothing left to carry him into another day. Heedless now of the coughing that tore his chest apart, he pushed along in the rain, hurrying to join his wife in the vigil over their dead.

JOYCE MARSHALL

b.1913

The Old Woman

He has changed, Molly thought, the instant she glimpsed her husband in the station at Montreal. He has changed. . . . The thought thudded hollowly through her mind, over and over during the long train-ride into northern Quebec.

It was more than the absence of uniform. His face seemed so still, and there was something about his mouth—a sort of slackness. And at times she would turn and find him looking at her, his eyes absorbed and watchful.

'I *am* glad to see you,' he kept saying. 'I thought you would never make it, Moll.'

'I know,' she said. 'But I had to wait till Mother was really well. . . . It *has* been a long three years, hasn't it?'

Apart from repeating his gladness at her arrival, he seemed to have little to say. He was just strange with her, she tried to soothe herself. They had known each other less than a year when they married in England during the war, and he had left for Canada so soon without her. He must have found it hard to hold a picture of her, just as she had found it hard to hold a picture of him. As soon as they got home—whatever home might be in this strange romantic north to which the train was drawing them—he would be more nearly the Toddy she had known.

It was grey dawn faintly disturbed with pink when they left the train, the only passengers for this little town of Missawani, at the tip of Lake St. John. The name on the greyed shingle reassured Molly a little. How often she had spelled out the strange syllables on letters to Toddy—the double s, the unexpected single n. Somewhere beyond this huddle of low wooden shacks, she knew, was the big Mason paper mill, and Toddy's power-house—one of several that supplied it with electricity—was more than thirty miles away. There was a road, Toddy had told her, but it was closed in winter.

A sullen youth waited behind the station with the dogs. Such beautiful dogs, black brindled with cream, their mouths spread wide in what seemed to Molly happy smiles of welcome. She put a hand towards the nose of the lead-dog, but he lunged and Toddy drew her back.

'They're brutes,' he told her. 'All of them wolfish brutes.'

It was a long strange journey over the snow, first through pink-streaked grey, then into a sun that first dazzled and then inflamed the eyes.

Snow that was flung up coarse and stinging from the feet of the dogs, black brittle fir-trees, birches gleaming like white silk. No sound but the panting breath of the dogs, the dry leatherlike squeak of the snow under the sleigh's runners, and Toddy's rare French-spoken commands to the dogs.

At last he poked her back wordlessly and pointed a mittened hand over her shoulder. For an instant the picture seemed to hang suspended before Molly's eyes: the bare hill with the square red house at its top, the dam level with the top of the hill, the waterfall steaming down to a white swirl of rapids, the power-house like a squat grey cylinder at its foot.

'My old woman,' Toddy shouted, and she saw that he was pointing, not up the hill towards the house where they would live, but to the power-house below.

In England his habit of personalizing an electric generating plant had charmed her, fitting her picturesque notions of the Canadian north. But now she felt uneasiness prod her. It was such a sinister-looking building, and the sound of falling water was so loud and engulfing.

The kitchen of the red house had what Molly thought of as a 'poor' smell about it. Still, no one expected a man to be a good housewife. As soon as she could shut the door and get rid of the sound of that water, she told herself, it would be better. She looked quickly behind her, but Toddy had shut the door already. There must be a window open somewhere. It couldn't be possible that the waterfall was going to live with them in the house like this. It couldn't be possible.

'Cheerful sort of sound,' said Toddy.

Molly looked at him vaguely, half-hearing. A window somewhere— there must be a window she could close.

He showed her quickly over the house, which was fairly well furnished and comfortably heated by electricity. Then he turned to her almost apologetically.

'I hope you won't mind if I go down right away,' he said. 'I'd like to see what kind of shape the old woman's got herself into while I've been away.'

He looked elated and eager, and she smiled at him.

'Go ahead,' she said, 'I'll be all right.'

After he had gone she unpacked her bags and went down to the living-room. It had a broad window, overlooking the power-house, the rapids, and a long snow-field disappearing into the black huddle of pine bush. Snow, she thought. I always thought snow was white, but it's blue. Blue and treacherous as steel. And fully for the first time she realized how cut off they were to be—cut off from town by thirty odd miles of snow and tangled bush and roadlessness.

She found a pail and mop and began to clean the kitchen. She would have it all fresh and nice by the time Toddy came back. She would have no time to look out into the almost instantly blinding glare of the snow. She might even be able to ignore the thundering of the water. She was going to have to spend a lot of time alone in this house. She would have to learn to keep busy.

Toddy did not come up till evening. The power-house was in very bad shape, he told her.

'Those French operators and assistants are a lazy bunch of bums. It's amazing how they can let things go to hell in just two days.'

Molly had set dinner on a little table in the living-room. Toddy had wolfed his meal, his face pre-occupied.

He *was* different. She hadn't just been imagining it. She had thought he would seem closer to her here, but he was more withdrawn than ever. For an instant she had a curious sense that none of this was real to him—not the dinner, nothing but the turbines and generators in the plant below.

Well, so you married this man, she told herself briskly, because you were thirty-eight and he looked nice in his officer's uniform. You followed him here because you were entranced with the idea of a strange and different place. So it is strange and different. And you have to start imagining things, just because your husband is a busy man who seems scarcely to notice that you are here.

'I'm going to make this place ever so much cosier,' she heard herself saying, in a voice so importunate she scarcely recognized it as her own.

'What—oh, yes—yes, fine. Make any changes you like.'

He finished eating and stood up.

'Well, I must be going back now.'

'Back?' He wasn't even apologizing this time, she realized dully. 'Won't your old woman give you an evening off—even when your wife has just come from the old country?'

'I've still things to do,' he said. 'You needn't be lonely. There's a radio—though I'm afraid the static's pretty bad on account of the plant. And I'll be only fifty feet away.'

It was a week before he considered the power-house in suitable shape to show her. He showed her around it proudly—the squat gleaming turbines lying like fat sleepers along the floor, one of the four dismantled so that he could explain the power-generator within, the gauges on the wall.

'It's very interesting, dear,' she said, trying to understand his love for these inanimates, his glowing delight in the meshing parts.

'Perhaps now she looks so slick,' she added, 'you won't have to give her so much of your time.'

'You'd be surprised how quickly she can go wrong,' said Toddy.

He continued to spend all his hours there, from eight in the morning until late at night, with only brief spaces for meals.

Molly worked vigorously about the house and soon it was cleaned and sparkling from top to bottom. After that it was harder to keep busy. She read all the books she had brought, even the ancient magazines she found about the house. She could not go out. It was impossible to do more than keep a path cleared down to the power-house. There were no skis or snow-shoes, and Toddy could not seem to find time to teach her to drive the dogs. There were no neighbours within miles, no telephone calls or visits from milkman or baker—only one of Toddy's sweepers coming in once a fortnight with supplies and mail from Missawani.

She looked forward almost wildly to these visits, for they meant a break as well as letters from home. The men all lived on the nearby concessions—'ranges' they were called here in northern Quebec—six or seven or eight miles away, driving back and forth to the power-house by dog-team. She tried to get them to tell her about their lives and their families, but they were taciturn, just barely polite, and she felt that they simply did not like this house of which she was a part.

She tried constantly to build up some sort of closeness between herself and Toddy. But he seemed only to become less talkative—he had always had a lot of cheerful small talk in England—and more absorbed in the power-house. He seemed to accept her presence as a fact which pleased him, but he had no companionship to spare for her.

'I wish,' she said to him one day, 'that you could go out with me soon and teach me to drive the dogs.'

'But where would you go?' he asked.

'Oh,' she said, 'around. Over the snow.'

'But I'm so busy,' he said. 'I'm sorry—but this is my work, and I'm so busy.'

As he spoke, she saw in his eyes again that look that had terrified her so the first day. Now she thought she recognized what it was. It was a watchful look, a powerful look, as if he were still in the presence of his machinery.

'But couldn't you take an afternoon? Those machines look as if they practically ran themselves. Couldn't you even take a Sunday, Toddy?'

'What if something went wrong while I was away?'

'Oh, Toddy, it can't need you every minute. I'm your wife and I need you too. You seemed so anxious for the time when I'd be able to come here. I can imagine how a person might get to hate being here alone, with that water always roaring and—'

Toddy's face became suddenly angry and wild.

'What do you mean?' he demanded.

'Just that you had three years here alone,' she began.

'I have never been bushed,' Toddy interrupted furiously. 'How dare you suggest that such a thing could ever happen to me? My God, apart from the war, I've lived in this country for twenty years.'

Bushed. The suggestion was his, and for a moment she allowed herself to think about it. She was familiar with the term. Toddy used it constantly about others who had come up north to live. He knew the country, but he had been away. And then he had returned alone to this place, where for so long every year the winter buried you, snow blinded you, the wind screamed up the hill at night, and the water thundered. . . .

'Toddy,' she said, afraid of the thought, putting it out of her mind, 'when spring comes, couldn't we get a cow or two. I *do* know about cattle—I wasn't in the Land Army all through the war for nothing. I think it would give me an interest.'

Toddy stared at her.

'Aren't you my wife?' he asked.

'Why yes—yes, of course.'

'Then how can you speak about needing an interest? Isn't there interest enough for you in simply being my wife?'

'But I'm—I'm left so much alone. You have your work, but I have so little to do.'

Toddy turned on his heel, preparing to go again to the power-house. At the door he glanced back over his shoulder, not speaking, merely watching her.

He doesn't want me to have an interest, thought Molly, her mind bruised with horror and fear. He looks at me watchfully, as if I were one of his machines. Perhaps that's what he wants me to be—a generator, quiet and docile, waiting for him here, moving only when he tells me to move.

And I am the sort of woman who must have work to do. If I don't, my mind will grow dim and misty. Already I can feel the long sweep of the snow trying to draw my thoughts out till they become diffused and vague. I can feel the sound of the water trying to crush and madden me.

After that, it seemed as if Toddy were trying to spend more time with her. Several times he sat and talked with her after dinner, telling her about the power-house and the catastrophes he had averted that day. But always his eyes would be turning to the window and the power-house showing grey and sullen against the snow.

'Oh, you can go down now, Toddy,' Molly would say. 'Obviously, that is where you wish to be.'

And then one day she found the work she wanted.

She looked up from her dishes to see Louis-Paul, one of the power-house oilers, standing in the doorway, snow leaking from his great felt boots on to the floor.

'Madame—' he said.

'Oh Louis, hello,' said Molly warmly, for she was friendlier with this slight fair youth than with any of Toddy's other workmen. They had long solemn conversations—she practising her French and he his English. 'But don't tell the Curé,' Louis would say. 'He does not like it if we speak English.'

'Did you come for my list?' Molly asked him. 'Are you going to town?'

'No, Madame, I have—how you say it? I am today in big trouble. My Lucienne—'

'Oh, the baby—has your baby been born, Louis-Paul?'

'Yes, madame—'

With a hopeless gesture he relinquished his English. From his rapid, desperate French, Molly learned that there was something that prevented Lucienne from nursing her child, and none of the cows on any of the ranges were giving milk that winter.

'If you could come, madame, you might know—you might do something—'

His team of yellow dogs was tied at the kitchen stoop. Together Louis-Paul and Molly dashed across the snow to the house at the first range. Just a little bit of a house that Louis-Paul's father had built for him six years ago when he divided his thin-soiled farm and his timber-lots among his sons. Its roof was the warm grey of weathered wood, almost as deeply curved as the roof of a Chinese pagoda.

In the kitchen Lucienne's mother and sisters and aunts in all their black wept noisily, one of them holding the crying child. And in the bedroom the girl Lucienne was sobbing, because she realized that the presence of her relatives in their best black meant that her child could not be saved.

Molly looked at her for a moment—the swarthy broad cheeks, the narrow eyes, that showed a tinge of Indian blood.

'Would you be shy with me, Lucienne?' she asked. 'Too shy to take off your nightgown while I am here?'

'I would never be shy with you, madame,' said Lucienne.

Something hot came into Molly's throat as she eased the nightgown from the girl's shoulders and went into the kitchen for hot and cold water and a quantity of cloths.

Tenderly she bathed the heavy breasts with alternate hot and cold water, explaining that the nipples were inverted and that this should bring them into place. And before she left, Lucienne was holding the baby's dark head against her breast, weeping silently, the wailing in the kitchen had ceased, and Louis-Paul was fixing stiff portions of whisky blanc and home-made wine, passing the one wine-glass around and around the assembly.

Not until she was back at the red house, actually stamping the snow from her boots on the kitchen stoop, did Molly realize that it was long past the early dinner that Toddy liked. She went in quickly.

Toddy was standing in the middle of the room, his hands dangling with a peculiar slackness at his sides. He looked at her, and there was a great empty bewilderment on his face.

'You have been out?' he asked.

'Yes,' she said, elated still from her afternoon. 'I went over to Louis-Paul's with him. His wife's had her baby and—'

'He asked you?' said Toddy.

'Yes,' she said. 'He was desperate, poor lad, so I just had to offer to do what I could.'

He's afraid I'll go away, she thought. He must have come up here and found the stove cold and thought I had gone forever. The thought alternately reassured and chilled her. It was simple and ordinary for him to be anxious, but his expression was neither simple nor ordinary. Now that she had explained, he should not be staring at her still, his gaze thinned by surprise and fear.

'I'm sorry about dinner,' she said, 'but I'll hurry and fix something easy. You have a smoke and I'll tell you all about it.'

She told him but he would not join in her enthusiasm.

'Another French-Canadian brat,' he said. 'Molly, you're a fool.'

A few weeks later she realized she now had a place even in this barren land. Louis-Paul appeared again in the kitchen, less shy, for now she was his friend. His sister-in-law was having a baby and something was wrong. They would have taken her to Missawani, but there was every sign of a blizzard blowing up. Madame had been so good with Lucienne. Perhaps she could do something for Marie-Claire as well.

'I don't see how I could,' said Molly. 'I've helped bring little calves and pigs into the world, but never a baby—'

'She may die,' said Louis. 'They say the baby is placed wrong. They have given her blood of a newborn calf to drink, but still—'

'All right,' said Molly, 'I'll go.'

She set a cold meal for Toddy and propped a note against his plate. The thought of him nudged her mind guiltily during the dash over the snow to the little house. But that was absurd. She would be away only a few hours. Toddy would have to learn to accept an occasional absence. He was a little—well, selfish about her. He would have to learn.

With some help from an ancient grandmother, Molly delivered a child on the kitchen table of the little house. An old Cornish farm-hand had showed her once how to turn a calf that was breached. Much the same thing was involved now—deftness, daring, a strong hand timed to the bitter contractions of the girl on the table.

When she returned home late in the evening, she had not thought of Toddy for hours.

This time he was angry, mumblingly, shakingly angry.

'Molly,' he shouted, 'you must put an end to this nonsensical—'

'But it's not nonsensical,' she said, serene still from the miracle of new life she had held across her hands. 'I brought a nice little boy into the world. He might never have been born except for me.'

'These women have been popping kids for years without you.'

'I know,' said Molly, 'but sometimes they lose them. And they're so—superstitious. I can help them, Toddy. I can.'

She paused, then spoke more gently.

'What is it, Toddy? Why don't you want me to go?'

The question caught him somehow, and his face, his whole expression became loosed, as if suddenly he did not understand his own rage.

'You're my wife,' he said. 'I want you here.'

'Well, cheer up,' she said, speaking lightly because his look had chilled her so. 'I am, usually.'

After that, no woman in any of the ranges ever had a baby without her husband's dogs whisking over the fields to the red house.

Molly now was famed for miles. She was good luck at a birth, and when something unexpected happened she could act with speed and ingenuity. She liked the people and felt that they liked her. Even the Curé, who hated the power-house and all it represented, bowed and passed the time of day when he and Molly met in a farm-house kitchen.

She sent away for government pamphlets and a handful of texts. Though it was true, as Toddy said, that these women had had babies without her, it pleased her that she was cutting down the percentage of early deaths.

Each of her errands meant a scene with Toddy. There was a struggle here, she felt, between her own need for life and work and what she tried to persuade herself was merely selfishness in him. In her new strength and happiness she felt that she ought to be able to draw Toddy into taking an interest in something beyond the power-house. But he would not be drawn.

Surely when the snows broke it would be possible. She would persuade him to take the old car in the barn and drive with her about the countryside. He was only a trifle bushed from the long winter. Though she had been shocked at first by the suggestion that he might be bushed, she found the hope edging into her mind more and more often now that it was nothing more.

And then one day it was Joe Blanchard's turn to come to get her. His wife was expecting her tenth child.

All day Molly was restless, going to the window to strain her eyes into the glare for a sight of Joe's sleigh and his tough yellow dogs winding out of the bush. Sunset came and she prepared dinner, and still he had not come.

Once she looked up from her plate and saw Toddy staring at her, his lips trembling in an odd small way.

'Is anything wrong?' she asked.

'No,' he said, 'nothing.'

'Toddy,' she said, gently, and under her gentleness afraid. 'I'll probably be going out tonight. I promised Joe Blanchard I'd help Mariette.'

Toddy looked at her, and his face blazed.

'No,' he shouted, 'by God—you will stay where you belong.'

'Why?' she asked, as she had before. 'Why don't you want me to go?'

He seemed to search through his mind for words.

'Because I won't have you going out at night with that ruffian—because, damn it, it's too dangerous.'

'Then you come too,' she said. 'You come with us.'

'Don't be a fool,' he said. 'How could I leave?'

'Well, stay home tonight,' she said. 'Stay here and—and rest. We'll decide what to do when Joe comes.'

'Rest—what do you mean?'

'I think you're—tired,' she said. 'I think you should stay home just one evening.'

Toddy scraped back his chair.

'Don't be a fool, Molly. Of course I can't stay. I can't.'

He walked to the door, then turned back to her.

'I shall find you here,' he said, 'when I return.'

The evening dragged between the two anxieties—between wondering when Joe would come and watching for Toddy's return.

Midnight came, and still neither Toddy nor Joe had come. Her anxiety grew. Toddy had never stayed this late before. It had been ten-thirty first, then eleven.

The sound of the back door opening sent her flying to the kitchen. Joe stood in the doorway, his broad face beaming.

'You ready, madame?'

Molly began to put on her heavy clothes, her snow-boots. Anxiety licked still in her mind. Past twelve o'clock and Toddy had not returned.

'Joe,' she said, 'you'll wait just a minute while I go down and tell my husband?'

Her feet slipped several times on the icy steps Toddy kept cut in the hillside. She felt a sudden terrible urgency. She must reassure herself of something. She didn't quite know what.

She pulled open the door of the power-house and was struck, as she had been before, by the way the thunder of the waterfall was suddenly replaced by a low even whine.

For an instant she did not see Toddy. Louis-Paul was propped in a straight chair dozing, across the room. Then she saw Toddy, his back, leaning towards one of the turbines. As she looked, he moved, with a curious scuttling speed, to one of the indicators on the wall. She saw the side of his face then, its expression totally absorbed, gloating.

'Toddy!' she called.

He turned, and for a long moment she felt that he did not know who she was. He did not speak.

'I didn't want you to worry,' she said. 'I'm going with Joe. If I shouldn't be back for breakfast—'

She stopped, for he did not seem to be listening.

'I probably *will* be back for breakfast,' she said.

He glared at her. He moved his lips as if to speak. Then his gaze broke and slid back to the bright indicator on the wall.

At that moment she understood. The struggle she had sensed without being able to give it a name had been between herself and the power-house. In an indistinct way Toddy had realized it when he said, 'I want you here.'

'Toddy!' she shouted.

He turned his back to her in a vague automatic way, and she saw that his face was quite empty except for a strange glitter that spread from his eyes over his face. He did not answer her.

For a moment she forgot that she was not alone with him, until a sound reminded her of Louis-Paul, awake now and standing by the door. And from the expression of sick shaking terror on his face she knew what the fear had been that she had never allowed herself to name.

'Oh Louis,' she said.

'Come madame,' he said. 'We can do nothing here. In the morning I will take you to Missawani. I will bring the doctor back.'

'But is he safe?' she asked. 'Will he—damage the machines perhaps?'

'Oh no. He would never hurt these machines. For years I watch him fall in love with her. Now she has him for herself.'

HELEN WEINZWEIG

b. 1915

Causation

The woman hesitated at first to let him in. 'Piano tuner,' Gyorgi Szigeti
said, then waited, leaning against the door frame. He waited for her to
decide whether he was a musician and therefore eligible to come in the
front door, or whether he was a tradesman to be directed to the rear
entrance. What she could not have known was that Gyorgi had no
intention of using the servants' entrance. He stood before her, proud in
his black bowler hat, his long white silk scarf knotted loosely and flowing
down over his shiny black leather jacket. 'Piano tuner,' he repeated to
the woman, who had not moved. She was transfixed. 'Oh my God,' she
said, 'not you, not you!' He did not question her words: by habit he took
no notice of the eccentricities of the rich. Slowly, slowly, she widened
the doorway.

No one ever had to show him where the piano was. He found it the
way a dog searches out a bone. Traversing miles, it seemed, of Oriental
carpets to reach the ebony grand piano at the other end of a vast room, he
experienced a numbness, a detachment, as if asleep and dreaming: he
had a sense of having once before covered the distance. And the short,
sturdy woman in a flowered housecoat (he had noticed) who was following
him—he knew her, too. But then, he knew a lot of women, some also
short and sturdy, and maybe that's all it was: so many women.

'It's my own piano,' she was saying. Her heavy hand clumped across
the keys. 'This B keeps getting out of tune,' striking the note five times
to let him hear how bad it was.

Gyorgi Szigeti almost fell to his knees. He was in the presence of a
Bechstein grand piano.

She was still talking. 'Everything you see in here, all the furniture in
the house, was chosen by my ex-husband. He lets me keep my piano
only because he is a music lover.'

Gyorgi removed his black leather jacket, draping it on the back of a
gilded chair with curved legs. The bowler hat and silk scarf he arranged

carefully on the seat. He ran his fingers over the piano keys. The sound was as brilliant as he remembered a Bechstein to be; the bass was resonant and the top notes vibrant. This was unexpected: in these wealthy homes the pianos were regarded as furniture and tuned only when an anticipated house guest was some sort of performer.

'I'm a singer. A concert artist. An opera star,' she announced. 'That is, I used to be an opera star.'

While Gyorgi worked, she sat on the piano bench, which he had moved aside. She hummed each note in unison with his repeated plunking as he tightened strings. She had perfect pitch. It spurred him on, this breathless attention of hers; then the two of them listening, listening together, both now intent on the climactic moments when he brought each white whole note and each black half note to perfection. He felt like the Creator of All Sound. When he tightened a string, he had a way of tightening his mouth, twisting the left corner upward into his cheek, which resulted in a threatening grimace. Once the ideal sound was achieved, his mouth loosened.

She rose to leave. 'Would you like some coffee?'

Gyorgi looks around, then re-enters the room in his mind, retraces his steps in imagination; but this time, instead of seeing her figure stride out the doorway, as it is doing at this very moment, he sees her laid out in a satin-lined coffin, in the same flowered housecoat; and instead of her sluttish make-up, the face in death is delicately tinted as if in the blush of youth. The mortician's skill has fixed the happiness he, Gyorgi, gave her. After the funeral he stays on in the old house, sleeping in one of the spare rooms, surprised at his delicacy, even in fantasy, in not using the bedroom where he had made her ecstatic. The letter from the lawyers comes, addressed to Gyorgi Szigeti, to this house. She has left him everything. Everything, including the beloved Bechstein, is his. Just in time, before her return interrupts his fateful vision, he recalls with a sudden clarity the source of his images: an account in this morning's newspaper: rich elderly widow . . . a young man of thirty-three . . . they married . . . she died . . . left him everything she owned . . . great wealth . . . her daughters suing . . . old mother was crazy . . . 'They're crazy,' the new heir had protested to the judge, 'she was more fascinating, more of a woman, than those two dried-up broads will ever be if they live to be a hundred.'

Over coffee, perhaps because he had already lived out the scene in his mind, Gyorgi leaned forward and said in a voice deep with sincerity:

'You are still a beautiful woman. you have so much to give . . .'

She eyed him silently. She was about fifty-five, but in her clear, light eyes, raised to meet his directly, age had been postponed. It was a matter of pride with him that in his persuasions Gyorgi rarely lied. In every woman he found qualities he could honestly admire. He went on, emboldened:

'Your eyes—they are the eyes of a girl.'

She denied nothing: that was all that mattered.

'These Bechsteins,' he ventured, 'do not take kindly to the extreme cold and intense heat of our climate. The wood . . . changes of temperature . . .' He brought out a small notebook from his back pocket. He could come back next week. To see if the tuning held.

Uppermost in her mind is the fact that his wide, curved mouth is at odds with his small, deep-set, dark eyes, suggesting to her an easygoing cruelty.

At his ring the following week she flung open the door. Her face was heavier than before with rouge and lipstick, her brows blacker, her lids greener. Gyorgi believed that if he ate enough of the stuff women put on their faces he would get cancer. In such cases he would put his lips to the bare hollows of her throat.

Today she ignored his pretence of tuning the perfectly tuned instrument. She didn't listen; she chattered.

'Once I was Violetta with the San Francisco Opera Company. Oswald, my former husband, loved *Traviata*. He loved me. He offered me the world if I would give up the stage and sing for him alone: wealth, babies, a fire in the hearth on Sunday nights. Oh, he knows his operas . . . I worked hard, practised every day. In the evening, with the two babies asleep in the nursery, I sang for him. I dressed for the part. The costumes accumulated: Cio-Cio San, Carmen, Tosca, Mignon.

'The idyll lasted almost five years. One morning I awoke to find him standing at the foot of the bed. The room was still dark so that I could not quite see his face, just the outline of his figure, fully dressed. He had been waiting, I sensed, for me to awaken. I sat up and then he spoke, slowly and distinctly:

' "You are not the great artist I thought you were. You cannot place your voice, and when it comes out from behind your big nose, the glorious music falls to the floor like a bag of cement. You are ridiculous in the clothes of the great heroines: you have the passion of a disposable lighter. You have deceived me." With that he left and never returned.'

'Did he leave you for another woman?' Gyorgi asked, for that is what he knew of the way of the world.

'No, no, he wouldn't do that. He is a very respectable man.'

'Did he marry again?'

'Ha! The only woman he'd consider would have to be a virgin who chose marriage to Oswald instead of entering a nunnery.' She gave him a sly smile. 'You know what? I think Oswald was jealous of my music. When I played the role of Mimi or Aïda or Desdemona, I became the woman I was portraying. I didn't mean to, but I escaped him each time—*that's* what he couldn't stand.'

Gyorgi tilted his head in a pretence of interest. He had no idea what she was talking about, but he realized that she was determined to reveal herself to him. It was as if women had to expose themselves—their defeats, their triumphs, their hopes and beliefs—before they undressed. In his opinion, a nude man in a raincoat was more honest. Gyorgi listened to women for their 'tone' quality, the same way he listened when he was tuning a piano. He noticed that her forehead glistened with perspiration.

'I can't pay you today,' she said. 'Oswald has gone to India to see his guru. Left me without a cent. Again.'

'It's all right,' he said gently, 'you can pay me any time.'

Even after she had paid him, Gyorgi took to dropping in, making his visits sporadic, so that they would seem compulsive, as if he couldn't resist seeing her. She was always unprepared, and would run to comb her hair and put on fresh lipstick. Once he stopped her, saying he liked her the way she was. Above all, he would want her to be perfectly natural with him. She was so moved by these sentiments, she wanted to do something for him in return.

'Would you like to hear Cio-Cio San's farewell aria? No? I see. But you obviously know everything about pianos.'

'I was an apprentice for five years in the Bechstein factory in Berlin.'

'What else can you do?'

'I can build a bomb shelter.'

'Good. Then you can take care of this house. What do you say—live here and look after things. Oh, you will go out to your work as you always have, but instead of a small room in a smelly boardinghouse—ah, I thought so!—you can stay here. Pick any of the five spare rooms. What do you say?'

Gyorgi couldn't speak. He put his hands on his lap lest she see how they shook. A mansion, a Bechstein—all within the space of a few weeks. He hung his head and assumed the obsequious manner of his youth.

Then he went through the house, taking the stairs two at a time. The rooms were full of the kind of masterpieces he had seen only behind thick silken cords in museums. Everything was old and massive or old and fragile; everything was forceful with value. She ran after him, unable to keep up, observing that he moved with an animal grace, as if he had lived all his life out of doors.

'I can't understand why a man would want to leave you. It's a wonderful house,' he said.

'Oswald doesn't care about material things—furniture, cars, clothes—he has no interest in them. He wants to touch the infinite, discover the ineffable; he is on a journey of the spirit, he is concerned only with his immortal soul.'

'So?' said Gyorgi. 'So?' he repeated. 'He has never had to work hard in order to eat.'

'You must know that I still love him.'

Suddenly she was crying, crying for no reason that he could see.

He waved an arm into the air, around and around. 'You have everything; you have it all!'

'Nothing! Nothing, I tell you. There is only the music, notes on a page, enduring, eternal, nothing else exists.' Then, in afterthought, her voice distant, she added, 'You are the exception.'

He chose the sixth bedroom. Hers. Awaiting her in the wide bed, he called out, 'And wash that damned crap off your face.'

When she came back into the room, she grasped the post at the foot of the huge bed, weaving slightly as if drunk, and intoned:

'I adore you, you are low-born, you have no character, you are inevitable. Ours will be an affair of terrible limits. Your insults are without principle. Whatever grief you will cause will come naturally and I shall recover as one does after slipping on ice. Most important, though, Oswald will no longer be able to draw blood with his blunt knives. I shall continue to go to him every week for money. But it will be for you. That will make it easy. No. More than that. I shall *enjoy* the humiliation. I will answer his interrogation: "Why is the butcher's bill so high?" "Because I have a tall, strong man to feed," I will sit in the leather chair in his office while he counts out the ten-dollar bills, slowly, sliding them halfway across the desk. I will lean forward and scoop them up and thank him. Oswald will unbutton his vest and look across at me like a judge with a three-time loser and condemn me, as he always does, with good advice. But I won't care. He has lost his power: tonight I hand it over to you.'

During the prolonged love-making that follows, she opens her eyes a few times. Once she sees his mouth tighten and a corner go up into his cheek into an ugly grimace.

Gyorgi moved in. It was then that he was faced with what he had missed that first time because his head had been bursting with the delirium of his good fortune. There was everywhere a fury of disorder, as if a bomb had gone off in each room separately. The halls had boxes and overshoes strewn about. There was dirt on every surface; old dust that had hardened; mouse droppings in the kitchen and cockroaches in the sinks. She shrugged off his dismay. 'Oswald won't pay for a cleaning woman.'

Gyorgi loved control and completeness. He set about to restore order, spending every weekend sweeping, scrubbing, repairing, room by room, starting with the bedroom. The kitchen alone took a month. The cellar, he figured, could occupy him as long as she lived.

There was no design to her life. Asleep when he left, off in a world of song when he got home; she could not remember what, if anything, she had accomplished, nor what had transpired during the day. 'Some phone calls. Nothing much. How was *your* day?' And showered him with kisses. One of the phone calls, he surmised, was for the frozen chicken pie and canned pea soup that he was eating for dinner. And he, who required a daily pattern to blanket his years, felt a chill of apprehension.

'Now, my handsome Magyar,' she crooned, 'I'll sing for you and you alone. I learned some Hungarian folk songs set by Kodàly.'

'I told you a dozen times, I hate Hungarian anything. Maybe there's a soccer game on TV.'

'Don't you ever tire of watching grown men kick a ball?'

'You have the memory of an imbecile: I told you: I was a professional soccer player. I toured Germany.'

Each day Gyorgi went out on his calls. He had given up his black leather jacket and now wore a navy blue blazer with a crest embroidered in red and white on the upper left pocket. He refused to part with his bowler hat and long white scarf. He no longer said, 'Piano tuner' at the front door. Instead, he presented, wordlessly, his business card with his name and elegant new address and *Pianos Tuned to Perfection* embossed in shiny black script. As the days got shorter, he came home earlier and earlier. Some cold days he did not go out at all. He would float about the house, content to hammer, force windows open, stop taps from dripping. She would follow him around like the small daughter he once had. While he worked, she would sit on the floor, always in the flowered housecoat, telling him stories about people she knew.

'You're making it up,' he sometimes accused her. 'No, no,' she protested, 'that's what he really did.' Or, 'She was desperate. A woman in that state will say anything.' His disbelief at times bordered on wonder: did people of wealth and substance really carry on crazy like that? Keeping his eyes on his work, never turning his head, pretending a lofty indifference, he would probe with ruttish questions: what had taken place with her and Oswald in bed; what had she done with other men; how many lovers; in what combinations. And she, without a second thought, would lay open intimacies as one spreads open an umbrella in the rain. And always she hugged her knees and chortled deep in her throat, 'But you, my darling, are the best, you are the champ.' On those days a camaraderie was struck between them and he felt himself to be her equal in the sense that she was no better than he. More than that: he felt himself elevated, and ceased to regret, once and for all, that he was so unschooled that she had to read to him the instructions on a can of varnish.

Every night he made love to her. He treated the whole business as his part of the bargain. In bed his movements were as easy and graceful as when he painted a wall or repaired a broken drainpipe. He was precise; he was unhurried. Afterwards, Gyorgi would turn over as if fatigued, although his exultation was boundless. He did this rather than listen to her. 'You talk too much,' he would say, 'people screw up by talking too much.'

Once she frightened him in the middle of the night by shaking him awake. The bedside lamp was on. She was sitting bolt upright.

'Quickly,' she said in an urgent voice, 'don't think, tell me, quickly, what is life?'

'Life,' he said obediently, 'is. Life is. That's all. You're either alive or dead.'

'Wrong!' she said sharply. 'Life is an imposition. Oswald refuses to admit it. He wants life to be raw, with the bones showing. Today he presented me with a new account book, with more spaces for more entries. He threatened me again: unless I am more exact about the money I spend, he will cut off my alimony. He *imposes* himself on my life.'

Gyorgi condescended. 'What are you complaining about? A short ride in the Mercedes and you're living fat for another week. Perfect octaves don't buy houses like this.'

'You comprehend nothing.' She turned from him. 'You know nothing of the malice that masquerades as virtue. You are young: you still make plans.'

He stared at the long, heavy drapes.

'After the war we were thrown out of Hungary and shipped in boxcars to Germany. We lived behind barbed wire, then in barracks, then in a shack somewhere outside Frankfurt. All night long we heard the screams of the tortured. My brothers and sisters and I jumped out of bed when we heard the cries. We took turns standing on a chair at the small, high window. We could see nothing. Our parents never woke up.'

She studied him: there was no humility in him. She laid her head on his chest and a hand on his shoulder. Gyorgi yawned and lay back with his hands under his head.

'Fate,' she whispered, 'weaves its mysteries in the dark; that is why we do not know our destiny in the light of day.'

'That's true,' he agreed, understanding nothing. He had no sense of the abstract, but he recognized, if not destiny, certainly an opportunity. 'You have a beautiful house. I'm surprised you never married again.'

'Oswald wouldn't like it. Besides, if I married I wouldn't have this beautiful house.'

Gyorgi, startled, heard only the first part: 'Oswald wouldn't like it.' What did Oswald have to do with her desire to marry again? His own life had been a series of divorcements so immutable that he never again saw his parents, his brothers and sisters, two wives, countless lovers, as well as a number of unreasonable employers. If his decision to part, made simply and honestly, was challenged, he used his soccer-field fists, elbows, knees, or boots to make his meaning clear.

'We are lovers now,' he pursued, 'let us be as if married. I will care for you as my father did for my mother; you will care for me as my mother did my father.'

'But you are already here, in my house, in my bed . . .'

Lack of sleep made Gyorgi irritable. She was missing the point.

'From now on,' he rasped, 'you will do a woman's work.'

'Oh, oh,' she moaned, 'more impositions . . .'

'We must speak of necessities,' he went on inexorably. 'Food is a necessity. Respect is a necessity. It is necessary to respect the place you eat and sleep in. The way you live now, you turn roses into shit. Starting tomorrow, you will keep the house clean, wash the clothes, cook the meals. I will take out the garbage, attend the mousetraps, spray the roach powder.'

'My music . . .'

'*Deine Stimme is zum Kotzen*,' he said as day dawned, 'you have the voice of a crow.'

'Yes, yes,' she said, falling in with his thought, 'I will buy a loom and learn to weave.'

'Don't be stupid. You're too clumsy.'

She flung her faith into the new day. Laughing now and clapping her hands she exclaimed:

'You noticed! Oh, how I do love you!'

She no longer rouges her lips and cheeks nor colours her eyelids. Gyorgi has convinced her of his preference for an unadorned face. This he has done by holding her head down in the bathroom sink filled with water. Her giggles spluttered, she choked, she lost consciousness. She has learned that he means what he says. She thinks he has helped her begin a new life. She telephones everyone she knows to tell them that she gets up in the morning and that she bakes bread.

Just before Christmas there was a party. Gyorgi was surprised, considering her indolence, that she had so many friends. Well, maybe he could understand: she was guileless; she harboured no ill will. He was sent to the convenience store on Summerhill Avenue for peanuts and chips and mixes. 'Not to worry,' she assured him, 'everyone brings a bottle. All we need are enough clean glasses.' He went back and bought five dozen plastic glasses.

Gyorgi dressed for the evening. He wore a white shirt and a patterned silk tie and real gold cuff links—gifts of grateful women. He looked distinguished, almost, in a suit. The synthetic brown cloth hung on his frame like an admiral's uniform. She introduced him: 'Isn't he gorgeous!' He walked behind her and watched gravely while she went about kissing men and 'adoring' them. In his turn he was careful not to flirt with women. He could take no chances: women mistook his compliments for confessions.

He assumed the dignity of the foreman he remembered in the Bechstein factory, hands behind his back, observing everyone, recording, alert to what might be expected of him. He mixed drinks, removed coats, and carried them upstairs; clipped pairs of galoshes and boots together with clothespins. After a while he realized that the guests made no distinction between him and themselves. An envoy from India invited him to a cricket match in Edwards Gardens next summer; Gyorgi invited him in return to a soccer match next summer, also in Edwards Gardens. A pretty psychiatrist wept on his breast in revealing an unhappy marriage;

he told her of his own two divorces. A stockbroker took him aside, confided that metals were going to be big, and gave him a business card. Gyorgi went upstairs and got his business card, which he gave to the stockbroker. Gyorgi was overcome by a sophistication he had never known before. In his new expansiveness he slid into discussions.

'Hitler never wanted war,' he said with the authority of one who also has an inside track to matters of importance. 'He waited outside Poland for word from Chamberlain, who double-crossed him and declared war on Germany. The Allies have falsified history. Hitler could have invaded Britain but ordered the generals to hold off, always hoping for peace. The Holocaust was a lie, spread by Jewish international bankers.'

She, meanwhile, had been circling. In the silence that followed his revelations she linked her arm through his and pulled him away just when he was about to heap fact upon startling fact. Tomorrow (he intends) he will tell her: 'It is not respectful for a woman to interrupt a man when he is speaking. You must never do that again.'

Instead, it was she who faced him when everyone had gone. She was calm; there was a hardness about her as she stood looking up at him without a flicker or a twinge. 'You must never, never again reveal your fascism. I will not permit racist talk in my house.'

When the spring sun began to stream through the shiny windows and the lawn gave off a yielding odour, Gyorgi, too, softened. He permitted her to sing for him in the evening, to wear costumes and a little make-up. She accompanied herself at the Bechstein, the rings on both hands flashing under the crystal lights. He listened to her stories of the operas, stories of terror and love and irony and death. He listened and planned. There would be the garden to attend to, storms to be taken down, screens to be installed, diningroom chairs to be repaired. Days of work; music and parties; nights of love. The picture of an old woman dying and leaving him her big house faded, then disappeared altogether.

This night she was dressed as Mimi, looking quite appealing, he thought, in a pink bonnet tied with satin ribbons under her chin. She looked girlish and demure. He even recognized the song in which Mimi asks for a muff to warm her poor, cold hands. Suddenly she broke off, rose abruptly from the piano, turned off the lights, lit a candle, and waving it high overhead, announced:

'I want to die slowly like Mimi.' She placed the candle on the table at the side of his chair and sank at his feet. 'Do you still want to marry me?'

'Marry me . . . ?' Gyorgi repeated, and his voice broke. He saw himself answering the ring at the front door, raising his eyebrows, and, if necessary, directing the caller to the servants' entrance. Forgiveness flowed over him. In his mind he sent money to his mother and father to come for a visit to see what he had made of himself. Then would come his brothers and sisters, each in turn. He drew her up on his lap. He removed Mimi's bonnet and stroked her head.

She, dreaming: 'I feel like Gretel,' cradling into him, 'we will be like Hansel and Gretel, alone in the forest. We will learn to live in innocence, like peasants, gathering nuts and berries, protected from evil by our happiness.'

'You people,' he said, shaking his head, 'I love the way you people want to play poor, with your budgets and your diets, with your gurus and your torn jeans.' Suddenly he became angry. 'It is all one big lie: you people couldn't survive a day's hunger.'

'I'm not pretending. When I marry, Oswald cuts off my alimony. This is his house, lock, stock, and four-poster. We will not be allowed to stay here.' Her teeth were clamped together. 'Oswald would never let us live in his house.'

Gyorgi felt evicted, dislodged from a place in his head. Somehow he did not find it odd that he should be striking out at her. But she was off his lap and out of range with a swiftness that surprised him: she must have expected something like this.

'You tricked me!' he shouted. 'The work . . . the hours . . . I cleaned up your bloody mess . . . it was to have been for me, for me, damn you . . . all this time I was busting my ass for him . . . for *his* house . . .'

In his fury he lunged at her. She ran from him and he after her with his fists extended. His anger also brought confusion: images of her friends, lawyers and judges and others in high places before whom he was powerless: he could smell the acid of a jail cell. He heard a crash. He stopped in his tracks as if shot and he heard her laugh. She was standing with her back to the Bechstein, her rump on the keys, her arms flung out and back in a posture of protection. He was astounded that she knew so little about him after all these days and nights that she could think him capable of harming a Bechstein. He banged his knuckles against each other and did not touch her. He opened his fingers and let his arms hang.

'What will become of you?' she taunted. 'You have been spoiled, spoiled by mahogany and fine linen and oil paintings on the walls. You are unfit now for rented rooms and tired waitresses and the hopes of check-out girls.'

So. They had come to the end of the game. It made him sad: he had liked her: he could have been satisfied. Then, doglike, shaking the discovery off himself, he withdrew, walking backwards. Gyorgi kept going, backwards, stepping over the thick carpets for the last time.

Where she is standing, in her shabby Mimi gown, arms still extended against her beloved piano, dry-eyed, ears strained towards the sounds of Gyorgi's departure, she knows already she will soon sit across the desk from fair, florid Oswald. She hears already his instructions: no calls. Hears Oswald's voice without a rise in it saying: 'What happened this time? Hmm. You got off easy. Give me the account.' She knows, too, that Oswald will lace his pale fingers across his chest and quote for the hundredth time: ' "Even among galley slaves there were ten percent volunteers." For God's sake, when will you stop inviting your own destruction.' She sees already her hungry hand as it moves across the desk. She will take the money to keep her safe for yet another little while.

MAVIS GALLANT

b. 1922

The Ice Wagon Going Down the Street

Now that they are out of world affairs and back where they started, Peter Frazier's wife says, 'Everybody else did well in the international thing except us.'

'You have to be crooked,' he tells her,

'Or smart. Pity we weren't.'

It is Sunday morning. They sit in the kitchen, drinking their coffee, slowly, remembering the past. They say the names of people as if they were magic. Peter thinks, *Agnes Brusen*, but there are hundreds of other names. As a private married joke, Peter and Sheilah wear the silk dressing gowns they bought in Hong Kong. Each thinks the other a peacock, rather splendid, but they pretend the dressing gowns are silly and worn in fun.

Peter and Sheilah and their two daughters, Sandra and Jennifer, are visiting Peter's unmarried sister, Lucille. They have been Lucille's guests seventeen weeks, ever since they returned to Toronto from the Far East. Their big old steamer trunk blocks a corner of the kitchen, making a problem of the refrigerator door; but even Lucille says the trunk may as well stay where it is, for the present. The Fraziers' future is so unsettled; everything is still in the air.

Lucille has given her bedroom to her two nieces, and sleeps on a camp cot in the hall. The parents have the living-room divan. They have no privileges here; they sleep after Lucille has seen the last television show that interests her. In the hall closet their clothes are crushed by winter overcoats. They know they are being judged for the first time. Sandra and Jennifer are waiting for Sheilah and Peter to decide. They are waiting to learn where these exotic parents will fly to next. What sort of climate will Sheilah consider? What job will Peter consent to accept? When the parents are ready, the children will make a decision of their own. It is just possible that Sandra and Jennifer will choose to stay with their aunt.

The peacock parents are watched by wrens. Lucille and her nieces are much the same—sandy-coloured, proudly plain. Neither of the girls has the father's insouciance or the mother's appearance—her height, her carriage, her thick hair, and sky-blue eyes. The children are more cautious than their parents; more Canadian. When they saw their aunt's apartment they had been away from Canada nine years, ever since they were two and four; and Jennifer, the elder, said, 'Well, now we're home.' Her voice is nasal and flat. Where did she learn that voice? And why should this be home? Peter's answer to anything about his mystifying children is, 'It must be in the blood.'

On Sunday morning Lucille takes her nieces to church. It seems to be the only condition she imposes on her relations: the children must be decent. The girls go willingly, with their new hats and purses and gloves and coral bracelets and strings of pearls. The parents, ramshackle, sleepy, dim in the brain because it is Sunday, sit down to their coffee and privacy and talk of the past.

'We weren't crooked,' says Peter. 'We weren't even smart.'

Sheilah's head bobs up; she is no drowner. It is wrong to say they have nothing to show for time. Sheilah has the Balenciaga. It is a black afternoon dress, stiff and boned at the waist; long for the fashions of now, but neither Sheilah nor Peter would change a thread. The Balenciaga is their talisman, their treasure; and after they remember it they touch hands and think that the years are not behind them but hazy and marvellous and still to be lived.

The first place they went to was Paris. In the early fifties the pick of the international jobs was there. Peter had inherited the last scrap of money he knew he was ever likely to see, and it was enough to get them over: Sheilah and Peter and the babies and the steamer trunk. To their joy and astonishment they had money in the bank. They said to each other, 'It should last a year.' Peter was fastidious about the new job; he hadn't come all this distance to accept just anything. In Paris he met Hugh Taylor, who was earning enough smuggling gasoline to keep his wife in Paris and a girl in Rome. That impressed Peter, because he remembered Taylor as a sour scholarship student without the slightest talent for life. Taylor had a job, of course. He hadn't said to himself, I'll go over to Europe and smuggle gasoline. It gave Peter an idea; he saw the shape of things. First you catch your fish. Later, at an international party, he met Johnny Hertzberg, who told him Germany was the place. Hertzberg said that anyone who came out of Germany broke now was too stupid to be here, and deserved to be back home at a desk. Peter nodded, as if he had already thought of that. He began to think about Germany. Paris was fine for a holiday, but it had been picked clean. Yes, Germany. His money was running low. He thought about Germany quite a lot.

That winter was moist and delicate; so fragile that they daren't speak of it now. There seemed to be plenty of everything and plenty of time. They were living the dream of a marriage, the fabric uncut, nothing slashed or spoiled. All winter they spent their money, and went to parties, and talked about Peter's future job. It lasted four months. They spent their money, lived in the future, and were never as happy again.

After four months they were suddenly moved away from Paris, but not to Germany—to Geneva. Peter thinks it was because of the incident at the Trudeau wedding at the Ritz. Paul Trudeau was a French Canadian Peter had known at school and in the Navy. Trudeau had turned into a snob, proud of his career and his Paris connections. He tried to make the difference felt, but Peter thought the difference was only for strangers. At the wedding reception Peter lay down on the floor and said he was dead. He held a white azalea in a brass pot on his chest, and sang, 'Oh, hear us when we cry to Thee for those in peril on the sea.' Sheilah bent over him and said, 'Pete, darling, get up. Pete, listen, every single person who can do something for you is in this room. If you love me, you'll get up.'

'I do love you,' he said, ready to engage in a serious conversation. 'She's so beautiful,' he told a second face. 'She's nearly as tall as I am. She was a model in London. I met her over in London in the war. I met her there in the war.' He lay on his back with the azalea on his chest, explaining their history. A waiter took the brass pot away, and after Peter had been hauled to his feet he knocked the waiter down. Trudeau's bride, who was freshly out of an Ursuline convent, became hysterical; and even though Paul Trudeau and Peter were old acquaintances, Trudeau never spoke to him again. Peter says now that French Canadians always have that bit of spite. He says Trudeau asked the Embassy to interfere. Luckily, back home there were still a few people to whom the name 'Frazier' meant something, and it was to these people that Peter appealed. He wrote letters saying that a French-Canadian combine was preventing his getting a decent job, and could anything be done? No one answered directly, but it was clear that what they settled for was exile to Geneva: a season of meditation and remorse, as he explained to Sheilah, and it was managed tactfully, through Lucille. Lucille wrote that a friend of hers, May Fergus, now a secretary in Geneva, had heard about a job. The job was filing pictures in the information service of an international agency in the Palais des Nations. The pay was so-so, but Lucille thought Peter must be getting fed up doing nothing.

Peter often asks his sister now who put her up to it—what important person told her to write that letter suggesting Peter go to Geneva?

'Nobody,' says Lucille. 'I mean, nobody in the way *you* mean. I really did have this girl friend working there, and I knew you must be running through your money pretty fast in Paris.'

'It must have been somebody pretty high up,' Peter says. He looks at his sister admiringly, as he has often looked at his wife.

Peter's wife had loved him in Paris. Whatever she wanted in marriage she found that winter, there. In Geneva, where Peter was a file clerk and they lived in a furnished flat, she pretended they were in Paris and life was still the same. Often, when the children were at supper, she changed as though she and Peter were dining out. She wore the Balenciaga, and put candles on the card table where she and Peter ate their meal. The neckline of the dress was soiled with make-up. Peter remembers her dabbing on the make-up with a wet sponge. He remembers her in the kitchen, in the soiled Balenciaga, patting on the make-up with a filthy sponge. Behind her, at the kitchen table, Sandra and Jennifer, in buttonless pajamas and bunny slippers, ate their supper of marmalade sandwiches and milk. When the children were asleep, the parents dined solemnly, ritually, Sheilah sitting straight as a queen.

It was a mysterious period of exile, and he had to wait for signs, or signals, to know when he was free to leave. He never saw the job any other way. He forgot he had applied for it. He thought he had been sent to Geneva because of a misdemeanor and had to wait to be released. Nobody pressed him at work. His immediate boss had resigned, and he was alone for months in a room with two desks. He read the *Herald-Tribune*, and tried to discover how things were here—how the others ran their lives on the pay they were officially getting. But it was a closed conspiracy. He was not dealing with adventures now but civil servants waiting for pension day. No one ever answered his questions. They pretended to think his questions were a form of wit. His only solace in exile was the few happy weekends he had in the late spring and early summer. He had met another old acquaintance, Mike Burleigh. Mike was a serious liberal who had married a serious heiress. The Burleighs had two guest lists. The first was composed of stuffy people they felt obliged to entertain, while the second was made up of their real friends, the friends they wanted. The real friends strove hard to become stuffy and dull and thus achieve the first guest list, but few succeeded. Peter went on the first list straight away. Possibly Mike didn't understand, at the beginning, why

Peter was pretending to be a file clerk. Peter had such an air—he might have been sent by a universal inspector to see how things in Geneva were being run.

Every Friday in May and June and part of July, the Fraziers rented a sky-blue Fiat and drove forty miles east of Geneva to the Burleighs' summer house. They brought the children, a suitcase, the children's tattered picture books, and a token bottle of gin. This, in memory, is a period of water and water birds, swans, roses, and singing birds. The children were small and still belonged to them. If they remember too much, their mouths water, their stomachs hurt. Peter says, 'it was fine while it lasted.' Enough. While it lasted Sheilah and Madge Burleigh were close. They abandoned their husbands and spent long summer afternoons comparing their mothers and praising each other's skin and hair. To Madge, and not to Peter, Sheilah opened her Liverpool childhood with the words 'rat poor'. Peter heard about it later, from Mike. The women's friendship seemed to Peter a bad beginning. He trusted women but not with each other. It lasted ten weeks. One Sunday, Madge said she needed the two bedrooms the Fraziers usually occupied for a party of sociologists from Pakistan, and that was the end. In November, the Fraziers heard that the summer house had been closed, and that the Burleighs were in Geneva, in their winter flat; they gave no sign. There was no help for it, and no appeal.

Now Peter began firing letters to anyone who had ever known his late father. He was living in a mild yellow autumn. Why does he remember the streets of the city dark, and the windows everywhere black with rain? He remembers being with Sheilah and the children as if they clung together while just outside their small shelter it rained and rained. The children slept in the bedroom of the flat because the window gave on the street and they could breathe air. Peter and Sheilah had the living-room couch. Their window was not a real window but a square on a well of cement. The flat seemed damp as a cave. Peter remembers steam in the kitchen, pools under the sink, sweat on the pipes. Water streamed on him from the children's clothes, washed and dripping overhead. The trunk, upended in the children's room, was not quite unpacked. Sheilah had not signed her name to this life; she had not given in. Once Peter heard her drop her aitches. 'You kids are lucky,' she said to the girls. 'I never 'ad so much as a sit-down meal. I ate chips out of a paper or I 'ad a butty out on the stairs.' He never asked her what a butty was. He thinks it means bread and cheese.

The day he heard 'You kids are lucky' he understood they were becoming in fact something they had only *appeared* to be until now—the shabby civil servant and his brood. If he had been European he would have ridden to work on a bicycle, in the uniform of his class and condition. He would have worn a tight coat, a turned collar, and a dirty tie. He wondered then if coming here had been a mistake, and if he should not, after all, still be in a place where his name meant something. Surely Peter Frazier should live where 'Frazier' counts? In Ontario even now when he says 'Frazier' an absent look comes over his hearer's face, as if its owner were consulting an interior guide. What is Frazier? What does it mean? Oil? Power? Politics? Wheat? Real estate? The creditors had the house sealed when Peter's father died. His aunt collapsed with a heart attack in somebody's bachelor apartment, leaving three sons and a widower to surmise they had never known her. Her will was a disappointment. None of that generation left enough. One made it: the granite Presbyterian immigrants from Scotland. Their children, a generation of daunted women and maiden men, held still. Peter's father's crowd spent: they were not afraid of their fathers, and their grandfathers were old. Peter and his sister and his cousins lived on the remains. They were left the rinds of income, of notions, and the memories of ideas rather than ideas intact. If Peter can choose his reincarnation, let him be the oppressed son of a Scottish parson. Let Peter grow up on cuffs and iron principles. Let him make the fortune! Let him flee the manse! When he was small his patrimony was squandered under his nose. He remembers people dancing in his father's house. He remembers seeing and nearly understanding adultery in a guest room, among a pile of wraps. He thought he had seen a murder; he never told. He remembers licking glasses wherever he found them—on window sills, on stairs, in the pantry. In his room he listened while Lucille read Beatrix Potter. The bad rabbit stole the carrot from the good rabbit without saying please, and downstairs was the noise of the party—the roar of the crouched lion. When his father died he saw the chairs upside down and the bailiff's chalk marks. Then the doors were sealed.

He has often tried to tell Sheilah why he cannot be defeated. He remembers his father saying, 'Nothing can touch us,' and Peter believed it and still does. It has prevented his taking his troubles too seriously. 'Nothing can be as bad as this,' he will tell himself. 'It is happening to me.' Even in Geneva, where his status was file clerk, where he sank and stopped on the level of the men who never emigrated, the men on the bicycles—even there he had a manner of strolling to work as if his office were a pastime, and his real life a secret so splendid he could share it with no one except himself.

In Geneva Peter worked for a woman—a girl. She was a Norwegian from a small town in Saskatchewan. He supposed they had been put together because they were Canadians; but they were as strange to each other as if 'Canadian' meant any number of things, or had no real meaning. Soon after Agnes Brusen came to the office she hung her framed university degree on the wall. It was one of the gritty, prideful gestures that stand for push, toil, and family sacrifice. He thought, then, that she must be one of a family of immigrants for whom education is everything. Hugh Taylor had told him that in some families the older children never marry until the youngest have finished school. Sometimes every second child is sacrificed and made to work for the education of the next born. Those who finish college spend years paying back. They are white-hot Protestants, and they live with a load of work and debt and obligation. Peter placed his new colleague on scraps of information. He had never been in the West.

She came to the office on a Monday morning in October. The office was overheated and painted cream. It contained two desks, the filing cabinets, a map of the world as it had been in 1945, and the Charter of the United Nations left behind by Agnes Brusen's predecessor. (She took down the Charter without asking Peter if he minded, with the impudence of gesture you find in women who wouldn't say boo to a goose; and then she hung her college degree on the nail where the Charter had been.) Three people brought her in—a whole committee. One of them said, 'Agnes, this is Pete Frazier. Pete, Agnes Brusen. Pete's Canadian, too, Agnes. He knows all about the office, so ask him anything.'

Of course he knew all about the office: he knew the exact spot where the cord of the venetian blind was frayed, obliging one to give an extra tug to the right.

The girl might have been twenty-three: no more. She wore a brown tweed suit with bone buttons, and a new silk scarf and new shoes. She clutched an unscratched brown purse. She seemed dressed in going-away presents. She said, 'Oh, I never smoke,' with a convulsive movement of her hand, when Peter offered his case. He was courteous, hiding his disappointment. The people he worked with had told him a Scandinavian girl was arriving, and he had expected a stunner. Agnes was a mole: she was small and brown, and round-shouldered as if she had always carried parcels or younger children in her arms. A mole's profile was turned when she said goodbye to her committee. If she had been foreign, ill-favoured though she was, he might have flirted a little, just to show that he was friendly; but their being Canadian, and suddenly left together, was a sexual damper. He sat down and lit his own cigarette. She smiled at him, questioningly, he thought, and sat as if she had never seen a chair before. He wondered if his smoking was annoying her. He wondered if she was fidgety about drafts, or allergic to anything, and whether she would want the blind up or down. His social compass was out of order because the others couldn't tell Peter and Agnes apart. There was a world of difference between them, yet it was she who had been brought in to sit at the larger of the two desks.

While he was thinking this she got up and walked around the office, almost on tiptoe, opening the doors of closets and pulling out the filing trays. She looked inside everything except the drawers of Peter's desk. (In any case, Peter's desk was locked. His desk is locked wherever he works. In Geneva he went into Personnel one morning, early, and pinched his application form. He had stated on the form that he had seven years' experience in public relations and could speak French, German, Spanish, and Italian. He has always collected anything important about himself— anything useful. But he can never get on with the final act, which is getting rid of the information. He has kept papers about for years, a constant source of worry.)

'I know this looks funny, Mr Ferris,' said the girl. 'I'm not really snooping or anything. I just can't feel easy in a new place unless I know where everything is. In a new place everything seems so hidden.'

If she had called him 'Ferris' and pretended not to know he was Frazier, it could only be because they had sent her here to spy on him and see if he had repented and was fit for a better place in life. 'You'll be all right here,' he said. 'Nothing's hidden. Most of us haven't got brains enough to have secrets. This is Rainbow Valley.' Depressed by the thought that they were having him watched now, he passed his hand over his hair and looked outside to the lawn and the parking lot and the peacocks someone gave the Palais des Nations years ago. The peacocks love no one. They wander about the parked cars looking elderly, bad-tempered, mournful, and lost.

Agnes had settled down again. She folded her silk scarf and placed it just so, with her gloves beside it. She opened her new purse and took out a notebook and a shiny gold pencil. She may have written

> Duster for desk
> Kleenex
> Glass jar for flowers
> Air-Wick because he smokes
> Paper for lining drawers

because the next day she brought each of these articles to work. She also brought a large black Bible, which she unwrapped lovingly and placed on the left-hand corner of her desk. The flower vase—empty—stood in the middle, and the Kleenex made a counterpoise for the Bible on the right.

When he saw the Bible he knew she had not been sent to spy on his work. The conspiracy was deeper. She might have been dispatched by ghosts. He knew everything about her, all in a moment: he saw the ambition, the terror, the dry pride. She was the true heir of the men from Scotland; she was at the start. She had been sent to tell him, 'You can begin, but not begin again.' She never opened the Bible, but she dusted it as she dusted her desk, her chair, and any surface the cleaning staff had overlooked. And Peter, the first days, watching her timid movements, her insignificant little face, felt, as you feel the approach of a storm, the charge of moral certainty round her, the belief in work, the faith in undertakings, the bread of the Black Sunday. He recognized and tasted all of it: ashes in the mouth.

After five days their working relations were settled. Of course, there was the Bible and all that went with it, but his tongue had never held the taste of ashes long. She was an inferior girl of poor quality. She had nothing in her favour except the degree on the wall. In the real world, he would not have invited her to his house except to mind the children. That was what he said to Sheilah. He said that Agnes was a mole, and a virgin, and that her tics and mannerisms were sending him round the bend. She had an infuriating habit of covering her mouth when she talked. Even at the telephone she put up her hand as if afraid of losing anything, even a word. Her voice was nasal and flat. She had two working costumes, both dull as the wall. One was the brown suit, the other a navy blue dress with changeable collars. She dressed for no one; she dressed for her desk, her jar of flowers, her Bible, and her box of Kleenex. One day she crossed the space between the two desks and stood over Peter, who was reading a newspaper. She could have spoken to him from her desk, but she may have felt that being on her feet gave her authority. She had plenty of courage, but authority was something else.

'I thought—I mean, they told me you were the person . . . ' She got on with it bravely: 'If you don't want to do the filing or any work, all right, Mr Frazier. I'm not saying anything about that. You might have poor health or your personal reasons. But it's got to be done, so if you'll kindly show me about the filing I'll do it. I've worked in Information before, but it was a different office, and every office is different.'

'My dear girl,' said Peter. He pushed back his chair and looked at her, astonished. 'You've been sitting there fretting, worrying. How insensitive of me. How trying for you. Usually I file on the last Wednesday of the month, so you see, you just haven't been around long enough to see a last Wednesday. Not another word, please. And let us not waste another minute.' He emptied the heaped baskets of photographs so swiftly, pushing 'Iran—Smallpox Control' into 'Irish Red Cross' (close enough), that the girl looked frightened, as if she had raised a whirlwind. She said slowly, 'If you'll only show me, Mr Frazier, instead of doing it so fast, I'll gladly look after it, because you might want to be doing other things, and I feel the filing should be done every day.' But Peter was too busy to answer, and so she sat down, holding the edge of her desk.

'There,' he said, beaming. 'All done,' His smile, his sunburst, was wasted, for the girl was staring round the room as if she feared she had not inspected everything the first day after all; some drawer, some cupboard, hid a monster. That evening Peter unlocked one of the drawers of his desk and took away the application form he had stolen from Personnel. The girl had not finished her search.

'How could you *not* know?' wailed Sheilah. 'You sit looking at her every day. You must talk about *something*. She must have told you.'

'She did tell me,' said Peter, 'and I've just told you.'

It was this: Agnes Brusen was on the Burleighs' guest list. How had the Burleighs met her? What did they see in her? Peter could not reply. He knew that Agnes lived in a bed-sitting room with a Swiss family and had her meals with them. She had been in Geneva three months, but no one had ever seen her outside the office. 'You *should* know,' said Sheilah. 'She must have something, more than you can see. Is she pretty? Is she brilliant? What is it?'

'We don't really talk,' Peter said. They talked in a way: Peter teased her and she took no notice. Agnes was not a sulker. She had taken her defeat like a sport. She did her work and a good deal of his. She sat behind her Bible, her flowers, and her Kleenex, and answered when Peter spoke. That was how he learned about the Burleighs—just by teasing and being bored. It was a January afternoon. He said, '*Miss* Brusen. Talk to me. Tell me everything. Pretend we have perfect rapport. Do you like Geneva?'

'It's a nice clean town,' she said. He can see to this day the red and blue anemones in the glass jar, and her bent head, and her small untended hands.

'Are you learning beautiful French with your Swiss family?'

'They speak English.'

'Why don't you take an apartment of your own?' he said. Peter was not usually impertinent. He was bored. 'You'd be independent then.'

'I am independent,' she said. 'I earn my living. I don't think it proves anything if you live by yourself. Mrs Burleigh wants me to live alone, too. She's looking for something for me. It mustn't be dear. I send money home.'

Here was the extraordinary thing about Agnes Brusen: she refused the use of Christian names and never spoke to Peter unless he spoke first, but she would tell anything, as if to say, 'Don't waste time fishing. Here it is.'

He learned all in one minute that she sent her salary home, and that she was a friend of the Burleighs. The first he had expected; the second knocked him flat.

'She's got to come to dinner,' Sheilah said. 'We should have had her right from the beginning. If only I'd known! But *you* were the one. You said she looked like—oh, I don't even remember. A Norwegian mole.'

She came to dinner one Saturday night in January, in her navy-blue dress, to which she had pinned an organdy gardenia. She sat upright on the edge of the sofa. Sheilah had ordered the meal from a restaurant. There was lobster, good wine, and a *pièce-montée* full of kirsch and cream. Agnes refused the lobster; she had never eaten anything from the sea unless it had been sterilized and tinned, and said so. She was afraid of skin poisoning. Someone in her family had skin poisoning after having eaten oysters. She touched her cheeks and neck to show where the poisoning had erupted. She sniffed her wine and put the glass down without tasting it. She could not eat the cake because of the alcohol it contained. She ate an egg, bread and butter, a sliced tomato, and drank a glass of ginger ale. She seemed unaware she was creating disaster and pain. She did not help clear away the dinner plates. She sat, adequately nourished, decently dressed, and waited to learn why she had been invited here that was the feeling Peter had. He folded the card table on which they had dined, and opened the window to air the room.

'It's not the same cold as Canada, but you feel it more,' he said, for something to say.

'Your blood has gotten thin,' said Agnes.

Sheilah returned from the kitchen and let herself fall into an armchair. With her eyes closed she held out her hand for a cigarette. She was performing the haughty-lady act that was a family joke. She flung her head back and looked at Agnes through half-closed lids; then she suddenly brought her head forward, widening her eyes.

'Are you skiing madly?' she said.

'Well, in the first place there hasn't been any snow,' said Agnes. 'So nobody's doing any skiing so far as I know. All I hear is people complaining because there's no snow. Personally, I don't ski. There isn't much skiing in the part of Canada I come from. Besides, my family never had that kind of leisure.'

'Heavens,' said Sheilah, as if her family had every kind.

I'll bet they had, thought Peter. On the dole.

Sheilah was wasting her act. He had a suspicion that Agnes knew it was an act but did not know it was also a joke. If so, it made Sheilah seem a fool, and he loved Sheilah too much to enjoy it.

'The Burleighs have been wonderful to me,' said Agnes. She seemed to have divined why she was here, and decided to give them all the information they wanted, so that she could put on her coat and go home to bed. 'They had me out to their place on the lake every weekend until the weather got cold and they moved back to town. They've rented a chalet for the winter, and they want me to come there, too. But I don't know if I will or not. I don't ski, and, oh, I don't know—I don't drink either, and I don't always see the point. Their friends are too rich and I'm too Canadian.'

She had delivered everything Sheilah wanted and more: Agnes was on the first guest list and didn't care. No, Peter corrected; doesn't know. Doesn't care and doesn't know.

'I thought with you Norwegians it was in the blood, skiing. And drinking,' Sheilah murmured.

'Drinking, maybe,' said Agnes. She covered her mouth and said behind her spread fingers, 'In our family we were religious. We didn't drink or smoke. My brother was in Norway in the war. He saw some cousins. Oh,' she said, unexpectedly loud, 'Harry said it was just terrible. They were so poor. They had flies in their kitchen. They gave him something to eat a fly had been on. They didn't have a real toilet, and they'd been in the same house about two hundred years. We've only recently built our own home, and we have a bathroom and two toilets. I'm from Saskatchewan,' she said. 'I'm not from any other place.'

Surely one winter here had been punishment enough? In the spring they would remember him and free him. He wrote Lucille, who said he was lucky to have a job at all. The Burleighs had sent the Fraziers a second-guest-list Christmas card. It showed a Moslem refugee child weeping outside a tent. They treasured the card and left it standing long after the others had been given to the children to cut up. Peter had discovered by now what had gone wrong in the friendship—Sheilah had charged a skirt at a dressmaker to Madge's account. Madge had told her she might, and then changed her mind. Poor Sheilah! She was new to this part of it—to the changing humours of independent friends. Paris was already a year in the past. At Mardi Gras, the Burleighs gave their annual party. They invited everyone, the damned and the dropped, with the prodigality of a child at prayers. The invitation said 'in costume', but the Fraziers were too happy to wear a disguise. They might not be recognized. Like many of the guests they expected to meet at the party, they had been disgraced, forgotten, and rehabilitated. They would be anxious to see one another as they were.

On the night of the party, the Fraziers rented a car they had never seen before and drove through the first snowstorm of the year. Peter had not driven since last summer's blissful trips in the Fiat. He could not find the switch for the windshield wiper in this car. He leaned over the wheel. 'Can you see on your side?' he asked. 'Can I make a left turn here? Does it look like a one-way?'

'I can't imagine why you took a car with a right-hand drive,' said Sheilah.

He had trouble finding a place to park; they crawled up and down unknown streets whose curbs were packed with snow-covered cars. When they stood at last on the pavement, safe and sound, Peter said, 'This is the first snow.'

'I can see that,' said Sheilah. 'Hurry, darling. My hair.'

'It's the first snow.'

'You're repeating yourself,' she said. 'Please hurry, darling. Think of my poor shoes. My *hair*.'

She was born in an ugly city, and so was Peter, but they have this difference: she does not know the importance of the first snow—the first clean thing in a dirty year. He would have told her then that this storm, which was wetting her feet and destroying her hair, was like the first day of the English spring, but she made a frightened gesture, trying to shield her head. The gesture told him he did not understand her beauty.

'Let me,' she said. He was fumbling with the key, trying to lock the car. She took the key without impatience and locked the door on the driver's side; and then, to show Peter she treasured him and was not afraid of wasting her life or her beauty, she took his arm and they walked in the snow down a street and around a corner to the apartment house where the Burleighs lived. They were, and are, a united couple. They were afraid of the party, and each of them knew it. When they walk together, holding arms, they give each other whatever each can spare.

Only six people had arrived in costume. Madge Burleigh was disguised as Manet's 'LoLa de Valence', which everyone mistook for Carmen. Mike was an Impressionist painter, with a straw hat and a glued-on beard. 'I am all of them,' he said. He would rather have dressed as a dentist, he said, welcoming the Fraziers as if he had parted from them the day before, but Madge wanted him to look as if he had created her. 'You know?' he said.

'Perfectly,' said Sheilah. Her shoes were stained and the snow had softened her lacquered hair. She was not wasted; she was the most beautiful woman here.

About an hour after their arrival, Peter found himself with no one to talk to. He had told about the Trudeau wedding in Paris and the pot of azaleas, and after he mislaid his audience he began to look round for Sheilah. She was on a window seat, partly concealed by a green velvet curtain. Facing her, so that their profiles were neat and perfect against the night, was a man. Their conversation was private and enclosed, as if they had in minutes covered leagues of time and arrived at the place where everything was implied, understood. Peter began working his way across the room, toward his wife, when he saw Agnes. He was granted the sight of her drowning face. She had dressed with comic intention, obviously with care, and now she was a ragged hobo, half tramp, half clown. Her hair was tucked up under a bowler hat. The six costumed guests who had made the same mistake—the ghost, the gypsy, the Athenian maiden, the geisha, the Martian, and the apache—were delighted to find a seventh; but Agnes was not amused; she was gasping for life. When a waiter passed with a crowded tray, she took a glass without seeing it; then a wave of the party took her away.

Sheilah's new friend was named Simpson. After Simpson said he thought perhaps he'd better circulate, Peter sat down where he had been. 'Now look, Sheilah,' he began. Their most intimate conversations have taken place at parties. Once at a party she told him she was leaving him; she didn't, of course. Smiling, blue-eyed, she gazed lovingly at Peter and said rapidly, 'Pete, shut up and listen. That man. The man you scared away. He's a big wheel in a company out in India or someplace like that. It's gorgeous out there. Pete, the *servants*. And it's warm. It never never snows. He says there's heaps of jobs. You pick them off the trees like . . . orchids. He says it's even easier now than when we owned all those places, because now the poor pets can't run anything and they'll pay *fortunes*. Pete, he says it's warm, it's heaven, and Pete, they pay.'

A few minutes later, Peter was alone again and Sheilah part of a closed, laughing group. Holding her elbow was the man from the place where jobs grew like orchids. Peter edged into the group and laughed at a story he hadn't heard. He heard only the last line, which was, 'Here comes another tunnel.' Looking out from the tight laughing ring, he saw Agnes again, and he thought, I'd be like Agnes if I didn't have Sheilah. Agnes put her glass down on a table and lurched toward the doorway, head forward. Madge Burleigh, who never stopped moving around the room and smiling, was still smiling when she paused and said in Peter's ear, 'Go with Agnes, Pete. See that she gets home. People will notice if Mike leaves.'

'She probably just wants to walk around the block,' said Peter. 'She'll be back.'

'Oh, stop thinking about yourself, for once, and see that that poor girl gets home,' said Madge. 'You've still got your Fiat, haven't you?'

He turned away as if he had been pushed. Any command is a release, in a way. He may not want to go in that particular direction, but at least he is going somewhere. And now Sheilah, who had moved inches nearer to hear what Madge and Peter were murmuring, said, 'Yes, go, darling,' as if he were leaving the gates of Troy.

Peter was to find Agnes and see that she reached home: this he repeated to himself as he stood on the landing, outside the Burleighs' flat, ringing for the elevator. Bored with waiting for it, he ran down the stairs, four flights, and saw that Agnes had stalled the lift by leaving the door open. She was crouched on the floor, propped on her fingertips. Her eyes were closed.

'Agnes,' said Peter. '*Miss* Brusen, I mean. That's no way to leave a party. Don't you know you're supposed to curtsey and say thanks? My God, Agnes, anybody going by here just now might have seen you! Come on, be a good girl. Time to go home.'

She got up without his help and, moving between invisible crevasses, shut the elevator door. Then she left the building and Peter followed, remembering he was to see that she got home. They walked along the snowy pavement, Peter a few steps behind her. When she turned right for no reason, he turned, too. He had no clear idea where they were going. Perhaps she lived close by. He had forgotten where the hired car was parked, or what it looked like; he could not remember its make or its colour. In any case, Sheilah had the key. Agnes walked on steadily, as if she knew their destination, and he thought, Agnes Brusen is drunk in the street in Geneva and dressed like a tramp. He wanted to say, 'This is the best thing that ever happened to you, Agnes; it will help you understand how things are for some of the rest of us.' But she stopped and turned and, leaning over a low hedge, retched on a frozen lawn. He held her clammy forehead and rested his hand on her arched back, on muscles as tight as a fist. She straightened up and drew a breath but the cold air made her cough. 'Don't breathe too deeply,' he said. 'It's the worst thing you can do. Have you got a handkerchief?' He passed his own handkerchief over her wet weeping face, upturned like the face of one of his little girls. 'I'm out without a coat,' he said, noticing it. 'We're a pair.'

'I never drink,' said Agnes. 'I'm just not used to it.' Her voice was sweet and quiet. He had never seen her so peaceful, so composed. He thought she must surely be all right, now, and perhaps he might leave her here. The trust in her tilted face had perplexed him. He wanted to get back to Sheilah and have her explain something. He had forgotten what it was, but Sheilah would know. 'Do you live around here?' he said. As he spoke, she let herself fall. He had wiped her face and now she trusted him to pick her up, set her on her feet, take her wherever she ought to be. He pulled her up and she stood, wordless, humble, as he brushed the snow from her tramp's clothes. Snow horizontally crossed the lamplight. The street was silent. Agnes had lost her hat. Snow, which he tasted, melted on her hands. His gesture of licking snow from her hands was as formal as a handshake. He tasted snow on her hands and then they walked on.

'I never drink,' she said. They stood on the edge of a broad avenue. The wrong turning now could lead them anywhere; it was the changeable avenue at the edge of towns that loses its houses and becomes a highway. She held his arm and spoke in a gentle voice. She said, 'In our house we didn't smoke or drink. My mother was ambitious for me, more than for Harry and the others.' She said, 'I've never been alone before. When I was a kid I would get up in the summer before the others, and I'd see the ice wagon going down the street. I'm alone now. Mrs Burleigh's found me an apartment. It's only one room. She likes it because it's in the old part of town. I don't like old houses. Old houses are dirty. You don't know who was there before.'

'I should have a car somewhere,' Peter said. 'I'm not sure where we are.'

He remembers that on this avenue they climbed into a taxi, but nothing about the drive. Perhaps he fell asleep. He does remember that when he paid the driver Agnes clutched his arm, trying to stop him. She pressed extra coins into the driver's palm. The driver was paid twice.

'I'll tell you one thing about us,' said Peter. 'We pay everything twice.' This was part of a much longer theory concerning North American behaviour, and it was not Peter's own. Mike Burleigh had held forth about it on summer afternoons.

Agnes pushed open a door between a stationer's shop and a grocery, and led the way up a narrow inside stair. They climbed one flight, frightening beetles. She had to search every pocket for the latchkey. She was shaking with cold. Her apartment seemed little warmer than the street. Without speaking to Peter she turned on all the lights. She looked inside the kitchen and the bathroom and then got down on her hands and knees and looked under the sofa. The room was neat and belonged to no one. She left him standing in this unclaimed room—she had forgotten him—and closed a door behind her. He looked for something to do—some useful action he could repeat to Madge. He turned on the electric radiator in the fireplace. Perhaps Agnes wouldn't thank him for it; perhaps she would rather undress in the cold. 'I'll be on my way,' he called to the bathroom door.

She had taken off the tramp's clothes and put on a dressing gown of orphanage wool. She came out of the bathroom and straight toward him. She pressed her face and rubbed her cheek on his shoulder as if hoping the contact would leave a scar. He saw her back and her profile and his own face in the mirror over the fireplace. He thought, This is how disasters happen. He saw floods of sea water moving with perfect punitive justice over reclaimed land; he saw lava covering vineyards and overtaking dogs and stragglers. A bridge over an abyss snapped in two and the long express train, suddenly V-shaped, floated like snow. He thought amiably of every kind of disaster and thought, This is how they occur.

Her eyes were closed. She said, 'I shouldn't be over here. In my family we didn't drink or smoke. My mother wanted a lot from me, more than from Harry and the others.' But he knew all that; he had known from the day of the Bible, and because once, at the beginning, she had made him afraid. He was not afraid of her now.

She said, 'It's no use staying here, is it?'

'If you mean what I think, no.'

'It wouldn't be better anywhere.'

She let him see full on her blotched face. He was not expected to do anything. He was not required to pick her up when she fell or wipe her tears. She was poor quality, really—he remembered having thought that once. She left him and went quietly into the bathroom and locked the door. He heard taps running and supposed it was a hot bath. He was pretty certain there would be no more tears. He looked at his watch: Sheilah must be home, now, wondering what had become of him. He descended the beetles' staircase and for forty minutes crossed the city under a windless fall of snow.

The neighbour's child who had stayed with Peter's children was asleep on the living-room sofa. Peter woke her and sent her, sleepwalking, to her own door. He sat down, wet to the bone, thinking, I'll call the Burleighs. In half an hour I'll call the police. He heard a car stop and the engine running and a confusion of two voices laughing and calling goodnight. Presently Sheilah let herself in, rosy-faced, smiling. She carried his trenchcoat over her arm. She said, 'How's Agnes?'

'Where were you?' he said. 'Whose car was that?'

Sheilah had gone into the children's room. He heard her shutting their window. She returned, undoing her dress, and said, 'Was Agnes all right?'

'Agnes is all right. Sheilah, this is about the worst . . . '

She stepped out of the Balenciaga and threw it over a chair. She stopped and looked at him and said, 'Poor old Pete, are you in love with Agnes?' And then, as if the answer were of so little importance she hadn't time for it, she locked her arms around him and said, 'My love, we're going to Ceylon.'

Two days later, when Peter strolled into his office, Agnes was at her desk. She wore the blue dress, with a spotless collar. White and yellow freesias were symmetrically arranged in the glass jar. The room was hot, and the spring snow, glued for a second when it touched the window, blurred the view of parked cars.

'Quite a party,' Peter said.

She did not look up. He sighed, sat down, and thought if the snow held he would be skiing at the Burleighs' very soon. Impressed by his kindness to Agnes, Madge had invited the family for the first possible weekend.

Presently Agnes said, 'I'll never drink again or go to a house where people are drinking. And I'll never bother anyone the way I bothered you.'

'You didn't bother me,' he said. 'I took you home. You were alone and it was late. It's normal.'

'Normal for you, maybe, but I'm used to getting home by myself. Please never tell what happened.'

He stared at her. He can still remember the freesias and the Bible and the heat in the room. She looked as if the elements had no power. She felt neither heat nor cold. 'Nothing happened,' he said.

'I behaved in a silly way. I had no right to. I led you to think I might do something wrong.'

'*I* might have tried something,' he said gallantly. 'But that would be my fault and not yours.'

She put her knuckle to her mouth and he could scarcely hear. 'It was because of you. I was afraid you might be blamed, or else you'd blame yourself.'

'There's no question of any blame,' he said. 'Nothing happened. We'd both had a lot to drink. Forget about it. Nothing *happened*. You'd remember if it had.'

She put down her hand. There was an expression on her face. Now she sees me, he thought. She had never looked at him after the first day. (He has since tried to put a name to the look on her face; but how can he, now, after so many voyages, after Ceylon, and Hong Kong, and Sheilah's nearly leaving him, and all their difficulties—the money owed, the rows with hotel managers, the lost and found steamer trunk, the children throwing up the foreign food?) She sees me now, he thought. What does she see?

She said, 'I'm from a big family. I'm not used to being alone. I'm not a suicidal person, but I could have done something after that party, just not to see any more, or think or listen or expect anything. What can I think when I see these people? All my life I heard, Educated people don't do this, educated people don't do that. And now I'm here, and you're all educated people, and you're nothing but pigs. You're educated and you drink and do everything wrong and you know what you're doing, and that makes you worse than pigs. My family worked to make me an educated person, but they didn't know you. But what if I didn't see and hear and expect anything more? It wouldn't change anything. You'd all be still the same. Only *you* might have thought it was your fault. You might have thought you were to blame. It could worry you all your life. It would have been wrong for me to worry you.'

He remembered that the rented car was still along a snowy curb somewhere in Geneva. He wondered if Sheilah had the key in her purse and if she remembered where they'd parked.

'I told you about the ice wagon,' Agnes said. 'I don't remember everything, so you're wrong about remembering. But I remember telling you that. That was the best. It's the best you can hope to have. In a big family, if you want to be alone, you have to get up before the rest of them. You get up early in the morning in the summer and it's you, you, once in your life alone in the universe. You think you know everything that can happen . . . Nothing is ever like that again.'

He looked at the smeared window and wondered if this day could end without disaster. In his mind he saw her falling in the snow wearing a tramp's costume, and he saw her coming to him in the orphanage dressing gown. He saw her drowning face at the party. He was afraid for himself. The story was still unfinished. It had to come to a climax, something threatening to him. But there was no climax. They talked that day, and afterward nothing else was said. They went on in the same office for a short time, until Peter left for Ceylon; until somebody read the right letter, passed it on for the right initials, and the Fraziers began the Oriental tour that should have made their fortune. Agnes and Peter were too tired to speak after that morning. They were like a married couple in danger, taking care.

But what were they talking about that day, so quietly, such old friends? They talked about dying, about being ambitious, about being religious, about different kinds of love. What did she see when she looked at him—taking her knuckle slowly away from her mouth, bringing her hand down to the desk, letting it rest there? They were both Canadians, so they had this much together—the knowledge of the little you dare admit. Death, near-death, the best thing, the wrong thing—God knows what they were telling each other. Anyway, nothing happened.

When, on Sunday mornings, Sheilah and Peter talk about those times, they take on the glamour of something still to come. It is then he remembers Agnes Brusen. He never says her name. Sheilah wouldn't remember Agnes. Agnes is the only secret Peter has from his wife, the only puzzle he pieces together without her help. He thinks about families in the West as they were fifteen, twenty years ago—the iron-cold ambition, and every member pushing the next one on. He thinks of his father's parties. When he thinks of his father he imagines him with Sheilah, in a crowd. Actually, Sheilah and Peter's father never met, but they might have liked each other. His father admired good-looking women. Peter wonders what they were doing over there in Geneva—not Sheilah and Peter, *Agnes* and Peter. It is almost as if they had once run away together, silly as children, irresponsible as lovers. Peter and Sheilah are back where they started. While they were out in world affairs picking up microbes and debts, always on the fringe of disaster, the fringe of a fortune, Agnes went on and did—what? They lost each other. He thinks of the ice wagon going down the street. He sees something he has never seen in his life—a Western town that belongs to Agnes. Here is Agnes—small, mole-faced, round-shouldered because she has always carried a younger child. She watches the ice wagon and the trail of ice water in a morning invented for her: hers. He sees the weak prairie trees and the shadows on the sidewalk. Nothing moves except the shadows and the ice wagon and the changing amber of the child's eyes. The child is Peter. He has seen the grain of the cement sidewalk and the grass in the cracks, and the dust, and the dandelions at the edge of the road. He is there. He has taken the morning that belongs to Agnes, he is up before the others, and he knows everything. There is nothing he doesn't know. He could keep the morning, if he wanted to, but what can Peter do with the start of a summer day? Sheilah is here, it is a true Sunday morning, with its dimness and headache and remorse and regrets, and this is life. He says, 'We have the Balenciaga.' He touches Sheilah's hand. The children have their aunt now, and he and Sheilah have each other. Everything works out, somehow or other. Let Agnes have the start of the day. Let Agnes think it was invented for her. Who wants to be alone in the universe? No, begin at the beginning: Peter lost Agnes. Agnes says to herself somewhere, Peter is lost.

NORMAN LEVINE

b. 1923

We All Begin in a
Little Magazine

We live in a small coastal town. And in the summer, when the place is looking its best, it becomes overcrowded with people who have come away from the cities for their annual holiday by the sea. It is then that we leave and go up to London for our holiday.

My wife usually finds a house by looking through *The Times*. In this way we had the house of a man who built hotels in the poor parts of Africa so that wealthy American Negroes could go back to see where their grandparents came from. Another summer it was an architect's house where just about everything was done by pushbutton control. A third time, it was in a house whose owner was in the middle of getting a divorce—for non-consummation—and wanted to be out of the country.

This June she saw an ad saying: DOCTOR'S HOUSE AVAILABLE IN LONDON FOR THREE WEEKS. REASONABLE RENT. She phoned the number. And we agreed to take it.

The advertised house was central, near South Kensington tube station, not far from the Gardens. The taxi took us from Paddington—how pale people looked in London on a hot summer's day—and brought us to a wide street, stopping in front of a detached all-white house with acacia trees in the front garden. A bottle of warm milk was on the doorstep. I opened the door with the key and brought our cases inside.

The phone was ringing.

'Hello,' I said.

'Is this *ABC*?' a youthful voice asked.

'I'm sorry,' I said. 'You have the wrong number.'

'What is your number?'

'Knightsbridge 4231,' I said.

'That *is* the number,' the voice said.

'There must be some mistake,' I said. 'This is a doctor's house.'

'Is the doctor there?'

'No,' I said. 'He's on holiday.'

'Can I leave a message for him?'

'Are you ill?'

'No,' he said. 'Tell him that David White rang. David White of Somerset. He has had my manuscript for over six months now. He said he would let me know over a month ago. I have written him four times.'

'I'll tell him,' I said.

'If he needs more time,' the young man said hesitantly, 'I don't mind—'

'OK,' I said and hung up.

'I don't know what's going on here,' I said to my wife.

But she and the children were busy exploring the rest of the house.

It was a large house and it looked as if it had been lived in. The front room was a children's room with all sorts of games and blackboards and toys and children's books and posters on the walls. There was the sitting-room, the bottom half of the walls were filled with books in shelves. There were more books in the hallway, on the sides of the stairs, and in shelves on every landing. There were three separate baths. A breakfast room where a friendly black cat slept most of the time on top of the oil-fired furnace. And a back garden with a lawn, flowerbeds on the sides, a pond with goldfish, water-lilies, and a copper beech tree at the end.

The phone rang and a shaky voice said,

'May I speak to Doctor Jones?'

'I'm sorry, he's on holiday.'

'When will he come back?'

'In three weeks,' I said.

'I can't wait that long,' the voice said. 'I'm going to New York tomorrow.'

'Would you,' I said, 'like to leave a message?'

'I can't hear what you're saying,' the voice said. 'Can you speak up? I'm a bit deaf and have to wear a hearing aid. The doctors have a cure for this now. If I'd been born two years later I would have been all right.'

'I said would you like to leave the doctor a message?'

'I don't think that will do any good,' he said. 'Could you look in his office and see if he has a poem of mine? It's called 'Goodbye'. If it is in proof, don't bother. I'll wait. But just find out. I am going over to teach creative writing in night school so I can make some money to come back here. The poem will probably be on the floor.'

'Hold on,' I said.

I went into the office at the top of the house. The floor was cluttered with papers and magazines and manuscripts with letters and envelopes attached. On a wooden table, a large snap file had correspondence. A box had cheques for small amounts. There were also several pound notes, loose change, a sheet of stamps, and two packages of cigarettes. (How trusting, I thought. The doctor doesn't know us—supposing we were crooks?) There was typing paper, large envelopes, a typewriter, a phone, telephone directories, and some galleys hanging on a nail on a wall. A smaller table had an in-and-out tray to do with his medical work, more letters, and copies of the *Lancet*. The neatest part of the room was the area where stacks of unsold copies of *ABC* were on the floor against the far wall.

'I'm sorry,' I said on the phone. 'I can't see it.'

'Oh,' he said. He sounded disappointed.

'Well, tell him that Arnold Mest called. M-E-S-T.'

'I've got that,' I said.

'Goodbye,' he said.

'You won't guess,' I told my wife. 'The doctor edits a little magazine.'

'We can't get away from it,' she said.

Early next morning the doorbell woke us. It was the postman. He gave me several bundles. There were letters from different parts of England and Europe and air mail ones from Canada, the States, Australia, and South America. There were two review copies of books from publishers. There were other little magazines, and what looked like medical journals, and a few bills.

As I put the envelopes and parcels on the chair in the office and saw the copies of *Horizon* and *New Writing*, the runs of *Encounter*, *London Magazine*, and a fine collection of contemporary books on the shelves right around the room—it brought back a time twenty years ago when I first came over.

There was still the bomb-damage to be seen, the queues, the ration books, the cigarettes under the counter. And a general seediness in people's clothes. Yet I remember it as one of my happiest times. Perhaps because we were young and full of hope and because we were so innocent of what writing involved. A lot of boys and girls had come to London from different parts. And we would meet in certain pubs, in certain restaurants, Joe Lyons, the French pub, Caves de France, the Mandrake. Then go on somewhere else. I remember going over to see another Canadian, from Montreal, who was writing a novel. He had a studio, by the Chelsea football grounds (we could always tell when a goal was scored). I remember best the cold damp winter days with the fog thick—you could just see the traffic lights—and then going inside and having some hot wine by the open fire and talking about writing, what we were writing, and where we had things out. We used to send our stories, optimistically, to the *New Yorker* and the *Atlantic*. But that was like taking a ticket in a lottery. It was the little magazines who published us, who gave us encouragement and kept us going.

I remember Miss Waters. She was in her late forties, a pale woman with thinning blonde hair and a docile tabby cat. She edited a little magazine founded by her great-grandfather. She had photographs of Tennyson on the wall, of Yeats and Dylan Thomas. And wooden pigeon-holes, like the sorting room at the post office, with some of the recent back issues. She didn't know when I was coming. But she always greeted me with:

'How nice to see you. Do come in.'

She walked ahead, into the dark living-room. Suggested that I take my winter coat off. Then she would bring out a decanter of sherry and fill a glass. Then take out a package of *Passing Clouds*, offer me a cigarette.

I was treated as a writer by this woman when I had very little published. And that did more than anything to keep up morale. And after another sherry, another *Passing Cloud*, and she had asked me what I was working on and seemed very interested in what I said, she told me that her great-grandfather paid Tennyson a thousand pounds for one of his short poems, and two thousand pounds to George Eliot for a short story. (Was she trying to tell me that there was money to be made out of writing?) Then she stood up. And we went into the other room. It was very neat and tidy. Magazines on a table laid out as at a newsagent's, books as in a library.

'Is there anything you would like to review?' she asked.

I would pick a novel or two, or a book of short stories.

Then she would say: 'And help yourself to four books from that pile.'

That pile consisted of books that she didn't want reviewed. She had told me, the first time, to take these books to a bookseller in the Strand who would give me half-price for them, and later sell them to the public libraries. But before I could get the money from him I had to sign my name in what looked like a visiting book. And I saw there, above me, the signatures of the leading Sunday and weekly reviewers—they were also selling their review copies for half-price.

And I remember how I would come to her place—with the brown envelopes lying behind the door—broke and depressed. And when I left her, I left feeling buoyed up, cheerful. There would be the few pounds from the review copies. Money enough for a hamburger and a coffee and a small cigar. And there was something to do—the books to review. She always paid in advance.

And before Miss Waters there were others. The press officer at the Norwegian Embassy—he ran a Norwegian little magazine, in English, from London. And another one, from India, also in English. My early stories appeared in both. And when I got a copy of the Indian magazine I saw that my Canadian characters had been turned into Indians. And there was another editor who would ask to borrow your box of matches. Then when you got back to your flat you found he had stuffed a pound note inside the box.

They are all gone—like their magazines.

And something has gone with them.

Those carefree days when you wrote when you felt like it. And slept in when you wanted to. And would be sure of seeing others like yourself at noon in certain places.

Now in the morning, after breakfast, I wait for the mail to come. Then I go upstairs and close the door behind me. And I make myself get on with the novel, the new story, or the article, which has been commissioned by a well-paying magazine. I take a break for lunch, then come back up here until four. Once in a while I might take a day off and go on a bus to see what the country is like. I forget that there is so much colour about. Or, for a change, take a train for the day to Plymouth. But otherwise, it is up the stairs to this room. All my energy now goes into work. I light up a small Dutch cigar and sometimes I talk to myself. I feel reasonably certain now that what I have written will be published. Writing has become my living.

Of course there are still the occasional days when things are going right and the excitement comes back from the work. Not like in those early days when writing and the life we were leading seemed so much to belong together. I had complete faith then in those little magazines. What I didn't know was that what they bred was infectious. They infected a lot of young people with the notion that to be involved with literature was somehow to be involved with the good life. And by the time you learned differently, it was usually too late.

On Friday I had to be up early. In the morning I was to be interviewed, in a rowing-boat on the Serpentine, for a Canadian television program on the 'Brain-Drain.' And later I was to meet my publisher for lunch.

It was very pleasant on the water early in the morning. The sun made patterns. People going to work stopped to watch. While I rowed the interviewer, the cameraman, the sound-recordist, and their equipment— and was asked why wasn't I living in Canada, and why did I write?

I met my publisher in his club. He is an American, from Boston, bald and short. We had a Martini. Then another. Then we went into the dining-room. Smoked salmon followed by duck with wine, then dessert. And ending with brandy and a large Havana cigar.

He asked me what type would I like for the book, could I send him the blurb for the dust-jacket? He told me the number of copies they would print, that one of the Sunday papers wanted to run a couple of extracts before publication. He told me some gossip about other writers, publishers, and agents. And what was I writing now? And which publishing season would he have it for?

I left him after four and caught a taxi back to the house.

'How did it go?' my wife asked.

'OK,' I said. 'How was the zoo?'

She began to tell me when we heard a noise. It sounded as if it was coming from the front door. We went to look and surprised a man with a key trying to open the door. He was in his late fifties, short and stocky and wearing a shabby raincoat.

'Is the doc in?' he said timidly.

'No,' I said. 'He's on holiday.'

'Oh,' he said. 'I've come up from Sussex. I always have a bed here when I come up.'

He spoke with an educated accent.

'I'm sorry,' I said. 'But we have the place for three weeks.'

'I always have a bed here when I come up.'

'There isn't room,' I said.

'My name is George Smith,' he said. '*ABC* publish me. I'm a poet.'

'How do you do,' I said. 'We'll be gone in ten days. Come in and have a drink.'

While I poured him a brandy, I asked what was the name of his last book.

He said he had enough work for a book and had sent the manuscript to—and here he named a well-known publisher.

'But I haven't heard,' he said.

'That's a good sign,' I said.

'Perhaps they have lost it,' he said. 'Or they are, like Doc, on holiday.'

He brought out a small tin and took some loose tobacco and began to roll his own cigarette and one for me.

'How long,' I asked, 'have they had it?'

'Nearly five months,' he said.

He finished his brandy. I poured him some more.

'I would ring them up and find out,' I said. 'Or drop them a line.'

'Do you think I should?'

'Yes,' I said.

I went to the door to see him out. And instead walked him to the bus stop.

The street was full of mountain ash and red berries were lying on the lawns, the sidewalk, and on the road.

'I had a letter from T.S. Eliot,' he said. 'I kept it all these years. But I sold it last month to Texas for fifty dollars,' he said proudly. 'My daughter was getting married. And I had to get her a present.'

I asked him where he would stay the night.

'I have one or two other places,' he said. 'I come up about once every six weeks. London is my commercial centre.'

I went and bought him a package of cigarettes.

'Thank you,' he said.

The red bus came and I watched him get on.

When I got back my wife said, 'Well, do you feel better?'

'No,' I said.

It went on like this—right through the time we were there. An assortment of people turned up at the door. There was a young blonde girl— she wanted to lick stamps for literature. There were visiting lecturers and professors from American and Canadian and English universities. There were housewives; one said, over the phone, 'I'll do anything to get into print.' There were long-distance telephone calls. One rang after midnight and woke us up. 'Nothing important,' the voice said. 'I just wanted to have a talk. We usually do now and then. I've had stories in *ABC*.'

There was, it seemed, a whole world that depended on the little magazine.

I tried to be out of the house as much as possible. I went to see my agent. He had a cheque for four hundred dollars, less his commission, waiting for me, for the sale of a story. He took me out for a meal. And we talked about the size of advances, the sort of money paperback publishers were paying these days, the way non-fiction was selling better than fiction. I met other writers in expensive clubs and restaurants. We gossiped about what middle-aged writer was leaving his middle-aged wife to live with a young girl. And what publisher was leaving his firm to form his own house. I was told what magazines were starting—who paid the best.

Then I would come back to the phone ringing, the piles of mail, and people turning up at the door eager to talk about the aesthetics of writing. I didn't mind the young. But it was the men and women who were around my age or older who made me uncomfortable. I didn't like the feeling of superiority I had when I was with them. Or was it guilt? I didn't know.

Meanwhile my wife and kids enjoyed themselves. They went to the Victoria and Albert Museum, the National Gallery, the Tate. And came back with postcard reproductions that they sent to friends. They went to a couple of Proms, to a play, had a day in Richmond Park, Hampton Court, and a boat ride on the Thames.

When the time came to go back—they didn't want to.

But I did.

I had passed through my *ABC* days. And I wanted to get away. Was it because it was a reminder of one's youth? Or of a time which promised more than it turned out to be? I told myself that there was an unreality about it all—that our lives then had no economic base—that it was a time of limbo. But despite knowing these things, I carry it with me. It represents a sort of innocence that has gone.

On the Saturday morning waiting for the taxi to come to take us to Paddington Station, the phone rang. And a young girl's voice wanted to know about her short story.

I said the doctor was away. He would be back later. She ought to ring this evening.

'What time?'

'After nine,' I said.

'Have you read the story?' she asked. 'What do you think of it?'

'We just rented the house,' I said. 'We were here for a holiday.'

'Oh,' she said. 'You're not one of us?'

'No,' I said.

Then the taxi came. And the driver began to load the cases into the back of the car.

MARGARET LAURENCE
b.1926

The Loons

Just below Manawaka, where the Wachakwa River ran brown and noisy over the pebbles, the scrub oak and grey-green willow and chokecherry bushes grew in a dense thicket. In a clearing at the centre of the thicket stood the Tonnerre family's shack. The basis of this dwelling was a small square cabin made of poplar poles and chinked with mud, which had been built by Jules Tonnerre some fifty years before, when he came back from Batoche with a bullet in his thigh, the year that Riel was hung and the voices of the Metis entered their long silence. Jules had only intended to stay the winter in the Wachakwa Valley, but the family was still there in the thirties, when I was a child. As the Tonnerres had increased, their settlement had been added to, until the clearing at the foot of the town hill was a chaos of lean-tos, wooden packing cases, warped lumber, discarded car tires, ramshackle chicken coops, tangled strands of barbed wire and rusty tin cans.

The Tonnerres were French halfbreeds, and among themselves they spoke a *patois* that was neither Cree nor French. Their English was broken and full of obscenities. They did not belong among the Cree of the Galloping Mountain reservation, further north, and they did not belong among the Scots-Irish and Ukrainians of Manawaka, either. They were, as my Grandmother MacLeod would have put it, neither flesh, fowl, nor good salt herring. When their men were not working at odd jobs or as section hands on the C.P.R., they lived on relief. In the summers, one of the Tonnerre youngsters, with a face that seemed totally unfamiliar with laughter, would knock at the doors of the town's brick houses and offer for sale a lard-pail full of bruised wild strawberries, and if he got as much as a quarter he would grab the coin and run before the customer had time to change her mind. Sometimes old Jules, or his son Lazarus, would get mixed up in a Saturday-night brawl, and would hit out at whoever was nearest, or howl drunkenly among the offended shoppers on Main Street, and then the Mountie would put them for the night in the barred cell underneath the Court House, and the next morning they would be quiet again.

Piquette Tonnerre, the daughter of Lazarus, was in my class at school. She was older than I, but she had failed several grades, perhaps because her attendance had alwayseen sporadic and her interest in school-work negligible. Part of the reason she had missed a lot of school was that she had had tuberculosis of the bone, and had once spent many months in hospital. I knew this because my father was the doctor who had looked after her. Her sickness was almost the only thing I knew about her, however. Otherwise, she existed for me only as a vaguely embarrassing presence, with her hoarse voice and her clumsy limping walk and her grimy cotton dresses that were always miles too long. I was neither friendly nor unfriendly towards her. She dwelt and moved somewhere within my scope of vision, but I did not actually notice her very much until that peculiar summer when I was eleven.

'I don't know what to do about that kid,' my father said at dinner one evening. 'Piquette Tonnerre, I mean. The damn bone's flared up again. I've had her in hospital for quite a while now, and it's under control all right, but I hate like the dickens to send her home again.'

'Couldn't you explain to her mother that she has to rest a lot?' my mother said.

'The mother's not there,' my father replied. 'She took off a few years back. Can't say I blame her. Piquette cooks for them, and she says Lazarus would never do anything for himself as long as she's there. Anyway, I don't think she'd take much care of herself, once she got back. She's only thirteen, after all. Beth, I was thinking—what about taking her up to Diamond Lake with us this summer? A couple of months rest would give that bone a much better chance.'

My mother looked stunned.

'But Ewen—what about Roddie and Vanessa?'

'She's not contagious,' my father said. 'And it would be company for Vanessa.'

'Oh dear,' my mother said in distress, 'I'll bet anything she has nits in her hair.'

'For Pete's sake,' my father said crossly, 'do you think Matron would let her stay in the hospital for all this time like that? Don't be silly, Beth.'

Grandmother MacLeod, her delicately featured face as rigid as a cameo, now brought her mauve-veined hands together as though she were about to begin a prayer.

'Ewen, if that half-breed youngster comes along to Diamond Lake, I'm not going,' she announced. 'I'll go to Morag's for the summer.'

I had trouble in stifling my urge to laugh, for my mother brightened visibly and quickly tried to hide it. If it came to a choice between Grandmother MacLeod and Piquette, Piquette would win hands down, nits or not.

'It might be quite nice for you, at that,' she mused. 'You haven't seen Morag for over a year, and you might enjoy being in the city for a while. Well, Ewen dear, you do what you think best. If you think it would do Piquette some good, then we'll be glad to have her, as long as she behaves herself.'

So it happened that several weels later, when we all piled into my father's old Nash, surrounded by suitcases and boxes of provisions and toys for my ten-month-old brother, Piquette was with us and Grandmother MacLeod, miraculously, was not. My father would only be staying at the cottage for a couple of weeks, for he had to get back to his practice, but the rest of us would stay at Diamond Lake until the end of August.

Our cottage was not named, as many were, 'Dew Drop Inn' or 'Bide-a-Wee,' or 'Bonnie Doon.' The sign on the roadway bore in austere letters only our name, MacLeod. It was not a large cottage, but it was on the lakefront. You could look out the windows and see, through the filigree of the spruce trees, the water glistening greenly as the sun caught it. All around the cottage were ferns, and sharp-branched raspberry bushes, and moss that had grown over fallen tree trunks. If you looked carefully among the weeds and grass, you could find wild strawberry plants which were in white flower now and in another month would bear fruit, the fragrant globes hanging like miniature scarlet lanterns on the thin hairy stems. The two grey squirrels were still there, gossiping at us from the tall spruce beside the cottage, and by the end of the summer they would again be tame enough to take pieces of crust from my hands. The broad moose antlers that hung above the back door were a little more bleached and fissured after the winter, but otherwise everything was the same. I raced joyfully around my kingdom, greeting all the places I had not seen for a year. My brother, Roderick, who had not been born when we were here last summer, sat on the car rug in the sunshine and examined a brown spruce cone, meticulously turning it round and round in his small and curious hands. My mother and father toted the luggage from car to cottage, exclaiming over how well the place had wintered, no broken windows, thank goodness, no apparent damage from storm-felled branches or snow.

Only after I had finished looking around did I notice Piquette. She was sitting on the swing, her lame leg held stiffly out, and her other foot scuffing the ground as she swung slowly back and forth. Her long hair hung black and straight around her shoulders, and her broad coarse-featured face bore no expression—it was blank, as though she no longer dwelt within her own skull, as though she had gone elsewhere. I approached her very hesitantly.

'Want to come and play?'

Piquette looked at me with a sudden flash of scorn.

'I ain't a kid,' she said.

Wounded, I stamped angrily away, swearing I would not speak to her for the rest of the summer. In the days that followed, however, Piquette began to interest me, and I began to want to interest her. My reasons did not appear bizarre to me. Unlikely as it may seem, I had only just realised that the Tonnerre family, whom I had always heard called half-breeds, were actually Indians, or as near as made no difference. My acquaintance with Indians was not extensive. I did not remember ever having seen a real Indian, and my new awareness that Piquette sprang from the people of Big Bear and Poundmaker, of Tecumseh, of the Iroquois who had eaten Father Brebeuf's heart—all this gave her an instant attraction in my eyes. I was a devoted reader of Pauline Johnson at this age, and sometimes would orate aloud and in an exalted voice, *West Wind, blow from your prairie nest; Blow from the mountains, blow from the west*—and so on. It seemed to me that Piquette must be in some way a daughter of the forest, a kind of junior prophetess of the wilds, who might impart to me, if I took the right approach, some of the secrets which she undoubtedly knew—where the whippoorwill made her nest, how the coyote reared her young, or whatever it was that it said in Hiawatha.

I set about gaining Piquette's trust. She was not allowed to go swimming, with her bad leg, but I managed to lure her down to the beach—or rather, she came because there was nothing else to do. The water was always icy, for the lake was fed by springs, but I swam like a dog, thrashing my arms and legs around at such speed and with such an output of energy that I never grew cold. Finally, when I had had enough, I came out and sat beside Piquette on the sand. When she saw me approaching, her hand squashed flat the sand castle she had been building, and she looked at me sullenly, without speaking.

'Do you like this place?' I asked, after a while, intending to lead on from there into the question of forest lore.

Piquette shrugged. 'It's okay. Good as anywhere.'

'I love it,' I said. 'We come here every summer.'

'So what?' Her voice was distant, and I glanced at her uncertainly, wondering what I could have said wrong.

'Do you want to come for a walk?' I asked her. 'We wouldn't need to go far. If you walk just around the point there, you come to a bay where great big reeds grow in the water, and all kinds of fish hang around there. Want to? Come on.'

She shook her head.

'Your dad said I ain't supposed to do no more walking than I got to.'

I tried another line.

'I bet you know a lot about the woods and all that, eh?' I began respectfully.

Piquette looked at me from her large dark unsmiling eyes.

'I don't know what in hell you're talkin' about,' she replied. 'You nuts or somethin'? If you mean where my old man, and me, and all them live, you better shut up, by Jesus, you hear?'

I was startled and my feelings were hurt, but I had a kind of dogged perseverance. I ignored her rebuff.

'You know something, Piquette? There's loons here, on this lake. You can see their nests just up the shore there, behind those logs. At night, you can hear them even from the cottage, but it's better to listen from the beach. My dad says we should listen and try to remember how they sound, because in a few years when more cottages are built at Diamond Lake and more people come in, the loons will go away.'

Piquette was picking up stones and snail shells and then dropping them again.

'Who gives a good goddamn?' she said

It became increasingly obvious that, as an Indian, Piquette was a dead loss. That evening I went out by myself, scrambling through the bushes that overhung the steep path, my feet slipping on the fallen spruce needles that covered the ground. When I reached the shore, I walked along the firm damp sand to the small pier that my father had built, and sat down there. I heard someone else crashing through the undergrowth and the bracken, and for a moment I thought Piquette had changed her mind, but it turned out to be my father. He sat beside me on the pier and we waited, without speaking.

At night the lake was like black glass with a streak of amber which was the path of the moon. All around, the spruce trees grew tall and close-set, branches blackly sharp against the sky, which was lightened by a cold flickering of stars. Then the loons began their calling. They rose like phantom birds from the nests on the shore, and flew out onto the dark still surface of the water.

No one can ever describe that ululating sound, the crying of the loons, and no one who has heard it can ever forget it. Plaintive, and yet with a quality of chilling mockery, those voices belonged to a world separated by aeons from our neat world of summer cottages and the lighted lamps of home.

'They must have sounded just like that,' my father remarked, 'before any person ever set foot here.'

Then he laughed. 'You could say the same, of course, about sparrows, or chipmunks, but somehow it only strikes you that way with the loons.'

'I know,' I said.

Neither of us suspected that this would be the last time we would ever sit here together on the shore, listening. We stayed for perhaps half an hour, and then we went back to the cottage. My mother was reading beside the fireplace. Piquette was looking at the burning birch log, and not doing anything.

'You should have come along,' I said, although in fact I was glad she had not.

'Not me,' Piquette said. 'You wouldn' catch me walkin' way down there jus' for a bunch of squawkin' birds.'

Piquette and I remained ill at ease with one another. I felt I had somehow failed my father, but I did not know what was the matter, nor why she would not or could not respond when I suggested exploring the woods or playing house. I thought it was probably her slow and difficult walking that held her back. She stayed most of the time in the cottage with my mother, helping her with the dishes or with Roddie, but hardly ever talking. Then the Duncans arrived at their cottage, and I spent my days with Mavis, who was my best friend. I could not reach Piquette at all, and I soon lost interest in trying. But all that summer she remained as both a reproach and a mystery to me.

That winter my father died of pneumonia, after less than a week's illness. For some time I saw nothing around me, being completely immersed in my own pain and my mother's. When I looked outward once more, I scarcely noticed that Piquette Tonnerre was no longer at school. I do not remember seeing her at all until four years later, one Saturday night when Mavis and I were having Cokes in the Regal Café. The jukebox was booming like tuneful thunder, and beside it, leaning lightly on its chrome and its rainbow glass, was a girl.

Piquette must have been seventeen then, although she looked about twenty. I stared at her, astounded that anyone could have changed so much. Her face, so stolid and expressionless before, was animated now with a gaiety that was almost violent. She laughed and talked very loudly with the boys around her. Her lipstick was bright carmine, and her hair was cut short and frizzily permed. She had not been pretty as a child, and she was not pretty now, for her features were still heavy and blunt. But her dark and slightly slanted eyes were beautiful, and her skin-tight skirt and orange sweater displayed to enviable advantage a soft and slender body.

She saw me, and walked over. She teetered a little, but it was not due to her once-tubercular leg, for her limp was almost gone.

'Hi, Vanessa.' Her voice still had the same hoarseness. 'Long time no see, eh?'

'Hi,' I said. 'Where've you been keeping yourself, Piquette?'

'Oh, I been around,' she said. 'I been away almost two years now. Been all over the place—Winnipeg, Regina, Saskatoon. Jesus, what I could tell you! I come back this summer, but I ain't stayin'. You kids goin' to the dance?'

'No,' I said abruptly, for this was a sore point with me. I was fifteen, and thought I was old enough to go to the Saturday-night dances at the Flamingo. My mother, however, thought otherwise.

'Y'oughta come,' Piquette said. 'I never miss one. It's just about the on'y thing in this jerkwater town that's any fun. Boy, you couldn' catch me stayin' here. I don't give a shit about this place. It stinks.'

She sat down beside me, and I caught the harsh over-sweetness of her perfume.

'Listen, you wanna know something, Vanessa?' she confided, her voice only slightly blurred. 'Your dad was the only person in Manawaka that ever done anything good to me.'

I nodded speechlessly. I was certain she was speaking the truth. I knew a little more than I had that summer at Diamond Lake, but I could not reach her now any more than I had then. I was ashamed, ashamed of my own timidity, the frightened tendency to look the other way. Yet I felt no real warmth towards her—I only felt that I ought to, because of that distant summer and because my father had hoped she would be company for me, or perhaps that I would be for her, but it had not happened that way. At this moment, meeting her again, I had to admit that she repelled and embarrassed me, and I could not help despising the self-pity in her voice. I wished she would go away. I did not want to see her. I did not know what to say to her. It seemed that we had nothing to say to one another.

'I'll tell you something else,' Piquette went on. 'All the old bitches an' biddies in this town will sure be surprised. I'm gettin' married this fall—my boyfriend, he's an English fella, works in the stockyards in the city there, a very tall guy, got blond wavy hair. Gee, is he ever handsome. Got this real classy name. Alvin Gerald Cummings—some handle, eh? They call him Al.'

For the merest instant, then, I saw her. I really did see her, for the first and only time in all the years we had both lived in the same town. Her defiant face, momentarily, became unguarded and unmasked, and in her eyes there was a terrifying hope.

'Gee, Piquette—' I burst out awkwardly, 'that's swell. That's really wonderful. Congratulations—good luck—I hope you'll be happy—'

As I mouthed the conventional phrases, I could only guess how great her need must have been, that she had been forced to seek the very things she so bitterly rejected.

When I was eighteen, I left Manawaka and went away to college. At the end of my first year, I came back home for the summer. I spent the first few days in talking non-stop with my mother, as we exchanged all the news that somehow had not found its way into letters—what had happened in my life and what had happened here in Manawaka while I was away. My mother searched her memory for events that concerned people I knew.

'Did I ever write you about Piquette Tonnerre, Vanessa?'' she asked one morning.

'No I don't think so,' I replied. 'Last I heard of her, she was going to marry some guy in the city. Is she still there?'

My mother looked perturbed, and it was a moment before she spoke, as though she did not know how to express what she had to tell and wished she did not need to try.

'She's dead,' she said at last. Then, as I stared at her, 'Oh, Vanessa, when it happened, I couldn't help thinking of her as she was that summer—so sullen and gauche and badly dressed. I couldn't help wondering if we could have done something more at that time—but what could we do? She used to be around in the cottage there with me all day, and honestly, it was all I could do to get a word out of her. She didn't even talk to your father very much, although I think she liked him, in her way.'

'What happened?' I asked.

'Either her husband left her, or she left him,' my mother said. 'I don't know which. Anyway, she came back here with two youngsters, both only babies—they must have been born very close together. She kept house, I guess, for Lazarus and her brothers, down in the valley there, in the old Tonnerre place. I used to see her on the street sometimes, but she never spoke to me. She'd put on an awful lot of weight, and she looked a mess, to tell you the truth, a real slattern, dressed any old how. She was up in court a couple of times—drunk and disorderly, of course. One Saturday night last winter, during the coldest weather, Piquette was alone in the shack with the children. The Tonnerres made home brew all the time, so I've heard, and Lazarus said later she'd been drinking most of the day when he and the boys went out that evening. They had an old woodstove there—you know the kind, with exposed pipes. The shack caught fire. Piquette didn't get out, and neither did the children.'

I did not say anything. As so often with Piquette, there did not seem to be anything to say. There was a kind of silence around the image in my mind of the fire and the snow, and I wished I could put from my memory the look that I had seen once in Piquette's eyes.

I went up to Diamond Lake for a few days that summer, with Mavis and her family. The MacLeod cottage had been sold after my father's death, and I did not even go to look at it, not wanting to witness my long-ago kingdom possessed now by strangers. But one evening I went down to the shore by myself.

The small pier which my father had built was gone, and in its place there was a large and solid pier built by the government, for Galloping Mountain was now a national park, and Diamond Lake had been re-named Lake Wapakata, for it was felt that an Indian name would have a greater appeal to tourists. The one store had become several dozen, and the settlement had all the attributes of a flourishing resort—hotels, a dance-hall, cafés with neon signs, the penetrating odours of potato chips and hot dogs.

I sat on the government pier and looked out across the water. At night the lake at least was the same as it had always been, darkly shining and bearing within its black glass the streak of amber that was the path of the moon. There was no wind that evening, and everything was quiet all around me. It seemed too quiet, and then I realized that the loons were no longer here. I listened for some time, to make sure, but never once did I hear that long-drawn call, half mocking and half plaintive, spearing through the stillness across the lake.

I did not know what had happened to the birds. Perhaps they had gone away to some far place of belonging. Perhaps they had been unable to find such a place, and had simply died out, having ceased to care any longer whether they lived or not.

I remembered how Piquette had scorned to come along, when my father and I sat there and listened to the lake birds. It seemed to me now that in some unconscious and totally unrecognised way, Piquette might have been the only one, after all, who had heard the crying of the loons.

JAMES REANEY
b.1926

The Bully

As a child I lived on a farm not far from a small town called Partridge. In the countryside about Partridge, thin roads of gravel and dust slide in and out among the hollows and hills. As roads go, they certainly aren't very brave, for quite often they go round a hill instead of up it and even in the flattest places they will jog and hesitate absurdly. But then this latter tendency often comes from some blunder a surveying engineer made a hundred years ago. And although his mind has long ago dissolved, its forgetfulness still pushes the country people crooked where they might have gone straight.

Some of the farm-houses on these ill-planned roads are made of red brick and have large barns and great cement silos and soft large strawstacks behind them. And other farm-houses are not made of brick, but of frame and clap-board that gleam with the silver film unpainted wood attains after years of wild rain and shrill wind beating upon it. The house where I was born was such a place, and I remember that whenever it rained, from top to bottom the whole outside of the house would turn jet-black as if it were blushing in shame or anger.

Perhaps it blushed because of my father who was not a very good farmer. He was what is known as an afternoon farmer. He could never get out into the fields till about half-past eleven in the morning and he never seemed to be able to grow much of anything except buckwheat which as everyone knows is the lazy farmer's crop. If you could make a living out of playing checkers and talking, then my father would have made enough to send us all to college, but as it was he did make enough to keep us alive, to buy tea and coffee, cake and pie, boots and stockings, and a basket of peaches once every summer. So it's really hard to be-grudge him a few games of checkers or a preference for talking instead of a preference for ploughing.

When I was six, my mother died of T.B. and I was brought up by my Aunt Coraline and by my two older sisters, Noreen and Kate. Noreen, the oldest of us, was a very husky, lively girl. She was really one of the liveliest girls I have ever seen. She rode every horse we had bare-back, sometimes not with a bridle at all but just by holding on to their manes. When she was fifteen, in a single day she wall-papered both our kitchen and our living-room. And when she was sixteen she helped my father draw in hay just like a hired man. When she was twelve she used to tease me an awful lot. Sometimes when she had teased me too much, I would store away scraps of food for days, and then go off down the side-road with the strong idea in my head that I was not going to come back. But then Noreen and Kate would run after me with tears in their eyes and, having persuaded me to throw away my large collection of breakfast toast crusts and agree to come back, they would both promise never to tease me again. Although Kate, goodness knows, had no need to promise that for she was always kind, would never have thought of teasing me. Kate was rather like me in being shy and in being rather weak. Noreen's strength and boldness made her despise Kate and me, but she was like us in some ways. For instance Noreen had a strange way of feeding the hens. Each night she would sprinkle the grain out on the ground in the shape of a letter or some other pattern, so that when the hens ate the grain, they were forced to spell out Noreen's initials or to form a cross and a circle. There were just enough hens to make this rather an interesting game. Sometimes, I know, Noreen spelt out whole sentences in this way, a letter or two each night, and I often wondered to whom she was writing up in the sky.

Aunt Coraline, who brought me up, was most of the time sick in bed and as a result was rather pettish and ill-tempered. In the summer time, she would spend most of the day in her room making bouquets out of any flowers we could bring her; even dandelions, Shepherd's Purse, or Queen Anne's Lace. She was very skilful at putting letters of the alphabet into a bouquet, with two kinds of flowers, you know, one for the letters and one for the background. Aunt Coraline's room was filled with all sorts of jars and bottles containing bouquets, some of them very ancient so that her room smelt up a bit, especially in the hot weather. She was the only one of us who had a room to herself. My father slept in the kitchen. Aunt Coraline's days were devoted to the medicine-bottle and the pill-box, making designs in bouquets, telling us stories, and bringing us up; her nights were spent in trying to get to sleep and crying softly to herself.

When we were children we never were worked to death, but still we didn't play or read books all of the time. In the summer we picked strawberries, currants, and raspberries. Sometimes we picked wild berries into milkpails for money, but after we had picked our pails full, before we could get the berries to the woman who had commissioned them, the berries would settle down in the pails and of course the woman would refuse then to pay what she had promised because we hadn't brought her full pails. Sometimes our father made us pick potato beetles off the potato plants. We would tap the plants on one side with a shingle and hold out a tin can on the other side to catch the potato bugs as they fell. And we went for cows and caught plough-horses for our father.

Every Saturday night we children all took turns bathing in the dish-pan and on Sundays, after Sunday-school, we would all sit out on the lawn and drink the lemonade that my father would make in a big glass pitcher. The lemonade was always slightly green and sour like the moon when it's high up in a summer sky. While we were drinking the lemonade, we would listen to our victrola gramophone which Noreen would carry out of the house along with a collection of records. These were all very old, very thick records and their names were: *I Know Where the Flies Go, The Big Rock Candy Mountain, Hand Me Down My Walking Cane*, and a dialogue about some people in a boarding-house that went like this:

'Why can't you eat this soup?'

Various praising replies about the soup and its fine, fine qualities by all the fifteen members of the boarding-house. Then:

'So WHY can't you eat this soup?'

And the non-appreciative boarder replies:

'Because I ain't got a spoon.'

Even if no one laughed, and of course we always did, the Record Company had thoughtfully put in some laughter just to fill up the centre. Those Sunday afternoons are all gone now and if I had known I was never to spend any more like them, I would have spent them more slowly.

We began to grow up. Noreen did so gladly but Kate and I secretly hated to. We were much too weak to face things as they were. We were weak enough to prefer what we had been as children rather than what we saw people often grew up to be, people who worked all day at dull, senseless things and slept all night and worked all day and slept all night and so on until they died. I think Aunt Coraline must have felt the same when she was young and decided to solve the problem by being ill. Unfortunately for us, neither Kate nor I could quite bring ourselves to take this line. I don't know what Kate decided, but at the age of eleven I decided that school-teaching looked neither too boring nor too hard so a schoolteacher I would be. It was my one chance to escape what my father had fallen into. To become a teacher one had to go to high school five years and go one year to Normal School. Two miles away in the town of Partridge there actually stood a high school.

It was not until the summer after I had passed my Entrance Examination that I began to feel rather frightened of the new life ahead of me. That spring, Noreen had gone into town to work for a lady as a housemaid. At my request, she went to look at the high school. It was situated right next the jail, and Noreen wrote home that of the two places she'd much rather go to the jail, even although they had just made the gates of the jail three feet higher. Of that summer I particularly remember one sultry Sunday afternoon in August when I walked listlessly out to the mail-box and, leaning against it, looked down the road in the general direction of town. The road went on past our house and then up a hill and then not over the top of the hill for it went crooked a bit, wavered and disappeared, somehow, on the other side. Somewhere on that road stood a huge building which would swallow me up for five years. Why I had ever wanted to leave all the familiar things around me, I could hardly understand. Why people had to grow up and leave home I could not understand either. I looked first at the road and then into the dull sky as I wondered at this. I tried to imagine what the high school would really be like, but all I could see or feel was a strong tide emerging from it to sweep me into something that would give me a good shaking up.

Early every morning, I walked into high school with my lunch-box and my school-books under my arm. And I walked home again at night. I have none of the textbooks now that were used at that school, for I sold them when I left. And I can't remember very much about them except that the French book was fat and blue. One took fifteen subjects in all: Business Practice (in this you learned how to write out cheques and pay electric light bills, a knowledge that so far has been of no use to me); there was English, Geography, Mathematics, French, Spelling, History, Physical Training, Music, Art, Science (here one was taught how to light a Bunsen Burner) and there must have been other subjects for I'm sure there were fifteen of them. I never got used to high school. There were so many rooms, so many people, so many teachers. The teachers were watchful as heathen deities and it was painful to displease them. Almost immediately I became the object of everyone's disgust and rage. The Geography teacher growled at me, the English teacher stood me up in corners. The History teacher denounced me as an idiot. The French teacher cursed my accent. In Physical Training I fell off innumerable parallel-bars showing, as the instructor remarked, that I could not and never would co-ordinate my mind with my body. My platoon of the cadet corps discovered that the only way to make progress possible in drill was to place me deep in the centre of the ranks away from all key positions. In Manual Training I broke all sorts of precious saws and was soundly strapped for something I did to the iron-lathe. For no reason that I could see, the Art teacher went purple in the face at me, took me out into the hall and struck my defenceless hands with a leather thong. The French teacher once put me out into the hall, a far worse fate than that of being put in a corner, for the halls were hourly stalked by the principal in search of game; anyone found in the halls he took off with him to his office where he administered a little something calculated to keep the receiver out of the halls thereafter.

Frankly, I must have been, and I was, a simpleton, but I did the silly things I did mainly because everyone expected me to do them. Very slowly I began to be able to control myself and give at least some sort of right answer when questioned. Each night when I came home at first, Kate would ask me how I liked high school. I would reply as stoutly as I could that I was getting on all right. But gradually I did begin to get along not too badly and might have been a little happy if something not connected with my studies had not thrown me back into a deeper misery.

This new unhappiness had something to do with the place where those students who came from the country ate their lunch. This place was called a cafeteria and was divided into a girls' cafeteria and a boys' one. After about a month of coming to the boys' cafeteria to eat my lunch, I noticed that a certain young man (he couldn't be called a boy) always sat near me with his back to me at the next long table. The cafeteria was a basement room filled with three long tables and rows of wire-mended chairs. Now my lunch always included a small bottle of milk. The bottle had originally been a vinegar bottle and was very difficult to drink from unless you put your head away back and gulped it fast. One day when I had finished my sandwiches and was drinking my milk, he turned around and said quietly: 'Does baby like his bottle?'

I blushed and immediately stopped drinking. Then I waited until he would finish his lunch and go away. While I waited with downcast eyes and a face red with shame, I felt a furious rush of anger against Kate and Aunt Coraline for sending milk for my lunch in a vinegar bottle. Finally, I began to see that he had finished his lunch and was not going to leave until I did. I put the vinegar bottle back in my lunchbox and walked as quickly as I could out of the boys' cafeteria, upstairs into the classroom left open during the noon-hour so that the country people could study there. He followed me there and sat in the seat opposite me with what I managed to discover in the two times I looked at him, a derisive smile upon his face. He had a North American Indian face and complexion, with heavy lips, and he wore a dark green shirt. With him sitting beside me, I had no chance of ever getting the products of New Zealand and Australia off by heart and so I failed the Geography test we had that afternoon. Day after day he tormented me. He never hit me. He would always just stay close to me, commenting on how I ate my food or didn't drink my vinegar and once he pulled a chair from beneath me. Since our first meeting I never drank anything while he was near me. Between him and my friends the teachers, my life in first form at high school was a sort of Hell with too many tormenting fiends and not enough of me to go round so they could all get satisfaction. If I'd had the slightest spark of courage I'd have burnt the high school down at least.

At last, in the middle of November, I hit upon the plan of going over to the public library after I had eaten my lunch. Lots of other country students went there too. Most of them either giggled at magazines or hunted up art prints and photographs of classical sculpture on which they made obscene additions, or if more than usually clever, obscene comments. For over one happy week the Bully seemed to have lost me, for he did not appear at the library. Then I looked up from a dull book I was reading and there he was. He had my cap in his hand and would not give it back to me. How he had got hold of it I couldn't imagine. How I was to get it back from him, I couldn't imagine either. He must have given it back to me, I can't remember just how. Of course it wasn't the sort of hat anyone else wore, as you might expect. It was a toque, a red-and-white woollen one that Noreen used to wear. Every other boy at school wore a fedora or at least a helmet.

During the library period of my bullying he sat as close up against me as he could and whispered obscenities in my ear. After two weeks of this, being rather desperate, I did not go to the boys' cafeteria to eat my lunch but took my books and my lunch and went out into the streets. This was in early December and there was deep snow everywhere. I ran past the jail, down into the civic gardens, across the river, under a bridge, and down the other side of the river as fast as I could go. I had no idea where I was going to eat my lunch until I saw the town cemetery just ahead of me. It seemed fairly safe. I could eat my sandwiches under a tree and then keep warm by reading the inscriptions on gravestones and walking about.

The second day or the third, I discovered that the doors of the cemetery's mausoleum were open and that there were two benches inside where you can be buried in a marble pigeon-hole instead of the cold ground. To this place I came day after day, and I revelled in the morbid quiet of the place. I sat on one of the walnut benches and whispered irregular French verbs to myself or memorized the mineral resources of Turkey or the history of the Upper Canada Rebellion. All around and all above me dead citizens lay in their coffins, their rings flashing in the darkness, their finger-nails grown long like white thin carrots, and the hair of the dead men grown out long and wild to their shoulders. No one ever disturbed me. People's finger-nails and hair do keep on growing after they're dead, you know. Aunt Coraline read it in a book.

No one ever disturbed me at the mausoleum. The wind howled about that dismal place but no other voice howled. Only once I had some trouble in getting the heavy doors open when the factory whistles blew and it was time to start walking back to school. I usually arrived back at school at twenty minutes after one. But one day the wind weakened the sound of the whistles and I arrived at school just at half-past one. If it had been allowed, I might have run in the girls' door and not been late. But it was not allowed and since the boys' door was at the other end of the building, by the time I had run to it, I was quite late and had to stay after four.

Just before Christmas they had an At Home at the school. The emphasis in pronouncing At Home is usually put on the AT. Everyone goes to the AT Home. The tickets are usually old tickets that weren't sold for last year's operetta, cut in half. Noreen forced me to take her because she wanted to see what an AT Home was like. She did not mind that I could not dance. She only wanted to sip at second-hand what she supposed to be the delightful joys of higher education. We first went into the rooms where schoolwork was exhibited. Noreen kept expecting some of my work to be up and kept being disappointed. I was very nervous with a paint-brush so none of my drawings were up in the art display. At the writing exhibit none of my writing was up. I had failed to master the free-hand stroke, although away from the writing teacher I could draw beautiful writing that looked as if it had been done by the freest hand imaginable. At the Geography exhibit not one of my charts of national resources had been pinned up. Noreen was heart-broken. I had learned not to care. For instance, almost everyone's window-stick got into the Manual Training show. Mine didn't because I had planed it down until it was about a quarter of an inch thick, and as the Manual Training teacher pointed out, it couldn't have held up a feather. But I didn't care.

Noreen and I went into the girls' gymnasium where we saw a short, brown-coloured movie that showed Dutch gardeners clipping hedges into the shapes of geese and chickens, ducks and peacocks. The Dutch gardeners cut away with their shears so fast that the ducks and peacocks seemed fairly to leap out of the hedges at you. Noreen and I wondered how these gardeners were going to keep employed if they carved up things that fast. Then we went into the boys' gym where young men stripped almost naked and covered with gold paint pretended to be statues. After watching them for a while Noreen and I went up to the Assembly Hall where dancing was in progress and young girls hovered shyly at the edge of the floor. Some of these shy young girls were dressed in handmade evening gowns that seemed to be made out of very thin mosquito netting coated with icing sugar. Noreen had one of her employer's old dresses on. It was certainly an old dress, made about 1932 I guess, for it had a hunch-back sack of cloth flying out of the middle of the back. Noreen, I know, thought she looked extremely distinctive. I only thought she looked extremely extraordinary.

And she did so want to dance. So we went up to the third floor and there Noreen tried to teach me how to dance in one lesson, but it was no use. She asked me to introduce her to some of my friends who danced. I had no friends but there was one boy who borrowed everything I owned almost daily. Here was a chance for him to repay me if he could dance. We soon captured him, but although Noreen clung tightly to him for a good deal of the evening and although we led him to the mouth of the Assembly Hall, all the time proclaiming quite loudly how nice it must be to dance, he didn't ask Noreen for a dance. So we went down into the basement to the Domestic Science Room where punch was being served and thin cookies with silver beads in the middle of them. There was a great crowd of people in the Domestic Science Room and before we knew it, he had given us the slip. Then Noreen said, 'Where do you eat your lunch? Kate was telling me how she makes it every night for you.'

I replied that I ate in the boys' cafeteria.

'Oh, what's that? Come on. Show me.'

'It's not very interesting,' I said.

'But show me it. Show me it,' Noreen insisted stubbornly.

'It's down here,' I said.

We went past the furnace room.

'That's the furnace room, Noreen. There's the girls' cafeteria. Here's the—'

It was dark inside the boys' cafeteria and I felt along the wall just beside the door for a light button. I could hear someone climbing in one of the windows. Someone who didn't want to buy a ticket, I supposed. Probably someone who came here regularly at noon and thought of leaving a window open for himself. Before I could tell her not to, Noreen had found the light switch ahead of me and turned it on. The person climbing in the window turned out to be my friend the Bully. Like a wild animal he stared for a second at us and then jumped back through the window.

'Well, who on earth was that? asked Noreen.

'I don't know,' I said, trembling all over.

'Don't tremble like a leaf!' said Noreen scornfully. 'Why you look and act exactly like you'd seen a ghost. What was so frightening about him?'

'Nothing,' I said, leaning against the wall and putting my hand to my forehead. 'Nothing.'

The Christmas holidays were haunted for me by my fear of what would happen at school when I went back there after New Year's. But I never complained to my father or Aunt Coraline. They would have been only too glad to hear me say that I didn't want to go back. I must somehow stick it until the spring and the end of first form at least. But I knew that before the spring came the Bully would track me down, and if I met him once again I knew it would be the end of me. I remember in those Christmas holidays that I went walking a lot with Kate over the fields that were dead white with snow. I wished then that we might always do that. I told Kate about my unhappiness at high school and it drew us closer together. If I had told Noreen she would only have called me a silly fool and made me hate her. But Kate was always more sympathetic towards me.

The first morning when I was back at school I found a note in my desk. All it said was this: *I want to see you eating where you should eat today, baby.* At noon I hid myself in the swarm of city students who were going home for lunch and arrived at the mausoleum by a round-about way. I couldn't get over the notion that someone was following me or watching me, which could easily have been true, since he had many friends.

I was just in the middle of eating my lunch. I was sitting on a bench in front of the Hon. Arthur P. Hingham's tomb. I saw the Bully trying to open the great doors to the mausoleum. But he couldn't seem to get them open. At last he did. All I can remember is seeing the advancing edge of the door for I toppled off the bench in a dead faint. By the time I came to it was half-past one so I started to walk home. My head ached violently as if someone had kicked it, which turned out to be the case, there being a red dent just below my left eye that turned blue after a few hours. On the way home that afternoon I had just reached a place in the road where you can see our house when I decided that I could not bear to go to high school any longer. So I went home and I told them that I had been expelled for walking in through the girls' door instead of the boys' door. They never doubted that this was true, so little did they know of high schools and their rules. Noreen doubted me, but by the time she heard about my being expelled it was too late to send me back. Aunt Coraline cried a bit over it all; my father told me the whole thing showed that I really belonged on the farm. Only Kate realized how much school had meant to me and how desperately I had tried to adapt myself to it.

That night as I lay in bed, while outside a cold strong river of wind roared about the house shaking everything and rattling the dishes in the cupboard downstairs, that night I dreamt three dreams. I have never been able to discover what they meant.

First I dreamt that Noreen was the Bully and that I caught her washing off her disguise in the water-trough in the yard. Then I dreamt I saw the Bully make love to Kate and she hugging and kissing him. The last dream I had was the longest of all. I dreamt that just before dawn I crept out of the house and went through the yard. And all the letters Noreen had ever made out of grain there while she was feeding the chickens had all sprouted up into green letters of grass and wheat. Someone touched me on the shoulder and said sadly, *I haven't got a spoon*, but I ran away without answering across the fields into the bush. There was a round pond there surrounded by a grove of young chokecherry trees. I pushed through these and came to the edge of the pond. There lay the Bully looking almost pitiful, his arms and legs bound with green ropes made out of nettles. He was drowned dead, half in the water and half out of it, but face up. And in the dim light of the dawn I knelt down and kissed him gently on the forehead.

HUGH HOOD

b.1928

Flying a Red Kite

The ride home began badly. Still almost a stranger to the city, tired, hot and dirty, and inattentive to his surroundings, Fred stood for ten minutes, shifting his parcels from arm to arm and his weight from one leg to the other, in a sweaty bath of shimmering glare from the sidewalk, next to a grimy yellow-and-black bus stop. To his left a line of murmuring would-be passengers lengthened until there were enough to fill any vehicle that might come for them. Finally an obese brown bus waddled up like an indecent old cow and stopped with an expiring moo at the head of the line. Fred was glad to be first in line, as there didn't seem to be room for more than a few to embus.

But as he stepped up he noticed a sign in the window which said *Côte des Neiges—Boulevard* and he recoiled as though bitten, trampling the toes of the woman behind him amd making her squeal. It was a Sixty-six bus, not the Sixty-five that he wanted. The woman pushed furiously past him while the remainder of the line clamoured in the rear. He stared at the number on the bus stop: Sixty-six, not his stop at all. Out of the corner of his eye he saw another coach pulling away from the stop on the northeast corner, the right stop, the Sixty-five, and the one he should have been standing under all this time. Giving his characteristic weary put-upon sigh, which he used before breakfast to annoy Naomi, he adjusted his parcels in both arms, feeling sweat run around his neck and down his collar between his shoulders, and crossed Saint Catherine against the light, drawing a Gallic sneer from a policeman, to stand for several more minutes at the head of a new queue, under the right sign. It was nearly four-thirty and the Saturday shopping crowds wanted to get home, out of the summer dust and heat, out of the jitter of the big July holiday weekend. They would all go home and sit on their balconies. All over the suburbs in duplexes and fourplexes, families would be enjoying cold suppers in the open air on their balconies; but the Calverts' apartment had none. Fred and Naomi had been ignorant of the meaning of the custom when they were apartment hunting. They had thought of Montreal as a city of the Sub-Arctic and in the summers they would have leisure to repent the misjudgment.

He had been shopping along the length of Saint Catherine between Peel and Guy, feeling guilty because he had heard for years that this was where all those pretty Montreal women made their promenade; he had wanted to watch without familial encumbrances. There had been girls enough but nothing outrageously special so he had beguiled the scorching afternoon making a great many small idle purchases, of the kind one does when trapped in a Woolworth's. A ball-point pen and a note-pad for Naomi, who was always stealing his and leaving it in the kitchen with long, wildly-optimistic, grocery lists scribbled in it. Six packages of cigarettes, some legal-size envelopes, two Dinky-toys, a long-playing record, two parcels of secondhand books, and the lightest of his burdens and the unhandiest, the kite he had bought for Deedee, two flimsy wooden sticks rolled up in red plastic film, and a ball of cheap thin string—not enough, by the look of it, if he should ever get the thing into the air.

When he'd gone fishing, as a boy, he'd never caught any fish; when playing hockey he had never been able to put the puck in the net. One by one the wholesome outdoor sports and games had defeated him. But he had gone on believing in them, in their curative moral values, and now he hoped that Deedee, though a girl, might sometime catch a fish; and though she obviously wouldn't play hockey, she might ski, or toboggan on the mountain. He had noticed that people treated kites and kite-flying as somehow holy. They were a natural symbol, thought Fred, and he felt uneasily sure that he would have trouble getting this one to fly.

The inside of the bus was shaped like a box-car with windows, but the windows were useless. You might have peeled off the bus as you'd peel the paper off a pound of butter, leaving an oblong yellow lump of thick solid heat, with the passengers embedded in it like hopeless breadcrumbs.

He elbowed and wriggled his way along the aisle, feeling a momentary sliver of pleasure as his palm rubbed accidentally along the back of a girl's skirt—once, a philosopher—the sort of thing you couldn't be charged with. But you couldn't get away with it twice and anyway the girl either didn't feel it, or had no idea who had caressed her. There were vacant seats towards the rear, which was odd because the bus was otherwise full, and he struggled towards them, trying not to break the wooden struts which might be persuaded to fly. The bus lurched forward and his feet moved with the floor, causing him to pop suddenly out of the crowd by the exit, into a square well of space next to the heat and stink of the engine. He swayed around and aimed himself at a narrow vacant seat, nearly dropping a parcel of books as he lowered himself precipitately into it.

The bus crossed Sherbrooke Street and began, intolerably slowly, to crawl up Côte des Neiges and around the western spur of the mountain. His ears began to pick up the usual melange of French and English and to sort it out; he was proud of his French and pleased that most of the people on the streets spoke a less correct, though more fluent, version than his own. He had found that he could make his customers understand him perfectly—he was a book salesman—but that people on the street were happier when he addressed them in English.

The chatter in the bus grew clearer and more interesting and he began to listen, grasping all at once why he had found a seat back here. He was sitting next to a couple of drunks who emitted an almost overpowering smell of beer. They were cheerfully exchanging indecencies and obscure jokes and in a minute they would speak to him. They always did, drunks and panhandlers, finding some soft fearfulness in his face which exposed him as a shrinking easy mark. Once in a railroad station he had been approached three times in twenty minutes by the same panhandler on his rounds. Each time he had given the man something, despising himself with each new weakness.

The cheerful pair sitting at right-angles to him grew louder and more blunt and the women within earshot grew glum. There was no harm in it; there never is. But you avoid your neighbour's eye, afraid of smiling awkwardly, or of looking offended and a prude.

'Now this Pearson,' said one of the revellers, 'he's just a little short-ass. He's just a little fellow without any brains. Why, some of the speeches he makes . . . I could make them myself. I'm an old Tory myself, an old Tory,'

'I'm an old Blue,' said the other.

'Is that so, now? That's fine, a fine thing.' Fred was sure he didn't know what a Blue was.

'I'm a Balliol man. Whoops!' They began to make monkey-like noises to annoy the passengers and amuse themselves. 'Whoops,' said the Oxford man again, 'hoo, hoo, there's one now, there's one for you.' He was talking about a girl on the sidewalk.

'She's a one, now, isn't she? Look at the legs on her, oh, look at them now, isn't that something?' There was a noisy clearing of throats and the same voice said something that sounded like 'Shaoil-na-baig.'

'Oh, good, good!' said the Balliol man.

'Shaoil-na-baig,' said the other loudly, 'I've not forgotten my Gaelic, do you see, shaoil-na-baig,' he said it loudly, and a woman up the aisle reddened and looked away. It sounded like a dirty phrase to Fred, delivered as though the speaker had forgotten all his Gaelic but the words for sexual intercourse.

'And how is your French, Father?' asked the Balliol man, and the title made Fred start in his seat. He pretended to drop a parcel and craned his head quickly sideways. The older of the two drunks, the one sitting by the window, examining the passing legs and skirts with the same impulse that Fred had felt on Saint Catherine Street, was indeed a priest, and couldn't possibly be an impostor. His clerical suit was too well-worn, egg-stained and blemished with candle-droppings, and fit its wearer too well, for it to be an assumed costume. The face was unmistakably a southern Irishman's. The priest darted a quick peek into Fred's eyes before he could turn them away, giving a monkey-like grimace that might have been a mixture of embarrassment and shame but probably wasn't.

He was a little grey-haired bucko of close to sixty, with a triangular sly mottled crimson face and uneven yellow teeth. His hands moved jerkily and expressively in his lap, in counterpoint to the lively intelligent movements of his face.

The other chap, the Balliol man, was a perfect type of English-speaking Montrealer, perhaps a bond salesman or minor functionary in a brokerage house on Saint James Street. He was about fifty with a round domed head, red hair beginning to go slightly white at the neck and ears, pink porcine skin, very neatly barbered and combed. He wore an expensive white shirt with a fine blue stripe and there was some sort of ring around his tie. He had his hands folded fatly on the knob of a stick, round face with deep laugh-lines in the cheeks, and a pair of cheerfully darting little blue-bloodshot eyes. Where could the pair have run into each other?

'I've forgotten my French years ago,' said the priest carelessly. 'I was down in New Brunswick for many years and I'd no use for it, the work I was doing. I'm Irish, you know.'

'I'm an old Blue.'

'That's right,' siad the priest, 'John's the boy. Oh, he's a sharp lad is John. He'll let them all get off, do you see, to Manitoba for the summer, and bang, BANG!' All the bus jumped. 'He'll call an election on them and then they'll run.' Something caught his eye and he turned to gaze out the window. The bus was moving slowly past the cemetery of Notre Dame des Neiges and the priest stared, half-sober, at the graves stretched up the mountainside in the sun.

'I'm not in there,' he said involuntarily.

'Indeed you're not,' said his companion, 'lot's of life in you yet, eh, Father?'

'Oh,' he said, 'oh, I don't think I'd know what to do with a girl if I fell over one.' He looked out at the cemetery for several moments. 'It's all a sham,' he said, half under his breath, 'they're in there for good.' He swung around and looked innocently at Fred. 'Are you going fishing, lad?'

'It's a kite that I bought for my little girl,' said Fred, more cheerfully than he felt.

'She'll enjoy that, she will,' said the priest, 'for it's grand sport.'

'Go fly a kite!' said the Oxford man hilariously. It amused him and he said it again. 'Go fly a kite!' He and the priest began to chant together, 'Hoo, hoo, whoops,' and they laughed and in a moment, clearly, would begin to sing.

The bus turned lumberingly onto Queen Mary Road. Fred stood up confusedly and began to push his way towards the rear door. As he turned away, the priest grinned impudently at him, stammering a jolly goodbye. Fred was too embarrassed to answer but he smiled uncertainly and fled. He heard them take up their chant anew.

'Hoo, there's a one for you, hoo. Shaoil-na-baig. Whoops!' Their laughter died out as the bus rolled heavily away.

He had heard about such men, naturally, and knew that they existed; but it was the first time in Fred's life that he had ever seen a priest misbehave himself publicly. There are so many priests in the city, he thought, that the number of bum ones must be in proportion. The explanation satisfied him but the incident left a disagreeable impression in his mind.

Safely home he took his shirt off and poured himself a Coke. Then he allowed Deedee, who was dancing around him with her terrible energy, to open the parcels.

'Give your Mummy the pad and pencil, sweetie,' he directed. She crossed obediently to Naomi's chair and handed her the cheap plastic case.

'Let me see you make a note in it,' he said, 'make a list of something, for God's sake, so you'll remember it's yours. And the one on the desk is mine. Got that?' He spoke without rancour or much interest; it was a rather overworked joke between them.

'What's this?' said Deedee, holding up the kite and allowing the ball of string to roll down the hall. He resisted a compulsive wish to get up and re-wind the string.

'It's for you. Don't you know what it is?'

'It's a red kite,' she said. She had wanted one for weeks but spoke now as if she weren't interested. Then all at once she grew very excited and eager. 'Can you put it together right now?' she begged.

'I think we'll wait till after supper, sweetheart,' he said, feeling mean. You raised their hopes and then dashed them; there was no real reason why they shouldn't put it together now, except his fatigue. He looked pleadingly at Naomi.

'Daddy's tired, Deedee,' she said obligingly, 'he's had a long hot afternoon.'

'But I want to see it,' said Deedee, fiddling with the flimsy red film and nearly puncturing it.

Fred was sorry he'd drunk a Coke; it bloated him and upset his stomach and had no true cooling effect.

'We'll have something to eat,' he said cajolingly, 'and then Mummy can put it together for you.' He turned to his wife. 'You don't mind, do you? I'd only spoil the thing.' Threading a needle or hanging a picture made the normal slight tremor of his hands accentuate itself almost embarrassingly.

'Of course not,' she said, smiling wryly. They had long ago worked out their areas of uselessness.

'There's a picture on it, and directions.'

'Yes. Well, we'll get it together somehow. Flying it . . . that's something else again.' She got up, holding the notepad, and went into the kitchen to put the supper on.

It was a good hot-weather supper, tossed greens with the correct proportions of vinegar and oil, croissants and butter, and cold sliced ham. As he ate, his spirits began to percolate a bit, and he gave Naomi a graphic sketch of the incident on the bus. 'It depressed me,' he told her. This came as no surprise to her; almost anything unusual, which he couldn't do anything to alter or relieve, depressed Fred nowadays. 'He must have been sixty. Oh, quite sixty, I should think, and you could tell that everything had come to pieces for him.'

'It's a standard story,' she said, 'and aren't you sentimentalizing it?'

'In what way?'

'The ''spoiled priest'' business, the empty man, the man without a calling. They all write about that. Graham Greene made his whole career out of that.'

'That isn't what the phrase means,' said Fred laboriously. 'It doesn't refer to a man who actually *is* a priest, though without a vocation.'

'No?' She lifted an eyebrow; she was better educated than he.

'No, it doesn't. It means somebody who never became a priest at all. The point is that you *had* a vocation but ignored it. That's what a spoiled priest is. It's an Irish phrase, and usually refers to somebody who is a failure and who drinks too much.' He laughed shortly. 'I don't qualify, on the second count.'

'You're not a failure.'

'No, I'm too young. Give me time!' There was no reason for him to talk like this; he was a very productive salesman.

'You certainly never wanted to be a priest,' she said positively, looking down at her breasts and laughing, thinking of some secret. 'I'll bet you never considered it, not with your habits.' She meant his bedroom habits, which were ardent, and in which she ardently acquiesced. She was an adept and enthusiastic partner, her greatest gift as a wife.

'Let's put that kite together,' said Deedee, getting up from her little table, with such adult decision that her parents chuckled. 'Come on,' she said, going to the sofa and bouncing up and down.

Naomi put a tear in the fabric right away, on account of the ambiguity of the directions. There should have been two holes in the kite, through which a lugging-string passed; but the holes hadn't been provided and when she put them there with the point of an icepick they immediately began to grow.

'Scotch tape,' she said, like a surgeon asking for sutures.

'There's a picture on the front,' said Fred, secretly cross but ostensibly helpful.

'I see it,' she said.

'Mummy puts holes in the kite,' said Deedee with alarm. 'Is she going to break it?'

'No,' said Fred. The directions were certainly ambiguous.

Naomi tied the struts at right-angles, using so much string that Fred was sure the kite would be too heavy. Then she strung the fabric on the notched ends of the struts and the thing began to take shape.

'It doesn't look quite right,' she said, puzzled and irritated.

'The surface has to be curved so there's a difference of air pressure.' He remembered this, rather unfairly, from high-school physics classes.

She bent the cross-piece and tied it in a bowed arc, and the red film pulled taut. 'There now,' she said.

'You've forgotten the lugging-string on the front,' said Fred critically, 'that's what you made the holes for, remember?'

'Why is Daddy mad?' said Deedee.

'I'M NOT MAD!'

It had begun to shower, great pear-shaped drops of rain falling with a plop on the sidewalk.

'That's as close as I can come,' said Naomi, staring at Fred, 'we aren't going to try it tonight, are we?'

'We promised her,' he said, 'and it's only a light rain.'

'Will we all go.'

'I wish you'd take her,' he said, 'because my stomach feels upset. I should never drink Coca-Cola.'

'It always bothers you. You should know that by now.'

'I'm not running out on you,' he said anxiously, 'and if you can't make it work, I'll take her up tomorrow afternoon.'

'I know,' she said, 'come on Deedee, we're going to take the kite up the hill.' They left the house and crossed the street. Fred watched them through the window as they started up the steep path hand in hand. He felt left out, and slightly nauseated.

They were back in half an hour, their spirits not at all dampened, which surprised him.

'No go, eh?'

'Much too wet, and not enough breeze. The rain knocks it flat.'

'O.K.!' he exclaimed with fervour. 'I'll try tomorrow.'

'We'll try again tomorrow,' said Deedee with equal determination— her parents mustn't forget their obligations.

Sunday afternoon the weather was nearly perfect, hot, clear, a firm steady breeze but not too much of it, and a cloudless sky. At two o'clock Fred took his daughter by the hand and they started up the mountain together, taking the path through the woods that led up to the University parking lots.

'We won't come down until we make it fly,' Fred swore, 'that's a promise.'

'Good,' she said, hanging on to his hand and letting him drag her up the steep path, 'there are lots of bugs in here, aren't there?'

'Yes,' he said briefly—he was being liberally bitten.

When they came to the end of the path, they saw that the campus was deserted and still, and there was all kinds of running room. Fred gave Deedee careful instructions about where to sit, and what to do if a car should come along, and then he paid out a little string and began to run across the parking lot towards the main building of the University. He felt a tug at the string and throwing a glance over his shoulder he saw the kite bobbing in the air, about twenty feet off the ground. He let out more string, trying to keep it filled with air, but he couldn't run quite fast enough, and in a moment it fell back to the ground.

'Nearly had it!' he shouted to Deedee, whom he'd left fifty yards behind.

'Daddy, Daddy, come back,' she hollered apprehensively. Rolling up the string as he went, he retraced his steps and prepared to try again. It was important to catch a gust of wind and run into it. On the second try the kite went higher than before but as he ran past the entrance to the University he felt the air pressure lapse and saw the kite waver and fall. He walked slowly back, realizing that the bulk of the main building was cutting off the air currents.

'We'll go up higher,' he told her, and she seized his hand and climbed obediently up the road beside him, around behind the main buiding, past ash barrels and trash heaps; they climbed a flight of wooden steps, crossed a parking lot next to L'Ecole Polytechnique and a slanting field further up, and at last came to a pebbly dirt road that ran along the top ridge of the mountain beside the cemetery. Fred remembered the priest as he looked across the fence and along the broad stretch of cemetery land rolling away down the slope of the mountain to the west. They were about six hundred feet above the river, he judged. He'd never been up this far before.

'My sturdy little brown legs are tired,' Deedee remarked, and he burst out laughing.

'Where did you hear that,' he said, 'who has sturdy little brown legs?'

She screwed her face up in a grin. 'The gingerbread man,' she said, beginning to sing, 'I can run away from you, I can, 'cause I'm the little gingerbread man.'

The air was dry and clear and without a trace of humidity and the sunshine was dazzling. On either side of the dirt road grew great clumps of wild flowers, yellow and blue, buttercups, daisies, and goldenrod, and cornflowers and clover. Deedee disappeared into the flowers—picking bouquets was her favourite game. He could see the shrubs and grasses heave and sway as she moved around. The scent of clover and of dry sweet grass was very keen here, and from the east, over the curved top of the mountain, the wind blew in a steady uneddying stream. Five or six miles off to the southwest he spied the wide intensely gray-white stripe of the river. He heard Deedee cry: 'Daddy, Daddy, come and look.' He pushed through the coarse grasses and found her.

'Berries,' she cried rapturously, 'look at all the berries! Can I eat them?' She had found a wild raspberry bush, a thing he hadn't seen since he was six years old. He'd never expected to find one growing in the middle of Montreal.

'Wild raspberries,' he said wonderingly, 'sure you can pick them dear; but be careful of the prickles.' They were all shades and degrees of ripeness from black to vermilion.

'Ouch,' said Deedee, pricking her fingers as she pulled off the berries. She put a handful in her mouth and looked wry.

'Are they bitter?'

'Juicy,' she mumbled with her mouth full. A trickle of dark juice ran down her chin.

'Eat some more,' he said, 'while I try the kite again.' She bent absorbedly to the task of hunting them out, and he walked down the road for some distance and then turned to run up towards her. This time he gave the kite plenty of string before he began to move; he ran as hard as he could, panting and handing the string out over his shoulders, burning his fingers as it slid through them. All at once he felt the line pull and pulse as if there were a living thing on the other end and he turned on his heel and watched while the kite danced into the upper air-currents above the treetops and began to soar up and up. He gave it more line and in an instant it pulled high up away from him across the fence, two hundred feet and more above him up over the cemetery where it steadied and hung, bright red in the sunshine. He thought flashingly of the priest saying 'It's all a sham,' and he knew all at once that the priest was wrong. Deedee came running down to him, laughing with excitement and pleasure and singing joyfully about the gingerbread man, and he knelt in the dusty roadway and put his arms around her, placing her hands on the line between his. They gazed, squinting in the sun, at the flying red thing, and he turned away and saw in the shadow of her cheek and on her lips and chin the dark rich red of the pulp and juice of the crushed raspberries.

TIMOTHY FINDLEY

b. 1930

Dinner Along the Amazon

For Robin Phillips

Perhaps the house was to blame. Once, it had been Olivia's pride; her safe, good place. Everyone else—including Michael—found it charming. Prestigious. Practical. North Seton Drive was a great location. Running out of Rosedale down towards the ravine, all its back yards were set with trees and rolling lawns. Autumn and spring, Olivia could happily walk or ride her bicycle to Branksome Hall, where she had been teaching now for six years. She really had no right to complain. Number 38 was handsome enough—its glass all shining; its paint unchipped.

Recently, however, Olivia had begun to balk at the physical act of arriving there; of being on the sidewalk and turning in towards the house, admitting that she belonged on that cement and was meant to walk through that front door. There was always something lying on the grass she would not allow was hers: a torn, wet *Star* or a bit of orange peel—(*I didn't put that there!*)—something left by a neighbour's child or someone else's dog. And even, once, a sinister pair of men's blue undershorts.

Inside, the house gave off the smell of discontent; of ashes in the sink and slippers prowling through the halls at night; of schisms rusting like a set of knives. Also the odour—faintly underarm—of Michael's petulance and Olivia's silence hiding in the closets. *Boo* . . . .

Today, on the twenty-eighth of April, Olivia entered the house with her arms full of flowers at five in the afternoon. The flowers were done up in green paper cones, but still the smell of them was rampant under her chin and she stood in the middle of the hall not speaking—only listening—dizzy with the scent of freesia.

Michael was in here somewhere. Up in the sun room, probably. Drunk.

Conrad's car was in the driveway, rubbing its already damaged bumper up against the garage. This could only signal they would both be drunk: not only Michael but Conrad, too. Old friends and empty bottles. Poor deadly Conrad, dragging the unwelcome past with all its frayed address books and stringy love affairs behind him, had come to 'visit for a while'—i.e. to crash until he'd pulled himself together. God damn old friends.

It could not be borne. There wasn't time for the past in their lives. Not now. Not ever. All it did was crowd you into corners and turn out the lights. Then it rattled you with guilt and regret and left you inarticulate and incapacitated. Who needs that? *I'm taking enough of a beating from the present, thank you very much;* Olivia thought. *Damn you, Conrad. Much as I love you, if you hadn't come, I could talk to Michael. Now. Tonight. I could tell him and get it over with.*

No I couldn't.

Olivia peered to her left, into the dim shuttered light of Michael's den. She tried to imagine the thing in her belly running through that doorway into those shadows to find its father. It was impossible. He would slam the door in its face. *Get out!*

She knew this was only a coward's excuse. Michael didn't hate children: he hated the future—and that was different. He hated anything he couldn't control: he hated anything he didn't know. Certainty was the only ally you could trust, in Michael's books. Certainty and literature. History—(maybe)—and a few poems written on the backs of envelopes. He *wanted* children, but he didn't want their lives to run beyond his own. He couldn't bear to inject them into the future—only into the past. Michael would like it best if his children had preceded him. Then he could say to them; 'Everything I told you was the truth. I have never lied. It is all borne out by what you have seen: the known—the safe.' The future was his enemy.

In Michael's den, there were piles and piles of notebooks and reams of paper. These were his diatribes—some of them four or six or ten years old. They were covered with marmalade fungi and peanut butter mushrooms. Olivia smiled. The rug was stained with his solipsisms. She had listened to him roaring there, amongst his books—knocking over his drinks—jabbing his fingers at her: 'Just you wait, Olivia! Every word I say is true. . . . ' Then he would have to verify every word—dragging down all the pertinent books, drawing out all the pertinent pieces of paper, going crazy—ranting—when he couldn't find what he wanted. In its way, it was a sad, dead room. Echoes hiding in the curtains. The roll-top desk had pigeon holes that smelled, Olivia swore, of pigeons: all the pigeons flown away with their messages—the words that Michael couldn't find. In a bowl, he kept all his paper clips attached to rubber bands—ready to fire at the passing parade or at any rash intruder who brought the future into his presence: man, woman or child . . .

No. There could be no child.

Olivia turned towards the kitchen, leaning her ear in the direction of the stairwell, hoping to hear the sound of sober conversation. Even of laughter. But there was nothing. Only the silence between drinks. Up there, sitting in the sun room, they were probably holding their breath: Michael and Conrad, hiding from Olivia. *Don't give away our secret, Connie.* Mustn't let her know we're only ten years old, when she thinks we're twelve, at least.

Olivia took a deep breath that left her gasping for another.

It *was* the house: its airlessness; its *culs-de-sac;* its bear pits waiting for the bears. It had lost its capacity to generate dreams. All it reflected, as you moved from room to room, was the tidy horror of what was really going to happen.

As Olivia entered the kitchen, the sun room made a creaking noise above her head. She looked up, thinking; *they're walking on tiptoe. How ridiculous. Two grown men . . .*

She crossed to the sink, making sure her heels could be heard as she went. Still clothed in all her outer garments, her tweed coat; her three layers of scarves; her soft, rich sweater; her wool lined boots—she set her briefcase on one cutting board and the packets of flowers on the other. She turned on the tap for a glass of water and reached to the left for a thick, red tumbler with a crack in it. Habit. It was always there, the last of its kind. There had once been eight—a gift from Conrad. Pinned to the curtain above the sink was one of Mrs Kemp's inimitable notes:

Mrs Penny I done the back room up for Mr Fastbinder and put a towel and a wash cloth on his burow. You run out of blue sheets so he only got one and the other ones yellow. Grennel is loss again. Hiden.

Olivia, reading, was holding the tumbler under the tap.

I could not find no more OLD DUTCH so have put down OLD DUTCH on the list. 4 large ones please as the bathroom really eats them up. Mr Fastbinder near creamed the garge. Dont let them tell you different. I will be in tomorrow to clean up after.

Lilah Kemp.

The cold water ran on Olivia's hands, comforting, numbing.

Ps Prof Penny did not eat his sandwhich. Toona if you want one.

All the usual digs at Michael were intact. Mortal enemies—Michael Penny and Mrs Kemp. And Grendel. Grendel was Michael's beloved dog and, like his master, he always hid from Mrs Kemp and her dreaded vacuum cleaner and her dreadful tuna sandwiches, the edges of which she always left in Grendel's dish.

Olivia set aside the tumbler and took down the note, threw it into the garbage pail and replaced the pin in the folds of the curtain. As she drank her water, she wondered where the dog might be this time. Lying poisoned, perhaps, in someone's flower bed—the victim of Mrs Kemp's 'toona'. The detritus of neglect. Poor old Grendel.

Poor old Grendel had a habit of lying dead in other people's flowerbeds, but his favourite place of all was in behind the curtain of the shower stall, where he portrayed with alarming veracity the corpses of his master and his mistress—one and then the other. Michael and Olivia, dead.

Olivia's hand went down to rest on her belly and the red tumbler, in the other hand, shook. *Michael first and then Olivia—dead.* I am not a murderer. Not. I am doing what is right. The only right thing: the only possible thing.

She began to cry—*(oh why am I crying?)*—her gaze shifting sideways, awash—*(please: it's so shaming)*—towards the flowers—*(and stupid: stop)*. What had the flowers been for, she wondered, setting the tumbler aside. To get her past the front door without throwing up? Not that. No. She could tolerate the tension one more week—so what had the flowers been for? Perhaps, she decided, they were for Grendel, always 'dying'. Or for Michael, still alive. Or for the undug grave in her belly. Pick a card—any card. Now put it back in the deck. Just don't tell me which card it was . . . .

'Hallo.'

Olivia grabbed the sink and nearly fell before she turned.

Standing in the doorway was a man she had never seen before. A man—a 'boy'. He was in his early twenties.

'Yes?' she said.

His arms were full of brown paper packages.

'Who are you?' he said, with casual, inbred impertinence.

Olivia was flabbergasted. 'I'm . . . Olivia Penny,' she said. *And this is my house*, she almost added. But didn't.

'Are you Professor Penny's sister, then?' The young man barged completely into the kitchen. The brown paper packages were clinking suspiciously like future toasts, and the young man was trying not to spill them before they could be proposed.

'No, I am not Professor Penny's God damn sister. I am Professor Penny's God damn wife,' said Olivia, stepping aside to avoid being trampled. 'And who the hell are you?'

'I'm with Conrad,' the young man said. He laid his loot—eight bottles of wine, four bottles of scotch—beside and on top of the flowers and turned to smile at Olivia. 'You're a scream,' he said, and put out his hand. 'Conrad didn't tell me you were *funny*,' he added. 'I'm Rodney Farquhar.' (His grip was like the proverbial vise.) 'Or should I say I'm Conrad's God damn lover?'

'Why are you here?' said Olivia.

Rodney Farquhar's face was emptied of all expression. Perhaps he didn't know the answer to the question.

'You've just set all your things on top of my flowers,' Olivia continued. 'Would you please find some other place?'

Rodney moved in on the bottles and began to shift them, two by two, onto the kitchen table.

'Why are you here?' Olivia repeated.

'I was sent to get the booze,' he said. 'I've just come back. . . .'

' I can see that. Booze for what?'

'For the party,' said Rodney. His back was to her.

Party?

'What party?' said Olivia. Her eyes had narrowed. Her blood was rising.

'Conrad's party,' said Rodney.

'Conrad is giving a party? Where?'

'Here, of course.'

Olivia ground her teeth and was speechless for a moment. Then she said, 'Am I invited?'

Conrad was lying in the bath. The bathroom was full of steam and the steam was scented with Conrad's favourite cologne: *Chanel 19*. Michael was seated on the toilet, the lid down—its grey fur cover slightly damp beneath him. Conrad could barely be seen in the fog.

'Aren't you going to boil yourself to death in there?' Michael asked.

'Never,' said Conrad. 'The heat is wonderful. It spreads the alcohol faster through the system. Give me another . . . .'

Conrad's hand, with goblet, appeared from the steam.

Michael poured more scotch and the hand withdrew and then Michael poured more sctoch into his own Waterford goblet and took a great, raw mouthful; 'ahhhh . . . ' He set the goblet on the floor, fingering its cut design. 'Always drink the best from the best,' he said. 'So, who have you invited?'

'Fabiana Holbach,' said Conrad.

'Yes. And who else?'

'Who cares who else? Fabiana Holbach. That's all that matters.'

'So I gather,' Michael sighed. He lighted a damp cigarette, with a damp recalcitrant match. 'Are you sure this is really a good idea? Inviting Fabiana after all these years?'

'All these years number precisely three,' said Conrad. 'Give me a cigarette.'

Michael handed over the one already lit and lighted another.

'You realize, of course,' he said, 'she's married, now.'

'People can always be convinced their current marriages don't work,' said Conrad.

Michael muttered 'yes' and 'amen' to this, but not loud enough for Conrad to hear.

'What's her name, now?' said Conrad.

'Mrs Jackman Powell.'

The bath fell silent. Not a ripple.

'You don't approve, I take it,' said Michael.

'It's neither here nor there,' said Conrad. 'Truth is, I always thought that *Jackman* had to be the most pretentious name a man could have. Isn't his brother's name plain old Tom?'

'Yes.'

'Maybe their mother's name was Jackman.'

'No. Their mother's name was Tompkins.'

Conrad laughed. Then sobered. 'Son-of-a-bitch,' he said. 'So she married Jackman Powell.'

'That's right.' Michael was watching all he could see of Conrad—the arm that lay along the rim of the tub; the shape of the neck; the thrust of the head as it bent to the glass to drink; above all, the tension in the hand that held the cigarette so hard against the tub, the cigarette broke and the lighted end of it fell to the floor. Conrad didn't even notice. All he did was mutter: 'sons-of-bitches.'

'Who?'

'All of them,' Conrad said with a kind of vehemence Michael had never heard from his friend before. 'All of the God damn Powells. God damn sons-of-bitches.' Conrad sat disconsolate, still barely visible.

What, Michael wondered, could have happened to Conrad—usually so resilient and now, apparently, defeated by the mention of a mere name. They had spent all their school days laughing. Not that a person could go on laughing forever. Michael was perfectly aware of this and of the darker things that had affected Conrad's life. But this was something new; unknown. As if the laughter had escaped and Conrad could not locate it.

'I suppose,' Conrad said, 'this means Fabiana will actually bring him with her. Jackman. I suppose this means I'll have to face him . . . stand there and actually shake his God damn hand.'

'I suppose so. Does it matter?'

'Yes. It matters.'

'Why?'

'Won't go into it. Later, maybe. After they've gone. Not now. The son-of-a-bitch . . . .'

'You've said that. Several times.'

'I know I have. Leave me alone.'

'You know I can't leave you alone, Con . . . .' (Michael was using a swishy, sibilant voice—the one he always used to tease Conrad.) 'I adore you.'

'Don't,' said Conrad. 'This isn't funny.'

'I'm sorry.' Michael lighted another cigarette and handed it through the mist to Conrad. Ever since Conrad's father had died, three years ago, there were things you couldn't talk about. Not always having to do with Fastbinder senior (whose name had been Karl). Sometimes with mysteries Michael wasn't privy to. The causes of Conrad's silence: the long sojourn abroad in Italy and Spain; his sudden reappearance; Rodney Farquhar; Fabiana Holbach Powell. . . . God knew, any or all of these things could and should be the centres of conversation. But, more often than not, they were the cause of snapping jaws and bitten tongues.

'Change the subject,' said Conrad. 'Help me understand what's wrong between you and Olivia. Give me something to laugh about.'

'You think we're going to laugh about *that*? said Michael.

'Maybe,' said Conrad. 'Is there another woman?'

'No,' said Michael. 'I wish there was.'

'What do you mean? Is there someone you love?'

'Yes.'

'Someone you can't have?'

'Yes. I suppose you could put it that way.'

'Who?'

'Olivia.'

'Oh.' Conrad drank from his glass and took a drag from his cigarette. 'Have you ever seriously thought of falling in love with me?' he said.

'I wouldn't know how to behave in bed,' said Michael, trying to be funny: failing. 'What *do* you do with Rodney?'

'I admire him, dear,' said Conrad. 'He adores it. I tell him he has the most beautiful pudendum known to man or boy. A palpable lie of course. But Rodney believes it. Sometimes I pull it for him.'

'Don't be so God damn crude. That's disgusting.'

'Well—you asked.'

'It's so childish.'

'Precisely. And Rodney is a child.'

'And you? What do you get out of all this?'

'Notoriety. Open doors. Rodney's connections are quite spectacular, you know.'

'But you don't need open doors, Con. Every door is open to you.'

Conrad was silent. Then he said: '*was.*'

'You mean to tell me you've taken up with that young man just to get through a few doors? It's grotesque.'

'How the hell else am I supposed to get through? Who else would take me? I'm a forty-year-old faggot without a cent to my name.'

'That's only temporary, Con.'

'You're damn right it is. Any minute now, I'm going to be a forty-*one*-year-old faggot without a cent to my name. And stop laughing! Rodney's getting restless. The young always do. They wake up one morning and they *see* you. That's why I always insist on separate rooms. Never let your lover see you, Michael. It's death.' Conrad held out his goblet. 'If anyone turns up here tonight, it's only going to be because Rodney Farquhar asked them. I may be the attraction—but it's Rodney's circus.'

Michael said, 'That's ridiculous' and poured more scotch.

'It's not ridiculous. Alas,' said Conrad, lying back in the bath. 'I overheard him on the phone. "*Do come and see old Conrad again. He's so amusing. Tells such wonderfully funny stories. Even gets drunk and falls down . . . but never loses consciousness. I tell you, it's a scream. He once had a whole conversation with the Princess of Rheims lying flat on his back in the middle of the floor. The whole room flocked to him. People were actually introduced while he lay there. The footmen brought him drinks and got on their knees to serve him.*" I heard him, Michael. He could sell tickets. But I can't. I'm the one they all come to see, lying down on the rug. You do have a rug, I hope.'

Michael could see Conrad, now. The steam was beginning to dissipate. His skin was alarmingly pale; his arms and shoulders lacked entirely the tension of muscles; his neck was like a girl's, stretching to hold the tremulous chin in place and the large, round head with its dank, stringy hair seemed unable to contain his skull which pushed against the skin like a swollen melon about to burst. His hands were almost ridiculously fine; waxen, beautifully shaped and manicured . . . .

'Please stop staring,' said Conrad. 'Tell me about Olivia.'

Michael did not say all of this that follows. He only said the parts he could articulate. The rest—the precision and the syntax—were in his mind, but silent under a cloud of scotch and daydreams. Downstairs, he could hear Olivia setting the table in the dining room—telling Rodney she didn't have anything that matched by way of crystal and china—all because Mrs Kemp had her own definition of the word 'set': '*break eight and leave four. . . .*' Rodney could also be heard on the telephone, ordering food from Fenton's. Grendel was found in the hall closet and came up the stairs to lie outside the bathroom door.

Michael said: 'When you said you always insisted on separate rooms, I understood. Our bed—Olivia's and mine—is divided down the middle by the Grand Canyon. We might as well live in separate hotels.'

Conrad glanced at Michael, huge and majestic, just a shape in the steam: backlit—hovering on the toilet seat—holding both the bottle and his goblet—his head turned sideways, looking for the words. Michael was six foot four and he had a club foot that no one ever talked about. It affected his walk, of course, but not outrageously and on the occasions when it pained him, he would remove the boot and rest the foot on a table or a chair. He was resting it now on the edge of the tub.

She's gone away somewhere, Con: gone without going, of course.

Conrad waved his hand in the soapy water, watching it vanish.

Now what am I? A sort of bachelor, living in her house; always on the periphery of Olivia's life. 'Goodbye, Michael.' 'Goodbye, Olivia.' 'I'm going to the other end of the sofa, now.' Gone. Like that.

I saw a movie once. One of those 'Nature of Things' on the CBC. It was a film about some tribe in Borneo. One of those primitive tribes—still living almost a prehistoric existence. Ceremonial killings. Sexual segregation. Ritual circumcision. Unbelievable savagery. The way they treated one another—slaughtered their animals—slaughtered their enemies. Three things stood out: three I will never forget. One was the pig thing.

The women with children lived in special houses—groups of women and children—until the children grew to be a certain age. And they had these pigs, you see, as pets. The women and the babies and pigs all lived together and, the way it was shown, they seemed to be quite happy. Then the men would decide it was time to have a nice feast of pork and they would come and drag away the pigs and they would kill them. The wom-

en's pets, you see. The children's pets. But it was only the men who got
to eat them. Pork was supposed to induce some special kind of magic. So
off they went—the men—to their bachelors' quarters where they'd roast
these pigs and sit around having magic dreams.

Another thing was the women killing their babies. But only their boy
babies. Only their boys. But it wasn't always . . . I mean, they didn't
necessarily kill every boy.

What you have to know is, the women did all the work. The only thing
they didn't do was hunt. But everything else was left up to them and they
had to do it all with their babies on their backs and their children dragging along behind them. You could see it must drive them mad; all these
children and all this work and, all of a sudden, there would be this
moment when one of them would take off down to the river. Where she
would drown her baby son. Not quite dispassionately—certainly with
anger—but suddenly: coldly—methodically—without remorse. It was
awful. You knew it was revenge for how the men had made them live and
for what the men had done to their pigs.

And then there was this other thing—the third thing I remember.

This is about the bachelors. Even the husbands were 'bachelors'. And
they moved in and out of the women's lives—mating with them—not
'making love' but truly mating, animal style. And stealing their pigs and
watching the women—always from a distance. There were these huts—
retreats—high up in the mountains where the bachelors went. Also,
there were these compounds where the growing boys were kept. Not just
kept with the men—but, really, kept apart from the women. And this was
some kind of privilege. Different, you see, from the dowdy huts and the
little, crowded farmyards where the women lived with all the pigs and
babies. The men and boys had contests. They played games and laughed.
They created a culture of male totems . . .

'Why?' said Conrad.

'Fear,' said Michael.

That was the basis of it. Fear. Partly disgust and a sort of mystical
distrust of the women because of menstruation. But also a childlike fear
of the power of women to give birth. And this fear was real and so tacit
that, even though the men had segregated the women—even though they
had succeeded in debasing them and disinheriting them, the women
taunted the men. And they got away with it. They stood on the hillsides
in groups and they laughed at the men in the compounds and they dared
the boys to come out and have sexual intercourse. Dared them with all
kinds of lewd, graphic gestures and always laughing. And, of course,
the boys wouldn't go. They were afraid. They backed off. They hid. Or
else, they came outside the compound in an army and they'd kill the

pigs. Sometimes, too, they made war on their neighbours. Anything, rather than go to the women.

'Are you sure it was really the women they were afraid of?'

Michael did not answer this.

Conrad pulled the plug and the water began to surge toward the drain. He lay back watching it ebbing, revealing his pallid, hairless body.

'Anyhow, that's how I see myself now,' Michael said. 'A kind of ritual bachelor, living in retreat. Taunted from the hillsides. Being watched and listened to. But silently . . .'

'What about her pigs?'

Michael thought of the yelling matches and the slamming doors and the undone, promised things. He also thought of the silence with which Olivia seemed to be rebuking him. 'I guess I've killed a few,' he said. 'But I haven't had the benefit of any God damn magic dreams.'

The last of the water drew away with a great, loud sucking noise and was gone. Conrad lay there in the empty tub, with his goblet in his hand and his toes sticking up.

After a moment, he spoke and he said, 'This is how they found my father. Just exactly three years ago. The twenty-ninth of April. With his wrists slashed.'

'Today's the twenty-eighth,' said Michael.

Outside the bathroom door, Grendel threw up the remnants of Mrs Kemp's toona sandwich. It was now 6:45. The guests would arrive at eight and still no one knew—but Rodney—who they would be.

'Conrad wants an egg.'

'But we're going to eat in an hour-and-a-half.'

'I don't think he wants it to eat,' said Michael.

'He's going to throw it at someone, is that it?' Olivia was undoing the boxes from Fenton's and setting the contents in bowls and souffle dishes. Rodney was arranging her flowers in crystal vases on the cutting board.

'All I know is, he wants an egg.'

'He wants it to lift his face with,' said Rodney. 'If you have a pastry brush, you'd better send that up, too. And a nice little dish to separate the egg in.'

'Has he been doing this long?' Michael asked.

'About a year,' said Rodney. 'And only at parties. It makes him look Chinese.'

'All we need,' said Michael. 'The Empress of China.'

They arrived in the first warm rain.

There was a girl whose name was Louellen Potts who had once been one of Michael's students. She was now out taking care of other people's children in a daycare centre, wasting her talents as a first rate critic. She had come, this evening, ostensibly as Rodney's 'date'—but she seemed to have an ulterior motive: at least, in Michael's view. She was one of those dreadful women who hound you with their beauty while they beat you with their mind. Michael cringed from the thought of what lay ahead: Louellen attempting to best him at every turn in the conversation, opening one and then two more buttons of her blouse and thrusting her breasts into the lamplight. If only she were less attractive, he could be sure of winning.

Olivia rather liked Louellen Potts. She was one of perhaps six students both she and Michael had encountered in the classroom and the lecture hall over the years. What Olivia instilled from *Heart of Darkness*, Michael destroyed with *Frankenstein*. Kurtz and the Monster, walking hand in hand: *that* was the future, according to Michael.

When Fabiana Holbach Powell arrived, she was not with her husband, but her husband's brother Tom and Tom's wife Betty. Fabiana's husband, Jackman, was enigmatically 'abroad'. The word 'abroad' was delivered by Tom, while Fabiana looked the other way.

They had drunk for half-an-hour, waiting for Conrad to come downstairs. Michael put on some passable tapes (acceptable to everyone, that is, except Louellen) and the atmosphere was actually bearable. Under the influence of Cleo Laine, things loosened up a bit. The sailing voice cut through the dreadful, early chit-chat and very soon people were asking freely for 'another scotch' or another glass of white wine. If only Louellen would stop exposing herself, life might be endurable.

Tom Powell was a cold-eyed blond who had just come back from Nassau. He had one of those infuriating tans and an even more infuriating physique. He didn't say much. The eyes said it all. They never left Fabiana, unless they were turned on Michael (perhaps *'through'* Michael would be more accurate) during the course of such questions as: 'When was the last time we saw you?' and statements, such as the patently ridiculous: 'You're looking well, Mike.'

Betty Powell just sat on the sofa and rummaged in her pocket book for something she never found.

Fabiana, on the other hand, was radiant—as always. She carried with her—just as she had as a child—that wonderful and wondrous sense of someone always on the verge of imparting the secret of life, if only she could remember the wording. Her gaze would drift away towards the answer—beautiful and oddly heartbreaking—only to return yet again with the words; 'no—that's not it . . . ' implicit in the wounded, blue confusion of her eyes. She had once been kidnapped and the ransom had been a million dollars. Lucien Holbach, her father, had refused to pay it—even though he had sixty millions and his wife twenty millions more. Fabiana had escaped, unharmed.

Or had she? Michael wondered.

At any rate, she had escaped and, shortly thereafter, she had been married to Jackman Powell—who was currently 'abroad'. She claimed to have never seen her captors, having been forced to wear a blindfold the whole time. It was when, after hours of silence, she had discovered she was standing in the middle of an empty house that she made her escape. All of this had happened in Jamaica: a place to which Fabiana had never returned.

Years and years and years ago—when they were children—Conrad Fastbinder had fallen in love with Fabiana Holbach and, for a while—in later years, before the kidnap, it seemed that Fabiana might return his love. But three things had happened in rapid succession, dashing all those hopes forever: until now. Fastbinder's father had died, leaving him penniless: Fabiana had been kidnapped and Jackman Powell—('that son-of-a-bitch!')—had married her.

Tonight, through some fortuitous twist of fate, she had turned up in Michael and Olivia Penny's living room without her husband—and only her brother-in-law ('that other son-of-a-bitch!') to watch over her.

Conrad waited for Cleo to begin singing '*Traces*' before he made his entrance.

'*A faded photograph,*
Covered, now, with lines and creases . . .'

Fabiana claimed not to recognize him.

Michael, never having seen his friend in lacquer before, tended to agree with Fabiana. Conrad, decked out in summer whites and with his hair plastered back, looked like someone trying to escape from a Somerset Maugham short story. His tie was a florid pink (admittedly, in fashion, if you glanced at the right magazines) and he reeked of Chanel 19. As for the face—it was true. Conrad Fastbinder had descended from the upper reaches in a Chinese mask.

The trouble was, he couldn't speak—whether because of all the scotch he had drunk in the afternoon, or because of the strictures of his 'facelift' or, perhaps, because of both. As a consequence, he merely bowed over Fabiana's hand, and kissed it—after which, they all went in to dinner.

Michael sat at the head of the table, leaning back in his chair. He was turned to one side in order to accommodate his foot which increasingly troubled him as the evening wore on. He watched his guests—or rather, Conrad's guests, through a haze of pain and liquor.

Far off, he could just make out Olivia seated at the other end of the table. She was smiling—oh rare event—and, though the smile was somewhat fixed, it appeared to be genuine. What could she be smiling about? Michael regretted he had not begun to count as soon as the smile had turned up—just to see how long it would stay. It was rather like a visitor: another guest at the table: a stranger. He should keep a little book, like Hamlet: 'My tables—meet it is, I set it down . . . Olivia smiled today for twenty seconds.'

Why?

Michael looked around the table.

See who's here; he thought. All the bachelors. This is a bachelors' dinner. Rodney, Conrad, me. And Tom Powell—*he's* a bachelor. So's his wife. Look at them! I bet they touch each other with tongs. Or perhaps they wear gloves. Louellen Potts is a bachelor. (Damn it.) So is Fabiana.

So is Olivia.

Every damn one of us, living alone.

Here we are on the hillside—having killed the pig—and about to fall beneath the spell of the magic dream, perhaps.

Louellen Potts was sitting beside him: green eyed and green in tailored tweed. Breathtaking: youthful. Budding. Hair that falls—every hair in place and smelling of skin and flesh, no perfumes, only air and apples and sitting with one hand near his own, turned up—so innocent—or was that innocence? Maybe it was disdain. Knowing the harmless impotence of pockmarked hosts in their cups . . .

Not pockmarked. No. Do not go cruel into that good face. Be kinder. Kinder to yourself. Be kind.

Then, on the other side of the table, next to that blazered booby—Rodney Farquhar, pal and pudendum to the fallen Conrad—there was someone weeping.

Fabiana.

Was it true? Was she weeping?

Tom had told the tale at dinner—the dinner just finished, the one whose little bones were scattered under the grape seeds even now mounting on the plates as the bachelors lingered over their wine.

Tom, without saying so, had made it clear that Fabiana was waiting for a divorce. Her husband, his brother Jackman, had disappeared. He was a civil engineer—or something—and, though Fabiana's lawyers (working, of course for *him*) had told her he had 'left her' and had gone somewhere, they would not say where. Not precisely. Only 'into the

Amazon region.' That was all. That was how they had put it to her: 'Jackman has gone'—into roughly speaking one million square green miles of rain forest. Now, he had been gone eight months and the lawyers had said, 'he is probably not coming back.'

So she could not get a divorce. She could only wait the mandatory seven years, after which she could declare herself a widow. Not that Jackman would be dead. He had gone there with her money. It was the money that was dead.

There was more, of course. Money. Enough for Conrad to cultivate, if he'd only take that egg off his face.

Michael watched Fabiana.

Just as Olivia's badge was neatness, Fabiana's badge was a restless wrist—her left—which she constantly massaged with her right hand, adjusting her watch and her bracelets and her bones, while the wrist turned slowly, this way and that. She also never looked at whoever was speaking, but set her eyes on those who were listening, watching perhaps for some clue as to the importance and meaning of what was being said. Now, it was Olivia who was speaking and Fabiana was watching Betty Powell, her sister-in-law. Betty Powell was cutting up an apple with a knife and there was blood on her napkin, of which she seemed to be entirely unaware.

Olivia was still smiling.

The subject under discussion had been famous mistresses and who had performed that function best in history. Olivia had just said something startling and amusing and even Michael was laughing.

Olivia had suggested that Antinous, the beloved of the Emperor Hadrian, had been the world's greatest mistress.

'Why?' Louellen Potts had asked.

'Because,' Olivia had answered, 'he couldn't bear children.'

'Do you mean he couldn't stand them?' Betty asked. 'Or just that he couldn't have them . . . '

She was ignored.

It was then that disaster struck, as it will out of silence.

Thinking he spoke in a confidential tone, and being quite drunk, Conrad turned towards Michael and reached out his hand as if to emphasize his words. As a result of the gesture, he knocked over Betty Powell's glass. Wine and blood and an apple core.

But that was not the disaster. The disaster was in what he said.

What he said was, 'There's your answer, Michael. You and Olivia should have a baby.'

Michael said; 'Thanks for the advice and shut up.'

Conrad said; 'Oh, I see . . .' and he laughed. 'You're afraid Olivia will kill it.'

For a moment, there was only the sound of dripping wine and of someone breathing and then Louellen Potts turned down the table in Conrad's direction and said, 'Do you think that's funny, Mr Fastbinder? Do you really think that's funny?' Then she turned to Michael and she said, 'Why don't you hit him? If I were you, I'd hit him.'

'You are not me, Miss Potts,' said Michael. He was looking at Olivia, who looked away.

Now, Louellen turned to her and she said, 'Mrs Penny? Don't you want to be defended?'

Olivia didn't answer her. She was looking at her napkin.

'Really, Professor Penny,' Louellen said—still standing—'I think it is outrageous. And if you won't hit him, I will!'

'Sit down, Potts.' (Michael)

'I will not sit down! This appalling man has just said the most appalling thing about your wife and . . .'

'SIT DOWN!'

'Michael . . .' This was Olivia. 'Leave her alone.'

'I beg your pardon,' said Michael, alarmed, his voice rising. 'I beg your bloody pardon?'

'You heard her,' said Louellen—somewhat tipsy herself. 'She says you're to leave me alone.'

Michael said, 'You condescending green-eyed bitch!'

'Michael!' said Olivia.

'Don't you "Michael" me—you down there in the dark! What the hell right has she to put herself in my shoes?'

'She's only expressing her feelings, Michael. And whether or not they're valid, she has a right to express them.'

'Not at my table, she hasn't!'

'This is our table, Michael. Not your table. Ours.' Olivia did not even raise her voice.

Michael snapped. 'Well she's sitting at my end!'

And Louellen said, with great vehemence, '*Standing!*'

And suddenly, everyone was laughing. Everyone, that is, except the Powells. They did not seem to know what to do in the presence of laughter.

Louellen Potts sat down and there was then a second, but minor disaster. Her hand had fallen onto the table rather near Michael's. And now, unthinking, Michael took it—merely as a gesture of forgiveness. Except that he did not let go.

Louellen looked at the table, not quite focusing on her upturned fingers resting under Michael's hand. Her main awareness was of Olivia's eyes.

Michael felt the reverberation and he, too, became aware of Olivia's eyes. He turned his hand away slowly and withdrew it all the way back to his head, where he pushed back his hair.

'Conrad,' he said.

'Yes, sir,' said Conrad.

'Tell us about the time you got lost in that hotel and ended up in Princess Diana's bedroom.'

In the living room, Conrad was lying on the rug, smoking a cigarette and staring at the ceiling. Michael, limping as unobtrusively as possible, was going about the room and bestowing second brandies into upheld glasses, including Conrad's.

Beyond them, the dining room glowed in the flickering light of its guttering candles. The table was an ordered ruin, with its eight distinct place settings, each distinctly destroyed by a separate pair of hands; the eight plates marred with the elegant parings of apples and cheese and pears; the wine glasses emptied to an exact degree, each one a signature; and the napkins, folded or thrown down and the chairs pushed back, reflective or violent or simply dispensed with—and the low, silver bowl of freesia, the flowers drooping as if they had been assaulted—and the mirrors that reflected mirrors that reflected mirrors—each one holding its perfect image a further remove, like sign posts down a road that led into darkness.

Rodney was playing the piano.

Otherwise—silence.

Olivia returned from the hallway, having opened the front door to let in some air. Outside, there was a spring rain and the strong smell of budding. She picked up her glass—allowed Michael to fill it—touched him with her pensiveness as he passed—and leaned against the door jamb, neither here nor there.

It was warm—and Fabiana's wrist was moving.

Slowly—it was imperceptible at first—as if a butterfly had entered the room and caught their attention only by degrees—Fabiana began to talk. She began in the middle of some interior monologue that perhaps had occupied her for some time—which yet seemed pertinent to the monologue of each of the others; one long sentence describing their mutual apprehension, whether it be about the past or the present or the future; arising out of that common literature which is the mind, peopled with common characters, moving over a common landscape, like a book they had all read—from which now one of their voices began to quote aloud:

'. . . I know he went there without me in order to escape me. And yet I never bothered or pursued him. I was always standing still, it seems. I hadn't wanted him at first; but only let myself be wanted. The way a dog will let itself be wanted, not understanding why, except that out of being wanted—wanting comes. And out of being chosen—choosing. And out of being longed for—longing. Con knows. I never gave my loving. Never trusted myself to give. Never let it happen. I was always the little sister—sitting in the front seat, watching in the mirror. Until I met him—Jackman Powell. He was like a drug you take at a party, for fun. And then you wonder what it was. And then you ask for more. And then you realize you're hooked. And you never stop to think they've hooked you on purpose. You only think what a lovely feeling it is—and all you want is more. Until one day, they refuse. *There isn't any more.* Or worse, *there is—but I'm not going to let you have it.* And then they hold it up—they keep on holding it up where you can see it—and saying to you: *no; no more, Fabiana. Never any more.* And then they shoot it into the air, they waste it before your eyes. And they walk away—and they leave you with this empty syringe—and nothing to fill it with. And nothing to fill your veins with. And they haven't told you what it was—so you don't know how to ask for more. Because it was unique; it was *theirs*—they grew it, manufactured it or conjured it out of the air. And then they get on a boat and they don't even wave good-bye. And they're gone. And then you get a message—telling you they've disappeared forever.'

Nobody watched her while she finished.

Instead, they each one welcomed the anaesthetic that prevented, if only for the moment, the idea that hope itself— anticipation—had disappeared for all of them into the Amazon region along with Jackman Powell.

Michael looked with a dreadful panic at Olivia.

Louellen Potts—the briefest of his dreams—got up to leave the room.

'It's time to go,' she whispered, having lost her voice in Fabiana's recitation. 'Late,' she said. And went upstairs to collect her coat.

3:00 a.m. and Grendel made a tour of the house, making his presence known to all the mice and to all the ghosts who haunted the dark, including the dark at the edge of everyone's dreams. Finally, he settled at the foot of the stairs, intermittently waking to stare out the open door through the screen at the sidewalks sparkling with rain—and to listen to the droning in the den, which to Grendel was like a cave, inhabited by bears or perhaps by giant, cave-dwelling birds whose wings were lifted in constant repetition, casting their immense shadows across the floor towards his paws. Michael's curtains. He eyed them with a careful wariness. He never completely slept. When there was thunder, the piano would echo its dying reverberations and the cello, in its corner, would hum a low, solemn note. The crystal prisms that hung from the candlesticks also sang and the dying fire in the grate made another song and the floorboards creaked in the faraway sun room and the windows sighed all over the house.

His ears hurt—chewed in a week-old battle—and his gums were tender, having been torn. All along his back, he ached. No position was comfortable.

Everyone had gone upstairs—and he was alone. All the food—anything of real interest—was locked away. Except . . .

One bone, he remembered—put down by Michael under the kitchen table.

Grendel got up and fetched the bone and brought it back to the foot of the stairs. All through the next hour, he held it tenderly between his paws and wrecked it—very slowly—with his chipped and broken teeth.

The sound of gnawing—bone against bone—was all that could be heard. That, and the sluicing of the rain. And Olivia's voice, as she lay in the bed with her gaze on the patterns running down the walls.

'Michael . . . ?'

She was smiling.

Far in the Amazon region, a pin dropped.

ALICE MUNRO

b. 1931

The Peace of Utrecht

I

I have been at home now for three weeks and it has not been a success. Maddy and I, though we speak cheerfully of our enjoyment of so long and intimate a visit, will be relieved when it is over. Silences disturb us. We laugh immoderately. I am afraid—very likely we are both afraid— that when the moment comes to say goodbye, unless we are very quick to kiss, and fervently mockingly squeeze each other's shoulders, we will have to look straight into the desert that is between us and acknowledge that we are not merely indifferent; at heart we reject each other, and as for that past we make so much of sharing we do not really share it at all, each of us keeping it jealously to herself, thinking privately that the other has turned alien, and forfeited her claim.

At night we often sit out on the steps of the verandah, and drink gin and smoke diligently to defeat the mosquitoes and postpone until very late the moment of going to bed. It is hot; the evening takes a long time to burn out. The high brick house, which stays fairly cool until midafternoon, holds the heat of the day trapped until long after dark. It was always like this, and Maddy and I recall how we used to drag our mattress down-stairs onto the verandah, where we lay counting falling stars and trying to stay awake till dawn. We never did, falling asleep each night about the time a chill drift of air came up off the river, carrying a smell of reeds and the black ooze of the riverbed. At half-past ten a bus goes through the town, not slowing much; we see it go by at the end of our street. It is the same bus I used to take when I came home from college, and I remember coming into Jubilee on some warm night, seeing the earth bare around the massive roots of the trees, the drinking fountain surrounded by little puddles of water on the main street, the soft scrawls of blue and red and orange light that said BILLIARDS and CAFE; feeling as I recognized these signs a queer kind of oppression and release, as I exchanged the whole holiday world of school, of friends and, later on, of love, for the dim world of continuing disaster, of home. Maddy making the same journey four years earlier must have felt the same thing. I want to ask her: it is possible that children growing up as we did lose the ability to believe in—to be at home in—any ordinary and peaceful reality? But I don't ask her; we never talk about any of that. No exorcising here, says Maddy in her thin, bright voice with the slangy quality I had forgotten, we're not going to depress each other. So we haven't.

One night Maddy took me to a party at the Lake, which is about thirty miles west of here. The party was held in a cottage a couple of women from Jubilee had rented for the week. Most of the women there seemed to be widowed, single, separated or divorced; the men were mostly young and unmarried—those from Jubilee so young that I remember them only as little boys in the lower grades. There were two or three older men, not with their wives. But the women—they reminded me surprisingly of certain women familiar to me in my childhood, though of course I never saw their party-going personalities, only their activities in the stores and offices, and not infrequently in the Sunday schools, of Jubilee. They differed from the married women in being more aware of themselves in the world, a little brisker, sharper and coarser (though I can think of only one or two whose respectability was ever in question). They wore resolutely stylish though matronly clothes, which tended to swish and rustle over their hard rubber corsets, and they put perfume, quite a lot of it, on their artificial flowers. Maddy's friends were considerably modernized; they had copper rinses on their hair, and blue eyelids, and a robust capacity for drink.

Maddy I thought did not look one of them, with her slight figure and her still carelessly worn dark hair; her face has grown thin and strained without losing entirely its girlish look of impertinence and pride. But she speaks with the harsh twang of the local accent, which we used to make fun of, and her expression as she romped and drank was determinedly undismayed. It seemed to me that she was making every effort to belong with these people and that shortly she would succeed. It seemed to me too that she wanted me to see her succeeding, to see her repudiating that secret, exhilarating, really monstrous snobbery which we cultivated when we were children together, and promised ourselves, of course, much bigger things than Jubilee.

During the game in which all the women put an article of clothing—it begins decorously with a shoe—in a basket, and then all the men come in and have a race trying to fit things on to their proper owners, I went out and sat in the car, where I felt lonely for my husband and my friends and listened to the hilarity of the party and the waves falling on the beach and presently went to sleep. Maddy came much later and said, 'For heaven's sake!' Then she laughed and said airily like a lady in an English movie, 'You find these goings-on distasteful?' We both laughed; I felt apologetic, and rather sick from drinking and not getting drunk. 'They may not be much on intellectual conversation but their hearts are in the right place, as the saying goes.' I did not dispute this and we drove at eighty miles an hour from Inverhuron to Jubilee. Since then we have not been to any more parties.

But we are not always alone when we sit out on the steps. Often we are joined by a man named Fred Powell. He was at the party, peaceably in the background remembering whose liquor was whose and amiably holding someone's head over the rickety porch railing. He grew up in Jubilee as we did but I do not remember him, I suppose because he went through school some years ahead of us and then went away to the war. Maddy surprised me by bringing him home to supper the first night I was here and then we spent the evening, as we have spent many since, making this strange man a present of our childhood, or of that version of our childhood which is safely preserved in anecdote, as in a kind of mental cellophane. And what fantasies we build around the frail figures of our childselves, so that they emerge beyond recognition incorrigible and gay. We tell stories together well. 'You girls have got good memories,' Fred Powell says, and sits watching us with an air of admiration and something else—reserve, embarrassment, deprecation—which appears on the faces of these mild deliberate people as they watch the keyed-up antics of their entertainers.

Now thinking of Fred Powell I admit that my reaction to this—this *situation* as I call it—is far more conventional than I would have expected; it is even absurd. And I do not know what situation it really is. I know that he is married. Maddy told me so, on the first evening, in a merely informative voice. His wife is an invalid. He has her at the Lake for the summer, Maddy says, he's very good to her. I do not know if he is Maddy's lover and she will never tell me. Why should it matter to me? Maddy is well over thirty. But I keep thinking of the way he sits on our steps with his hands set flat on his spread knees, his mild full face turned almost indulgently toward Maddy as she talks; he has an affable masculine look of being diverted but unimpressed. And Maddy teases him, tells him he is too fat, will not smoke his cigarettes, involves him in private, nervous, tender arguments which have no meaning and no end. He allows it. (And this is what frightens me, I know it now: he allows it;

she needs it.) When she is a little drunk she says in tones of half-pleading mockery that he is her only real friend. He speaks the same language, she says. Nobody else does. I have no answer to that.

Then again I begin to wonder: *is* he only her friend? I had forgotten certain restrictions of life in Jubilee—and this holds good whatever the pocket novels are saying about small towns—and also what strong, respectable, never overtly sexual friendships can flourish within these restrictions and be fed by them, so that in the end such relationships may consume half a life. This thought depresses me (unconsummated relationships depress outsiders perhaps more than anybody else) so much that I find myself wishing for them to be honest lovers.

The rhythm of life in Jubilee is primitively seasonal. Deaths occur in the winter; marriages are celebrated in the summer. There is good reason for this; the winters are long and full of hardship and the old and weak cannot always get through them. Last winter was a catastrophe, such as may be expected every ten or twelve years; you can see how the pavement in the streets is broken up, as if the town had survived a minor bombardment. A death is dealt with then in the middle of great difficulties; there comes time now in the summer to think about it, and talk. I find that people stop me in the street to talk about my mother. I have heard from them about her funeral, what flowers she had and what the weather was like on that day. And now that she is dead I no longer feel that when they say the words 'your mother' they deal a knowing, cunning blow at my pride. I used to feel that; at those words I felt my whole identity, that pretentious adolescent construction, come crumbling down.

Now I listen to them speak of her, so gently and ceremoniously, and I realize that she became one of the town's possessions and oddities, its brief legends. This she achieved in spite of us, for we tried, both crudely and artfully, to keep her at home, away from that sad notoriety; not for her sake, but for ours, who suffered such unnecessary humiliation at the sight of her eyes rolling back in her head in a temporary paralysis of the eye muscles, at the sound of her thickened voice, whose embarrassing pronouncements it was our job to interpret to outsiders. So bizarre was the disease she had in its effects that it made us feel like crying out in apology (though we stayed stiff and white) as if we were accompanying a particularly tasteless sideshow. All wasted, our pride; our purging its rage in wild caricatures we did for each other (no, not caricatures, for she was one herself; imitations). We should have let the town have her; it would have treated her better.

About Maddy and her ten-year's vigil they say very little; perhaps they want to spare my feelings, remembering that I was the one who went away and here are my two children to show for it, while Maddy is alone and has nothing but that discouraging house. But I don't think so; in Jubilee the feelings are not spared this way. And they ask me point-blank why I did not come home for the funeral; I am glad I have the excuse of the blizzard that halted air travel that week, for I do not know if I would have come anyway, after Maddy had written so vehemently urging me to stay away. I felt strongly that she had a right to be left alone with it, if she wanted to be, after all this time.

After all this time. Maddy was the one who stayed. First, she went away to college, then I went. You give me four years, I'll give you four years, she said. But I got married. She was not surprised; she was exasperated at me for my wretched useless feelings of guilt. She said that she had always meant to stay. She said that Mother no longer 'bothered' her. 'Our Gothic Mother,' she said, 'I play it out now, I let her be. I don't keep trying to make her *human* any more. You know.' It would simplify things so much to say that Maddy was religious, that she felt the joys of self-sacrifice, the strong, mystical appeal of total rejection. But about Maddy who could say that? When we were in our teens, and our old aunts, Aunt Annie and Auntie Lou, spoke to us of some dutiful son or daughter who had given up everything for an ailing parent, Maddy would quote impiously the opinions of modern psychiatry. Yet she stayed. All I can think about that, all I have ever been able to think, to comfort me, is that she may have been able and may even have chosen to live without time and in perfect imaginary freedom as children do, the future untampered with, all choices always possible.

To change the subject, people ask me what it is like to be back in Jubilee. But I don't know, I am still waiting for something to tell me, to make me understand that I am back. The day I drove up from Toronto with my children in the back seat of the car I was very tired, on the last lap of a twenty-five-hundred-mile trip. I had to follow a complicated system of highways and sideroads, for there is no easy way to get to Jubilee from anywhere on earth. Then about two o'clock in the afternoon I saw ahead of me, so familiar and unexpected, the gaudy, peeling cupola of the town hall, which is no relation to any of the rest of the town's squarely-built, dingy grey-and-red-brick architecture. (Underneath it hangs a great bell, to be rung in the event of some mythical disaster.) I drove up the main street—a new service station, new stucco front on the Queen's Hotel—and turned into the quiet, decaying side streets where old maids live, and have birdbaths and blue delphiniums in their gardens. The big brick houses that I knew, with their wooden verandahs and gaping, dark-screened windows, seemed to me plausible but unreal. (Anyone to whom I have mentioned the dreaming, sunken feeling of these streets wants to take me out to the north side of town where there is a new soft-drink bottling plant, some new ranch-style houses and a Tastee-Freez.) Then I parked my car in a little splash of shade in front of the house where I used to live. My little girl, whose name is Margaret, said neutrally yet with some disbelief, 'Mother, is that your house?'

And I felt that my daughter's voice expressed a complex disappointment—to which, characteristically, she seemed resigned, or even resigned *in advance*; it contained the whole flatness and strangeness of the moment in which is revealed the source of legends, the unsatisfactory, apologetic and persistent reality. The red brick of which the house is built looked harsh and hot in the sun and was marked in two or three places by long grimacing cracks; the verandah, which always had the air of an insubstantial decoration, was visibly falling away. There was—there *is*— a little blind window of coloured glass beside the front door. I sat staring at it with a puzzled lack of emotional recognition. I sat and looked at the house and the window shades did not move, the door did not fly open, no one came out on the verandah; there was no one at home. This was as I had expected, since Maddy works now in the office of the town clerk, yet I was surprised to see the house take on such a closed, bare, impoverished look, merely by being left empty. And it was brought home to me, as I walked across the front yard to the steps, that after all these summers on the Coast I had forgotten the immense inland heat, which makes you feel as if you have to carry the whole burning sky on your head.

A sign pinned to the front door announced, in Maddy's rather sloppy and flamboyant hand: VISITORS WELCOME, CHILDREN FREE, RATES TO BE ARRANGED LATER (YOU'LL BE SORRY) WALK IN. On the hall table was a bouquet of pink phlox whose velvety scent filled the hot air of a closed house on a summer afternoon. 'Upstairs!' I said to the children, and I took the hand of the little girl and her smaller brother, who had slept in the car and who rubbed against me, whimpering, as he walked. Then I paused, one foot on the bottom step, and turned to greet, matter-of-factly, the reflection of a thin, tanned, habitually watchful woman, recognizably a Young Mother, whose hair, pulled into a knot on top of her head, exposed a jawline no longer softly fleshed, a brown neck rising with a look of tension from the little sharp knobs of the collarbone—this in the hall mirror that had shown me, last time I looked, a commonplace pretty girl, with a face as smooth and insensitive as an apple, no matter what panic and disorder lay behind it.

But this was not what I had turned for; I realized that I must have been waiting for my mother to call, from her couch in the dining-room, where she lay with the blinds down in the summer heat, drinking cups of tea which she never finished, eating—she had dispensed altogether with mealtimes, like a sickly child—little bowls of preserved fruit and crumblings of cake. It seemed to me that I could not close the door behind me without hearing my mother's ruined voice call out to me, and feeling myself go heavy all over as I prepared to answer it. Calling, *Who's there?*

I led my children to the big bedroom at the back of the house, where Maddy and I used to sleep. It has thin, almost worn-out white curtains at the windows and a square of linoleum on the floor; there is a double bed, a washstand which Maddy and I used as a desk when we were in high school, and a cardboard wardrobe with little mirrors on the inside of the doors. As I talked to my children I was thinking—but carefully, not in a rush—of my mother's state of mind when she called out *Who's there?* I was allowing myself to hear—as if I had not dared before—the cry for help—undisguised, oh, shamefully undisguised and raw and supplicating—that sounded in her voice. A cry repeated so often, and, things being as they were, so uselessly, that Maddy and I recognized it only as one of those household sounds which must be dealt with, so that worse may not follow. *You go and deal with Mother,* we would say to each other, or *I'll be out in a minute, I have to deal with Mother.*

It might be that we had to perform some of the trivial and unpleasant services endlessly required, or that we had to supply five minutes' expediently cheerful conversation, so remorselessly casual that never for a moment was there a recognition of the real state of affairs, never a glint of pity to open the way for one of her long debilitating sieges of tears. But the pity denied, the tears might come anyway; so that we were defeated, we were forced—to stop that noise—into parodies of love. But we grew cunning, unfailing in cold solicitude; we took away from her our anger and impatience and disgust, took all emotion away from our dealings with her, as you might take away meat from a prisoner to weaken him, till he died.

We would tell her to read, to listen to music and enjoy the changes of season and be grateful that she did not have cancer. We added that she did not suffer any pain, and that is true—if imprisonment is not pain. While she demanded our love in every way she knew, without shame or sense, as a child will. And how could we have loved her, I say desperately to myself, the resources of love we had were not enough, the demand on us was too great. Nor would it have changed anything.

'Everything has been taken away from me,' she would say. To strangers, to friends of ours whom we tried always unsuccessfully to keep separate from her, to old friends of hers who came guiltily infrequently to see her, she would speak like this, in the very slow and mournful voice that was not intelligible or quite human; we would have to interpret. Such theatricality humiliated us almost to death; yet now I think that without that egotism feeding stubbornly even on disaster she might have sunk rapidly into some dim vegetable life. She kept herself as much in the world as she could, not troubling about her welcome; restlessly she wandered through the house and into the streets of Jubilee. Oh, she was not resigned; she must have wept and struggled in that house of stone (as I can, but will not, imagine) until the very end.

But I find the picture is still not complete. Our Gothic Mother, with the cold appalling mask of the Shaking Palsy laid across her features, shuffling, weeping, devouring attention wherever she can get it, eyes dead and burning, fixed inward on herself; this is not all. For the disease is erratic and leisurely in its progress; some mornings (gradually growing fewer and fewer and farther apart) she wakes up better; she goes out to the yard and straightens up a plant in such a simple housewifely way; she says something calm and lucid to us; she listens attentively to the news. She has wakened out of a bad dream; she tries to make up for lost time, tidying the house, forcing her stiff trembling hands to work a little while at the sewing machine. She makes us one of her specialties, a banana cake or a lemon meringue pie. Occasionally since she died I have dreams of her (I never dreamt of her when she was alive) in which she is doing something like this, and I think, why did I exaggerate so to myself, see, she is all right, only that her hands are trembling—

At the end of these periods of calm a kind of ravaging energy would come over her; she would make conversation insistently and with less and less coherence; she would demand that we rouge her cheeks and fix her hair; sometimes she might even hire a dressmaker to come in and make clothes for her, working in the dining room where she could watch—spending her time again more and more on the couch. This was extravagant, unnecessary from any practical point of view (for why did she need these clothes, where did she wear them?) and nerve-racking, because the dressmaker did not understand what she wanted and sometimes neither did we. I remember after I went away receiving from Maddy several amusing, distracted, quietly overwrought letters describing these sessions with the dressmaker. I read them with sympathy but without being able to enter into the once-familiar atmosphere of frenzy and frustration which my mother's demands could produce. In the ordinary world it was not possible to re-create her. The picture of her face which I carried in my mind seemed too terrible, unreal. Similarly the complex strain of living with her, the feelings of hysteria which Maddy and I once dissipated in a great deal of brutal laughter, now began to seem partly imaginary; I felt the beginnings of a secret, guilty estrangement.

I stayed in the room with my children for a little while because it was a strange place, for them it was only another strange place to go to sleep. Looking at them in this room I felt that they were particularly fortunate and that their life was safe and easy, which may be what most parents think at one time or another. I looked in the wardrobe but there was nothing there, only a hat trimmed with flowers from the five-and-ten, which one of us must have made for some flossy Easter. When I opened the drawer of the washstand I saw that it was crammed full of pages from a loose-leaf notebook. I read: "The Peace of Utrecht, 1713, brought an end to the War of the Spanish Succession.' It struck me that the handwriting was my own. Strange to think of it lying here for ten years—more; it looked as if I might have written it that day.

For some reason reading these words had a strong effect on me; I felt as if my old life was lying around me, waiting to be picked up again. Only then for a few moments in our old room did I have this feeling. The brown halls of the old High School (a building since torn down) were re-opened for me, and I remembered the Saturday nights in spring, after the snow had melted and all the country people crowded into town. I thought of us walking up and down the main street, arm in arm with two or three other girls, until it got dark, then going in to Al's to dance, under a string of little coloured lights. The windows in the dance hall were open; they let in the raw spring air with its smell of earth and the river; the hands of farm boys crumpled and stained our white blouses when we danced. And now an experience which seemed not at all memorable at the time (in fact Al's was a dismal place and the ritual of walking up and down the street to show ourselves off we thought crude and ridiculous, though we could not resist it) had been transformed into something curiously meaningful for me, and complete; it took in more than the girls dancing and the single street, it spread over the whole town, its rudimentary pattern of streets and its bare trees and muddy yards just free of the snow, over the dirt roads where the lights of cars appeared, jolting towards the town, under an immense pale wash of sky.

Also: we wore ballerina shoes, and full black taffeta skirts, and short coats of such colours as robin's egg blue, cerise red, lime green. Maddy wore a great funereal bow at the neck of her blouse and a wreath of artificial daisies in her hair. These were the fashions, or so we believed, of one of the years after the war. Maddy; her bright skeptical look; my sister.

I ask Maddy, 'Do you ever remember what she was like before?'

'No,' says Maddy. 'No, I can't.'

'I sometimes think I can,' I say hesitantly. 'Not very often.' Cowardly tender nostalgia, trying to get back to a gentler truth.

'I think you would have to have been away,' Maddy says, 'You would have to have been away these last—quite a few—years to get those kind of memories.'

It was then she said: No exorcising.

And the only other thing she said was, 'She spent a lot of time sorting things. All kinds of things. Greeting cards. Buttons and yarn. Sorting and putting them into little piles. It would keep her quiet by the hour.'

II

I have been to visit Aunt Annie and Auntie Lou. This is the third time I have been there since I came home and each time they have been spending the afternoon making rugs out of dyed rags. They are very old now. They sit in a hot little porch that is shaded by bamboo blinds; the rags and the half-finished rugs make an encouraging, domestic sort of disorder around them. They do not go out any more, but they get up early in the mornings, wash and powder themselves and put on their shapeless print dresses trimmed with rickrack and white braid. They make coffee and porridge and then they clean the house, Aunt Annie working upstairs and Auntie Lou down. Their house is very clean, dark and varnished, and it smells of vinegar and apples. In the afternoon they lie down for an hour and then put on their afternoon dresses, with brooches at the neck, and sit down to do hand work.

They are the sort of women whose flesh melts or mysteriously falls away as they get older. Auntie Lou's hair is still black, but it looks stiff and dry in its net as the dead end of hair on a ripe ear of corn. She sits straight and moves her bone-thin arms in very fine, slow movements; she looks like an Egyptian, with her long neck and small sharp face and greatly wrinkled, greatly darkened skin. Aunt Annie, perhaps because of her gentler, even coquettish manner, seems more humanly fragile and worn. Her hair is nearly all gone, and she keeps on her head one of those pretty caps designed for young wives who wear curlers to bed. She calls my attention to this and asks if I do not think it is becoming. They are both adept at these little ironies, and take a mild delight in pointing out whatever is grotesque about themselves. Their company manners are exceedingly lighthearted and their conversation with each other falls into an accomplished pattern of teasing and protest. I have a fascinated glimpse of Maddy and myself, grown old, caught back in the web of sisterhood after everything else has disappeared, making tea for some young, loved, and essentially unimportant relative—and exhibiting just such a polished relationship; what will anyone ever know of us? As I watch my entertaining old aunts I wonder if old people play such stylized and simplified roles with us because they are afraid that anything more honest might try our patience; or if they do it out of delicacy—to fill the social time—when in reality they feel so far away from us that there is no possibility of communicating with us at all.

At any rate I felt held at a distance by them, at least until this third afternoon when they showed in front of me some signs of disagreement with each other. I believe this is the first time that has happened. Certainly I never saw them argue in all the years when Maddy and I used to visit them, and we used to visit them often—not only out of duty but because we found the atmosphere of sense and bustle reassuring after the comparative anarchy, the threatened melodrama, of our house at home.

Aunt Annie wanted to take me upstairs to show me something. Auntie Lou objected, looking remote and offended, as if the whole subject embarrassed her. And such is the feeling for discretion, the tradition of circumlocution in that house, that it was unthinkable for me to ask them what they were talking about.

'Oh, let her have her tea,' Auntie Lou said, and Aunt Annie said, 'Well. When she's *had* her tea.'

'Do as you like then. That upstairs is hot.'

'Will you come up, Lou?'

'Then who's going to watch the children?'

'Oh, the children. I forgot.'

So Aunt Annie and I withdrew into the darker parts of the house. It occurred to me, absurdly, that she was going to give me a five-dollar bill. I remembered that sometimes she used to draw me into the front hall in this mysterious way and open her purse. I do not think that Auntie Lou was included in that secret either. But we went on upstairs, and into Aunt Annie's own bedroom, which looked so neat and virginal, papered with timid flowery wallpaper, the dressers spread with white scarves. It was really very hot, as Auntie Lou had said.

'Now,' Aunt Annie said, a little breathless. 'Get me down that box on the top shelf of the closet.'

I did, and she opened it and said with her wistful conspirator's gaiety, 'Now I guess you wondered what became of all your mother's clothes?'

I had not thought of it. I sat down on the bed, forgetting that in this house the beds were not to be sat on; the bedrooms had one straight chair apiece, for that. Aunt Annie did not check me. She began to lift things out, saying, 'Maddy never mentioned them, did she?'

'I never asked her,' I said.

'No. Nor I wouldn't. I wouldn't say a word about it to Maddy. But I thought I might as well show you. Why not? Look,' she said. 'We washed and ironed what we could and what we couldn't we sent to the cleaners. I paid the cleaning myself. Then we mended anything needed mending. It's all in good condition, see?'

I watched helplessly while she held up for my inspection the under-wear which was on top. She showed me where things had been expertly darned and mended and where the elastic had been renewed. She showed me a slip which had been worn, she said, only once. She took out nightgowns, a dressing gown, knitted bed-jackets. 'This was what she had on the last time I saw her,' she said. 'I think it was. Yes.' I recognized with alarm the peach-coloured bed-jacket I had sent for Christmas.

'You can see it's hardly used. Why, it's hardly used at all.'

'No,' I said.

'Underneath is her dresses.' Her hands rummaged down through those brocades and flowered silks, growing yearly more exotic, in which my mother had wished to costume herself. Thinking of her in these peacock colours, even Aunt Annie seemed to hesitate. She drew up a blouse. 'I washed this by hand, it looks like new. There's a coat hanging up in the closet. Perfectly good. She never wore a coat. She wore it when she went into the hospital, that was all. Wouldn't it fit you?'

'No,' I said. '*No.*' For Aunt Annie was already moving towards the closet. 'I just got a new coat. I have several coats. Aunt Annie!'

'But why should you go and buy,' Aunt Annie went on in her mild stubborn way, 'when there are things here as good as new.'

'I would rather buy,' I said, and was immediately sorry for the cold-ness in my voice. Nevertheless I continued, 'When I need something, I do go and buy it.' This suggestion that I was not poor any more brought a look of reproach and aloofness into my aunt's face. She said nothing. I went and looked at a picture of Aunt Annie and Auntie Lou and their older brothers and their mother and father which hung over the bureau. They stared back at me with grave accusing Protestant faces, for I had run up against the simple unprepossessing materialism which was the rock of their lives. Things must be used; everything must be used up, saved and mended and made into something else and used again; clothes were to be worn. I felt that I had hurt Aunt Annie's feelings and that furthermore I had probably borne out a prediction of Auntie Lou's, for she was sensitive to certain attitudes in the world that were too sophisticated for Aunt Annie to bother about, and she had very likely said that I would not want my mother's clothes.

'She was gone sooner than anybody would have expected,' Aunt Annie said. I turned around surprised and she said, 'Your mother.' Then I wondered if the clothes had been the main thing after all; perhaps they were only to serve as the introduction to a conversation about my mother's death, which Aunt Annie might feel to be a necessary part of our visit. Auntie Lou would feel differently; she had an almost superstitious dislike of certain rituals of emotionalism; such a conversation could never take place with her about.

'Two months after she went into the hospital,' Aunt Annie said. 'She was gone in two months.' I saw that she was crying distractedly, as old people do, with miserable scanty tears. She pulled a handkerchief out of her dress and rubbed at her face.

'Maddy told her it was nothing but a check-up,' she said. 'Maddy told her it would be about three weeks. Your mother went in there and she thought she was coming out in three weeks.' She was whispering as if she was afraid of us being overheard. 'Do you think she wanted to stay in there where nobody could make out what she was saying and they wouldn't let her out of her bed? She wanted to come home!'

'But she was too sick,' I said.

'No, she wasn't, she was just the way she'd always been, just getting a little worse and a little worse as time went on. But after she went in there she felt she would die, everything kind of closed in around her, and she went down so fast.'

'Maybe it would have happened anyway,' I said. 'Maybe it was just the time.'

Aunt Annie paid no attention to me. 'I went up to see her,' she said. 'She was so glad to see me because I could tell what she was saying. She said Aunt Annie, they won't keep me in here for good, will they? And I said to her, No. I said, No.

'And she said, Aunt Annie ask Maddy to take me home again or I'm going to die. She didn't want to die. Don't you ever think a person wants to die, just because it seems to everybody else they have got no reason to go on living. So I told Maddy. But she didn't say anything. She went to the hospital every day and saw your mother and she wouldn't take her home. Your mother told me Maddy said to her, I won't take you home.'

'Mother didn't always tell the truth,' I said. 'Aunt Annie, you know that.'

'*Did you know your mother got out of the hospital?*'

'No,' I said. But strangely I felt no surprise, only a vague physical sense of terror, a longing not to be told—and beyond this a feeling that what I would be told I already knew, I had always known.

'Maddy, didn't she tell you?'

'No.'

'Well she got *out*. She got out the side door where the ambulance comes in, it's the only door that isn't locked. It was at night when they haven't so many nurses to watch them. She got her dressing gown and her slippers on, the first time she ever got anything on herself in years, and she went out and there it was January, snowing, but she didn't go back in. She was away down the street when they caught her. After that they put the board across her bed.'

The snow, the dressing gown and slippers, the board across the bed. It was a picture I was much inclined to resist. Yet I had no doubt that this was true, all this was true and exactly as it happened. It was what she would do; all her life as long as I had known her led up to that flight.

'Where was she going?' I said, but I knew there was no answer.

'I don't know. Maybe I shouldn't have told you. Oh, Helen, when they came after her she tried to run. She tried to *run*.'

The flight that concerns everybody. Even behind my aunt's soft familiar face there is another, more primitive old woman, capable of panic in some place her faith has never touched.

She began folding the clothes up and putting them back in the box. 'They nailed a board across her bed. I saw it. You can't blame the nurses. They can't watch everybody. They haven't the time.

'I said to Maddy after the funeral, Maddy, may it never happen like that to you. I couldn't help it, that's what I said.' She sat down on the bed herself now, folding things and putting them back in the box, making an effort to bring her voice back to normal—and pretty soon succeeding, for having lived this long who would not be an old hand at grief and self-control?

'We thought it was hard,' she said finally. 'Lou and I thought it was hard.'

Is this the last function of old women, beyond making rag rugs and giving us five-dollar bills—making sure the haunts we have contracted for are with us, not one gone without?

She was afraid of Maddy—through fear, had cast her out for good. I thought of what Maddy had said: nobody speaks the same language.

When I got home Maddy was out in the back kitchen making a salad. Rectangles of sunlight lay on the rough linoleum. She had taken off her high-heeled shoes and was standing there in her bare feet. The back kitchen is a large untidy pleasant room with a view, behind the stove and the drying dishtowels, of the sloping backyard, the CPR station and the golden, marshy river that almost encircles the town of Jubilee. My children who had felt a little repressed in the other house immediately began to play under the table.

'Where have you been?' Maddy said.

'Nowhere. Just to see the Aunts.'

'Oh, how are they?'

'They're fine. They're indestructible.'

'Are they? Yes I guess they are. I haven't been to see them for a while. I don't actually see that much of them any more.'

'Don't you?' I said, and she knew then what they had told me.

'They were beginning to get on my nerves a bit, after the funeral. And Fred got me this job and everything and I've been so busy—' She looked at me, waiting for what I would say, smiling a little derisively, patiently.

'Don't be guilty, Maddy,' I said softly. All this time the children were running in and out and shrieking at each other between our legs.

'I'm not guilty,' she said. 'Where did you get that? I'm not guilty.' She went to turn on the radio, talking to me over her shoulder. 'Fred's going to eat with us again since he's alone. I got some raspberries for dessert. Raspberries are almost over for this year. Do they look all right to you?'

'They look all right,' I said. 'Do you want me to finish this?'

'Fine,' she said. 'I'll go and get a bowl.'

She went into the dining room and came back carrying a pink cut-glass bowl, for the raspberries.

'I couldn't go on,' she said. 'I wanted my life.'

She was standing on the little step between the kitchen and the dining room and suddenly she lost her grip on the bowl, either because her hands had begun to shake or because she had not picked it up properly in the first place; it was quite a heavy and elaborate old bowl. It slipped out of her hands and she tried to catch it and it smashed on the floor.

Maddy began to laugh. 'Oh, hell,' she said. 'Oh, hell, oh *Hel*-en,' she said, using one of our old foolish ritual phrases of despair. 'Look what I've done now. In my bare feet yet. Get me a broom.'

'Take your life, Maddy. Take it.'

'Yes I will,' Maddy said. 'Yes I will.'

'Go away, don't stay here.'

'Yes I will.'

Then she bent down and began picking up the pieces of broken pink glass. My children stood back looking at her with awe and she was laughing and saying, 'It's no loss to me. I've got a whole shelf full of glass bowls. I've got enough glass bowls to do me the rest of my life. Oh, don't stand there looking at me, go and get me a broom!' I went around the kitchen looking for a broom because I seemed to have forgotten where it was kept and she said, 'But why can't I, Helen? *Why can't I?*'

MORDECAI RICHLER

b. 1931

The Summer My Grandmother Was Supposed to Die

Dr Katzman discovered the gangrene on one of his monthly visits. 'She won't last a month,' he said.

He said the same the second month, the third and the fourth, and now she lay dying in the heat of the back bedroom.

'God in heaven,' my mother said, 'what's she holding on for?'

The summer my grandmother was supposed to die we did not chip in with the Greenbaums to take a cottage in the Laurentians. My grandmother, already bed-ridden for seven years, could not be moved again. The doctor came twice a week. The only thing was to stay in the city and wait for her to die or, as my mother said, pass away. It was a hot summer, her bedroom was just behind the kitchen, and when we sat down to eat we could smell her. The dressings on my grandmother's left leg had to be changed several times a day and, according to Dr Katzman, any day might be her last in this world. 'It's in the hands of the Almighty,' he said.

'It won't be long now,' my father said, 'and she'll be better off, if you know what I mean?'

A nurse came every day from the Royal Victorian Order. She arrived punctually at noon and at five to twelve I'd join the rest of the boys under the outside staircase to peek up her dress as she climbed to our second-storey flat. Miss Bailey favoured absolutely beguiling pink panties, edged with lace, and that was better than waiting under the stairs for Cousin Bessie, for instance, who wore enormous cotton bloomers, rain or shine.

I was sent out to play as often as possible, because my mother felt it was not good for me to see somebody dying. Usually, I would just roam the scorched streets. There was Duddy, Gas sometimes, Hershey, Stan, Arty and me.

'Before your grandmaw kicks off,' Duddy said, 'she's going to roll her eyes and gurgle. That's what they call the death-rattle.'

'Aw, you know everything. *Putz*.'

'I read it, you jerk,' Duddy said, whacking me one, 'in Perry Mason.'

Home again I would usually find my mother sour and spent. Sometimes she wept.

'She's dying by inches,' she said to my father one stifling night, 'and none of them ever come to see her. Oh, such children,' she added, going on to curse them vehemently in Yiddish.

'They're not behaving right. It's certainly not according to Hoyle,' my father said.

Dr Katzman continued to be astonished. 'It must be will-power alone that keeps her going,' he said. 'That, and your excellent care.'

'It's not my mother any more in the back room, Doctor. It's an animal. I want her to die.'

'Hush. You don't mean it. You're tired.' Dr Katzman dug into his black bag and produced pills for her to take. 'Your wife's a remarkable woman,' he told my father.

'You don't so say,' my father replied, embarrassed.

'A born nurse.'

My sister and I used to lie awake talking about our grandmother. 'After she dies,' I said, 'her hair will go on growing for another twenty-four hours.'

'Says who?'

'Duddy Kravitz. Do you think Uncle Lou will come from New York for the funeral?'

'I suppose so.'

'Boy, that means another fiver for me. Even more for you.'

'You shouldn't say things like that or her ghost will come back to haunt you.'

'Well, I'll be able to go to her funeral anyway. I'm not too young any more.'

I was only six years old when my grandfather died, and so I wasn't allowed to go to his funeral.

I have one imperishable memory of my grandfather. Once he called me into his study, set me down on his lap, and made a drawing of a horse for me. On the horse he drew a rider. While I watched and giggled he gave the rider a beard and the fur-trimmed round hat of a rabbi, a *straimel*, just like he wore.

My grandfather had been a Zaddik, one of the Righteous, and I've been assured that to study Talmud with him had been an illuminating experience. I wasn't allowed to go to his funeral, but years later I was shown the telegrams of condolence that had come from Eire and Poland and even Japan. My grandfather had written many books: a translation of the Book of Splendour (the Zohar) into modern Hebrew, some twenty years work, and lots of slender volumes of sermons, hasidic tales, and rabbinical commentaries. His books had been published in Warsaw and later in New York.

'At the funeral,' my mother said, 'they had to have six motorcycle policemen to control the crowds. It was such a heat that twelve women fainted—and I'm *not* counting Mrs Waxman from upstairs. With her, you know, *anything* to fall into a man's arms. Even Pinsky's. And did I tell you that there was even a French Canadian priest there?'

'Aw, you're kidding me.'

'The priest was some *knacker*. A bishop maybe. He used to study with the *zeyda*. The *zeyda* was a real personality, you know. Spiritual and worldly-wise at the same time. Such personalities they don't make any more. Today rabbis and peanuts come in the same size.'

But, according to my father, the *zeyda* (his father-in-law) hadn't been as celebrated as all that. 'There are things I could say,' he told me. 'There was another side to him.'

My grandfather had sprung from generations and generations of rabbis, his youngest son was a rabbi, but none of his grandchildren would be one. My Cousin Jerry was already a militant socialist. I once heard him say, 'When the men at the kosher bakeries went out on strike the *zeyda* spoke up against them on the streets and in the *shuls*. It was of no consequence to him that the men were grossly underpaid. His superstitious followers had to have bread. Grandpappy,' Jerry said, 'was a prize reactionary.'

A week after my grandfather died my grandmother suffered a stroke. Her right side was completely paralysed. She couldn't speak. At first it's true, she could manage a coherent word or two and move her right hand enough to write her name in Hebrew. Her name was Malka. But her condition soon began to deteriorate.

My grandmother had six children and seven step-children, for my grandfather had been married before. His first wife had died in the old country. Two years later he had married my grandmother, the only daughter of the most affluent man in the *shtetl*, and their marriage had been a singularly happy one. My grandmother had been a beautiful girl. She had also been a shrewd, resourceful, and patient wife. Qualities, I fear, indispensable to life with a Zaddik. For the synagogue paid my grandfather no stipulated salary and much of the money he picked up here and there he had habitually distributed among rabbinical students, needy immigrants and widows. A vice, for such it was to his impecunious family, which made him as unreliable a provider as a drinker. To carry the analogy further, my grandmother had to make hurried, surreptitious trips to the pawnbroker with her jewellery. Not all of it to be redeemed, either. But her children had been looked after. The youngest, her favourite, was a rabbi in Boston, the oldest was the actor-manager of a Yiddish theatre in New York, and another was a lawyer. One daughter lived in Montreal, two in Toronto. My mother was the youngest daughter and when my grandmother had her stroke there was a family conclave and it was decided that my mother would take care of her. This was my father's fault. All the other husbands spoke up—they protested hotly that their wives had too much work—they could never manage it—but my father detested quarrels and so he was silent. And my grandmother came to stay with us.

Her bedroom, the back bedroom, had actually been promised to me for my seventh birthday, but now I had to go on sharing a room with my sister. So naturally I was resentful when each morning before I left for school my mother insisted that I go in and kiss my grandmother goodbye.

'Bouyo-bouyo,' was the only sound my grandmother could make.

During those first hopeful months—'Twenty years ago who would have thought there'd be a cure for diabetes?' my father asked. 'Where there's life, you know.'—my grandmother would smile and try to speak, her eyes charged with effort; and I wondered if she knew that I was waiting for her room.

Even later there were times when she pressed my hand urgently to her bosom with her surprisingly strong left arm. But as her illness dragged on and on she became a condition in the house, something beyond hope or reproach, like the leaky ice-box, there was less recognition and more ritual in those kisses. I came to dread her room. A clutter of sticky medicine bottles and the cracked toilet chair beside the bed; glazed but imploring eyes and a feeble smile, the wet smack of her crooked lips against my cheeks. I flinched from her touch. And after two years, I protested to my mother, 'What's the use of telling her I'm going here or I'm going there? She doesn't even recognize me any more.'

'Don't be fresh. She's your grandmother.'

My uncle who was in the theatre in New York sent money regularly to help support my grandmother and, for the first few months, so did the other children. But once the initial and sustaining excitement had passed the children seldom came to our house any more. Anxious weekly visits—

'And how is she today, poor lamb?'—quickly dwindled to a dutiful monthly looking in, then a semi-annual visit, and these always on the way to somewhere.

When the children did come my mother was severe with them. 'I have to lift her on that chair three times a day maybe. And what makes you think I always catch her in time? Sometimes I have to change her linen twice a day. That's a job I'd like to see your wife do,' she said to my uncle, the rabbi.

'We could send her to the Old People's Home.'

'Now there's an idea,' my father said.

'Not so long as I'm alive.' My mother shot my father a scalding look, 'Say something, Sam.'

'Quarrelling will get us nowhere. It only creates bad feelings.'

Meanwhile, Dr Katzman came once a month. 'It's astonishing,' he would say each time. 'She's as strong as a horse.'

'Some life for a person,' my father said. 'She can't speak—she doesn't recognize anybody—what is there for her?'

The doctor was a cultivated man; he spoke often for women's clubs, sometimes on Yiddish literature and other times, his rubicund face hot with menace, the voice taking on a doomsday tone, on the cancer threat. 'Who are we to judge?' he asked.

Every evening, during the first few months of my grandmother's illness, my mother would read her a story by Sholem Aleichem. 'Tonight she smiled,' my mother would report defiantly, 'She understood. I can tell.'

Bright afternoons my mother would lift the old lady into a wheelchair and put her out in the sun and once a week she gave her a manicure. Somebody always had to stay in the house in case my grandmother called. Often, during the night, she would begin to wail unaccountably and my mother would get up and rock her mother in her arms for hours. But in the fourth year of my grandmother's illness the strain began to tell. Besides looking after my grandmother, my mother had to keep house for a husband and two children. She became scornful of my father and began to find fault with my sister and me. My father started to spend his evenings playing pinochle at Tansky's Cigar & Soda. Weekends he took me to visit his brothers and sisters. Wherever my father went people had little snippets of advice for him.

'Sam, you might as well be a bachelor. One of the other children should take the old lady for a while. You're just going to have to put your foot down for once.'

'Yeah, in your face, maybe.'

My Cousin Libby, who was at McGill, said, 'This could have a very damaging effect on the development of your children. These are their formative years, Uncle Samuel, and the omnipresence of death in the house . . .'

'What you need is a boy friend,' my father said. '*And how.*'

After supper my mother took to falling asleep in her chair, even in the middle of Lux Radio Theatre. One minute she would be sewing a patch in my breeches or making a list of girls to call for a bingo party, proceeds for the Talmud Torah, and the next she would be snoring. Then, inevitably, there came the morning she just couldn't get out of bed and Dr Katzman had to come round a week before his regular visit. 'Well, well, this won't do, will it?'

Dr Katzman led my father into the kitchen. 'Your wife's got a gallstone condition,' he said.

My grandmother's children met again, this time without my mother, and decided to put the old lady in the Jewish Old People's Home on Esplanade Street. While my mother slept an ambulance came to take my grandmother away.

'It's for the best,' Dr Katzman said, but my father was in the back room when my grandmother held on tenaciously to the bedpost, not wanting to be moved by the two men in white.

'Easy does it, granny,' the younger man said.

Afterwards my father did not go in to see my mother. He went out for a walk.

When my mother got out of bed two weeks later her cheeks had regained their normal pinkish hue; for the first time in months, she actually joked with me. She became increasingly curious about how I was doing in school and whether or not I shined my shoes regularly. She began to cook special dishes for my father again and resumed old friendships with the girls on the parochial school board. Not only did my father's temper improve, but he stopped going to Tansky's every night and began to come home early from work. But my grandmother's name was seldom mentioned. Until one evening, after I'd had a fight with my sister, I said, 'Why can't I move into the back bedroom now?'

My father glared at me. 'Big-mouth.'

'It's empty, isn't it?'

The next afternoon my mother put on her best dress and coat and new spring hat.

'Don't go looking for trouble,' my father said.

'It's been a month. Maybe they're not treating her right.'

'They're experts.'

'Did you think I was never going to visit her? I'm not inhuman, you know.'

'Alright, go.' But after she had gone my father stood by the window and said, 'I was born lucky, and that's it.'

I sat on the outside stoop watching the cars go by. My father waited on the balcony above, cracking peanuts. It was six o'clock, maybe later, when the ambulance slowed down and rocked to a stop right in front of our house. 'I knew it,' my father said. 'I was born with all the luck.'

My mother got out first, her eyes red and swollen, and hurried upstairs to make my grandmother's bed.

'You'll get sick again,' my father said.

'I'm sorry, Sam, but what could I do? From the moment she saw me she cried and cried. It was terrible.'

'They're recognized experts there. They know how to take care of her better than you do.'

'Experts? Expert murderers you mean. She's got bedsores, Sam. Those dirty little Irish nurses they don't change her linen often enough they hate her. She must have lost twenty pounds in there.'

'Another month and you'll be flat on your back again. I'll write you a guarantee, if you want.'

My father became a regular at Tansky's again and, once more, I had to go in and kiss my grandmother in the morning. Amazingly, she had begun to look like a man. Little hairs had sprouted on her chin, she had grown a spiky grey moustache, and she was practically bald.

Yet again my uncles and aunts sent five dollar bills, though erratically, to help pay for my grandmother's support. Elderly people, former followers of my grandfather, came to inquire about the old lady's health. They sat in the back bedroom with her, leaning on their canes, talking to themselves and rocking to and fro. 'The Holy Shakers,' my father called them. I avoided the seamed, shrunken old men because they always wanted to pinch my cheeks or trick me with a dash of snuff and laugh when I sneezed. When the visit with my grandmother was over the old people would unfailingly sit in the kitchen with my mother for another hour, watching her make *lokshen*, slurping lemon tea out of a saucer. They would recall the sayings and books and charitable deeds of the late Zaddik.

'At the funeral,' my mother never wearied of telling them, 'they had to have six motorcycle policemen to control the crowds.'

In the next two years there was no significant change in my grandmother's condition, though fatigue, ill-temper, and even morbidity enveloped my mother again. She fought with her brothers and sisters and once, after a particularly bitter quarrel, I found her sitting with her head in her hands. 'If, God forbid, I had a stroke,' she said, 'would you send me to the Old People's Home?'

'Of course not.'

'I hope that never in my life do I have to count on my children for anything.'

The seventh summer of my grandmother's illness she was supposed to die and we did not know from day to day when it would happen. I was often sent out to eat at an aunt's or at my other grandmother's house. I was hardly ever at home. In those days they let boys into the left-field bleachers of Delormier Downs free during the week and Duddy, Gas sometimes, Hershey, Stan, Arty and me spent many an afternoon at the ball park. The Montreal Royals, kingpin of the Dodger farm system, had a marvellous club at the time. There was Jackie Robinson, Roy Campanella, Lou Ortiz, Red Durrett, Honest John Gabbard, and Kermit Kitman. Kitman was our hero. It used to give us a charge to watch that crafty little Jew, one of ours, running around out there with all those tall dumb southern crackers. 'Hey, Kitman,' we would yell, 'Hey, shmohead, if your father knew you played ball on *shabus*—' Kitman, alas, was all field and no hit. He never made the majors. 'There goes Kermit Kitman,' we would holler, after he had gone down swinging again, 'the first Jewish strike-out king of the International League.' This we promptly followed up by bellowing choice imprecations in Yiddish.

It was after one of these games, on a Friday afternoon, that I came home to find a crowd gathered in front of our house.

'That's the grandson,' somebody said.

A knot of old people stood staring at our front door from across the street. A taxi pulled up and my aunt hurried out, hiding her face in her hands.

'After so many years,' a woman said.

'And probably next year they'll discover a cure. Isn't that always the case?'

The flat was clotted. Uncles and aunts from my father's side of the family, strangers, Dr Katzman, neighbours, were all milling around and talking in hushed voices. My father was in the kitchen, getting out the apricot brandy. 'Your grandmother's dead,' he said.

'Where's Maw?'

'In the bedroom with . . . You'd better not go in.'

'I want to see her.'

My mother wore a black shawl and glared down at a knot of handkerchief clutched in a fist that had been cracked by washing soda. 'Don't come in here,' she said.

Several bearded round-shouldered men in shiny black coats surrounded the bed. I couldn't see my grandmother.

'Your grandmother's dead.'

'Daddy told me.'

'Go wash your face and comb your hair.'

'Yes.'

'You'll have to get your own supper.'

'Sure.'

'One minute. The *baba* left some jewellery. The necklace is for Rifka and the ring is for your wife.'

'Who's getting married?'

'Better go and wash your face. Remember behind the ears, please.'

Telegrams were sent, the obligatory long distance calls were made, and all through the evening relatives and neighbours and old followers of the Zaddik poured into the house. Finally, the man from the funeral parlour arrived.

'There goes the only Jewish businessman in town,' Segal said, 'who wishes all his customers were German.'

'This is no time for jokes.'

'Listen, life goes on.'

My Cousin Jerry had begun to affect a cigarette holder. 'Soon the religious mumbo-jumbo starts,' he said to me.

'Wha'?'

'Everybody is going to be sickeningly sentimental.'

The next day was the sabbath and so, according to law, my grandmother couldn't be buried until Sunday. She would have to lie on the floor all night. Two grizzly women in white came to move and wash the body and a professional mourner arrived to sit up and pray for her. 'I don't trust his face,' my mother said. 'He'll fall asleep.'

'He won't fall asleep.'

'You watch him, Sam.'

'A fat lot of good prayers will do her now. Alright! Okay! I'll watch him.'

My father was in a fury with Segal.

'The way he goes after the apricot brandy you'd think he never saw a bottle in his life before.'

Rifka and I were sent to bed, but we couldn't sleep. My aunt was sobbing over the body in the living room; there was the old man praying, coughing and spitting into his handkerchief whenever he woke; and the hushed voices and whimpering from the kitchen, where my father and mother sat. Rifka allowed me a few drags off her cigarette.

'Well, *pisherke*, this is our last night together. Tomorrow you can take over the back room.'

'Are you crazy?'

'You always wanted it for yourself, didn't you?'

'She died in there, but.'

'So?'

'I couldn't sleep in there now.'

'Good night and happy dreams.'

'Hey, let's talk some more.'

'Did you know,' Rifka said, 'that when they hang a man the last thing that happens is that he has an orgasm?'

'A wha'?'

'Skip it. I forgot you were still in kindergarten.'

'Kiss my Royal Canadian—'

'At the funeral, they're going to open the coffin and throw dirt in her face. It's supposed to be earth from Eretz. They open it and you're going to have to look.'

'Says you.'

A little while after the lights had been turned out Rifka approached my bed, her head covered with a sheet and her arms raised high. 'Bouyo-bouyo. Who's that sleeping in my bed? Woo-woo.'

My uncle who was in the theatre and my aunt from Toronto came to the funeral. My uncle, the rabbi, was there too.

'As long as she was alive,' my mother said, 'he couldn't even send her five dollars a month. I don't want him in the house, Sam. I can't bear the sight of him.'

'You're upset,' Dr Katzman said, 'and you don't know what you're saying.'

'Maybe you'd better give her a sedative,' the rabbi said.

'Sam will you speak up for once, please.'

Flushed, eyes heated, my father stepped up to the rabbi. 'I'll tell you this straight to your face, Israel,' he said. 'You've gone down in my estimation.'

The rabbi smiled a little.

'Year by year,' my father continued, his face burning a brighter red, 'your stock has gone down with me.'

My mother began to weep and she was led unwillingly to a bed. While my father tried his utmost to comfort her, as he muttered consoling things, Dr Katzman plunged a needle into her arm. 'There we are,' he said.

I went to sit on the stoop outside with Duddy. My uncle, the rabbi, and Dr Katzman stepped into the sun to light cigarettes.

'I know exactly how you feel,' Dr Katzman said. 'There's been a death in the family and the world seems indifferent to your loss. Your heart is broken and yet it's a splendid summer day . . . a day made for love and laughter . . . and that must seem very cruel to you.'

The rabbi nodded; he sighed.

'Actually,' Dr Katzman said, 'it's remarkable that she held out for so long.'

'Remarkable?' the rabbi said. 'It's written that if a man has been married twice he will spend as much time with his first wife in heaven as he did on earth. My father, may he rest in peace, was married to his first wife for seven years and my mother, may she rest in peace, has managed to keep alive for seven years. Today in heaven she will be able to join my father, may he rest in peace.'

Dr Katzman shook his head. 'It's amazing,' he said. He told my uncle that he was writing a book based on his experiences as a healer. 'The mysteries of the human heart.'

'Yes.'

'Astonishing.'

My father hurried outside. 'Dr Katzman, please. It's my wife. Maybe the injection wasn't strong enough. She just doesn't stop crying. It's like a tap. Can you come in, please?'

'Excuse me,' Dr Katzman said to my uncle.

'Of course.' My uncle turned to Duddy and me. 'Well, boys,' he said, 'what would you like to be when you grow up?'

JANE RULE
b. 1931

Slogans

Jessica did not say, 'I am dying.' She said, 'I live from day to day,' that cliché of terminal therapy. Some people never did learn to say the word, *cancer*, but nearly everyone could master a slogan.

Already divorced before her first bout, the children all away at school or college, Jessica bought a wig, took a lover, and in the first remission went with him to Europe.

'Serious about him? Of course not,' she explained to a friend they visited. 'I'm not serious about anything.'

After the second bout, she put a pool in at her summer place and then nearly regretted it.

'The children come home not only with lovers but with pets. I am being overrun with dogs and budgies and a bob-tailed cat.'

'It's given her permission to be selfish,' her critical sister observed.

'She's finally doing what she pleases,' explained an admiring friend.

'I live from day to day,' was Jessica's only answer.

For some that obviously meant doing what they'd always done, going to work every day or not dropping out of the bridge club or still having everyone for Christmas. For Jessica it meant something quite different, lovers, trips, and swimming pools. Finally, at the end of her second remission, when she discovered it was not arthritis in her back but cancer of the spine, she took a trip across the continent to see her birthplace, to attend her twenty-fifth reunion at college, to resurrect old friends who had not been much more than signatures on Christmas cards for years.

'If I'd known you were planning to go to the reunion,' Nancy wrote, 'I would have planned to go myself,' a lie, for not having married, given birth, or divorced, Nancy was uncertain what she might say to friends of twenty-five years ago, even if it was also to be Jessica's premature wake. 'Come and see me on your way home,' she added.

When Jessica accepted her invitation, Nancy tried to remember what kind of a friendship theirs had been. They lived in the same dorm, and they both had clownish reputations, teeth too strong, brows too high to be pretty. So they were funny instead, co-operatively so, setting each other up in song or gag or prank, protecting each other, too, from being thought to be just fools. Jessica had been clever as well, good at winning elections, and Nancy was smart. They were never roommates, never a team, but Jessica was in the crowd Nancy took home for a week of spring skiing, and Nancy was among the few friends Jessica took home singly to keep her holiday company in the house of a much younger sister, reclusive father and put-up-with-it mother, both long since dead of wasting diseases. Nancy's parents were still skiing the slopes, and, if she needed a slogan, it was learning how to live forever.

Jessica and Nancy hadn't much confided in each other, but they came to depend on each other in a casual way, more like sisters than like friends but without sisterly intolerance. Nancy knew first hand about what Jessica called 'the gloom of the ancestral mansion', and Jessica knew that Nancy didn't care a fig about the slopes. 'Oh God . . .' they were apt to say to each other just before Christmas holidays.

But one evening, towards the end of their senior year, Nancy went to Jessica's room to borrow a book or check an assignment and stayed for a cigarette, then another. Jessica was obviously in a mood she was trying to joke herself out of.

'Mother says I must simply resign myself to a tailored exterior. I don't tell her about my underwear. I give half a dozen pairs of white cotton pants to the Good Will every year and spend my pocket money on black lace and apricot ruffles. Do you believe me?'

Jessica opened a bureau drawer to reveal stacks of what Nancy's mother would have called 'whorish' underwear.

'Some people are too rich to worry about being old maids,' Jessica said.

'I won't even be able to afford to marry a poor man.'

Had Jessica actually asked Nancy what she was going to do, or had she, out of embarrassment at Jessica's vulnerability or some moody need of her own, simply offered her confession?

'I'm a lesbian. I don't suppose I will marry.'

'Oh, God,' Jessica said. 'What is it about me that people are always telling me such awful things? Why do I have to bear it?'

It was years before Nancy again risked a friendship with that information. It did seem to her that she had taken unfair advantage of Jessica, presumed far too much on her good will. Jessica hadn't dropped her, but they were both careful, in the months before graduation, to avoid being alone together.

They had met only once in the years since by accident on the street in Edinburgh, both there for the same festival, Nancy with Ann, her lover, and Jessica with her stiff young husband, George. They were glad to see each other and raucous about it, like the college girls they had recently been.

'Come help me buy a set of bagpipes,' Nancy suggested. 'I've decided I can't have them unless I can manage to play them.'

While an embarrassed Ann and George stood by, Nancy blew mightily into the instrument they found without being able to make a sound over Jessica's laughter. Only when Nancy had left the bagpipes on the counter and crossed the shop to consider the kilts, did there come a soft groan of air like a creature expiring.

'That doesn't count,' Jessica said firmly.

When they were back in the street, taking their leave of each other, Jessica explained, 'We're having to cut our trip short. My father's dying.'

Faithfully over the years, they wrote their Christmas notes to each other, Jessica reporting the progress of her children, the success of her husband's business, the move to a city apartment when the last child went to boarding school, Nancy describing her work, the house she and Ann had bought together, the progress of nieces and nephews, the health of parents.

They had nothing in common really. What held them to their ritual was the shadow of guilt that one evening had cast over their otherwise easy friendship, Nancy's for her burdensome indiscretion, Jessica's probably for her lack of sympathy. That they had both aged into a more permissive climate made that guilt nothing more than a seasoning for their yearly good will. Yet without it, there would have been no reason for putting a good face on year after year.

Then Jessica divorced, apparently with great relief. She asked Nancy some practical questions about getting a job, and Nancy gave what advice she could, but across a continent and the years, Nancy could not easily imagine with Jessica what she might do. It became obvious that Jessica entertained the idea of a job only to be entertained. When the children weren't at home, she found cruises, courses in art history, and shopping for new clothes enough to occupy her. Probably the post-cancer lover had not been the first. Remembering the underwear, Nancy speculated that he might have been one of many over the years.

Now with a spine of fast multiplying cells which would this time surely kill her, Jessica was crossing the continent and coming for dinner and the night.

Ann was fixing the guest room, twin-bedded now that Nancy's parents preferred it when they were away from their own king-sized. It was an arrangement that suited an increasing number of their friends, a less melodramatic symbol of decline than a visit from a dying friend, but it saddened Nancy simply. She had decided, she wasn't sure why, to bake cookies. Motherly gestures, whatever the occasion, occurred to her more and more often these days. She wondered if she'd ever said, in one of her Christmas notes, that she was white-haired now.

'Are you going to smoke in front of her?' Ann asked.

'I hadn't thought about it,' Nancy said, handing Ann a cookie to sample.

Nancy got out the large cookie tin, brought to them once by a would-be lover neither of them had liked, partly for that reason. They had kept the tin because they did like it, a wreath of old fashioned flowers stencilled on the lid, in the centre of which was the motto·

> To the House
> of a Friend
> The Road is
> Never long.

It reminded Nancy of the petit-pointed mottoes of her great-grandmother and her great-aunts which used to hang in the stairwell of an old summer house. In childhood, Nancy had been surrounded by protective, promising slogans and superstitions, making wishes on everything from a load of hay to the first raspberries of the season, crossing fingers against her own white lies, wearing a small cache of herbs around her neck to ward off germs.

The tin was too large to put on the table unless they had a crowd. Then always someone began to read the verses stencilled on its four sides.

> Monday's child is
> Fair of Face
> Tuesday's child is
> Full of Grace

Nancy could never remember the day she was born. She knew it was one of the hard ones, either 'Thursday's child has far to go,' or 'Saturday's child works hard for a living.' It was easy to remember that Ann was Friday's child.

Friends usually didn't know their own days either. Nancy didn't always tell them to look in the back of the phone book where the years were blocked out, in silly dread that someone would discover a Wednesday birthday and be 'full of woe'.

'I'd better put the cookies on a plate,' Nancy decided.

'Doesn't Jessica know?' Ann asked surprised.

'Oh, that, sure, I told her years ago when we were still in college.'

The tin was also, of course, an 'in' joke, which was why it had been given them:

> The child that is born
> on the Sabbath Day
> Is bonny, blythe, good
> and gay.

It was Wednesday, not Sunday, from which Nancy wished she could protect Jessica.

Coming towards Nancy through the clutter of people at the baggage claim area, Jessica didn't look as if she needed protection. Though her hair was short and the flesh had begun to fall away from her jaw line, she looked very much like herself. Only when they embraced, a gesture that startled Nancy, could she feel Jessica's thinness under her disguising clothes. Then Jessica was standing her off to look at her.

'I've decided there are two categories of classmates: totally unrecognizable or made up to play the part of a forty-six-year-old woman. You're in category two. That hair's fantastic. Is it a wig?'

'No, my very own.'

'So's mine,' Jessica said proudly, taking a handful to demonstrate. 'But not as distinguished as yours. And mine's a suspicious length. I look like a man recently out of the army or prison.'

'You look elegant,' Nancy said and meant it.

Jessica hadn't rejected her mother's advice. But the suit she wore, a combination of suede and cashmere, was expensively soft and becoming.

'Do you like it?' Jessica asked, looking down at herself. 'It's even more important to divorce a rich man once you've married him. I bought it at Carmel last week.'

Claiming her bag, walking to the car, driving home, they talked in their old casual easiness. There were, after all, all those people and those four years they had in common, a larger store than Nancy had imagined, not coming directly from a reunion.

'Vera, do you remember Vera?' Jessica asked. 'Sure you do. She was that little blonde who was funny *and* pretty. Well, she's still the belle of the ball. She divorced her husband, got a huge settlement, the house, alimony, and now he's moved back in and wants to marry her again. Nothing doing! She likes him better as a star boarder. She says it's much more romantic and practical, because now she's the only woman he can afford.'

'Was Larsen there?' Nancy asked.

'Oh, no. The really colourful ones, the really interesting ones, like Larsen, like you, don't go to reunions.'

'Like me?' Nancy asked surprised.

'Being a lesbian by now, even in those conservative circles is, well, admirably scandalous. And then you have a career . . .'

'I call it a job,' Nancy answered.

'Well, we weren't trained to have jobs, were we? Not like girls today. Even mine. The college is a different place, you know. No curfew, men in the rooms. Some of our classmates were shocked about that. But I said the only thing that shocked me was how stupid we were to put up with all those rules.'

'Do you remember,' Nancy said, 'when we got campused for a weekend for opening a side door after six o'clock?'

'We'd probably be expelled now. There are locks everywhere, even on the rooms. If you want to go out, even to the library, after dark, you have to call the campus escort,' Jessica said.

'What about Dr Ryan?' Nancy asked.

'She gave the dinner speech. She retires next year. She's *old*, Nancy, dottery.'

Once they arrived at the house and Nancy could look directly at Jessica, she saw the sudden death's head strain in Jessica's face.

'Rest?' she asked.

'Yes,' Jessica agreed simply.

Jessica was still in the guest room when Ann got home from work.

'How is she?'

'Just the same . . . and dying,' Nancy answered. 'I don't know.'

'How are you?'

'Very glad she's come,' Nancy said, 'and frightened for her.'

'Can she talk about it?'

'She hasn't.'

They began to prepare dinner together without exchanging the ordinary bits of their separate days.

By the time Jessica joined them she had refreshed herself. She embraced

Ann as warmly as she had Nancy, as if to include her in that old friendship though they had met only once.

'No drink, thanks. Do go ahead,' she encouraged. 'And if you smoke, please smoke. I can't stand the role of Hamlet's ghost.'

' "Swear," ' Nancy intoned dramatically, remembering that they used to say that, not remembering why.

'I also hate to waste time resting,' Jessica said. 'They'll have to put me in again and do something about me when I get home.'

'It must be awful,' Nancy said.

'It is,' Jessica answered. 'Do you know what I hate most? All those articles about the "cancer personality", trying to make you feel guilty as well as sick.'

'It's the medical profession, passing the buck,' Ann said.

'And the friends and relatives. My daughter thinks it's God's wrath for my wicked ways. I said to her, "Ducky, the only reason I have to die is that we all do. You find me a survivor, and I'll repent." '

'Why is everyone so stuck on cause and effect, I wonder?' Ann asked.

'A combination of Newtonian physics and Christianity,' Nancy suggested, 'when we need Einstein and possibly Zen.'

'Nobody said anything remotely like that at the reunion,' Jessica said, laughing. 'Nancy, you don't disappoint me.'

Nancy remembered how little anyone at college had ever talked about what interested her, how Jessica had always covered for her accidents of seriousness and turned them into a joke.

'Well, as one of our gallant classmates put it, if divorce makes you a high risk for cancer, at least it lowers the risk of being found chopped in pieces.'

'What a ghoulish way of putting it,' Nancy said.

'But Josie Enright (she was in one of the hill halls, do you remember?) had that distinction, haven't you heard, and her "widower" got off scot free,' Jessica said.

'It's not the sort of thing that gets into the class newsletter,' Nancy said.

'She was in the obits. In the *Quarterly*, not with the gory details. "Suddenly," I think it said,' Jessica said.

'Is the general consensus against marriage by now?' Ann asked.

'Oh, I don't suppose so: Sore heads tend to congregate. Ninety percent of us were really majoring in marriage after all. The awards go to those getting ready for their silver anniversaries with one pregnant child or child-in-law. On some, smugness is even becoming. Do you remember Judy Framton?'

Nancy nodded as she got up to clear the table.

'Well, she's proto-grandmother of the first category, totally unrecognizable.'

'I wouldn't have the courage to go back,' Ann said.

'It was fun,' Jessica said. 'I haven't laughed that much in a long time.'

Nancy brought the plate of cookies to the table.

'Home made?' Jessica asked.

'It's what lesbians do when they're alone together,' Nancy said.

'Now I wish I'd known *that* before the reunion,' Jessica said. 'There are still sheltered lives among us. Gosh, I haven't baked cookies in years. Do you remember the enormous chocolate chip cookies they used to make at college? They still do.'

Nancy remembered the short-and-thicks, milkshakes you had to eat with a spoon, and fresh orange juice at the college shop.

'I had to buy the whole pitcher of it once,' Jessica remembered, 'because Donna (she was my roommate) was so hungover she couldn't write her exam without it.'

The remembering went on over coffee, which Jessica didn't drink. She and Nancy apologized to Ann, who said she knew some of the stories as well as they did and could even join in on a punch line or two. But Jessica was tiring.

'You have a long trip tomorrow,' Nancy said.

'Oh, I know,' Jessica said.

Ann and Nancy went into the kitchen to finish loading the dishwasher.

'What about Einstein and Zen?' Ann asked.

'We have to accept the random. We know all the leaves are going to fall, but we have no way of knowing when any particular one . . .'

They heard Jessica coming down the hall to the bathroom. She stopped at the kitchen door.

'I forgot to say about the flowers in my room. They're lovely. Goodnight.'

For a few moments they moved around the kitchen without speaking. Then Nancy said, 'Zen masters write death poems. Odd things like:

> Seventy-seven long years
> I've reviled the Scriptures,
> Zen itself. A failure through
> And through, I piss on Brahma.'

Ann gave a startled laugh and then said, 'Maybe you should have . . .'

Nancy shook her head, 'It's just another slogan.'

AUSTIN C. CLARKE
b. 1932

Griff!

Griff was a black man from Barbados who sometimes denied he was black. Among black Americans who visited Toronto, he was black: 'Right on!' 'Peace and love, Brother!' and 'Power to the people!' would suddenly become his vocabulary. He had emigrated to Toronto from Britain, and as a result, thought of himself as a black Englishman. But he was blacker than most immigrants. In colour, that is. It must have been this double indemnity of being British and black that caused him to despise his blackness. To his friends, and his so-called friends, he flaunted his British experience, and the 'civilized' bearing that came with it; and he liked being referred to as a West Indian who had lived in London, for he was convinced that he had an edge, in breeding, over those West Indians who had come straight to Canada from the canefields in the islands. He had attended Ascot many times and he had seen the Queen in her box. He hated to be regarded as just black.

'Griff, but you're blasted black, man,' Clynn said once, at a party in his own home, 'and the sooner you realize that fact, the more rass-hole wiser you would be!' Clynn usually wasn't so honest, but that night he was drunk.

What bothered Griff along with his blackness was that most of his friends were 'getting through': cars and houses and 'swinging parties' every Friday night, and a yearly trip back home for Christmas and for Carnival. Griff didn't have a cent in the bank. 'And you don't even have *one* blasted child, neither!' Clynn told him that same night.

But Griff was the best-dressed man present. They all envied him for that. And nobody but his wife really knew how poor he was in pocket. Griff smiled at them from behind his dark-green dark glasses. His wife smiled too, covering her embarrassment for her husband. She never criticized him in public, by gesture or by attitude, and she said very little to him about his ways, in their incensed apartment. Nevertheless, she carried many burdens of fear and failure for her husband's apparent ambitionless attitudes. England had wiped some British manners on her, too. Deep down inside, Griff was saying to Clynn and the others, *godblindyougodblindyou*!

'Griffy, dear, pour your wife a Scotch, darling. I've decided to enjoy myself.' She was breathing as her yoga teacher had taught her to do.

And Griffy said, *godblindyougodblindyou*! again, to Clynn; poured his wife her drink, poured himself a large Scotch on the rocks, and vowed, *I am going to drink all your Scotch tonight, boy*! This was his only consolation. Clynn's words had become wounds. Griff grew so centred around his own problems that he did not, for one moment, consider any emotion coming from his wife. 'She's just a nice kid,' he told Clynn once, behind her back. He had draped his wife in an aura of sanctity; and he would become angry to the point of violence, and scare anybody, when he thought his friends' conversation had touched the cloud and virginity of the sanctity in which he had clothed her: like taking her out on Friday and Saturday nights to the Cancer Calypso Club, in the entrails of the city, where pimps and doctors and lonely immigrants hustled women and brushed reputations in a brotherhood of illegal liquor. And if the Club got too crowded, Griff would feign a headache, and somehow make his wife feel the throbbing pain of his migraine, and would take her home in a taxi, and would recover miraculously on his way back along Sherbourne Street, and with the tact of a good barrister, would make tracks back to the Cancer and dance the rest of the limp-shirt night with a woman picked from among the lonely West Indian stags: his jacket let loose to the sweat and the freedom, his body sweet with the music rejoicing in the happy absence of his wife in the sweet presence of this woman.

But after these hiatuses of dance, free as the perspiration pouring down his face, his wife would be put to bed around midnight, high up in the elevator, high off the invisible hog of credit, high up on the Chargex Card, and Griff would be tense, for days. It was a tenseness which almost gripped his body in a paralysis, as it strangled the blood in his body when the payments of loans for furniture and for debts approached, and they always coincided with the approaching of his paycheque, already earmarked against its exact face value. In times of this kind of stress, like his anxiety at the racetrack, when the performance of a horse contradicted his knowledge of the Racing Form and left him broke, he would grumble, 'Money is *naught* all.'

Losing his money would cause him to ride on streetcars, and he hated any kind of public transportation. He seemed to realize his blackness more intensely; white people looking at him hard—questioning his presence, it seemed. It might be nothing more than the way his colour changed colour, going through a kaleidoscope of tints and shades under the varying ceiling lights of the streetcar. Griff never saw it this way. To him, it was staring. And his British breeding told him that to look at a person you didn't know (except she was a woman) was *infra dig*. *Infra dig* was the term he chose when he told Clynn about these incidents of people staring at him on the streetcars. The term formed itself on his broad thin lips, and he could never get the courage to spit it at the white people staring at him.

When he lost his money, his wife, after not having had dinner nor the money to buy food (the landlord locked the apartment door with a padlock one night while they were at a party), would smile in that half-censuring smile, a smile that told you she had been forced against the truth of her circumstances, to believe with him, that money was 'not all, at-all.' But left to herself, left to the ramblings of her mind and her aspirations and her fingers over the new broadloom in her girl-friend's home, where her hand clutched the tight sweating glass of Scotch on the rocks, her Scotch seeming to absorb her arriving unhappiness with the testimony of her friend's broadloom, or in Clynn's recreation room, which she called a 'den'; in her new sponge of happiness, fabricated like the house in her dreams, she would put her smile around her husband's losses, and in the embrace they would both feel higher than anybody present, because, 'Griffy, dear, you were the only one there with a Master of Arts.'

'I have more brains than *any one* there. They only coming-on strong. But I don't have to come on strong, uh mean, I don't *have* to come on strong, but . . . '

One day, at Greenwood Race Track, Griff put his hand into his pocket and pulled out five twenty-dollar bills, and put them on one race: he put three twenty-dollar bills on Number Six, on *the fucking nose—to win! Eh?* (he had been drinking earlier at the Pilot Tavern); and he also put two twenty-dollar bills on Number Six, *to show*. He had studied the Racing Form like a man studying torts: he would put it into his pocket, take it out again, read it in the bathroom as he trimmed his moustache; he studied it on the sweet-smelling toilet bowl, he studied it as he might have studied laws in Britain; and when he spoke of his knowledge in the Racing Form, it was as if he had received his degrees in the Laws of Averages, and not in English Literature and Language.

And he 'gave' a horse to a stranger that same day at Greenwood. 'Buy Number Three, man. I read the Form for three days, taking notes. It *got* to be Number Three!' The man thanked him because he himself was no expert; and he spent five dollars (more than he had ever betted before) on Number Three, to *win*. 'I read the Form like a blasted book, man!' Griff told him. He slipped away to the wicket farthest away; and like a thief, he bought his own tickets: 'Number Six! Sixty on the nose! forty to show!' and to himself he said, smiling, 'Law o' averages, man, law of averages.'

Tearing up Number Six after the race, he said to the man who had looked for him to thank him, and who thanked him and shook his hand and smiled with him, 'I don't have to come on strong, man, I *mastered* that Form.' He looked across the field to the board at the price paid on Number Three, and then he said to the man, 'Lend me two dollars for the next race, man. I need a bet.'

The man gave him three two-dollar bills and told him, '*Any* time, pardner, any time! Keep the six dollars. Thank *you*!'

Griff was broke. Money is *naught* all, he was telling the same man who, seeing him waiting by the streetcar stop, had picked him up. Griff settled himself back into the soft leather of the new Riviera, going west, and said again to the man, 'Money is naught all! But I don't like to come on strong. Uh mean, you see how I mastered the *Form*, did you?'

'You damn right, boy!' the man said, adjusting the tone of the tape-deck. 'How you like my new car?'

The elevator was silent that evening, on the way up to the twenty-fifth floor; and he could not even lose his temper with it: 'This country is uncivilized—even the elevators—they make too much noise a man can't even think in them; this place only has money but it doesn't have any culture or breeding or style so everybody is grabbing for money money money.' The elevator that evening didn't make a comment. And neither did his wife: she had been waiting for him to come from work, straight, with the money untouched in his monthly paycheque. But Griff had studied the Racing Form thoroughly all week, and had worked out the laws and averages and notations in red felt-pen ink; had circled all the 'longshots' in green, and had moved through the 'donkeys' (the slow horses) with waves of blue lines; had had three 'sure ones' for that day; and had averaged his wins against heavy bets against his monthly salary, it was such a 'goddamn cinch'! He had developed a migraine headache immediately after lunch, sipped through the emergency exit at the side, holding his head in his hand, his head full of tips and cinches, and had caught the taxi which miraculously had been waiting there, with the meter ticking; had run through the entrance of the racetrack, up the stairs, straight for the wicket to bet on the Daily Double; had invested fifty dollars on a 'long shot' (worked out scientifically from his red-

marked, green-and-blue wavy-line Form), and had placed 'two goddamn dollars' on the favourite'—just to be sure!—and went into the
clubhouse. The favourite won. Griff lost fifty dollars by the first race.
But he had won two dollars on his two-dollar bet.

'I didn't want to come on strong,' he told the man who was then a
stranger to him. The man could not understand what he was talking
about: and he asked for no explanation. 'I didn't want to come on strong,
but I worked out all the winners today, since ten o'clock last night. I
picked them, man. I can pick them. But I was going for the 'long shot'.
Hell, what is a little bread? Fifty dollars! Man, that isn't no bread, at all.
If I put my hand in my pocket now, look . . . *this is* bread! . . . five
hundred dollars. I can lose, man, I can afford to lose bread. Money don't
mean anything to me, man, money is no *big* thing! . . . money is *naught*
all.'

His wife remained sitting on the Scandinavian couch, which had the
habit of whispering to them, once a month, 'Fifty-nine thirty-five owing
on me!' in payments. She looked up at Griff as he gruffed through the
door. She smiled. Her face did not change its form, or its feeling, but she
smiled. Griff grew stiff at the smile. She got up from the couch. She
brushed the anxiety of time from her waiting miniskirt ('My wife must
dress well, and look *sharp*, even in the house!'), she tidied the already-
tidy hairdo she had just got from Azans, and she went into the kitchen,
which was now a wall separating Griff from her. Griff looked at the
furniture, and wished he could sell it all in time for the races tomorrow
afternoon: the new unpaid-for living-room couch, desk, matching executive chair, the table and matching chairs where they ate, desk pens
thrown in, into the bargain the salesman swore he was giving them, ten
Friday nights ago down Yonge Street, scatter rugs, Scandinavian-type
settee with its matching chairs, like Denmark in the fall season, in style
and design; he looked at the motto, CHRIST IS THE HEAD OF THIS
HOME, which his wife had insisted upon taking as another 'bargain';
and he thought of how relaxed he felt driving in the man's new Riviera.
He took the new Racing Form, folded in half and already notated, from
his breast pocket, and sat on the edge of the bed, in the wisteria-smelling
bedroom. The wife had been working, he said to himself, as he noticed
he was sitting on his clean folded pyjamas. But he left them there and
perused the handicaps and histories of the horses. The bundle buggy for
shopping was rolling over the polished wood of the living-room floor.
The hinges of the doors of the clothes cupboard in the hallway were
talking. A clothes hanger dropped on the skating rink of the floor. The
cupboard door was closed. The bundle buggy rolled down from its prop
against the cupboard and jangled onto the hardboard ice. Griff looked up

and saw a smooth brown, black-maned horse standing before him. It was his wife.

'Griffy, dear? I am ready.' She had cleaned out her pocketbook of old papers, useless personal and business cards accumulated over drinks and at parties; and she had made a budget of her month's allowance, allowing a place in the tidied wallet section for her husband's arrival. The horse in Griff's mind changed into a donkey. 'Clynn called. He's having a party tonight. Tennish. After the supermarket, I want to go round to the corner, to the cleaners' and stop off at the liquor store for a bottle of wine. My sisters're coming over for dinner, and they're bringing their boy-friends. I want to have a roast. Should I also buy you a bottle of Black-and-White, Griffy, dear?': *they're at post! they're off!* . . . *as they come into the backstretch, moving for the wire . . . it's Phil Kingston by two lengths, Crimson Admiral, third, True Willie . . . Phil Kingston, Crimson Admiral, True Willie . . .* but Griff had already moved downstairs, in the direction of the cashiers' wicket: 'Long-shot in your arse! Uh got it, this time, old man!' *True Willie is making a move. True Willie! . . . Phil Kingston now by one length, True Willie is coming on the outside! True Willie! It's True Willie!*

'It's almost time for the supermarket to close, Griff dear, and I won't like to be running about like a race horse, sweating and perspiring. I planned my housework and I tried to finish all my housework on time so I'll be fresh for when you came home. I took my time, too, doing my housework and I took a shower so I won't get excited by the time my sisters come and I didn't bother to go to my yoga class' *it's True Willie by a neck! True Willie! What a run, ladies and gentlemen! what a run! True Willie's the winner, and it's now official!* 'and I even made a promise to budget this month so we'll have some money for all these bills we have to pay. We have to pay these bills and we never seem to be paying them off and the rent's due in two days, no, today! oh, I forgot to tell you that the bank manager called about your loan, to say that' *it's True Willie, by a neck!*

Griff smashed all the furniture in the apartment in his mind, and then walked through the door. 'Oh Griffy, dear! Stooly called to say he's getting a lift to the races tomorrow and if you're going he wants you to . . .'

Griff was standing in the midst of a group of middle-aged West Indians, all of whom pretended through the amount of liquor they drank, and the 'gashes they lashed' that they were still young black studs.

'Man, when I entered that door, she knew better than to open her fucking mouth to me! To *me*? *Me*?' The listening red eyes understood the unspoken chastisement in his threatening voice. 'Godblindyou! she knew better than, *that*; me? if she'd only opened her fucking mouth, I would have . . . ' They raised their glasses, all of them, to their mouths, not exactly at the same time, but sufficiently together, to make it a ritualistic harmony among men. 'As man!' Griff said, and then wet his lips. They would, each of them, have chastised their women in precisely the same way that Griff was boasting about disciplining his. But he never did. He could never even put his hand to his wife's mouth to stop her from talking. And she was not the kind of woman you would want to beat: she was much too delicate. The history of their marriage had coincided with her history of a woman's illness which had been kept silent among them; and its physical manifestation, in the form of a large scar that crawled halfway around her neck, darker in colour than the natural shade of her skin, had always, from the day of recovery after the operation, been covered by a neckline on each of her dresses. And this became her natural style and fashion in clothes. Sometimes, in more daring moods, she would wear a silk scarf to hide the scar. 'If my wife wasn't so blasted sickly, I would've put my hand in her arse, *many times*! many times I've thought o' putting my hand in her arse, after a bad day at the races!' He had even thought of doing something drastic about her smile and about his losses at the track and at poker. It was not clearly shaped in his mind: and at times, with this violent intent, he could not think of whom he would perform this drastic act on. After a bad day at the track, the thought of the drastic act, like a cloud over his thoughts, would beat him down and take its toll out of his slim body which itself seemed to refuse to bend under the great psychological pressure of losing, all the time. He had just lost one hundred dollars at Woodbine Race Track, when one evening as he entered Clynn's living-room, for the usual Friday night party of Scotch and West Indian peas and rice and chicken, which Clynn's Polish wife cooked and spoiled and learned how to cook as she spoiled the food, he had just had time to adjust his shoulders in the over-sized sports jacket, when he said, braggingly, 'I just dropped a hundred. At Woodbine.' He wet his lips and smiled.

'Dollars?' It was Clynn's voice, coming from the dark corner where he poured drinks. Clynn was a man who wouldn't lend his sister, nor his mother—if she was still alive—more than five dollars at one time.

'Money don't mean anything, man.'

'A *hundred* dollars?' Clynn suddenly thought of the amount of Scotch Griff had been drinking in his house.

'Money is *naught* all.'

'You're a blasted . . . boy, do you lose *just* for fun, or wha'?' Clynn sputtered. 'Why the arse you don't become a *groom*, if you like racehorse so much? Or you's a . . . a *paffological* loser?'

'Uh mean, I don't like to come on strong, or anything, but, money is *naught* all . . . '

'Rass-hole put down my Scotch, then! You drinking my fucking Scotch!'

And it rested there. It rested there because Griff suddenly remembered he was among men who knew him: who knew his losses both in Britain and Canada. It rested there also, because Clynn and the others knew that his manner and attitude towards money, and his wife's expressionless smile, were perhaps lying expressions of a turbulent inner feeling of failure. 'He prob'ly got rass-hole ulcers, too'! Clynn said, and then spluttered into a laugh. Griff thought about it, and wondered whether he had indeed caused his wife to be changed into a different woman altogether. But he couldn't know that. Her smile covered a granite of silent and apparent contentment. He wondered whether he hated her, to the bone, and whether she hated him. He felt a spasm through his body as he thought of her hating him, and not knowing about it. For so many years living together, both here and in Britain; and she was always smiling. Her constancy and her cool exterior, her smiles, all made him wonder now, with the Scotch in his hand, about her undying devotion to him, her faithfulness, pure as the sheets in their sweet-smelling bedroom; he wondered whether 'I should throw my hand in her arse, *just* to see what she would do.' But Clynn had made up his own mind that she was, completely, destroyed inside: her guts, her spirit, her aspirations, her procreative mechanism, 'Hysterectomy all shot to pieces!' Clynn said cruelly, destroyed beyond repair, beneath the silent consolation and support which he saw her giving to her husband; at home among friends and relations, and in public among his sometimes silently criticizing friends. 'I don't mean to come on strong, but . . . '

'You really want to know what's wrong with Griff?' Clynn's sister, Princess, asked one day. 'He want a *stiff* lash in his backside! He don't know that he's gambling-'way his wife's life? He doesn't know that? Look, he don't have chick nor child. Wife working in a good job, for *decent* money, and they don't even live in a decent apartment that you could say, well, rent eating out his sal'ry. Don't own no record-player. *Nothing*. And all he doing is walking 'bout Toronto with his blasted head high in the air! He ain' know this is Northamerica? Christ, he don't even speak to poor people. He ain' have no motto-car, like some. Well, you tell me then, what the hell is Griff doing with thirteen-thousand Canadian dollars a year? Supporting race-horse? No, man, you can't tell me that, 'cause not even the *most* wutless o' Wessindians living in Toronto, could gamble'-way thirteen thousand dollars! Jesuschrist! that is twenty-six thousand back in Barbados! Think o' the land he could buy back home wid thirteen-thousand Canadian dollars. And spending it 'pon a race-horse? What the hell is a race-horse? *Thirteen thousand*? But lissen to me! one o' these mornings, that wife o' his going get up and tell him that she with-child, that she *pregnunt* . . . ' ('She can't get pregnunt, though, Princess, 'cause she already had one o' them operations!') 'Anyhow, if his wife was a diff'rent person, she would 'ave walked-out on his arse *long ago*! Or else, break his two blasted hands! And she won't spend a *day* in jail!'

When Griff heard what Princess had said about him, he shrugged his shoulders and said, 'I don't have to come on strong, but if I was a different man, I would really show these West Indian women something . . . ' He ran his thin, long, black fingers over the length of his old-fashioned slim tie, he shrugged the grey sports jacket that was a size too large, at the shoulders, into shape and place, wet his lips twice, and said, 'Grimme another Scotch, man.' While Clynn fixed the Scotch, he ran his thumb and index finger of his left hand down the razor edge of his dark brown trouser seams. He inhaled and tucked his shirt and tie neatly beneath the middle button of his sports jacket. He took the Scotch, which he liked to drink on the rocks, and he said, 'I don't have to come on strong, but I am going to tell you something . . . '

The next Friday night was the first day of fête in the long weekend. There hadn't been a long weekend in Canada for a long time. Everybody was tired of just going to work, coming home, watching CBC television, bad movies on the TV, and then going to bed. 'There ain' no action in this fucking town,' Clynn was saying for days, before the weekend appeared like raindrops on a farmer's dry-season head. And everybody agreed with him. It was so. Friday night was here, and the boys, their wives, their girl-friends, and their 'outside women' were noisy and drunk and happy. Some of the men were showing off their new bell-bottom trousers and broad leather belts worn under their bulging bellies, to make them look younger. The women, their heads shining like wet West Indian tar roads, the smell from the cosmetics and grease that went into their kinky hair and on their faces, to make them look sleek and smooth, all these smells and these women mixed with the cheap and domestic perfumes they used, whenever Avon called; and some women, wives whose husbands 'were getting through', were wearing good-looking dresses, in style and fashion; others were still back home in their style, poured in against their wishes and the better judgement of their bulging bodies; backsides big, sometimes too big, breasts bigger, waists fading into the turbulence of their middle age and their behinds, all poured against the shape of their noisy bodies, into evil-fitting, shiny material, made on sleepy nights after work, on a borrowed sewing machine. But everybody was happy. They had all forgotten now, through the flavour of the calypso and the peas and the rice, the fried chicken, the curry-chicken, that they were still living in a white man's country; and it didn't seem to bother them now, nor touch them now. Tonight, none of them would tell you that they hated Canada; that they wanted to go back home; that they were going 'to make a little money, first'; that they were only waiting till then; that they were going to go back before the 'blasted Canadian tourisses buy-up the blasted Caribbean'; they wouldn't tell you tonight that they all suffered some form of racial discrimination in Canada, and that that was to be expected, since 'there are certain things with this place that are not just right'; not tonight. Tonight, Friday night, was forgetting night. West Indian night. And they were at the Cancer Club to forget and to drink and to get drunk. To make plans for some strange woman's (or man's) body and bed, to spend 'some time' with a real West Indian 'thing', to eat her boiled mackerel and green bananas, which their wives and women had, in their ambitions to be 'decent' and Canadian, forgotten how to cook, and had left out of their diets, espe-cially when Canadian friends were coming to dinner, because that kind of food was 'plain West Indian stupidness'. Tonight, they would forget and drink, forget and dance, and dance to forget.

'Oh-Jesus-Christ, Griff!' Stooly shouted, as if he was singing a calypso. He greeted Griff this way each time he came to the Club, and each time it was as if Stooly hadn't seen Griff in months, although they might have been together at the track the same afternoon. It was just the way Stooly was. 'Oh-Jesus-Christ, Griff!' he would shout, and then he would rush past Griff, ignoring him, and make straight for Griff's wife. He would wrap his arms round her slender body (once his left hand squeezed a nipple, and Griff saw, and said to himself, 'Uh mean, I won't like to come on strong about it, but . . . '; and did nothing about it), pulling up her new minidress above the length of decency, worn for the first time tonight, exposing the expensive lace which bordered the tip of her slip. The veins of her hidden age, visible only at the back of her legs, would be exposed to Griff, who would stand and stare and feel 'funny', and feel, as another man inquired with his hands all over his wife's body, the blood and the passion and the love mix with the rum in his mouth. Sometimes, when in a passion of brandy, he would make love to his wife as if she was a different woman, as if she was no different from one of the lost women found after midnight on the crowded familiar floor of the Cancer.

'Haiii! How?' the wife would say, all the time her body was being crushed. She would say, 'Haiii! How?' every time it happened; and it happened every time; and every time it happened, Griff would stand and stare, and do nothing about it, because his memory of British breeding told him so; but he would feel mad and helpless afterwards, all night; and he would always want to kill Stooly, or kill his wife for doing it; but he always felt she was so fragile. He would want to kill Stooly more than he would want to kill his wife. But Stooly came from the same island as his wife. Griff would tell Clynn the next day, on the telephone, that he should have done something about it; but he 'didn't want to come on strong'. Apparently, he was not strong enough to rescue his wife from the rape of Stooly's arms, as he rubbed his body against hers, like a dog scratching its fleas against a tree.

Once, a complete stranger saw it happen. Griff had just ordered three drinks: one for his wife, one for himself, and one for Stooly, his friend. Griff looked at the man, and in an expansive mood (he had made the 'long shot' in the last race at Woodbine that afternoon), he asked the stranger, 'What're you drinking?'

'Rum, sah!'

'I am going to buy you a goddamn drink, just because I like you, man.'

The stranger did not change the mask on his face, but stood there, looking at Griff's dark-green lenses. Then he said, 'You isn' no blasted man at all, man!' He then looked behind: Stooly was still embracing Griff's wife. It looked as if he was feeling her up. The man took the drink from Griff, and said, 'You is no man, sah!'

Griff laughed; but no noise came out of his mouth. 'Man, that's all right. They went to school together in Trinidad.'

'In *my* books, you still ain' no fucking man, boy!' The stranger turned away from Griff: and when he got to the door of the dance floor, he said, 'Thanks for the drink, *boy*.'

The wife was standing beside Griff now, smiling as if she was a queen parading through admiring lines of subjects. She looked, as she smiled, like she was under the floodlights of some première performance she had prepared herself for a long time. She smiled, although no one in particular expected a smile from her. Her smiling went hand in hand with her new outfit. It had to be worn with a smile. It looked good, as usual, on her; and it probably understood that it could only continue to look good and express her personality if she continued smiling. At intervals, during the night, when you looked at her, it seemed as if she had taken the smile from her handbag, and had then powdered it onto her face. She could have taken it off any time, but she chose to wear it the whole night. 'Griffy, dear?' she said, although she wasn't asking him anything, or telling him anything, or even looking in his direction. 'Haiii! How?' she said to a man who brushed against her hips as he passed. The man looked suddenly frightened, because he wanted his advance to remain stealthy and masculine. When he passed back from the bar, with five glasses of cheap rum-and-Cokes in his hands, he walked far from her.

Griff was now leaning on the bar, facing the part-time barman, and talking about the results of the last race that day; his wife, her back to the bar, was looking at the men and the women, and smiling; when someone passed, who noticed her, and lingered in the recognition, she would say, 'Haiii! How?'

A large, black, badly dressed Jamaican (he was talking his way through the crowd) passed. He stared at her. She smiled. He put out his calloused construction hand, and with a little effort, he said, 'May I have this dance, gal?' Griff was still talking. But in his mind he wondered whether his wife would dance with the Jamaican. He became ashamed with himself for thinking about it. He went back to talking, and got into an argument with the part-time barman, Masher, over a certain horse that was running in the feature race the next day at Greenwood. Masher, ever watchful over the women, especially other men's, couldn't help notice that the calloused-hand Jamaican was holding on to Griff's wife's hand. With his shark-eyes he tried to get Griff's attention off horses and onto his wife. But Griff was too preoccupied. His wife placed her drink on the counter beside him, her left hand still in the paws of the Jamaican construction worker, whom nobody had seen before, and she said, 'Griffy, dear?' The man's hand on her manicured fingers had just come into his consciousness, when he wheeled around to give her her drink. He was upset. But he tried to be cool. It was the blackness of the Jamaican. And his size. Masher knew he was upset. The Jamaican reminded Griff of the 'Congo-man' in one of Sparrow's calypsos. Masher started to laugh in his spitting kee-kee laugh. And when Griff saw that everybody was laughing, and had seen the Congojamaican walk off with his wife, he too decided to laugh.

'It's all right, man,' he said, more than twice, to no one in particular, although he could have been consoling the Jamaicancongo man, or Masher, or the people nearby, or himself.

'I sorry, suh,' the Jamaican said. He smiled to show Griff that he was not a rough fellow. 'I am sorry, suh. I didn't know you was with the missis. I thought the missis was by-sheself, tonight, again, suh.'

'It's no *big* thing, man,' Griff said, turning back to talk to Masher, who by now had lost all interest in horses. Masher had had his eyes on Griff's wife, too. But Griff was worried by something new now: the man had said, '*by-sheself, tonight, again, suh*'; and that could mean only one thing: that his wife went places, like this very Club, when he wasn't with her; and he had never thought of this, and never even imagined her doing a thing like this; and he wasn't sure that it was not merely the bad grammar of the Jamaican, and not the accusation in that bad grammar, *'but language is a funny thing, a man could kill a person with language, and the accusation can't be comprehended outside of the structure of the language . . . wonder how you would parse this sentence, Clynn . . . a Jamaican fella told me last night, "by-sheself, tonight, again, suh"; now, do you put any emphasis on the position of the adverb, more than the conditional phrase?'* Griff was already dozing off into the next day's dreams of action, thinking already of what he would tell Clynn about the accident: *'Which is the most important word in that fellow's sentence structure? "By-sheself", "again", or "tonight"?'*

'Never mind the fellow looks like a canecutter, he's still a brother, Griff said to Masher, but he could have been talking into the future, the next day, to Clynn; or even to himself. 'I don't want to come on strong, but he's a brother.' The CBC television news that night dealt with the Black Power nationalism in the States. The Jamaican man and Griff's wife were now on the dance floor. Griff stole a glimpse at them, to make sure the man was not holding his wife in the same friendly way Stooly, who was a friend, would hold her. He thought he would be able to find the meaning of *'by-sheself'*, *'again'*, and *'tonight'* in the way the man held his wife. Had the Jamaican done so, Griff would have had to think even more seriously about the three words. But the Jamaican was about two hundred and fifty pounds of muscle and mackerel and green bananas. 'Some other fellow would have come on strong, just because a rough-looking chap like him, held on . . . '

'Man, Griff, you's a rass-hole idiot, man!' Masher said. He crept under the bar counter, came out, faced Griff, broke into his sneering laugh, and said, 'You's a rass-hole!' Griff laughed too, in his voiceless laugh. 'You ain' hear that man say, *'by-sheself'*, *'tonight'*, *'again'*? If I had a woman like that, I would kiss her arse, be-Christ, just for *looking* at a man like that Jamaikian-man!' Masher laughed some more, and walked away, singing the calypso the amateur band was trying to play: *'Oh Mister Walker, Uh come to see your daughter . . . '*

Griff wet his lips. His bottom lip disappeared inside his mouth, under his top lip; then he did the same thing with his top lip. He adjusted his dark glasses, and ran his right hand, with a cigarette in it, over his slim tie. His right hand was trembling. He shrugged his sports jacket into place and shape on his shoulders . . . *'Oh, Mister Walker, uh come to see ya daughterrrrr . . . '* He stood by himself in the crowd of West Indians at the door, and he seemed to be alone on a sun-setting beach back home. Only the waves of the calypsonian, and the rumbling of the congo drum, and the whispering, the loud whispering in the breakers of the people standing nearby, were with him. He was like the sea. He was like a man in the sea. He was a man at sea . . . *'tell she is the man from Sangre Grande . . . '*

The dance floor was suddenly crowded, jam-packed. Hands were going up in the air, and some under dresses, in exuberance after the music; the words in the calypso were tickling some appetites; he thought of his wife's appetite and of the Jamaican's, who could no longer be seen in the gloom of the thick number of black people; and tomorrow was races, and he had again mastered the Form. And Griff suddenly became terrifed about his wife's safety and purity, and the three words came back to him: *'by-sheself'*, *'tonight'*, *'again'*. Out of the crowd, he could see Masher's big red eyes and his teeth, skinned in mocking laugh. Masher was singing the words of the calypso: *'Tell she I come for she . . . '* The music and the waves on the beach, when the sun went behind the happy afternoon, came up like a gigantic sea, swelling and roaring as it came to where he was standing in the wet white sand; and the people beside him, whispering like birds going home to branches and rooftops, some whispering, some humming like the sea, fishing for fish and supper and for happiness, no longer in sight against the blackening dusk . . . *'she know me well, I had she already! . . . '* Stooly walked in front of him, like the lightning that jigsawed over the rushing waves; and behind Stooly was a woman, noisy and Trinidadian, 'this part-tee can't done till morning come!' like an empty tin can tied to a motor car bumper. All of a sudden, the fishermen and the fishing boats were walking back to shore, climbing out of their boats, laden with catches, their legs wet up to their knees; and they walked with their boats up to the brink of the sand. In their hands were fish. Stooly still held the hand of a woman who laughed and talked loud, 'Fête for so!' She was like a barracuda. Masher, raucous and happy, and harmless, and a woman he didn't know, were walking like Siamese twins. One of his hands could not be seen. Out of the sea, now resting from the turbulent congo drumming of the waves in the calypso, came the Jamaicancongoman, and his wife.

'Thank you very much, suh' he said, handing Griff his wife's hand. With the other hand, she was pulling her miniskirt into place. 'She is a first class dancer, suh.'

'Don't have to come on *strong*, man.'

'If I may, some other time, I would like to . . . ' the man said, smiling and wiping perspiration from his face with a red handkerchief. His voice was pleasant and it had an English accent hidden somewhere in it. But all the words Griff heard were 'I know she well, I had she already.' . . . '*by-sheself*', '*again*', '*tonight*' . . . and there were races tomorrow. His wife was smiling, smiling like the everlasting sea at calm.

'Haiii!' she said, and smiled some more. The Jamaicanman moved back into the sea for some more dancing and fish. The beach was still crowded; and in Griff's mind it was crowded, but there was no one but he standing among the broken forgotten pieces of fish: heads and tails, and empty glasses and cigarette butts, and some scales broken off in a bargain, or by chance, and the ripped-up tickets of wrong bets.

Masher appeared and said in his ear, 'If she was my wife, be-Christ, I tell you . . . ' and he left the rest for the imagination.

Griff's wife's voice continued, 'Griffy, dear?'

Masher came back from the bar with a Coke for the woman he was with. When he got close to Griff, he said in his ear, 'Even if she was only just a screw like that one I have there . . . '

'Griffy, dear, let's go home, I am feeling . . . '

' . . . and if you was *something*,' Masher was now screaming down the stairs after them. Griff was thinking of the three little words which had brought such a great lump of weakness within the pit of his stomach.

'Masher seems very happy tonight, eh, Griffy, dear? I never quite saw Masher so happy.'

' . . . you, *boy*! you, *boy*! . . .

'Masher, Haiii! How?'

'If it was mine,' Masher shouted, trying to hide the meaning of his message, 'if it was mine, and I had put only a two-dollar bet 'pon that horse, that horse that we was talking about, and, and that horse *behave*' *so*, well, I would have to *lash* that horse, till . . . *unnerstan?*'

'Griffy, dear? Masher really love horses, doesn't he, eh?'

They were around the first corner, going down the last flight of stairs, holding the rails on the right-hand side. Griff realized that the stairs were smelling of stale urine, although he could not tell why. His wife put her arm round his waist. It was the first for the day. 'I had a *great* time, a real ball, a *lovely* time!' Griff said nothing. He was tired, but he was also tense inside; still he didn't have the strength or the courage, which-ever it was he needed, to tell her how he felt, how she had humiliated him, in that peculiar West Indian way of looking at small matters, in front of all those people, he could not tell her how he felt each time he watched Stooly put his arms round her slender body; and how he felt when the strange Jamaican man, with his cluttered use of grammar broken beyond meaning and comprehending, had destroyed something, like a dream, which he had had about her for all these fifteen years of marriage. He just couldn't talk to her. He wet his lips and ran his fingers over the slim tie. All she did (for he wanted to know that he was married to a woman who could, through all the years of living together, read his mind, so he won't have to talk) was smile. That goddamn smile, he cursed. The sports jacket shoulders were shrugged into place and shape.

'Griffy, dear? Didn't you enjoy yourself?' Her voice was like a flower, tender and caressing. The calypso band, upstairs, had just started up again. And the quiet waltz-like tune seemed to have been chosen to make him look foolish, behind his back. He could hear the scrambling of men and crabs trying to find dancing partners. He could imagine himself in the rush of fishermen after catches. He was thinking of getting his wife home quickly and coming back, to face Stooly and the Jamaican man; and he wished that if he did come back, that they would both be gone, so he won't have to come on strong; but he was thinking more of getting rid of his wife and coming back to dance and discuss the Racing Form; and tomorrow was races, again. He imagined the large rough Jamaican man searching for women again. He saw Stooly grabbing some woman's hand, some woman whom he had never seen before. But it was *his* Club. He saw Masher, his eyes bulging and his mouth wide open, red and white, in joy. And Griff found himself not knowing what to do with his hands. He took his hands out of his jacket pockets; and his wife, examining her minidress in the reflection of the glass in the street door they were approaching, and where they always waited for the taxicab to stop for them, removed her arm from his waist. Griff placed his hand on her shoulder, near the scar, and she shuddered a little, and then he placed both hands on her shoulders; and she straightened up, with her smile on her face, waiting for the kiss (he always kissed her like that), which would be fun, which was the only logical thing to do with his hands in that position round her neck, which would be fun and a little naughty for their ages like the old times in Britain; and his wife, expecting this reminder of happier nights in unhappy London, relaxed, unexcited, remembering both her doctor and her yoga teacher, and in the excitement of her usually unexcitable nature, relaxed a little, and was about to adjust her body to his, and lean her scarred neck just a little bit backward to make it easy for him, to get the blessing of his silent lips, (she remembered then that the Jamaican held her as if he was her husband) when she realized that Griff's hands had walked up from her shoulders, and were now caressing the hidden bracelet of the scar on her neck, hidden tonight by a paisley scarf. She shuddered in anticipation. He thought of Stooly, as she thought of the Jamaican, as he thought of

Masher, as he squeezed, and of the races—tomorrow the first race goes at 1:45 P.M. And the more he squeezed the less he thought of other things, and the less those other things bothered him, and the less he thought of the bracelet of flesh under his fingers, the bracelet which had become visible, as his hands rumpled the neckline. He was not quite sure what he was doing, what he wanted to do; for he was a man who always insisted that he didn't like to come on strong, and to be standing up here in a grubby hallway killing his wife, would be coming on strong: he was not sure whether he was rapping his hands round her neck in a passionate embrace imitating the Jamaican, or whether he was merely kissing her.

But she was still smiling, the usual smile. He even expected her to say, 'Haiii! How?' But she didn't. She couldn't. He didn't know where his kiss began and ended; and he didn't know where his hands stopped squeezing her neck. He looked back up the stairs, and he wanted so desperately to go back up into the Club and show them, or talk to them, although he did not, at the moment, know exactly why, and what he would have done had he gone back into the Club. His wife's smile was still on her body. Her paisley scarf was falling down her bosom like a rich spatter of baby food, pumpkin and tomato sauce; and she was like a child, propped against a corner, in anticipation of its first step, toddling into movement. But there was no movement. The smile was there, and that was all. He was on the beach again, and he was looking down at a fish, into the eye of reflected lead, a fish left by a fisherman on the beach. He thought he saw the scales moving up and down, like small billows, but there was no movement. He had killed her. But he did not kill her smile. He wanted to kill her smile more than he wanted to kill his wife.

Griff wet his lips, and walked back up the stairs. His wife was standing against the wall by the door, and she looked as if she was dead, and at the same time she looked as if she was living. It must have been the smile. Griff thought he heard her whisper, 'Griffy, dear?' as he reached the door. Stooly, with his arm round a strange woman's body, took away his arm, and rushed to Griff, and screamed as if he was bellowing out a calypso line, 'Oh-Jesus-Christ-Griff!'

Masher heard the name called, and came laughing and shouting, 'Jesus-Christ, boy! You get rid o' the wife real quick, man! As man, *us man*.' Griff was wetting his lips again; he shrugged his sports jacket into place, and his mind wandered . . . 'show me the kiss-me-arse Racing Form, man. We going to the races tomorrow . . . '

GLORIA SAWAI

b. 1932

The Day I Sat with Jesus on the Sun Deck and a Wind Came Up and Blew My Kimono Open and He Saw My Breasts

When an extraordinary event takes place in your life, you're apt to remember with unnatural clarity the details surrounding it. You remember shapes and sounds that weren't directly related to the occurrence but hovered there in the periphery of the experience. This can even happen when you read a great book for the first time—one that unsettles you and startles you into thought. You remember where you read it, what room, who was nearby.

I can remember, for instance, where I read *Of Human Bondage*. I was lying on a top bunk in our high school dormitory, wrapped in a blue bedspread. I lived in a dormitory then because of my father. He was a religious man and wanted me to get a spiritual kind of education: to hear the WORD and know the LORD, as he put it. So he sent me to St John's Lutheran Academy in Regina for two years. He was confident, I guess, that's where I'd hear the WORD. Anyway, I can still hear Mrs Sverdren, our housemother, knocking on the door at midnight and whispering in her Norwegian accent, 'Now, Gloria, it iss 12 o'clock. Time to turn off the lights. Right now.' Then scuffing down the corridor in her bedroom slippers. What's interesting here is that I don't remember anything about the book itself except that someone in it had a club foot. But it must have moved me deeply when I was sixteen, which is some time ago now.

You can imagine then how distinctly I remember the day Jesus of Nazareth, in person, climbed the hill in our back yard to our house, then up the outside stairs to the sundeck where I was sitting. And how he stayed with me for a while. You can surely understand how clear those details rest in my memory.

The event occurred on Monday morning, 11 September, 1972 in Moose Jaw, Saskatchewan. These facts in themselves are more unusual than they may appear to be at first glance. September's my favourite month, Monday my favourite day, morning my favourite time. And although Moose Jaw may not be the most magnificent place in the world, even so, if you happen to be there on a Monday morning in September it has its beauty.

It's not hard to figure out why these are my favourites, by the way. I have five children and a husband. Things get hectic, especially on weekends and holidays. Kids hanging around the house, eating, arguing, asking me every hour what there is to do in Moose Jaw. And television. The programs are always the same; only the names change! Roughriders, Stampeders, Blue Bombers, whatever. So when school starts in September I bask in freedom, especially on Monday. No quarrels. No TV. The morning, crisp and lovely. A new day. A fresh start.

On the morning of 11 September, I got up at 7, the usual time, cooked Cream of Wheat for the kids, fried a bit of sausage for Fred, waved them all out of the house, drank a second cup of coffee in peace and decided to get at last week's ironing. I wasn't dressed yet but still in the pink kimono I'd bought years ago on my trip to Japan—my one and only overseas trip, a $300 quick tour of Tokyo and other cities. I'd saved for this while working as a library technician in Regina, and I'm glad I did. Since then I've hardly been out of Saskatchewan. Once in a while a trip to Winnipeg, and a few times down to Medicine Lake, Montana, to visit my sister.

I set up the ironing-board and hauled out the basket of week-old sprinkled clothes. When I unrolled the first shirt it was completely dry and smelled stale. The second was covered with little grey blots of mould. So was the third. Fred teaches junior-high science here in Moose Jaw. He uses a lot of shirts. I decided I'd have to unwrap the whole basketful and air everything out. This I did, spreading the pungent garments about the living-room. While they were airing I would go outside and sit on the deck for a while since it was such a clear and sunny day.

If you know Moose Jaw at all, you'll know about the new subdivision at the southeast end called Hillhurst. That's where we live, right on the edge of the city. In fact, our deck looks out on flat land as far as the eye can see, except for the backyard itself, which is a fairly steep hill leading down to a stone quarry. But from the quarry the land straightens out into the Saskatchewan prairie. One clump of poplars stands beyond the quarry to the right, and high weeds have grown up among the rocks. Other than that it's plain—just earth and sky. But when the sun rises new in the morning, weeds and rocks take on an orange and rusty glow that is pleasing. To me at least.

I unplugged the iron and returned to the kitchen. I'd take a cup of coffee out there, or maybe some orange juice. To reach the juice at the back of the fridge my hand passed right next to a bottle of dry red Calona. Now here was a better idea. A little wine on Monday morning, a little relaxation after a rowdy weekend. I held the familiar bottle comfortably in my hand and poured, anticipating a pleasant day.

I slid open the glass door leading to the deck. I pulled an old canvas folding-chair into the sun, and sat. Sat and sipped. Beauty and tranquillity floated toward me on Monday morning, 11 September, around 9.40.

First he was a little bump on the far, far-off prairie. Then he was a mole way beyond the quarry. Then a larger animal, a dog perhaps, moving out there through the grass. Nearing the quarry, he became a person. No doubt about that. A woman perhaps, still in her bathrobe. But edging out from the rocks, through the weeds, toward the hill, he was clear to me. I knew then who he was. I knew it just as I knew the sun was shining.

The reason I knew is that he looked exactly the way I'd seen him 5000 times in pictures, in books and Sunday School pamphlets. If there was ever a person I'd seen and heard about, over and over, this was the one. Even in grade school those terrible questions. Do you love the Lord? Are you saved by grace alone through faith? Are you awaiting eagerly the glorious day of his Second Coming? And will you be ready on that Great Day? I'd sometimes hidden under the bed when I was a child, wondering if I really had been saved by grace alone, or, without realizing it, I'd been trying some other method, like the Catholics, who were saved by their good works and would land in hell. Except for a few who knew in their hearts it was really grace, but they didn't want to leave the church because of their relatives. And was this it? Would the trumpet sound tonight and the sky split in two? Would the great Lord and King, Alpha and Omega, holding aloft the seven candlesticks, accompanied by a heavenly host that no man could number, descend from heaven with a mighty shout? And was I ready? Rev. Hanson in his high pulpit in Swift Current, Saskatchewan, roared in my ears and clashed against my eardrums.

And there he was. Coming. Climbing the hill in our backyard, his body bent against the climb, his robes ruffling in the wind. He was coming. And I was not ready. All those mouldy clothes scattered about the living-room, and me in this faded old thing, made in Japan, and drinking—in the middle of the morning.

He had reached the steps now. His hand touched the railing. His right hand was on my railing. Jesus' fingers were curled around my railing. He was coming up. He was ascending. He was coming up to me here on the sundeck.

He stood on the top step and looked at me. I looked at him. He looked exactly right, exactly the same as all the pictures: white robe, purple stole, bronze hair, creamy skin. How had all those queer artists, illustrators of Sunday School papers, how had they gotten him exactly right like that?

He stood at the top of the stairs. I sat there holding my glass. What do you say to Jesus when he comes? How do you address him? Do you call him *Jesus*? I supposed that was his first name. Or *Christ*? I remembered the woman at the well, the one living in adultery who'd called him *Sir*. Perhaps I could try that. Or maybe I should pretend not to recognize him. Maybe, for some reason, he didn't mean for me to recognize him. Then he spoke.

'Good morning,' he said. 'My name is Jesus.'

'How do you do,' I said. 'My name is Gloria Johnson.'

My name is Gloria Johnson. That's what I said, all right. As if he didn't know.

He smiled, standing there at the top of the stairs. I thought of what I should do next. Then I got up and unfolded another canvas chair.

'You have a nice view here,' he said, leaning back against the canvas and pressing his sandaled feet against the iron bars of the railing.

'Thank you,' I said. 'We like it.'

Nice view. Those were his very words. Everyone who comes to our house and stands on the deck says that. Everyone.

'I wasn't expecting company today.' I straightened the folds of my pink kimono and tightened the cloth more securely over my knees. I picked up the glass from the floor where I'd laid it.

'I was passing through on my way to Winnipeg. I thought I'd drop by.'

'I've heard a lot about you,' I said. 'You look quite a bit like your pictures.' I raised the glass to my mouth and saw that his hands were empty. I should offer him something to drink. Tea? Milk? How should I ask him what he'd like to drink? What words should I use?

'It gets pretty dusty out there,' I finally said. 'Would you care for something to drink?' He looked at the glass in my hand. 'I could make you some tea,' I added.

'Thanks,' he said. 'What are you drinking?'

'Well, on Mondays I like to relax a bit after the busy weekend with the family all home. I have five children you know. So sometimes after breakfast I have a little wine.'

'That would be fine,' he said.

By luck I found a clean tumbler in the cupboard. I stood by the sink, pouring the wine. And then, like a bolt of lightning, I realized my situation. Oh, Johann Sebastian Bach. Glory. Honour. Wisdom. Power. George Frederick Handel. King of Kings and Lord of Lords. He's on my sundeck. Today he's sitting on my sundeck. I can ask him any question under the sun, anything at all, he'll know the answer. Hallelujah. Hallelujah. Well now, wasn't this something for a Monday morning in Moose Jaw.

I opened the fridge door to replace the bottle. And I saw my father. It was New Year's morning. My father was sitting at the kitchen table. Mother sat across from him. She'd covered the oatmeal pot to let it simmer on the stove. I could hear the lid bumping against the rim, quietly. Sigrid and Freda sat on one side of the table, Raymond and I on the other. We were holding hymn books, little black books turned to page one. It was dark outside. On New Year's morning we got up before sunrise. Daddy was looking at us with his chin pointed out. It meant be still and sit straight. Raymond sat as straight and stiff as a soldier, waiting for Daddy to notice how nice and stiff he sat. We began singing. Page one. Hymn for the New Year. Philipp Nicolai. 1599. We didn't really need the books. We'd sung the same song every New Year's since the time of our conception. Daddy always sang the loudest.

The Morning Star upon us gleams; How full of grace and truth His beams,
How passing fair His splendour. Good Shepherd, David's proper heir,
My King in heav'n Thou dost me bear Upon Thy bosom tender.
Near—est, Dear—est, High—est, Bright—est, Thou delight—est.
Still to love me, Thou so high enthroned a—bove me.

I didn't mind, actually, singing hymns on New Year's, as long as I was sure no-one else would find out. I'd have been rather embarrassed if any of my friends ever found out how we spent New Year's. It's easy at a certain age to be embarrassed about your family. I remember Alice Olson, how embarrassed she was about her father, Elmer Olson. He was an alcoholic and couldn't control his urine. Her mother always had to clean up after him. Even so, the house smelled. I suppose she couldn't get it all. Anyway, I know Alice was embarrassed when we saw Elmer all tousled and sick-looking, with urine stains on his trousers. Actually, I don't know what would be harder on a kid—having a father who's a drunk, or one who's sober on New Year's and sings *The Morning Star*.

I walked across the deck and handed Jesus the wine. I sat down, resting my glass on the flap of my kimono. Jesus was looking out over the prairie. He seemed to be noticing everything out there. He was obviously in no hurry to leave, but he didn't have much to say. I thought of what to say next.

'I suppose you're more used to the sea than to the prairie.'

'Yes,' he answered. 'I've lived most of my life near water. But I like the prairie too. There's something nice about the prairie.' He turned his face to the wind, stronger now, coming toward us from the east.

Nice again. If I'd ever used that word to describe the prairie, in an English theme at St John's, for example, it would have had three red circles around it. At least three. I raised my glass to the wind. Good old St John's. Good old Pastor Solberg, standing in front of the wooden altar, holding the gospel aloft in his hand.

> In the beginning wass the Word,
> And the Word wass with God,
> And the Word wass God.
>
> All things were made by him;
> And without him wass not anything made
> That wass made.

I was sitting on a bench by Paul Thorson. We were sharing a hymnal. Our thumbs touched at the centre of the book. It was winter. The chapel was cold—an army barracks left over from World War 2. We wore parkas and sat close together. Paul fooled around with his thumb, pushing my thumb to my own side of the book, then pulling it back to his side. The wind howled outside. We watched our breath as we sang the hymn.

> *In thine arms I rest me, Foes who would molest me*
> *Cannot reach me here; Tho' the earth be shak—ing,*
> *Ev—ry heart be quak—ing, Jesus calms my fear;*
> *Fires may flash and thunder crash,*
> *Yea, and sin and hell as—sail me,*
> *Jesus will not fai—l me. . . .*

And here he was. Alpha and Omega. The Word. Sitting on my canvas chair, telling me the prairie's nice. What could I say to that?

'I like it too,' I said.

Jesus was watching a magpie circling above the poplars just beyond the quarry. He seemed very nice actually. But he wasn't like my father. My father was perfect, mind you, but you know about perfect people— busy, busy. He wasn't as busy as Elsie though. Elsie was the busy one. You could never visit there without her having to do something else at the same time. Wash the leaves of her plants with milk or fold socks in the basement while you sat on a bench by the washing-machine. I wouldn't mind sitting on a bench in the basement if that was all she had, but her living-room was full of big soft chairs that no-one ever sat in. Now Christ here didn't seem to have any work to do at all.

The wind had risen now. His robes puffed about his legs. His hair swirled around his face. I set my glass down and held my kimono together at my knees. The wind was coming stronger now out of the east. My kimono flapped about my ankles. I bent down to secure the bottom, pressing the moving cloth close against my legs. A Saskatchewan wind comes up in a hurry, let me tell you. Then it happened. A gust of wind hit me straight on, seeping into the folds of my kimono, reaching down into the bodice, billowing the cloth out, until above the sash, the robe was fully open. I knew without looking. The wind was suddenly blowing on my breasts. I felt it cool on both my breasts. Then as quickly as it came, it left, and we sat in the small breeze of before.

I looked at Jesus. He was looking at me. And at my breasts. Looking right at them. Jesus was sitting there on the sundeck, looking at my breasts.

What should I do? Say excuse me and push them back into the kimono? Make a little joke of it? Look what the wind blew in, or something? Or should I say nothing? Just tuck them in as inconspicuously as possible? What do you say when a wind comes up and blows your kimono open and he sees your breasts?

Now, there are ways and there are ways of exposing your breasts. I know a few things. I read books. And I've learned a lot from my cousin Millie. Millie's the black sheep in the family. She left the Academy without graduating to become an artist's model in Winnipeg. A dancer too. Anyway, Millie's told me a few things about body exposure. She says, for instance, that when an artist wants to draw his model he has her either completely nude and stretching and bending in various positions so he can sketch her from different angles. Or he drapes her with cloth, satin usually. He covers one section of the body with the material and leaves the rest exposed. But he does so in a graceful manner, draping the cloth over her stomach or ankle. Never over the breasts. So I realized that my appearance right then wasn't actually pleasing, either aesthetically or erotically—from Millie's point of view. My breasts were just sticking out from the top of my old kimono. And for some reason that I certainly can't explain, even to this day, I did nothing about it. I just sat there.

Jesus must have recognized my confusion, because right then he said, quite sincerely I thought, 'You have nice breasts.'

'Thanks,' I said. I didn't know what else to say, so I asked him if he'd like more wine.

'Yes, I would,' he said, and I left to refill the glass. When I returned he was watching the magpie swishing about in the tall weeds of the quarry. I sat down and watched with him.

Then I got a very, very peculiar sensation. I know it was just an illusion, but it was so strong it scared me. It's hard to explain because nothing like it had ever happened to me before. The magpie began to float toward Jesus. I saw it fluttering toward him in the air as if some vacuum were sucking it in. When it reached him, it flapped about on his chest, which was bare now because the top of his robe had slipped down. It nibbled at his little brown nipples and squawked and disappeared. For all the world, it seemed to disappear right into his pores. Then the same thing happened with a rock. A rock floating up from the quarry and landing on the breast of Jesus, melting into his skin. It was very strange, let me tell you, Jesus and I sitting there together with that happening. It made me dizzy, so I closed my eyes.

I saw the women in a public bath in Tokyo. Black-haired women and children. Some were squatting by faucets that lined a wall. They were running hot water into their basins, washing themselves with white cloths, rubbing each other's backs with the soapy washcloths, then emptying their basins and filling them again, pouring clean water over their bodies for the rinse. Water and suds swirled about on the tiled floor. Others were sitting in the hot pool on the far side, soaking themselves in the steamy water as they jabbered away to one another. Then I saw her. The woman without the breasts. She was squatting by a faucet near the door. The oldest woman I've ever seen. The thinnest woman I've ever witnessed. Skin and bones. Literally. Just skin and bones. She bowed and smiled at everyone who entered. She had three teeth. When she hunched over her basin, I saw the little creases of skin where her breasts had been. When she stood up the wrinkles disappeared. In their place were two shallow caves. Even the nipples seemed to have disappeared into the small brown caves of her breasts.

I opened my eyes and looked at Jesus. Fortunately, everything had stopped floating.

'Have you ever been to Japan?' I asked.

'Yes,' he said, 'a few times.'

I paid no attention to his answer but went on telling him about Japan as if he'd never been there. I couldn't seem to stop talking about that old woman and her breasts.

'You should have seen her,' I said. 'She wasn't flat-chested like some women even here in Moose Jaw. It wasn't like that at all. Her breasts weren't just flat. They were caved in, as if the flesh had sunk right there. Have you ever seen breasts like that before?'

Jesus' eyes were getting darker. He seemed to have sunk farther down into his chair.

'Japanese women have smaller breasts to begin with, usually,' he said.

But he'd misunderstood me. It wasn't just her breasts that held me. It was her jaws, teeth, neck, ankles, heels. Not just her breasts. I said nothing for a while, Jesus, too, was not talking.

Finally I asked, 'Well, what do you think of breasts like that?'

I knew immediately that I'd asked the wrong question. If you want personal and specific answers, you ask personal and specific questions. It's as simple as that. I should have asked him, for instance, what he thought of them from a sexual point of view. If he were a lover, let's say, would he like to hold such breasts in his hand and play on them with his teeth and fingers? Would he now? The woman, brown and shiny, was bending over her basin. Tiny bubbles of soap drifted from the creases of her chest down to her navel. Hold them. Ha.

Or I could have asked for some kind of aesthetic opinion. If he were an artist, a sculptor, let's say, would he travel to Italy and spend weeks excavating the best marble from the hills near Florence, and then would he stay up night and day in his studio, without eating or bathing, and with matted hair and glazed eyes, chisel out those little creases from his great stone slab?

Or if he were a curator in a large museum in Paris, would he place these wrinkles on a silver pedestal in the centre of the foyer?

Or if he were a patron of the arts, would he attend the opening of this grand exhibition and stand in front of these white caves in his purple turtleneck, sipping champagne and nibbling on the little cracker with the shrimp in the middle, and would he turn to the one beside him, the one in the sleek black pants, and would he say to her, 'Look, darling. Did you see this marvellous piece? Do you see how the artist has captured the very essence of the female form?'

These are some of the things I could have said if I'd had my wits about me. But my wits certainly left me that day. All I did say, and I didn't mean to—it just came out—was, 'It's not nice and I don't like it.'

I lifted my face, threw my head back, and let the wind blow on my neck and breasts. It was blowing harder again. I felt small grains of sand scrape against my skin.

Jesus lover of my soul, let me to thy bosom fly.
While the nearer waters roll, while the tempest still is nigh . . .

When I looked at him again, his eyes were blacker still and his body had shrunk considerably. He looked almost like Jimmy that time in Prince Albert. Jimmy's an old neighbour from Regina. On his twenty-seventh birthday he joined a motorcycle gang, The Grim Reapers to be exact, and got into a lot of trouble. He ended up in maximum security in PA. One summer on a camping trip up north we stopped to see him—Fred and the kids and I. It wasn't a good visit, by the way. If you're going to visit inmates you should do it regularly. I realize this now. Anyway, that's when his eyes looked black like that. But maybe he'd been smoking. It's probably not the same thing. Jimmy Lebrun. He never did think it was funny when I'd call him a Midnight Raider instead of a Grim Reaper. People are sensitive about their names.

Then Jesus finally answered. Everything seemed to take him a long time, even answering simple questions.

But I'm not sure what he said because something so strange happened that whatever he did say was swept away. Right then the wind blew against my face, pulling my hair back. My kimono swirled about every which way, and I was swinging my arms in the air, like swimming. And there right below my eyes was the roof of our house. I was looking down on the top of the roof. I saw the row of shingles ripped loose from the August hail storm. And I remember thinking—Fred hasn't fixed those shingles yet. I'll have to remind him when he gets home from work. If it rains again the back bedroom will get soaked. Before I knew it I was circling over the sundeck, looking down on the top of Jesus' head. Only I wasn't. I was sitting in the canvas chair watching myself hover over his shoulders. Only it wasn't me hovering. It was the old woman in Tokyo. I saw her grey hair twisting in the wind and her shiny little bum raised in the air, like a baby's. Water was dripping from her chin and toes. And soap bubbles trailed from her elbows like tinsel. She was floating down toward his chest. Only it wasn't her. It was me. I could taste bits of suds sticking to the corners of my mouth and feel the wind on my wet back and in the hollow caves of my breasts. I was smiling and bowing, and the wind was blowing in narrow wisps against my toothless gums. Then quickly, so quickly, like a flock of winter sparrows diving through snow into the branches of the poplar, I was splitting up into millions and millions of pieces and sinking into the tiny, tiny, holes in his chest. It was like the magpie and the rock, like I had come apart into atoms or molecules, or whatever it is we really are.

After that I was dizzy. I began to feel nauseated, there on my canvas chair. Jesus looked sick too. Sad and sick and lonesome. Oh, Christ, I thought, why are we sitting here on such a fine day pouring our sorrows into each other?

I had to get up and walk around. I'd go into the kitchen and make some tea.

I put the kettle on to boil. What on earth had gotten into me? Why had I spent this perfectly good morning talking about breasts? My one chance in a lifetime and I'd let it go. Why didn't I have better control? Why was I always letting things get out of hand? *Breasts.* And why was my name Gloria? Such a pious name for one who can't think of anything else to talk about but breasts. Why wasn't it Lucille? Or Millie? You could talk about breasts all day if your name was Millie. But Gloria. Gloria. Glo-o-o-o-o-o-o-oria. I knew then why so many Glorias hang around bars, talking too loud, laughing shrilly at stupid jokes, making sure everyone hears them laugh at the dirty jokes. They're just trying to live down their name, that's all. I brought out the cups and poured the tea.

Everything was back to normal when I returned except that Jesus still looked desolate sitting there in my canvas chair. I handed him the tea and sat down beside him.

Oh, Daddy. And Phillip Nicolai. Oh, Bernard of Clairvoux. Oh, Sacred Head Now Wounded. Go away for a little while and let us sit together quietly, here in this small space under the sun.

I sipped the tea and watched his face. He looked so sorrowful I reached out and put my hand on his wrist. I sat there a long while, rubbing the little hairs on his wrist with my fingers. I couldn't help it. After that he put his arm on my shoulder and his hand on the back of my neck, stroking the muscles there. It felt good. Whenever anything exciting or unusual happens to me my neck is the first to feel it. It gets stiff and knotted up. Then I usually get a headache, and frequently I become nauseous. So it felt very good having my neck rubbed.

I've never been able to handle sensation very well. I remember when I was in grade three and my folks took us to the Saskatoon Exhibition. We went to see the grandstand show—the battle of Wolfe and Montcalm on the Plains of Abraham. The stage was filled with Indians and pioneers and ladies in red, white and blue dresses, singing 'In Days of Yore From Britain's Shore'. It was very spectacular but too much for me. My stomach was upset and my neck ached. I had to keep my head on my mother's lap the whole time, just opening my eyes once in a while so I wouldn't miss everything.

So it felt really good having my neck stroked like that. I could almost feel the knots untying and my body becoming warmer and more restful. Jesus too seemed to be feeling better. His body was back to normal. His eyes looked natural again.

Then, all of a sudden, he started to laugh. He held his hand on my neck and laughed out loud. I don't know to this day what he was laughing about. There was nothing funny there at all. But hearing him made me laugh too. I couldn't stop. He was laughing so hard he spilled the tea over his purple stole. When I saw that I laughed even harder. I'd never thought of Jesus spilling his tea before. And when Jesus saw me laugh so hard and when he looked at my breasts shaking, he laughed harder still, till he wiped tears from his eyes.

After that we just sat there. I don't know how long. I know we watched the magpie carve black waves in the air above the rocks. And the rocks stiff and lovely among the swaying weeds. We watched the poplars twist and bend and rise again beyond the quarry. And then he had to leave.

'Goodbye, Gloria Johnson,' he said rising from his chair. 'Thanks for the hospitality.'

He leaned over and kissed me on my mouth. Then he flicked my nipple with his finger. And off he went. Down the hill. Through the quarry, and into the prairie. I stood on the sundeck and watched. I watched until I could see him no longer. Until he was only some dim and ancient star on the far horizon.

I went inside the house. Well, now, wasn't that a nice visit. Wasn't that something. I examined the clothes, dry and sour in the living-room. I'd have to put them back in the wash, that's all. I couldn't stand the smell. I tucked my breasts back into my kimono and lugged the basket downstairs.

That's what happened to me in Moose Jaw in 1972. It was the main thing that happened to me that year.

MARIAN ENGEL
1933–1985

Anita's Dance

It was a morning fit to convert any pessimist, and a Sunday to boot. Anita spent part of it in the garden virtuously weeding; then she poured enough coffee to float an army into her special mug and brought it out into the garden. Instead of reading, she sat stretching her neck to the sun and thinking how lucky she was; nothing to do but please herself all day. From time to time friends lectured her about being selfish and set in her ways, an old maid. And it was true she was sometimes lonely. She had, however, no reason to feel sorry for herself when she compared her life to theirs. She had a house, a garden, a car, a piano. A good job. A greedy, bad-tempered cat. Two eyes, a nose, and ten fingers, all in good working order. What did she have to feel sorry about? And was happiness selfish?

She mused over her library book. She had never really wanted to get married, except for a brief and embarrassing episode when she was at university. A boy she was very fond of had wanted her to drop her scholarship, marry him and put him through law school. Her fondness had ceased abruptly when he argued that, being male, he had more right to an education than she had. Winning the argument had hurt a lot.

Those days were over, she thought, and if she was wrong, she had no daughter to tell her so in exemplary form. I have my house, she thought, my garden with delphiniums and daisies and poppies. My piano, on which I have taught myself to play the simplest and saddest waltzes of Chopin. I have company in the form of a bad-tempered cat. What is more, I have a date with Clive this afternoon. I feel good with Clive. The something that is between us is nothing; there is no self-consciousness. We swim towards each other as if the water were our element. All's right with the world.

She had wanted to study literature but on practical grounds had chosen economics instead. She still, however, attempted to keep up with good books and now she was reading a novel by a man in England called

Berger, who was supposed to be both good and avant garde. She opened
it now, and put on her sun-glasses.

It was good: his main characters were small souls, which showed a
sort of left-wing point of view, but she liked the way he got into both
their heads at once and managed to stay there, so she could feel both the
room they were in and the beating of their rather constricted hearts.

It took place in a small employment agency; both characters, the
owner and his clerk, were weighing large changes in their private lives
while appearing to deal with clients. The owner, a fiftyish man who had
always lived with his sister, was considering independence: marriage
even.

She looked up and smiled at the sun. That was funny. She read on.

A woman came into the agency to look for a housekeeping job. A
largish, comfortable, middle-aged woman. The proprietor had an instant
vision of the comfort she could provide for him: a well-kept house—not
too well-kept, Canadian and mowed in the lawn departments, just a sort
of comfy English house, fish and chips for tea, a kettle on the hob.

'I could live with that,' Anita said to herself. 'What I couldn't live
with, not ever, is a set-up like this plus a job, plus three children and
entertaining for a junior executive now portly and senior. No wonder
I'm the way I am.'

She frowned at the book, closed it, and put it down. It had revealed to
her a seam of domesticity she had been avoiding recognizing: it was
cosy, and it was basically English working class, and basically (except
for a mob of children) what she had come from.

She had never wanted her mother's life, one of flying elbows and fits
of bad temper and aspirations that were a muddle of impulses. Her
mother had never seemed to be able to think anything through, she was
always anaemic from childbearing and exhausted from scrubbing; crying
out 'You girls . . .' Get this, fetch that, turn off the soup, scrub the sink,
do the dishes, iron that. When she was an old woman they had bought
her an automatic washing machine with a window in the door and found
her sitting on the basement steps watching it like television. 'I was
remembering the day Lanie got her hair caught in the wringer,' she said.

Anita shuddered: that dream of cosy domesticity was a male dream;
she'd been living in a man's world too long. The real thing she'd lived
through and it was what had made her so happy to get a scholarship to
university. Never mind that she'd had to char and work in a grocery store
to put herself through.

She stretched lazily. The cat was scowling at her through the kitchen window; he didn't like her to be happy. Too bad for him. She was going to enjoy this day. Clive and she weren't meeting until two and she didn't even have to change.

She heard scuffling footsteps on the gravel, the footsteps of her brother Jack. 'Oh damn,' she thought. 'He's found me.'

'Hi Nita, how's tricks?'

'Where did you come from, Jack?'

He was big and he was stupid, something of a bad dream: the one who hadn't succeeded. 'Oh well, you know,' he said, plunking himself down on the chaise longue so it clicked and shivered. 'I was wondering if you had any jobs for me, like.'

'Broke again, eh? Want some coffee?'

'Sure.'

She slammed the kitchen door as she went in. The cat gave her a satisfied look, pleased that her moment of glory was over. She poured Jack a coffee, creamed and sugared it, and stumbled as she went out, staining her white summer pants. 'Here,' she thrust it at him.

He sat up like a patient in bed and began not so much to drink as to inhale it. He looked badly hung over. 'What have you been doing lately?' she asked.

'I been doing . . . well, littla this, littla that. Delivering leaflets. You know.'

She knew. He was no good, Jack, and that was that.

'I keep up with the work around here myself,' she said. 'I don't really have anything for you to do.'

'There must be something, the way you lie around reading all the time.'

She refused to rise to the bait.

'Lanie's poorly,' he said. 'I was there yesterday.'

He must be making the rounds again, she thought, borrowing from all of us.

'She's got cancer,' he said, almost with satisfaction: the voice of the child at school announcing family bad news for current events class. 'She looks awful, and she can hardly move.'

'She's doing all right,' Anita said.

'Gotta get worse before you get better, eh? I don't think she'll get better. Ross is scared out of his wits. You should take the kids.'

'I can't. I go out to work, remember?'

'I remember,' he said and continued to stare at her, trying to put her in the wrong before he asked her for money.

'I wrote to Rosie but she's just had an operation. Kit's on the sick list too. Bill won't open the door to me. In the old days, a family stuck together.'

'Maybe we still do,' she said evenly, furious with him. 'Look, I have to go out and see a man about a dog. If ten dollars would do you, I could see you on your way.'

'Drop me off somewhere?'

It wasn't the clothes he was wearing, it was the condition he was in: tousled and dirty. 'Ten bucks and a subway ticket. That's it, Jack.'

'You always were a tight old broad.'

She went inside again, slamming the door, and pounded to the front of the house so hard that the petals shivered off the poppies she had set in a bowl in the front hall. She dashed upstairs and changed into another pair of trousers. As she went down again she made sure the front door was locked, then the back. 'Here,' she said, handing him ten dollars and a ticket. 'You can stay and finish your coffee. I have to be off.' She put her library book in her purse and strode off without looking behind her.

She was meeting Clive at the end of the subway line and they were going out in the country to browse through antique shops. That way he wouldn't have to drive downtown to her place first. That way, she thought grimly, he avoided Jack, thank God.

She had known him for only a few months and hadn't taken him seriously at first. An ordinary man with an ordinary job, he had seemed: indeed there was nothing special about him except the fact that they got on together, very well indeed. They were still in the wonderful time stage, however, and she wondered vaguely if that would change. He was divorced, and he had made it plain he wanted to set up housekeeping with someone again. She didn't know whether she wanted to live with anyone else: it had been so long since she hadn't had the morning paper and the morning clock and the morning coffee to herself that she was afraid she would resent an intruder.

She saw him swing into the parking lot and smiled to herself. An intruder! He got out of the car and came towards her, a smile on his face. He had a wide, rather shy smile, a funny walk. 'Hi,' she said, and ran towards him. 'Marvellous day.'

'Wonderful.' He put her into the car like the gentleman he was, said, 'Belt up, now,' and headed north.

Ordinarily, this act of merely strapping herself in beside him made her happy, but today it was different. Jack niggled and danced in her mind. Being mean to Jack made her feel like the mean, ignorant child she no doubt had been, that Jack still was.

'What's the matter?' Clive said. 'You're twitchy.'

'I'm mean-tempered today,' she said. 'As bad as Martha the cat. My brother Jack turned up. The no-good one.'

'You have one of those, have you? Most people do. I always used to wonder why they felt sorry for me being an only child. How much did you give him?'

So that was on her face too. He read her well. 'I was having such a good time,' she said, 'reading in the garden. Then in stomped Jack, and I still feel shattered.'

'Whom were you reading?'

'John Berger.'

'I'm always amazed at your taste: hardly anyone's heard of him. Look, about your brother, you'd better tell me about him and get it off your mind. No use having a day in the country if we're not in good spirits. Was he mother's blue-eyed boy?'

Suddenly she heard her mother yell, 'You girls, Nita, Rosie, look after that Jackie and make sure he don't fall in the well.' She hunched herself and said, 'First, you have to understand we were small-town people and not what you'd call well off.' She had used the genteel phrase for so long it didn't surprise her any more.

'Born with a plastic spoon?'

'Tin. My father was a sergeant in the army.'

'Powerful influence?'

'When he was there. There were four girls, then Jackie and Bill. Jackie tore the wings off flies and drowned our kitten in the rain barrel: we hated him. I'm sure he was disturbed or something, but I don't bleed for him; he was an awful kid and he's an awful man.'

'I was a social worker in my first incarnation,' he said, profile to the wind against a blue and scudding sky. 'No good at it, but I met a lot of them, awful boys who never grew up. I suppose they radicalized a lot of big sisters in their day. How often has he been inside?'

'I suppose three or four times: petty theft, drunkenness, nothing big or skilful. We were no help to him, you know. He needed a lot of attention from adults, not sisters who'd rather be doing something else.'

'Don't flog yourself, for heaven's sake. There are bad apples, and handing them the barrel doesn't help. Where is he now?'

'In my backyard on the chaise, I suppose. I gave him ten bucks and a subway ticket. But there's no real hope he's gone yet.'

Clive looked at her and slowed the car down. 'I think,' he said, 'that we'd better go back . . .'

'Clive, I don't want to spoil your day in the country.'

'You're more important than a day in the country and you're miserable. And that oaf is probably inside drinking the liquor cabinet: you can't win with those guys, Nita.'

'I locked the doors.'

'He's probably got Martha to open up for him by now; come on.'

He turned the car and drove very fast down the half-empty Sunday highway into town. They were home in twenty minutes.

They went in the front door and found Jack reclining with his work boots on the white corduroy sofa. He was drinking Nita's precious duty-free French cognac from her last trip to Europe from a kitchen glass.

'Jack!' she roared.

'Snob,' he said with an impish smile. 'So you caught me, you and your fine feller here. Nice coat he's got on. You're coming up and up and up in the world, aren't you, girl? Ma would be proud of you.' But he swung his boots off the chesterfield.

'I think you'd better go,' Clive said. 'You're bothering Anita.'

'Do you think so, Mr Prettyboy? What are you doing hanging around our Nita? Don't you know she's our Educated Woman, too good for a man? Why, all she cares about is white velvet and books and doilies. She don't even go to visit the sick and the dying, she . . .' He spoke in a stage Irishman's accent. Anita's blood began to rise and she could hear children in the background chanting, 'Nita's a nitwit, Nita's a nobody . . .'

'Jack,' she said. 'Get out.'

'And why would I want to get out, with a fine house to come to and a fine sister to look after me?'

'You should go,' said Clive, being reasonable, trying, being also, Anita thought, very sweet and middle class, 'because your sister has asked you to go.'

'Oh, I never did nothing Nita told me. It was Rosie had the good left hook. Nita was nothing, all skin and bone and no bust. No wonder she never got married or nothing. But then you wouldn't be so foolish, mister, would you, as not to open a package before you put it on the shelf?' His mouth turned down and he leered at Clive. He stood up and prepared to raise the bottle to his lips.

On the one hand, Anita wanted to laugh because he was being a self-defeating grotesque, asking for punishment, exile, anything: he had always been like that. But she was also very, very angry. She could hear all the fourteen-year-old boys in the world whispering, 'Nita Nobody, got no tits . . .' and the rest of it, which was worse. The rest of us reclaimed ourselves, she thought, as Mother wanted us to. We got out of misery and brutality. We stopped swearing, read books, got at least a smattering of education: cleaned up the family act.

Jack took a swig from the bottle. Clive balled his fists. Nita looked at the two of them and sized them: Clive was taller, but Clive was nervous. Clive had never had to punch anyone out.

Jack put the bottle down. Nita took his measure and lashed out, one two, one two, and bang bang bang on his falling head with her fists. Jack went down like a lamb.

Nita sat down on the sofa and started to cry. Clive sat down beside her and put his arm around her. Jack came to.

'Nita, you shouldn't ought to have done that. Nita, you damn well broke me false teeth.'

'Get out, Jack,' she said. 'Get flaming well out of this house and don't come back. If you don't, or if you ever come back, I'll flaming well . . . I'll call your probation officer.'

Jack stood up, holding his head, trying again. 'Nita, you're a hard woman. You should know,' he said to Clive, 'this is the kind of woman you're after: she's got no heart, she's all hollow.'

'Shut up, Jack, and go and tell your government psychiatrist you're persecuted by your sister,' Nita said. 'Get out. Get on with you. Go home and tell your mother she wants you.'

He went.

Anita sat trying to pull herself together. In the scuffle she had lost more than a lamp: the brandy bottle oozed on the carpet, the glass was broken. She sat up and sighed. She looked at Clive.

'Well,' she said. 'Now you know.'

Clive got up and reappeared with a cloth. He began sponging the brandy out of the carpet. 'Look,' he said, 'there's something I should tell you, but I want to know first how you did that?'

'What?'

'That wonderful kayo; I've never seen anything like it.'

'I wasn't born a lady and a scholar,' she said. 'I was born on the outskirts of Camp Borden, a longer time ago than you were, I have to come clean and tell you that. I was one of six children. Circumstances were not good. But in addition to being a sergeant, my father was a fighter, and when he got a beer or two into him he'd spar with anyone he could find. We saved my mother a lot.'

Clive disappeared for a moment again. She picked up the fallen glass, looked at herself in the mirror, smoothed down her hair. Thought desperately: now he knows. It's over.

Clive reappeared with a tray and glasses. 'It's our turn for a drink. There's something I said I would tell you, and I will. The real reason my wife and I got divorced was boredom. We never got quite so low as Graham Greene, who had a tooth out once when he couldn't stand it any more. But we got bored in a terrible way; we got so bored we felt we needed some kind of violence; we knew it wasn't for us, but we started to pick fights because we drove each other crazy. All our friends celebrated when they heard we were getting a divorce. Perfection drives everybody up the wall.'

She managed to look up at him and smile.

'So drink up, love. I don't care what happens between us; I know it won't bore me. But if we ever do take up living together and things get all sedate and cosy, would you . . .'

'I'd do anything for you,' she heard herself say, not believing she had said it, but hearing it anyway.

'Well, I'm not really that way, but . . . well, hell, Nita: you're magnificent in the boxing ring.'

Much later he said, after tangling with her, 'It wasn't that I wanted violence: I wanted a feeling that I was alive, that you were alive, that even our hair was growing.'

She smiled at her professor again and rubbed her bruised hands together.

LEON ROOKE

b. 1934

The Woman
Who Talked to Horses

'That's right,' she said, 'I talk to them. They will talk to me when they
will talk to no one else.'

'But they *can* talk,' I said.

'Oh, sure.'

'To each other?'

'All the time.'

I looked over at the horses. They were in their stalls, eating hay, their
rumps and hind legs about all I could see of them. They looked the same
as they always had. I didn't believe they talked. I certainly didn't believe
they would talk to her.

'What's your fee?' I asked.

She looked off at the horses, too, then glanced at me, then worked one
toe into the ground and looked at that. She was wearing blue cloth shoes
with thick white shoelaces—all very clean. Too clean. She looked clean
all over. I didn't think she knew snot about horseflesh or about anything
else. I figured she was a straight-out phoney.

'Your fee,' I said.

She had a little itch behind one ear. She scratched there.

'Before we go into my fee structure,' she said, 'we need to have a quiet
discussion.'

Fee structures? Holy Christ.

I had a good mind to turn and walk away.

'You won't tell me your fee?'

She pawed the ground again and the hand again went up to get at that
itch. I stared at that hand. She had long, slender fingers and white
immaculate skin with hardly any fuzz on it, and wrists no thicker than
my thumb. All very feminine. She wasn't wearing a ring; I noticed that.
I had her figured by this time. She was another one of those frail,

263

inhibited, emaciated females who knew nothing about the real world but like to think they could tell you about horses. One of those grim, pitiful creatures who was forever saying to themselves and to each other, *I can relate to horses.*

I'd had my share of that lot back when I had been boarding.

'I can't tell you my fee,' she said, 'until I know what you want of me and why you want it.'

I nearly laughed in her face. The whole business was stupid. I didn't know why I'd let myself get talked into calling her. I wished now that she'd just get in her car and go away, so I could go into the house and tell Sarah, 'Well, Sarah, you got any more of your dumb ideas? Let's hear them, Sarah.' Something like that. And watch her shrivel up. Watch her mew and sob and burn and hide away.

Christ, the time I was wasting. *All* the time I had wasted, listening to Sarah. Trying to take her seriously. Giving in when I knew it would prove a waste of time, all to keep a little peace in the house. To keep poor Sarah upright and not shrivelling.

I stared up at the house. Wondering if Sarah was watching. If she wasn't up there gritting her teeth, gnawing the woodwork, the broom in one hand, shoving hair out of her eyes with another, as she pressed her scared little face against a secret window. That was Sarah. Ever spying. The one way she had—so she'd tell it—of keeping her guard up.

'Mr Gaddis?' the woman said.

'Yes, what is it?'

'All I need to know is what trouble it is you are having. With your horses. Then we can talk price.'

'How about we talk *method*,' I said. '*Then* price. You going to go up and whisper sweet nothings in these horses' ears? Is that what I'm paying you for?'

The woman eyed me peculiarly. Her head tilted, her mouth a shade open. It wasn't dislike so much—though I knew she did. Nor was she making judgements. I didn't know what it was. A quiet distance. A watching.

Disapproval, too: that was there.

'I don't know what the trouble is,' I said. 'That's why I called you. I want to know what's going on. All I know is they've been acting funny lately.'

'Funny how?'

'It's hard to say. Standoffish, maybe.'

'Horses are like that. Can't horses have moods, Mr Gaddis?'

'Not on my time,' I said. 'They're not producing. You'd think the bastards had gone on vacation. Zombies, the lot of them.'

'I see,' the woman said.

Bull. She saw nothing.

I stared at her open throat. She had on this soft cottony blouse, tinted like old rose, with a wide, folded collar, and at her throat a gold necklace no thicker than a fish line.

She had on these black britches.

Up at the house Sarah had all the doors and windows shut up tight and outside not a hint of wind was stirring. Even the grass wasn't growing. It seemed to me all the life had gone out of that house. It looked dumb and impenetrable and cold.

'Sure they can have moods,' I said. 'And they do. All the time. But this time it's different. This time it's affecting me.'

She closed the blouse and held the hand at her throat.

'How do you mean?'

'I'm losing. I haven't had a horse in the running all year.'

'That could be bad luck. It could be that the other horses are better.'

'Could be but it isn't,' I said. 'These are good horses.'

She glanced up at the house. Then she went on to the roofline and from there up to the hills behind it. She wanted me to know she'd heard that story a thousand times before. Every owner thought he had good horses.

I thought to tell her I had a fortune tied up in these horses. That they were top dollar. Then I thought I had better not. You didn't talk fortune and top dollar when some nut was trying to get it from you. Especially a nut who imagined she could talk to horses.

'About fees,' she said. 'Naturally, if your horses that now are losing begin winning after I've had my chat with them, then my fee will be higher.'

'A chat!' I said. 'You're going to have a chat with them?'

'A serious discussion. Do you like that better?'

'I don't like any of it,' I said. 'You wouldn't be here if—' I stopped. I didn't see any point in raking up the family history.

'I didn't invite myself, Mr Gaddis. You invited me.'

She didn't say that with any anger. She was playing it very cool.

We both heard a door slam, and turned. Over at the back door of the house my wife stood, splashing out water from a white enamel pot. Then she swayed a little, standing there with her head bowed. Something must have told her we were looking. She glared our way, then flung her pot into the yard, and strutted back inside.

The woman beside me laughed.

I was pretty surprised myself. Sarah is prone to the odd explosion now and then—for reasons totally incomprehensible—but she'd never done anything like this before, not when someone else was around. Meek and long-suffering: that was the word for Sarah.

'I gather your wife dislikes that pot,' the woman said. She laughed again, a velvety, softly arching laugh. I wanted to tell her it was none of her business.

'Forget Sarah,' I said. 'A minute ago you were saying something about your fee structure and my hypothetical winnings.'

'Was I?'

For no reason at all this woman suddenly squatted down on her legs and began rooting through the thin grass with her long fingers. I couldn't make it out. I couldn't tell whether she was searching for rock or flower or clover, or for nothing at all. Maybe she had dropped a nickel. I had no idea what the hell she was doing. I moved a little closer. I was tempted to step on her hand. Her blouse ballooned out and I could see down her neckline to her breasts. She wasn't wearing any brassiere.

Maybe that's why she was kneeling there.

She began speaking without lifting her head. 'Yes,' she said, 'I think that's fair. Obviously much more is involved, more work for me, if I am to talk to your horses, root out their troubles, and get them winning. On the other hand, if you simply want me to walk over to the stalls and ask how they're doing today—"How you making it, kid," that sort of thing— and then come back here and simply repeat to you what they said, well in that case my fee would be minimum. Thirty dollars, let's say. Is that what you want?'

My wife was standing at the back door again. She had this fixed, zombielike expression which altered even as I watched. The skin reddened, her lips twitched, and in a moment she was twitching all over.

Then she pitched a pillow out into the yard. One of our big bed-pillows with the green slipcover still on it. Then she retreated.

The horse lady, down on the grass, hadn't noticed.

I had got around so that my back was to the door. 'I was looking for something more solid,' I told her. 'Something tangible that I could act on. *Useful*, you know. Useful information. I *have heard* that you get good results.'

She stood up. She turned and silently regarded the pillow in the yard.

'But you want my services for free, is that it, Mr Gaddis?'

This made me mad. It was clear to me that this woman carried some sort of chip around on her shoulder. That she had no use for men. One of *those*, I thought.

'Now listen,' I said. 'George Gaddis pays for goods and services properly rendered, and he always has. He pays top dollar. But it's crazy for me to fork over hundreds of dollars just to watch you go over there for an hour or two and whisper into the ears of my horses.'

She stopped studying the pillow and looked across at the door. No one was at the door. Sarah had closed the screen door, then she'd closed the cedar door behind it. It was quiet as a tomb in there.

'I don't often whisper, Mr Gaddis,' she said. 'I speak distinctly and usually with some force, and if you'll allow me, most horses do the same.'

Haughty and reproving. She seemed to think I deserved this.

'Their powers of articulation are quite well-developed, Mr Gaddis. Perhaps more so than our own.'

'They *do* talk?'

She bristled. '*Yes, they talk!*'

She struck off, moving down towards the fence at a determined pace. She truly disliked me. There, she stood leaning up against the fence with her hands in her pockets. She had narrow shoulders and narrow bony hips that would fit in a cigar box. She was a woman all right, but she was too mean and skimpy for me.

'That filly I got from Quebec,' I said, 'she'd be speaking French, I suppose? *J'ai lu mort dans mon â, J'ai la mort dans mon â, mon coeur se tend comme un lourd fardeau.*'

She spun and stared directly at me, her face burning. Mercy, one of the horses, plodded up to the fence and nuzzled her neck and shoulders. I wasn't impressed. Mercy was a dreamer. She liked people.

The woman strolled back, calm once more.

'We are getting nowhere,' she said, 'and my time is valuable. I did not drive out here to give you a free estimate, or to illustrate my capabilities, or to listen to your troubles. No, Mr Gaddis, the horses do not *talk* as such, not as we are talking, but they do think and develop their thoughts logically, except in dire cases. I am able, in a word, to read their minds.'

'ESP, you mean?'

'Something like that.' She fluttered a vague hand.

'You can guarantee this?'

'I do not give guarantees. I can swear to you that I shall talk to your horses, but the effectiveness with which you utilize the information I glean is clearly out of my hands.'

'All right,' I said. 'Suppose I employ you and make good use of your information, and my horses begin winning. What's your standard contract? How much do you get?'

'Normally, ten percent.'

'Good God! As much as that?'

'Yes. But in this instance I shall demand twenty-five.'

She shot that out. She wasn't negotiating any more.

'You're out of your mind,' I told her. 'You got a screw loose.'

'You are a difficult person to talk to,' she said. 'You are a distrusting person, a bullying one, and I should imagine your horses have picked up these traits or are responding to them. It will make my job that much more difficult.'

'Twenty-five *percent*!' I laughed. I still couldn't believe it. 'Hell, lady, you'd be costing me more than my trainer does!'

'Then let your trainer talk to your horses.'

It was my turn to walk down to the fence. Mercy saw me coming, and plodded away.

'I'll have to think about this,' I said. 'I don't know if any of it makes any sense.'

'You have my literature, sir,' she said. 'You have my testimonials. Call or not call, as you wish.'

She started over to her car, a low convertible, red and shining and new, which stood in my driveway with the top down. Very expensive. Just as she was.

'I'd much prefer you *didn't* call,' she said, stopping. 'I don't believe I like you. Your situation does not attract my interest.'

I waited until she got in the car.

'I don't suppose you like my horses *either*,' I said. 'I suppose you find *them* dull, too. I suppose you're one of those sanctified, scrubbed-out bitches who puts the dollar sign first. I don't suppose you care one crap about my horses' well-being.'

Go for the throat, I thought. Get them in the old jugular.

She wasn't offended. Her expression was placid, composed, even a little amused. I knew that look. It was the look Sarah had when she found me in something foolish. The look would last about two minutes, then she'd begin slamming doors.

She started the engine.

I stayed by the fence, close to laughter, waiting to see if this was a woman who knew how to drive a car.

She cut the engine. She stared a long time over at my house, her hands still up on the wheel, that same benign, watchful, untroubled look in her face. Then she turned in her seat and looked down at my fences and barn. All four horses had come out. Mercy had her nose between the lowest boards, trying to get at grass, but the other three had their necks out over the fence, looking at the woman in the car.

Something funny happened in the woman's eyes and in her whole face. She went soft. You could see it soaking through her, warming her flesh.

'Go on,' I said. 'Get out of here.'

She wasn't listening to me. She seemed, for the moment, unaware of my presence. She was attuned to something else. Her jaw dropped open—not prettily . . . she *was* a pretty woman—her brows went up, she grinned, and a second later her face broke out into a full-fledged smile. Then a good solid laugh.

She had a nice laugh. It was the only time since her arrival that I had liked her.

'What is it?' I asked.

'Your stallion,' she said. 'Egorinski, is that his name? He was telling me a joke. Not very flattering to you.'

Her eyes sparkled. She was genuinely enjoying herself. I looked over at Egor. The damned beast had his rear end turned to me. His head, too. He seemed to be laughing.

She got her car started again and slapped it up into first gear. 'I shall send you a bill for my time,' she said. 'Goodbye, Mr Gaddis.'

As she drove out, down the narrow, circling lane, throwing up dust behind her and over the white fence, I could still hear her laughing. I imagined I heard her—sportive now, cackling, giving full rein to her pleasure—even as she turned her spiffy car out onto the highway.

Sarah was at the yard pump. She'd picked up the enamel pot and was filling it with water. She was wearing her print work-dress, but for some reason she'd put back on the high heels she'd been wearing last night. She'd put on her lipstick. The little scratch on her forehead was still there. It had swollen some.

She'd brought out a blanket and dumped that out in the yard beside the pillow.

As I approached, she glanced up, severe and meaning business.

'Stay away,' she said. 'Don't touch me. Go on with whatever you were doing.'

I could see now wasn't the time. That the time hadn't come. That maybe it would be a long time before it did.

I went on down to the barn, scooted up the ladder, and sat on a bale of hay at the loft door. I looked out over the stables, over the fields, over the workout track and the further pasture and out over all of the long valley. I looked at the grey ring of hills. I wondered what had gone wrong with my life. How I had become this bad person.

RUDY WIEBE

b. 1934

Where Is the Voice Coming From?

Almighty Voice (1874–97), a Cree Indian, was arrested in 1895 for slaughtering a cow on a reserve near Duck Lake, N.W.T. He escaped, shot and killed a North West Mounted Police officer who was pursuing him, and became a hero to the Crees before he was finally killed by the police.

The problem is to make the story.

One difficulty of this making may have been excellently stated by Teilhard de Chardin: 'We are continually inclined to isolate ourselves from the things and events which surround us . . . as though we were spectators, not elements, in what goes on.' Arnold Toynbee does venture, 'For all that we know, Reality is the undifferentiated unity of the mystical experience,' but that need not here be considered. This story ended long ago; it is one of finite acts, of orders, of elemental feelings and reactions, of obvious legal restrictions and requirements.

Presumably all the parts of the story are themselves available. A difficulty is that they are, as always, available only in bits and pieces. Though the acts themselves seem quite clear, some written reports of the acts contradict each other. As if these acts were, at one time, too well known; as if the original nodule of each particular fact had from somewhere received non-factual accretions; or even more, as if, since the basic facts were so clear perhaps there were a larger number of facts than any one reporter, or several, or even any reporter had ever attempted to record. About facts that are still simply told by this mouth to that ear, of course, even less can be expected.

An affair seventy-five years old should acquire some of the shiny transparency of an old man's skin. It should.

Sometimes it would seem that it would be enough—perhaps more than enough—to hear the names only. The grandfather One Arrow; the mother Spotted Calf; the father Sounding Sky; the wife (wives rather, but only one of them seems to have a name, though their fathers are Napaise, Kapahoo, Old Dust, The Rump)—the one wife named, of all things, Pale Face; the cousin Going-Up-To-Sky; the brother-in-law (again, of all things) Dublin. The names of the police sound very much alike; they all begin with Constable or Corporal or Sergeant, but here and there an Inspector, then a Superintendent and eventually all the resonance of an Assistant Commissioner echoes down. More. Herself: Victoria, by the Grace of God etc., etc., QUEEN, defender of the Faith, etc., etc.; and witness 'Our Right Trusty and Right Well-beloved Cousin and Council- lor the Right Honorable Sir John Campbell Hamilton-Gordon, Earl of Aberdeen; Viscount Formartine, Baron Haddo, Methlic, Tarves and Kellie, in the Peerage of Scotland; Viscount Gordon of Aberdeen, County of Aberdeen, in the Peerage of the United Kingdom; Baronet of Nova Scotia, Knight Grand Cross of Our Most Distinguished Order of Saint Michael and Saint George, etc., Governor General of Canada'. And of course himself: in the award proclamation named 'Jean-Baptiste' but otherwise known only as Almighty Voice.

But hearing cannot be enough; not even hearing all the thunder of A Proclamation: 'Now Hear Ye that a reward of FIVE HUNDRED DOLLARS will be paid to any person or persons who will give such information as will lead . . . (etc., etc.) this Twentieth day of April, in the year of Our Lord one thousand eight hundred and ninety-six, and the Fifty-ninth year of Our Reign . . .' etc. and etc.

Such hearing cannot be enough. The first item to be seen is the piece of white bone. It is almost triangular, slightly convex—concave actually as it is positioned at this moment with its corners slightly raised—graduating from perhaps a strong eighth to a weak quarter of an inch in thickness, its scattered pore structure varying between larger and smaller on its per- haps polished, certainly shiny surface. Precision is difficult since the glass showcase is at least thirteen inches deep and therefore an eye cannot be brought as close as the minute inspection of such a small, though certainly quite adequate, sample of skull would normally require. Also, because of the position it cannot be determined whether the several hairs, well over a foot long, are still in some manner attached or not.

The seven-pounder cannon can be seen standing almost shyly between the showcase and the interior wall. Officially it is known as a gun, not a cannon, and clearly its bore is not large enough to admit a large man's fist. Even if it can be believed that this gun was used in the 1885 Rebellion and that on the evening of Saturday, May 29, 1897 (while the nine-pounder, now unidentified, was in the process of arriving with the police on the special train from Regina), seven shells (all that were available in Prince Albert at that time) from it were sent shrieking into the poplar bluffs as night fell, clearly such shelling could not and would not disembowel the whole earth. Its carriage is now nicely lacquered, the perhaps oak spokes of its petite wheels (little higher than a knee) have been recently scraped, puttied and varnished; the brilliant burnish of its brass breeching testifies with what meticulous care charmen and women have used nationally-advertised cleaners and restorers.

Though it can also be seen, even a careless glance reveals that the same concern has not been expended on the one (of two) .44 calibre 1866 model Winchesters apparently found at the last in the pit with Almighty Voice. It also is preserved in a glass case; the number 1536735 is still, though barely, distinguishable on the brass cartridge section just below the brass saddle ring. However, perhaps because the case was imperfectly sealed at one time (though sealed enough not to warrant disturbance now), or because of simple neglect, the rifle is obviously spotted here and there with blotches of rust and the brass itself reveals discolorations almost like mildew. The rifle bore, the three long strands of hair themselves, actually bristle with clots of dust. It may be that this museum cannot afford to be as concerned as the other; conversely, the disfiguration may be something inherent in the items themselves.

The small building which was the police guardroom at Duck Lake, Saskatchewan Territory, in 1895 may also be seen. It had subsequently been moved from its original place and used to house small animals, chickens perhaps, or pigs—such as a woman might be expected to have under her responsibility. It is, of course, now perfectly empty, and clean so that the public may enter with no more discomfort than a bend under the doorway and a heavy encounter with disinfectant. The door-jamb has obviously been replaced; the bar network at one window is, however, said to be original; smooth still, very smooth. The logs inside have been smeared again and again with whitewash, perhaps paint, to an insistent point of identity-defying characterlessness. Within the small rectangular box of these logs not a sound can be heard from the streets of the, probably dead, town.

> *Hey Injun you'll get hung for stealing that steer*
> *Hey Injun for killing that government cow you'll get three*
> *weeks on the woodpile Hey Injun*

The place named Kinistino seems to have disappeared from the map but the Minnechinass Hills have not. Whether they have ever been on a map is doubtful but they will, of course, not disappear from the landscape as long as the grass grows and the rivers run. Contrary to general report and belief, the Canadian prairies are rarely, if ever, flat and the Minnechinass (spelled five different ways and translated sometimes as 'The Outside Hill', sometimes as 'Beautiful Bare Hills') are dissimilar from any other of the numberless hills that everywhere block out the prairie horizon. They are bare; poplars lie tattered along their tops, almost black against the straw-pale grass and sharp green against the grey soil of the plowing laid in half-mile rectangular blocks upon their western slopes. Poles holding various wires stick out of the fields, back down the bend of the valley; what was once a farmhouse is weathering into the cultivated earth. The poplar bluff where Almighty Voice made his stand has, of course, disappeared.

The policemen he shot and killed (not the ones he wounded, of course) are easily located. Six miles east, thirty-nine miles north in Prince Albert, the English Cemetery. Sergeant Colin Campbell Colebrook, North West Mounted Police Registration Number 605, lies presumably under a gravestone there. His name is seventeenth in a very long 'list of non-commissioned officers and men who have died in the service since the inception of the force.' The date is October 29, 1895, and the cause of death is anonymous: 'Shot by escaping Indian prisoner near Prince Albert.' At the foot of this grave are two others: Constable John R. Kerr, No. 3040, and Corporal C. H. S. Hockin, No. 3106. Their cause of death on May 28, 1897 is even more anonymous, but the place is relatively precise: 'Shot by Indians at Min-etch-inass Hills, Prince Albert District.'

The gravestone, if he has one, of the fourth man Almighty Voice killed is more difficult to locate. Mr Ernest Grundy, postmaster at Duck Lake in 1897, apparently shut his window the afternoon of Friday, May 28, armed himself, rode east twenty miles, participated in the second charge into the bluff at about 6:30 p.m., and on the third sweep of that charge was shot dead at the edge of the pit. It would seem that he thereby contributed substantially not only to the Indians' bullet supply, but his clothing warmed them as well.

The burial place of Dublin and Going-Up-To-Sky is unknown, as is the grave of Almighty Voice. It is said that a Métis named Henry Smith lifted the latter's body from the pit in the bluff and gave it to Spotted Calf. The place of burial is not, of course, of ultimate significance. A gravestone is always less evidence than a triangular piece of skull, provided it is large enough.

Whatever further evidence there is to be gathered may rest on pictures.

There are, presumably, almost numberless pictures of the policemen in the case, but the only one with direct bearing is one of Sergeant Colebrook who apparently insisted on advancing to complete an arrest after being warned three times that if he took another step he would be shot. The picture must have been taken before he joined the force; it reveals him a large-eared young man, hair brush-cut and ascot tie, his eyelids slightly drooping, almost hooded under thick brows. Unfortunately a picture of Constable R. C. Dickson, into whose charge Almighty Voice was apparently committed in that guardroom and who after Colebrook's death was convicted of negligence, sentenced to two months hard labour and discharged, does not seem to be available.

There are no pictures to be found of either Dublin (killed early by rifle fire) or Going-Up-To-Sky (killed in the pit), the two teenage boys who gave their ultimate fealty to Almighty Voice. There is, however, one said to be of Almighty Voice, Junior. He may have been born to Pale Face during the year, two hundred and twenty-one days that his father was a fugitive. In the picture he is kneeling before what could be a tent, he wears striped denim overalls and displays twin babies whose sex cannot be determined from the double-laced dark bonnets they wear. In the supposed picture of Spotted Calf and Sounding Sky, Sounding Sky stands slightly before his wife; he wears a white shirt and a striped blanket folded over his left shoulder in such a manner that the arm in which he cradles a long rifle cannot be seen. His head is thrown back; the rim of his hat appears as a black half-moon above eyes that are pressed shut in, as it were, profound concentration; above a mouth clenched thin in a downward curve. Spotted Calf wears a long dress, a sweater which could also be a man's dress coat, and a large fringed and embroidered shawl which would appear distinctly Dukhobour in origin if the scroll patterns on it were more irregular. Her head is small and turned slightly towards her husband so as to reveal her right ear. There is what can only be called a quizzical expression on her crumpled face; it may be she does not understand what is happening and that she would have asked a question, perhaps of her husband, perhaps of the photographers, perhaps even of anyone, anywhere in the world if such questioning were possible for an Indian lady.

There is one final picture. That is one of Almighty Voice himself. At least it is purported to be of Almighty Voice himself. In the Royal Canadian Mounted Police Museum on the Barracks Grounds just off Dewdney Avenue in Regina, Saskatchewan, it lies in the same showcase, as a matter of fact immediately beside, that triangular piece of skull. Both are unequivocally labelled, and it must be assumed that a police force with a world-wide reputation would not label *such* evidence incorrectly. But here emerges an ultimate problem in making the story.

There are two official descriptions of Almighty Voice. The first reads: 'Height about five feet, ten inches, slight build, rather good looking, a sharp hooked nose with a remarkably flat point. Has a bullet scar on the left side of his face about 1½ inches long running from near corner of mouth towards ear. The scar cannot be noticed when his face is painted but otherwise is plain. Skin fair for an Indian.' The second description is on the Award Proclamation: 'About twenty-two years old, five feet ten inches in height, weight about eleven stone, slightly erect, neat small feet and hands; complexion inclined to be fair, wavey dark hair to shoulders, large dark eyes, broad forehead, sharp features and parrot nose with flat tip, scar on left cheek running from mouth towards ear, feminine appearance.'

So run the descriptions that were, presumably, to identify a well-known fugitive in so precise a manner that an informant could collect five hundred dollars—a considerable sum when a police constable earned between one and two dollars a day. The nexus of the problems appears when these supposed official descriptions are compared to the supposed official picture. The man in the picture is standing on a small rug. The fingers of his left hand touch a curved Victorian settee, behind him a photographer's backdrop of scrolled patterns merges to vaguely paradisiacal trees and perhaps a sky. The moccasins he wears make it impossible to deduce whether his feet are 'neat small'. He may be five feet, ten inches tall, may weigh eleven stone, he certainly is 'rather good looking' and, though it is a frontal view, it may be that the point of his long and flaring nose could be 'remarkably flat'. The photograph is slightly over-illuminated and so the unpainted complexion could be 'inclined to be fair'; however, nothing can be seen of a scar, the hair is not wavy and shoulder-length but hangs almost to the waist in two thick straight braids worked through with beads, fur, ribbons and cords. The right hand that holds the corner of the blanket-like coat in position is large and, even in the high illumination, heavily veined. The neck is concealed under coiled beads and the forehead seems more low than 'broad'.

Perhaps, somehow, these picture details could be reconciled with the official description if the face as a whole were not so devastating.

On a cloth-backed sheet two feet by two and one-half feet in size, under the Great Seal of the Lion and the Unicorn, dignified by the names of the Deputy of the Minister of Justice, the Secretary of State, the

Queen herself and all the heaped detail of her 'Right Trusty and Right Well Beloved Cousin', this description concludes: 'feminine appearance'. But the pictures: any face of history, any believed face that the world acknowledges as *man*—Socrates, Jesus, Attila, Genghis Khan, Mahatma Gandhi, Joseph Stalin—no believed face is more *man* than this face. The mouth, the nose, the clenched brows, the eyes—the eyes are large, yes, and dark, but even in this watered-down reproduction of unending reproductions of that original, a steady look into those eyes cannot be endured. It is a face like an ax.

It is now evident that the de Chardin statement quoted at the beginning has relevance only as it proves itself inadequate to explain what has happened. At the same time, the inadequacy of Aristotle's much more famous statement becomes evident: 'The true difference [between the historian and the poet] is that one relates what *has* happened, the other what *may* happen.' These statements cannot explain the storyteller's activity since, despite the most rigid application of impersonal investigation, the elements of the story have now run me aground. If ever I could, I can no longer pretend to objective, omnipotent disinterestedness. I am no longer *spectator* of what *has* happened or what *may* happen: I am become *element* in what is happening at this very moment.

For it is, of course, I myself who cannot endure the shadows on that paper which are those eyes. It is I who stand beside this broken veranda post where two corner shingles have been torn away, where barbed wire tangles the dead weeds on the edge of this field. The bluff that sheltered Almighty Voice and his two friends has not disappeared from the slope of the Minnechinass, no more than the sound of Constable Dickson's voice in that guardhouse is silent. The sound of his speaking is there even if it has never been recorded in an official report:

> *hey injun you'll get*
> *hung*
> *for stealing that steer*
> *hey injun for killing that government*
> *cow you'll get three*
> *weeks on the woodpile hey injun*

The unknown contradictory words about an unprovable act that move a boy to defiance, an implacable Cree warrior long after the three-hundred-and-fifty-year war is ended, a war already lost the day the Cree watch Cartier hoist his gun ashore at Hochelaga and they begin the long retreat west; these words of incomprehension, of threatened incomprehensible law are there to be heard just as the unmoving tableau of the three-day siege is there to be seen on the slopes of the Minnechinass. Sounding Sky is somewhere not there, under arrest, but Spotted Calf stands on a shoulder of the Hills a little to the left, her arms upraised to the setting sun. Her mouth is open. A horse rears, riderless, above the scrub willow at the edge of the bluff, smoke puffs, screams tangle in rifle barrage, there are wounds, somewhere. The bluff is so green this spring, it will not burn and the ragged line of seven police and two civilians is staggering through, faces twisted in rage, terror, and rifles sputter. Nothing moves. There is no sound of frogs in the night; twenty-seven policemen and five civilians stand in cordon at thirty-yard intervals and a body also lies in the shelter of a gully. Only a voice rises from the bluff:

We have fought well
You have died like braves
I have worked hard and am hungry
Give me food

but nothing moves. The bluff lies, a bright green island on the grassy slope surrounded by men hunched forward rigid over their long rifles, men clumped out of rifle-range, thirty-five men dressed as for fall hunting on a sharp spring day, a small gun positioned on a ridge above. A crow is falling out of the sky into the bluff, its feathers sprayed as by an explosion. The first gun and the second gun are in position, the beginning and end of the bristling surround of thirty-five Prince Albert Volunteers, thirteen civilians and fifty-six policemen in position relative to the bluff and relative to the unnumbered whites astride their horses, standing up in their carts, staring and pointing across the valley, in position relative to the bluff and the unnumbered Indians squatting silent along the higher ridges of the Hills, motionless mounds, faceless against the Sunday morning sunlight edging between and over them down along the tree tips, down into the shadows of the bluff. Nothing moves. Beside the second gun the red-coated officer has flung a handful of grass into the motionless air, almost to the rim of the red sun.

And there is a voice. It is an incredible voice that rises from among the young poplars ripped of their spring bark, from among the dead somewhere lying there, out of the arm-deep pit shorter than a man; a voice rises over the exploding smoke and thunder of guns that reel back in their positions, worked over, serviced by the grimed motionless men in bright coats and glinting buttons, a voice so high and clear, so unbelievably high and strong in its unending wordless cry.

The voice of 'Gitchie-Manitou Wayo'—interpreted as 'voice of the Great Spirit'—that is, The Almighty Voice. His death chant no less incredible in its beauty than in its incomprehensible happiness.

I say 'wordless cry' because that is the way it sounds to me. I could be more accurate if I had a reliable interpreter who would make a reliable interpretation. For I do not, of course, understand the Cree myself.

GEORGE BOWERING

b. 1935

A Short Story

Setting

It was that slightly disappointing moment in the year when the cherry blossoms have been blown off the trees, or shrunken to brown lace out of which little hard green pebbles are beginning to appear. The orchardists were running tractors between the rows of trees, disking the late spring weeds into the precious topsoil left there by the glacier that long ago receded from the desert valley.

Starlings were growing impatient with the season, tired of competing for scraps behind the Safeway store in town, eager for those high blue days when the cherries would be plump & pink, when they could laugh at the sunburnt men in high gum boots, who would again try to deceive them with fake cannons & old shirts stretcht between the branches.

High over Dog Lake a jet contrail was widening & drifting south. The orchards on the west bank were in shadow already, & sunlight sparkled off windows of the new housing development on the other shore. The lake was spotted with brown weeds dying underwater, where the newest poison had been dumpt by the government two weeks before.

Evening swallows were already dipping & soaring around the Jacobsen house, nabbing insects in their first minutes of activity after a warm day's sleep. The house was like many of the remodelled orchard homes in the southern part of the valley, its shiplap sides now covered with pastel aluminum, metallic screen doors here & there, a stone chimney marking the outside end of the living-room. Fifteen years ago the living-room had been used only when relatives from other valley towns came to visit. Now it was panelled with knotty cedar, animal heads looking across at one another from the walls, & the Jacobsens sat there after all the evening chores were done, watching Spokane television in colour, and reading this week's paper, or perhaps having some toast & raspberry jam.

The rug was a pastel shade fairly close to that of the outside surface. The Jacobsens lived with it, though neither of them particularly liked it. One of them had, once, when it was new; the other never thought of offering an opinion, or holding one.

Characters

The Jacobsens did not discuss things. They spoke short sentences to one another in the course of a card game, or while deciding which re-run was more worth watching on the mammoth television set parkt under a deer head on the west wall of the living-room.

'We haven't seen this Carol show, have we?' suggested Mrs Jacobsen. 'I think it must have been on the night we played bridge with Stu & Ronnie.'

'No, we saw it,' said Mr Jacobsen from behind his sixteen-page newspaper. 'This is the one where her & Harvey are on that jet plane that gets highjackt to South America.'

'Sky-jackt.'

'The same thing. But if you want to watch it again, go ahead.'

'I cant remember a sky-jack one.'

'Go ahead. I'll probably fall asleep in the middle, anyway,' said Mr Jacobsen.

Art Jacobsen was tired every night. As soon as the after-supper card game was over, & his short legs were up on the aquamarine hassock, his eyes would begin to droop. He was 61 years old, & still working eleven hours a day in the orchard. Like most valley orchardists, he wore a shirt only during the early hours of the morning, when the dew was still on every leaf. His body was tanned & muscled, but it was getting more rectangular every year.

Audrey Jacobsen was ten years younger. She had only recently taken to colouring her hair, often a kind of brownish-red she mistakenly remembered from her youth. Her first husband used to tease her about having red hair, though it wasnt true. By the time that Ordie Michaels had died & Art Jacobsen had started courting her on rainy days, her hair was a good plain brown, usually under a kerchief.

She'd taken to wearing the kerchief, as all the women did, while sorting fruit at the Coop packing-house. By the time Donna was five, Audrey had assumed the habit of wearing it all the time, except when she went for drives with Art Jacobsen.

They had been watching Carol on television for five years now, & she didn't know whether she liked the show.

Point of View

It is not that I know all about the Jacobsens & Donna Michaels before I start telling you about them. I am what they call omniscient, all right, but there isnt any Jacobsen family until I commit them to this medium. I have some hazy ideas or images, rather, of their story, a sort of past & a present, I suppose, but really, for me the story is waiting somewhere in the future. Or I should say that I'm waiting for a time in the future when I will have the time to come to it, here. As a matter of fact, you dont have to, now, wait as long for it as I do.

So I am in the position ascribed to the narrator with the totally omniscient point of view. A know-it-all. Dont you believe it! 'God-like.' Dont you believe it!

For instance, I've been thinking about writing this story for two years. Just a month ago I began to imagine a woman visiting her mother & stepfather at their orchard home, & that common emotional violence later on. But I just got the names while I was writing the first parts of the story, & I didn't imagine the Jacobsen house near the lake—I thought it would be 40 kilometres farther south.

Do I have to mention that there is something difficult to explain about a third-person omniscient narrative having all these 'I's' in it? Point of view dictates distance. Well, I would like to keep you closer than your usual 'god' will allow (except for people such as yourself, Leda) (no, that's not what I'm trying to do to you, reader: dont be so suspicious).

From up here I can see the Jacobsen house as a little square surrounded by trees that have nearly lost their blossoms & are just producing leaves. I have good eyes, I need them to see all that thru the drifting jet contrail.

By the way, have you noticed that when the narrator speaks in the first person, he makes you the second person? When he speaks of others in the third person, you are perhaps standing beside him, only the parallax preventing your seeing exactly what he is seeing. That makes for a greater distance produced by the first-person narrative. You must have noticed that.

Protagonist

Donna Michaels, an attractive honey-blonde in her early twenties, was about four kilometres from the Jacobsen house, driving along the lakeside road in her dented Morris Minor convertible. She had already gone thru her rite of passage between innocent childhood & knowledgeable maturity, involving strong Freudian implications. Now she was driving thru a warm valley evening, wishing that she had come a week ago, when the cherry blossoms were still at the beginning of their decline.

She had not been home during blossom time for seven years, & perhaps this more than anything else told her that she had really ceast to be a valley kid, that she was a Coast person. Looking to her right she could see, even in the shadows made by the hills over the water, splotches of brown weeds under the surface of the lake. A part of her that still wanted to be a valley person was hurt by that.

She thought about taking a Valium before she got there, only two kilometres to go now. It was not really the time to appear. She should have arrived while Art was still out in the orchard, so she could have a calm talk with her mother. When Art was there, making his blustery remarks or criticisms about her language, her mother could be depended on to remain silent, just as she had always done during family hassles, just as she had done then.

'I love him, Donna. What am I supposed to do?' she had said.

'More than you love me?' That newcomer.

'I *chose* him.'

That was the last time her mother had ever said anything so devastatingly open.

She got out of the car & took a Valium. One gets adept at swallowing them without water. She was mildly surprised that she was walking slowly toward the single little Ponderosa pine that used to be her going-to-be-alone place in the far corner of their orchard. It had perhaps grown four inches taller. Looking farther up, she could see Star Bright. She made a trivial wish & walkt slowly back to the dusty car.

What a beautiful sight she was, with her long legs & summer dress, sunglasses percht on top of her short feathery blondish hair.

Symbolism

Donna got back into the dented Morris Minor, & before she let the clutch out, she unaccountably thought about the animal heads protruding from her stepfather's walls. The first time she had seen one, she had gone to the room next door, to see whether the elk's body stuck out from that side. What had ever been done with the bodies, she wondered now. Were they discarded, left on the forest floor for the delectation of ants? Did the family eat them? She couldn't remember eating mountain goat or moose, & she had been a picky eater as a child.

She decided that whatever had been done with the torso & legs, Art was only really interested in the trophy. He talkt about nature a lot, but he was quite comfortable under the stare of the big glass eyes.

Her dog Bridey passed away after a fit when she was twelve. Quickly, before he would have a chance to take her to the taxidermist, Donna put the heavy & limp body along with an adult's shovel into a wheelbarrow & pusht it for half an hour thru the crumbling earth, to the Ponderosa. There she wasted no time looking at Bridey's fur & tight-closed eyes. She dug a deep hole & dropt her in & covered her up, without looking. She left no marker. She knew where Bridey was, & that was all that was necessary.

Now, she reflected, looking at the sagebrush growing around her tree, they probably knew too, he probably saw the wheel tracks the next morning.

She let out the clutch & drove the last kilometre slowly, having pulled on the lights. Just in time, a mother quail & her five little ones raced in a line to the safety of the roadside weeds. She smiled as she imagined the mother there, counting them.

Then she was at the turn just before their driveway, where the truck & the new Toyota were parkt in a sharp vee. People here along Rawleigh Road never pulled their drapes. Thru the window she could see Mr & Mrs Jacobsen, an over-coloured Carol, & a deer she used to call Bambi, first childishly, then later to needle her stepfather.

Her car's wheels crruncht over the driveway. Before she got out she did up her two top buttons.

Conflict

Donna had driven 400 kilometres to be there, but she didn't want to go inside the house. Of course in a setting such as this, they would know that somebody had driven up the gravel driveway, & one of them, probably her mother, would be walking to the door at this moment.

Donna wanted to be with her mother, & especially because she never wrote letters home. She did not even imagine writing 'Mrs A. Jacobsen' on an envelope. She felt as if, yes, she still loved her mother, that strange older woman in polyester slacks, though they had not once spoken to each other on the telephone since Jacobsen had mounted her as his casual season's trophy. What ambiguity in the delivery of the thought. When it was accomplisht, & all three knew, what depressing decisions & solitudes.

Donna could not stay in that family where her first love, her first world face, lost all hope & fell in, decided to stay with the bringer of death. What polluted language in the formerly unchallenged eden. Why? How, rather.

'But I chose him. I made my choice.'

'Do you love him? Can you?'

'I chose him.'

She was not a woman then, but she was not a valley girl, either. She left Dog Lake, she had to, & there was no question but the city on the coast, several ruinous jobs & some solitary education.

Now the door opened & it was Audrey who was illuminated by the porch light. Donna was momentarily ashamed with disappointment that her mother, Mrs Michaels, was not the picture of a defeated lustreless farm wife, the sensitive buffeted by life, such as one expected to find in the Canadian novels she had been reading.

'Donna! For the Lord's sake! Why didnt you tell us you were coming? Come in, you rascal,' the woman said, her arms outstretcht as if offering the red knitting she had been doing while watching television.

Donna held her mother's elbows & kissed her nose as she felt the screen door bat against her rear. Her mother chattered with a little confusion as the pretty blonde deposited her purse & a book & something wrapt in party paper on the telephone table.

'Well, well,' said Art Jacobsen, looking up from his paper, his feet still stretcht out on the hassock.

Dialogue

'I wish I'd gotten here while the blossoms were in full bloom,' said Donna. It was the perfect little bit of business to get thru the awkwardness of their surprise.

'Oh, we had a wonderful year for blossoms,' said her mother. 'When a breeze came up the whole valley smelled like a garden.'

'It *is* a garden,' said Donna, getting herself a cup of coffee from the pot on the stove. She came back thru the arch into the living-room, where her mother was still standing with the knitting in her hands. 'At least that's how we Coast people think of it.'

Art shook his paper to a new page.

It's not the blossoms that count. It's the bees.'

'The workers, you mean,' said Donna, a little edge on her voice. She sat down with her coffee, not looking at him.

'Yeah, the queen sits at home, getting fatter & fatter, while the workers bring her the honey,' said Art, his eyes looking at a news photo of the local skeet-shooting champs.

'Have you had any supper, dear?' Audrey piped in.

'Yes, I stopt at the Princeton bus station cafe, for old times sake,' said Donna.

That was a nice shot. It was there that she had abandoned Art's truck that night, with the keys in the dash. She'd taken the bus to Vancouver with no baggage, not even clean underwear. Just two apples & her purse.

Art didn't say a word now.

'Well, well,' said Audrey Jacobsen.

There was a silence. Even the knitting-needles crost & opened without a sound. It was pitch dark outside. A mirrored deer lookt in from between two young Lombardy poplars.

'How are all your aches & pains, Mom?' Donna askt at last, idly looking at snapshots from a glass bowl on the table beside her chair. Carol was over, & Art raised his remote control & shot the set off.

'Oh, the osteopath in Penticton said I did something to my lower spine when I was a girl, & I can never expect to be a hundred percent.'

'Does that mean you're not all there?' askt Art.

Flashback

When he seemed absolutely ready to give it up, give up on it, to settle for some costly talk then, she offered him a cigarette, which he took politely, & lit one herself. It was the only sort of occasion upon which she smoked, anything. They were always grateful, the talkers, when she by her gestures allowed them a certain comfort, a freedom from embarrassment.

'Thank you,' he said, & lay on his back beside her, carefully sharing the ashtray she kept on her belly.

'You needn't feel badly.' Her voice was soft & sure, caring & casual, it seemed. 'You might be surprised how often it happens. You had a lot to drink, I would imagine, it was only enough to make you think you wanted me. Happens quite a lot.'

'No, that's not it. Well, it might be a little, but that's not really it. It's . . .'

She did not offer the interruption he was waiting for. She just smoked her cigarette. She butted it out in the ashtray, & handed the ashtray to him. So he had something to do with his free hand.

'It's just that you are about exactly the age of my daughter,' he said.

'No kidding,' she said, with a twiggy edge to her voice, & that was his first hint that it was time to go back to his hotel.

Foreshadowing

After he had left, she got the scissors & clipped her toenails. Having done five, she lay back & imagined the john walking back to his hotel. He did not seem like the taxi-taking kind.

She pictured him lying on her, brought by her to the margin of success. Then she yanked the scissors toward her, fetching a jolt as they sank into the flesh of his back. It was not an old movie on midnight television. The points of her scissors were just below the joining of her ribcage, forcing the skin a little.

I wonder whether I could just throw a few clothes into the car & drive to Montreal, she thought.

Maybe you could work your way across the country, she replied.

She clipped five toenails again. They were the same ones.

Plot

The spare bedroom of the Jacobsen house was also a kind of store-room. It contained a gun-rack in which one could find a pump-action shotgun, a .22 calibre repeater rifle, an old .303 that once belonged to the Canadian Army, a .44 handgun in a tooled holster, a 30-30 with a scope sight, & a collector's .30 calibre machine-gun with a plugged barrel. This is where Donna was, taking off her light cardigan & shoes, finding the toothbrush & dental floss in the bottom of her big-city street bag, looking at herself, untanned, in the vanity mirror. A severed goat head lookt over her shoulder.

Thru two walls she could hear the Jacobsens disputing. Art's voice rose & rose, & at the end of a declarative sentence fragment it uttered the word 'slut', followed by an exclamation point.

One would expect the ammunition to be lockt up, & it was, in a cabinet with glass-panel doors. Donna shook the pillow out of one of the pillow-cases, wrapt the pillowcase around her fist, & puncht one of the glass panels three times, each time with greater force.

The male voice rose to the word 'hell!' & stopt. A door banged against a wall, & heavy footsteps approacht. Donna threw the pillowcase onto the bed beside her sweater. When Art propelled the bedroom door open, Donna was pointing a loaded shotgun at his head.

Art backt out of the bedroom & walkt backward all the way to the living-room. There he observed a slight movement of the dark holes he had wiped clean just the night before, & sat down in his favourite chair. He was on top of Audrey's knitting, but he felt convinced that he should not bring attention to such a minor problem.

Audrey Jacobsen, usually a chatterbox, found it hard to find the words she should say.

She said, 'Donna . . .'

It was very frightening that Donna did not say a word. Art looked depressed. He was a heavy man in his chair. Donna blew out her breath.

'For God's sake, girl, that's my husband!'
Donna did not breathe in.
'He's my husband, he's all I have!'
Donna turned a smooth quick arc, & shot her mother's face off.

Theme

Donna walkt from the house & into the orchard, the shotgun still dangling. She had no shoes on. No-one followed her, & she did not look
behind. She was walking between two rows of cherry trees, so that when
a quick hard breeze came around a rock outface it blew a snow of
exhausted blossoms over her head.

Donna walkt down the slope, not flinching when a clacking sprinkler
spun slowly & soakt her dress from the waist down. It was really dark
out now, & she could see the lights of the retirement village on the far
side of the lake.

The gun had made a dreadful noise. But now the night life was speaking again, crickets nearby & frogs from down by the lake. They were
calling each other to come & do it.

Donna walkt till she came to the dirt road with the row of couchgrass
down the middle, & followed it till she arrived at her ponderosa. There
she sat down with her back to its narrow trunk, & dropt the shotgun to the
dry ground. The sky was filled with bright stars that seemed to have
edges, & black behind them. One never saw anything like that from the
streets in Vancouver. She thought of the universality speaking thru her
condition.

Nearby, her dog lay curled, waiting for her to signal something to her.
But she ignored her, as she fought to remember what had happened in the
last hour, or was it some years? An airline jet with powerful landing
lights appeared from the other side of the hills & descended over the
lake, heavily pulling back on its fall toward the airstrip at the end.

Now that her eyes were adjusted to the late spring darkness of the
valley, she saw a bat flipping from direction to direction above her. She
remembered the fear that it might get caught in your hair. Bats dont get
caught in your hair.

I'm not very old, Donna thought, I'm not very old & here I am
already. She pickt up the shotgun & fired the other barrel, & threw it
over the side of the hill.

W.P. KINSELLA
b. 1935

The Thrill of the Grass

1981: the summer the baseball players went on strike. The dull weeks drag by, the summer deepens, the strike is nearly a month old. Outside the city the corn rustles and ripens in the sun. Summer without baseball: a disruption to the psyche. An unexplainable aimlessness engulfs me. I stay later and later each evening in the small office at the rear of my shop. Now, driving home after work, the worst of the rush hour traffic over, it is the time of evening I would normally be heading for the stadium.

I enjoy arriving an hour early, parking in a far corner of the lot, walking slowly toward the stadium, rays of sun dropping softly over my shoulders like tangerine ropes, my shadow gliding with me, black as an umbrella. I like to watch young families beside their campers, the mothers in shorts, grilling hamburgers, their men drinking beer. I enjoy seeing little boys dressed in the home team uniform, barely toddling, clutching hotdogs in upraised hands.

I am a failed shortstop. As a young man, I saw myself diving to my left, graceful as a toppling tree, fielding high grounders like a cat leaping for butterflies, bracing my right foot and tossing to first, the throw true as if a steel ribbon connected my hand and the first baseman's glove. I dreamed of leading the American League in hitting—being inducted into the Hall of Fame. I batted .217 in my senior year of high school and averaged 1.3 errors per nine innings.

I know the stadium will be deserted; nevertheless I wheel my car down off the freeway, park, and walk across the silent lot, my footsteps rasping and mournful. Strangle-grass and creeping charlie are already inching up through the gravel, surreptitious, surprised at their own ease. Faded bottle caps, rusted bits of chrome, an occasional paper clip, recede into the earth. I circle a ticket booth, sun-faded, empty, the door closed by an oversized padlock. I walk beside the tall, machinery-green, board fence. A half mile away a few cars hiss along the freeway; overhead a single-engine plane fizzes lazily. The whole place is silent as an empty classroom, like a house suddenly without children.

It is then that I spot the door-shape. I have to check twice to be sure it is there: a door cut in the deep green boards of the fence, more the promise of a door than the real thing, the kind of door, as children, we cut in the sides of cardboard boxes with our mother's paring knives. As I move closer, a golden circle of lock, like an acrimonious eye, establishes its certainty.

I stand, my nose so close to the door I can smell the faint odour of paint, the golden eye of a lock inches from my own eyes. My desire to be inside the ballpark is so great that for the first time in my life I commit a criminal act. I have been a locksmith for over forty years. I take the small tools from the pocket of my jacket, and in less time than it would take a speedy runner to circle the bases I am inside the stadium. Though the ballpark is open-air, it smells of abandonment; the walkways and seating areas are cold as basements. I breathe the odours of rancid popcorn and wilted cardboard.

The maintenance staff were laid off when the strike began. Synthetic grass does not need to be cut or watered. I stare down at the ball diamond, where just to the right of the pitcher's mound, a single weed, perhaps two inches high, stands defiant in the rain-pocked dirt.

The field sits breathless in the orangy glow of the evening sun. I stare at the potato-coloured earth of the infield, that wide, dun arc, surrounded by plastic grass. As I contemplate the prickly turf, which scorches the thighs and buttocks of a sliding player as if he were being seared by hot steel, it stares back in its uniform ugliness. The seams that send routinely hit ground balls veering at tortuous angles, are vivid, grey as scars.

I remember the ballfields of my childhood, the outfields full of soft hummocks and brown-eyed gopher holes.

I stride down from the stands and walk out to the middle of the field. I touch the stubble that is called grass, take off my shoes, but find it is like walking on a row of toothbrushes. It was an evil day when they stripped the sod from this ballpark, cut it into yard-wide swathes, rolled it, memories and all, into great green-and-black cinnamonroll shapes, trucked it away. Nature temporarily defeated. But Nature is patient.

Over the next few days an idea forms within me, ripening, swelling, pushing everything else into a corner. It is like knowing a new, wonderful joke and not being able to share. I need an accomplice.

I go to see a man I don't know personally, though I have seen his face peering at me from the financial pages of the local newspaper, and the *Wall Street Journal*, and I have been watching his profile at the baseball stadium, two boxes to the right of me, for several years. He is a fan. Really a fan. When the weather is intemperate, or the game not close, the people around us disappear like flowers closing at sunset, but we are always there until the last pitch. I know he is a man who attends because of the beauty and mystery of the game, a man who can sit during the last of the ninth with the game decided innings ago, and draw joy from watching the first baseman adjust the angle of his glove as the pitcher goes into his windup.

He, like me, is a first-base-side fan. I've always watched baseball from behind first base. The positions fans choose at sporting events are like politics, religion, or philosophy: a view of the world, a way of seeing the universe. They make no sense to anyone, have no basis in anything but stubbornness.

I brought up my daughters to watch baseball from the first-base side. One lives in Japan and sends me box scores from Japanese newspapers, and Japanese baseball magazines with pictures of superstars politely bowing to one another. She has a season ticket in Yokohama; on the first-base side.

'Tell him a baseball fan is here to see him,' is all I will say to his secretary. His office is in a skyscraper, from which he can look out over the city to where the prairie rolls green as mountain water to the limits of the eye. I wait all afternoon in the artificially cool, glassy reception area with its yellow and mauve chairs, chrome and glass coffee tables. Finally, in the late afternoon, my message is passed along.

'I've seen you at the baseball stadium,' I say, not introducing my-self.

'Yes,' he says. 'I recognize you. Three rows back, about eight seats to my left. You have a red scorebook and you often bring your daughter . . .'

'Granddaughter. Yes, she goes to sleep in my lap in the late innings, but she knows how to calculate an ERA and she's only in Grade 2.'

'One of my greatest regrets,' says this tall man, whose moustache and carefully styled hair are polar-bear white, 'is that my grandchildren all live over a thousand miles away. You're very lucky. Now, what can I do for you?'

'I have an idea,' I say. 'One that's been creeping towards me like a first baseman when the bunt sign is on. What do you think about artificial turf?'

'Hmmmf,' he snorts, 'that's what the strike should be about. Baseball is meant to be played on summer evenings and Sunday afternoons, on grass just cut by a horse-drawn mower,' and we smile as our eyes meet.

'I've discovered the ballpark is open, to me anyway,' I go on. 'There's no one there while the strike is on. The wind blows through the high top of the grandstand, whining until the pigeons in the rafters flutter. It's lonely as a ghost town.'

'And what is it you do there, alone with the pigeons?'

'I dream.'

'And where do I come in?'

'You've always struck me as a man who dreams. I think we have things in common. I think you might like to come with me. I could show you what I dream, paint you pictures, suggest what might happen . . . '

He studies me carefully for a moment, like a pitcher trying to decide if he can trust the sign his catcher has just given him.

'Tonight?' he says. 'Would tonight be too soon?'

'Park in the northwest corner of the lot about 1:00 a.m. There is a door about fifty yards to the right of the main gate. I'll open it when I hear you.'

He nods.

I turn and leave.

The night is clear and cotton warm when he arrives. 'Oh, my,' he says, staring at the stadium turned chrome-blue by a full moon. 'Oh, my,' he says again, breathing in the faint odours of baseball, the reminder of fans and players not long gone.

'Let's go down to the field,' I say. I am carrying a cardboard pizza box, holding it on the upturned palms of my hands, like an offering.

When we reach the field, he first stands on the mound, makes an awkward attempt at a windup, then does a little sprint from first to about half-way to second. 'I think I know what you've brought,' he says, gesturing toward the box, 'but let me see anyway.'

I open the box in which rests a square foot of sod, the grass smooth and pure, cool as a swatch of satin, fragile as baby's hair.

'Ohhh,' the man says, reaching out a finger to test the moistness of it. 'Oh, I see.'

We walk across the field, the harsh, prickly turf making the bottoms of my feet tingle, to the left-field corner where, in the angle formed by the foul line and the warning track, I lay down the square foot of sod. 'That's beautiful,' my friend says, kneeling beside me, placing his hand, fingers spread wide, on the verdant square, leaving a print faint as a veronica.

I take from my belt a sickle-shaped blade, the kind used for cutting carpet. I measure along the edge of the sod, dig the point in and pull carefully toward me. There is a ripping sound, like tearing an old bed sheet. I hold up the square of artificial turf like something freshly killed, while all the time digging the sharp point into the packed earth I have exposed. I replace the sod lovingly, covering the newly bared surface.

'A protest,' I say.

'But it could be more,' the man replies.

'I hoped you'd say that. It could be. If you'd like to come back . . . '

'Tomorrow night?'

'Tomorrow night would be fine. But there will be an admission charge. . .'

'A square of sod?'

'A square of sod two inches thick . . .'

'Of the same grass?'

'Of the same grass. But there's more.'

'I suspected as much.'

'You must have a friend . . .'

'Who would join us?'

'Yes.'

'I have two. Would that be all right?'

'I trust your judgement.'

'My father. He's over eighty,' my friend says. 'You might have seen him with me once or twice. He lives over fifty miles from here, but if I call him he'll come. And my friend . . .'

'If they pay their admission they'll be welcome . . .'

'And *they* may have friends . . .'

'Indeed they may. But what will we do with this?' I say, holding up the sticky-backed square of turf, which smells of glue and fabric.

'We could mail them anonymously to baseball executives, politicians, clergymen.'

'Gentle reminders not to tamper with Nature.'

We dance toward the exit, rampant with excitement.

'You will come back? You'll bring the others?'

'Count on it,' says my friend.

They do come, those trusted friends, and friends of friends, each making a live, green deposit. At first, a tiny row of sod squares begins to inch along toward left-centre field. The next night even more people arrive, the following night more again, and the night after there is positively a crowd. Those who come once seem always to return accompanied by friends, occasionally a son or young brother, but mostly men my age or older, for we are the ones who remember the grass.

Night after night the pilgrimage continues. The first night I stand inside the deep green door, listening. I hear a vehicle stop; hear a car door close with a snug thud. I open the door when the sound of soft soled shoes on gravel tells me it is time. The door swings silent as a snake. We nod curt greetings to each other. Two men pass me, each carrying a grasshopper-legged sprinkler. Later, each sprinkler will sizzle like frying onions as it wheels, a silver sparkler in the moonlight.

During the nights that follow, I stand sentinel-like at the top of the grandstand, watching as my cohorts arrive. Old men walking across a parking lot in a row, in the dark, carrying coiled hoses, looking like the many wheels of a locomotive, old men who have slipped away from their homes, skulked down their sturdy sidewalks, breathing the cool, grassy, after-midnight air. They have left behind their sleeping, grey-haired women, their immaculate bungalows, their manicured lawns. They continue to walk across the parking lot, while occasionally a soft wheeze, a nibbling, breathy sound like an old horse might make, divulges their humanity. They move methodically toward the baseball stadium which hulks against the moon-blue sky like a small mountain. Beneath the tint of starlight, the tall light standards which rise above the fences and grandstand glow purple, necks bent forward, like sunflowers heavy with seed.

My other daughter lives in this city, is married to a fan, but one who watches baseball from behind third base. And like marrying outside the faith, she has been converted to the third-base side. They have their own season tickets, twelve rows up just to the outfield side of third base. I love her, but I don't trust her enough to let her in on my secret.

I could trust my granddaughter, but she is too young. At her age she shouldn't have to face such responsibility. I remember my own daughter, the one who lives in Japan, remember her at nine, all knees, elbows and missing teeth—remember peering in her room, seeing her asleep, a shower of well-thumbed baseball cards scattered over her chest and pillow.

I haven't been able to tell my wife—it is like my compatriots and I are involved in a ritual for true believers only. Maggie, who knew me when I still dreamed of playing professionally myself—Maggie, after over half a lifetime together, comes and sits in my lap in the comfortable easy chair which has adjusted through the years to my thickening shape, just as she has. I love to hold the lightness of her, her tongue exploring my mouth, gently as a baby's finger.

'Where do you go?' she asks sleepily when I crawl into bed at dawn.

I mumble a reply. I know she doesn't sleep well when I'm gone. I can feel her body rhythms change as I slip out of bed after midnight.

'Aren't you too old to be having a change of life,' she says, placing her toast-warm hand on my cold thigh.

I am not the only one with this problem.

'I'm developing a reputation,' whispers an affable man at the ballpark. 'I imagine any number of private investigators following any number of cars across the city. I imagine them creeping about the parking lot, shining pen-lights on licence plates, trying to guess what we're up to. Think of the reports they must prepare. I wonder if our wives are disappointed that we're not out discoing with frizzy-haired teenagers?'

Night after night, virtually no words are spoken. Each man seems to know his assignment. Not all bring sod. Some carry rakes, some hoes, some hoses, which, when joined together, snake across the infield and outfield, dispensing the blessing of water. Others cradle in their arms bags of earth for building up the infield to meet the thick, living sod.

I often remain high in the stadium, looking down on the men moving over the earth, dark as ants, each sodding, cutting, watering, shaping. Occasionally the moon finds a knife blade as it trims the sod or slices away a chunk of artificial turf, and tosses the reflection skyward like a bright ball. My body tingles. There should be symphony music playing. Everyone should be humming 'America The Beautiful'.

Towards dawn, I watch the men walking away in groups, like small patrols of soldiers, carrying instead of arms, the tools and utensils which breathe life back into the arid ballfield.

Row by row, night by night, we lay the little squares of sod, moist as chocolate cake with green icing. Where did all the sod come from? I picture many men, in many parts of the city, surreptitiously cutting chunks out of their own lawns in the leafy midnight darkness, listening to the uncomprehending protests of their wives the next day—pretending to know nothing of it—pretending to have called the police to investigate.

When the strike is over I know we will all be here to watch the workouts, to hear the recalcitrant joints crackling like twigs after the forced inactivity. We will sit in our regular seats, scattered like popcorn throughout the stadium, and we'll nod as we pass on the way to the exits, exchange secret smiles, proud as new fathers.

For me, the best part of all will be the surprise. I feel like a magician who has gestured hypnotically and produced an elephant from thin air. I know I am not alone in my wonder. I know that rockets shoot off in half-a-hundred chests, the excitement of birthday mornings, Christmas eves, and home-town doubleheaders, boils within each of my conspirators. Our secret rites have been performed with love, like delivering a valentine to a sweetheart's door in that blue-steel span of morning just before dawn.

Players and management are meeting round the clock. A settlement is imminent. I have watched the stadium covered square foot by square foot until it looks like green graph paper. I have stood and felt the cool odours of the grass rise up and touch my face. I have studied the lines between each small square, watched those lines fade until they were visible to my eyes alone, then not even to them.

What will the players think, as they straggle into the stadium and find the miracle we have created? The old-timers will raise their heads like ponies, as far away as the parking lot, when the thrill of the grass reaches their nostrils. And, as they dress, they'll recall sprawling in the lush outfields of childhood, the grass as cool as a mother's hand on a forehead.

'Goodbye, goodbye,' we say at the gate, the smell of water, of sod, of sweat, small perfumes in the air. Our secrets are safe with each other. We go our separate ways.

Alone in the stadium in the last chill darkness before dawn, I drop to my hands and knees in the centre of the outfield. My palms are sodden. Water touches the skin between my spread fingers. I lower my face to the silvered grass, which, wonder of wonders, already has the ephemeral odours of baseball about it.

AUDREY THOMAS

b.1935

Kill Day on the Government Wharf

'I only wish,' she said, refilling his coffee mug, 'that it was all a little more primitive.'

The man, intent on his fried bread and tomato, did not hear or chose to ignore the wistfulness in her voice. Mouth full, he chuckled, and then, swallowing, 'All what?'

'All *this*,' she said impatiently, gesturing towards the inside of the little cabin. They were sitting by the window, having breakfast. It was nine o'clock on a Sunday morning and the sky outside bulged and sagged with heavy bundles of dirty-looking clouds. He wanted to get back out on the water before it rained.

'I thought you liked it here,' he said, challenging her with a smile. She was playing games again.

'I do. I love it. I really don't ever want to go back. But,' she said, looking at him over the rim of her mug, 'seeing that the old man died only a few months later, don't you think it was rather unkind of Fate to have suggested plumbing and electricity to him? I mean,' she added with a smile, 'also seeing as how we were going to be the reluctant beneficiaries of all that expense.'

'You may be reluctant,' he said, wiping his mouth, 'I'm not. I think we were damned lucky myself.'

She shrugged and stood up to clear the table, rubbing the small of her back unconsciously. She had acquired a slight tan in the ten days she'd been away and he thought how well she looked. There was a sprinkling of pale greeny-coppery freckles across her nose and along her arms. She looked strong and self-reliant and almost pretty as she stood by the window with the stacked plates in her hand. It was not a myth, he thought, or a white lie to make them feel better. Women really do look better when they're pregnant. Sometimes she would say to him, quite seriously,

'Tom, do you think I'm pretty?' or

'Tom, what would you say about me if you saw me across the room?'

Her questions made him impatient and embarrassed and he usually ended up by returning some smart remark because he was both a shy and a truthful man. He wished she would ask him now, but he did not volunteer his vision. Instead he got up and said,

'Where's Robert?'

'Right on the porch. I can see him. He has a dish full of oysters and clams and a hermit crab in a whelk shell. He's been fascinated by it for two days now. I didn't know,' she added, 'that barnacles were little creatures. They've got little hand-like things which come out and scoop the water, looking for food.'

'Yes, I believe those are actually their feet,' he said. 'My grandfather told me that years ago. They stand on their heads, once they become fixed, and kick the food into their mouths for the rest of their lives. Now *that's* primitive for you.' He drew on his pullover again. 'How would you feel if I had another little fish-around before it rains? Then I'll take Robert for a walk and let you have some peace.'

'Oh, he's alright, except sometimes when he wants to crawl all over me. He's actually better here than at home. Everything excites him. He could live here forever as well.'

'You must come back soon,' he reminded her gently, 'whether you like it or not.'

'I don't want to. I hate the city. And I like it better now,' she said, 'than later on, when all the summer people come.'

'You don't get lonely?'

'No, not at all.' She was embarrassed to admit it and irritated he had asked. 'I walk and sit and look and read my books at night or listen to the radio. And there's Robert of course. He's become afraid of the dark, though,' she said thoughtfully, 'I wonder why. He wakes me up at night.'

'Weren't you?' he challenged. 'I was.'

She turned surprised. She had been of course, but she was a very nervous, sickly child. This big sturdy, competent man who seemed afraid of nothing!

'Yes,' she stood at the sink, soapy hands held out of the water, poised over a plate, remembering. 'I used to lie very still because I was absolutely sure there was someone in the room. If he knew I was awake, or if I should call out, he would strangle me or slit my throat.'

'Footsteps on stairs,' he said, rolling a cigarette.

'Faces outside windowpanes,' she countered.

'And don't forget,' he added, 'the boy may actually have seen something. A deer, or even the Hoopers' dog. I've seen him stand up and pull that curtain back after his nap. Leave the light on.' He put the tobacco tin back on the window sill and got up. 'Leave the bathroom light on. It won't break us.'

'Won't that make him weak?' she cried, 'Isn't that giving in to his fears?'

'Not really. He'll outgrow it. I think maybe that kind of strength comes from reassurance.' He kissed the back of her hair. 'See you later on.'

'Bring us back a fish,' she said, reminding him of his role as provider, knowing in her heart it was all one to him whether he landed a fish or not. She was jealous of his relationship with the little boat, the oars, the sea. He would come back with a look of almost sensual pleasure on his face.

He went out, banging the door and she could hear him teasing the little boy, explaining something. She left the dishes to dry and poured herself another cup of coffee. The baby kicked and she patted her abdomen as though to reassure it. Boy or girl, dark or light, she wondered idly but not very earnestly. It was out of her hands, like the weather and the tides. But would she really like to have it out here, maybe alone, with Robert crying from the prison of his crib or huddled at the foot of her bed, marked and possibly maimed forever by the groaning and the blood. Robert had been quick, amazingly and blessedly quick for a first child; the doctor had told her this indicated a rapid labour for the second. In her own way she was shy, particularly about physical things. Could she really go along to old Mrs Hooper's and ask for help, or accept the possibility of being taken off the Island by one of the local fishing boats, observed by the taciturn, sun-baked faces of the men to whom she would be, if known at all, simply another one of the summer folk.

It was easier in the old days, she felt, when there were no choices. She smiled at herself, for Tom, if he had been listening, would have added 'and childbed fever, and babies dying, the women worn out before they'd hardly begun.' He called her a romantic and accused her of never thinking things through. *He* was the one who could really have survived here without complaint, in the old days. He was the one who had the strength to drag up driftwood from the little rocky beach, and saw it up by hand, and the knowledge which enabled him to mend things or to start a perfect fire every time. He hauled his little rowboat down to the wharf below their place on a triangular carrier he'd made from old wheels off a discarded pram, pulled it down the narrow ramp, which could be very steep when the tide was out, lowered it over the side, stepped in carefully and rowed away. She was jealous of his strength and his knowledge when he was around—he had grown up in the country and by the sea. She was a city girl and forever yearning after the names of things. She dreamed; he did. Her hands were terribly clumsy, except when loving her husband or her son and she often lamented that she had never learned to knit or weave or even to play an instrument. She liked to read and to walk and to talk and felt herself to be shallow and effete.

Yet since they had found the cabin she had experienced a certain degree of content and growing self-respect. She had learned to bake good, heavy bread in the little two-burner hot-plate/oven which she hoped to replace, eventually, with an old, iron wood- or oil-burning stove; she had learned about ammonia for wasp stings and how to recognize the edible mushrooms which grew in profusion near the abandoned school house. She could even light a fire, even if not a perfect fire, and almost every time.

She had bought a booklet on edible plants and was secretly learning something about the sustaining nature of the various weeds and plants which grew in profusion around her. She had started a herb garden in an old bureau drawer and already had visions of bunches of herbs drying from the kitchen ceiling, jars of rose-hip and blackberry jam, mushrooms keeping in brine in heavy earthenware crocks. Things could be learned from books and by experiment. She got a pencil and jotted down on a piece of drawing paper a list:

cod	thistles	pick salad
salmon	stinging nettles	? maybe sell some of our
oysters	blackberries	apples,
mussels	apples	? my bread
	mushrooms	
	dandelions	

plant a garden, make beer, ? a goat and chickens for Robert and the baby.

Then she laughed and crumpled up the paper and threw it in the pot-belly stove (her pride and joy and a present discovered for her by Tom) which heated the little kitchen. The fire was nearly out. She would set some bread and then take Robert down on the dock until Tom returned.

'Robbie,' she called, knocking on the window, 'd'you want to help me make bread?' From his expression she could tell he hadn't heard so she went to the other side of the room—Tom had knocked most of the wall out to make one big room out of two—and opened the front door. It was chilly and she shivered. 'Hey, d'you want to help me make bread?'

He nodded, sturdy and solemn like his father, but with her light skin and hair. She undid his jacket and kissed him. His cheeks were very red.

'Your ears are cold,' she laughed, holding his head, like a ball, between her hands. 'And you smell like the sea. Where did you put your cap?'

'I dunno. I want some juice.' He wriggled away from her and she thought with a stab of regret 'So soon?' and tried to fix him as he was at just that moment, red cheeked and fat, with his bird-bright eyes and cool, sea smelling skin, to remember him like that forever.

'Come on,' he said, tugging at her skirt, 'juice and cookies.'

'Who said anything about cookies?' she asked in mock severity.

'Juice,' he repeated, quite sure of himself. 'And two cookies. I'm allowed two cookies.'

'Says who.'

'Juice and two cookies,' he said, climbing onto a chair by the kitchen table.

Afterwards, after they had smelled the yeast and kneaded the dough and made a tiny loaf for Robert in a muffin tin, she covered the bread and left it near the still-warm stove and took the child down on the wharf to watch the fishermen. There were three boats in—the *Trincomali*, the *Sutil* and the *Mary T.*—and they jostled one another in the slightly choppy water. She looked out towards the other islands for Tom, but couldn't see him. Then carefully she and the little boy went down the ramp to the lower dock, where most of the activity was taking place. A few of the Indians she knew by sight, had seen them along the road or in the little store which served that end of the island; but most of the ten or so people on the dock or sitting on the decks of boats were strangers to her and she felt suddenly rather presumptuous about coming down at all, like some sightseer—which was, of course, exactly what she was.

'Do you mind if we come down?' she called above the noise of the hysterical gulls and a radio which was blaring in one of the cabins. The two young men in identical red-plaid lumberjackets were drinking beer and taking a break on the deck of the *Mary T*. They looked up at her as she spoke, looked without curiosity, she felt, but simply recognizing her as a fact, like the gulls or the flapping fish, of their Sunday morning.

'Suit yourself, Missus,' said an older man who seemed to be in charge. 'But mind you don't slip on them boards.'

She looked down. He was right, of course. The main part of the lower dock was, by now, viscous and treacherous with blood and the remains of fish gut. The men in their gum-boots stepped carefully. The kill had been going on for at least an hour and the smell of fish and the cry of gulls hung thick in the heavy air. There was an almost palpable curtain of smell and sound and that, with the sight of the gasping fish, made her dizzy for a moment, turned the wharf into an old-fashioned wood-planked round-about such as she had clung to, in parks, as a child, while she, the little boy, the Indians, the gulls, the small-eyed, gasping fish, the grey and swollen sky spun round and round in a cacophony of sound and smell and pure sensation. She willed herself to stop, but felt slightly sick—as she often had on the actual round-abouts of her childhood—and buried her face in the sweet-smelling hair of her child, as though he had been a posy. She breathed deeply, sat up, and smiled. No one had seen—except perhaps the two young Indians. Everyone else was busy. She smiled and began to enjoy and register what she was seeing.

Everywhere there were fish in various stages of life or death. Live cod swam beneath the decks of the little boats, round and round, bumping into one another as though they were part of some mad children's game, seeking desperately for a way out to open sea. Then one of the men, with a net, would scoop up a fish, fling it onto the wharf where it would be clubbed by another man, and disemboweled swiftly by a third, the guts flung overboard to the racous gulls. Often the fish were not dead when they were gutted, she could see that, and it should have mattered. The whole thing should have mattered: the clubbing, the disembowelment, the sad stupid faces of the cod with their receding chins and silly china-men's beards. Yet instead of bothering, it thrilled her, this strange Sunday morning ritual of death and survival.

The fish were piled haphazardly in garbage cans crammed in, tails any old way, and carried up the ramp by two of the men to be weighed on the scales at the top. The sole woman, also Indian and quite young, her hair done up in curlers under a pale pink chiffon scarf, carefully wrote down the weights as they were called out: 'Ninety-nine.' 'Seventy-eight.' Hundreds of pounds of cod to be packed in ice until the truck came and took them to the city on the evening ferry boat. And at how much a pound, she wondered. Fish was expensive in the city—too expensive, she thought—and wondered how much, in fact, went to these hard-working fishermen. But she dared not ask. Their faces, if not hostile, were closed to her, intent upon the task at hand. There was almost a rhythm to it, and although they did not sing, she felt the instinctual lift and drop and slice of the three who were actually responsible for the kill. If she had been a composer she could have written it down. One question from her and it might all be ruined. For a moment the sun slipped out, like a letter shoved under a heavy door, and she turned her face upwards feeling very happy and alive just to be there, on this particular morning, watching the hands of these fishermen, hands which glittered with scales, like mica, in the sunlight, listening to the thud of the fish, the creaking

and wheeling of the gulls. A year ago she felt, the whole scene would
have sickened her—now, in a strange way, she understood and was part
of it. Crab-like, she could feel a new self forming underneath the old,
brittle, shell—could feel herself expanding, breaking free. The child
kicked, as though in recognition —a crab within a crab. If only Tom—
But the living child tugged at her arm.

'I'm hungry.'

'Ah, Robert. Wait a while.' She was resentful. Sulky. He knew how to
beat her.

'I want to pee. I want to pee *and* poop,' he added defiantly.

She sighed. 'O.K. you win. Let's go.' She got up stiffly, from sitting in
one position for so long. A cod's heart beat by itself just below the ramp.
Carefully she avoided it, walking in a heavy dream up the now steeper
ramp (the tide was going out already) and up the path to her cabin.

Still in a dream she cared for the child and wiped his bottom and
punched the bread, turning the little oven on to heat. After the child had
been given a sandwich she put him down for a nap and sat at the kitchen
table, dreaming. The first few drops of rain began to fall but these she
did not see. She saw Tom and a fishing boat and living out their lives
together here away from the noise and terror of the city. Fish—and
apples—and bread. Making love in the early morning, rising to love with
the sun, the two of them— and Robert—and the baby. She put the bread
in the oven, wishing now that Tom would come back so that she could
talk to him.

'You only like the island,' he had said, 'because you know you can get
off. Any time. You are playing at being a primitive. Like still life of dead
ducks or partridges or peonies with just one ant. Just let it be.'

'What is wrong with wanting to be simple and uncluttered,' she had
cried.

'Nothing,' he replied,'if that is what you really are.'

She began a pie, suddenly restless, when there was a knock on the
door. It startled her and the baby kicked again.

'Hello' she said, too-conscious of her rolled-up sleeves and floury
hands. 'Can I help you?'

It was one of the young Indians.

'The fellows say you have a telephone, Missus. Could I use it? My
brother-in-law wuz supposed to pick us up and he ain't come.'

'Of course. It's right there.' She retreated to the kitchen and sliced
apples, trying not to listen. But of course there was no wall. Short of
covering her ears there was little she could do.

'Hey. Thelma. Is that you Thelma? Well where the hell is Joe? Yeah.

All morning. Naw. I'm calling from the house up above. Oh yeah? Well tell him to get the hell up here quick. Yeah. O.K. Be seeing you.'

She heard the phone replaced and then he came around the big fireplace, which, with the pot-belly stove, divided the one large room partially into two. 'Say,' he said, 'I got blood all over your phone. Have you got a rag?'

She looked at his hands, which were all scored with shallow cuts she could see, and the blood still bright orange-red and seeping.

'You're hurt.'

'Naw,' he said proudly, standing with his weight on one leg, 'it's always like that when we do the cod. The knives is too sharp. *You* know,' he added with a smile, as though she really did. Little drops of blood fell as he spoke, spattering on the linoleum floor.

'Don't you want some band-aids, at least?'

'Wouldn't last two minutes in that wet,' he said, 'but give me a rag to clean up the phone.'

'I'll do it,' she said, bending awkwardly to one of the bottom cupboards to get a floor cloth. She preceded him into the living room. He was right. The receiver was bright with blood, and some spots of blood decorated an air-letter, like notary's seals, which she had left open on the desk. Snow white in her paleness. He became Rose Red. 'What am I thinking of?' She blushed.

'I sure am sorry,' he said, looking at her with his dark bright eyes. 'I didn't mean to mess up your things.' She stood before him, the cloth bright with his blood, accepting his youth, his maleness, his arrogance. Her own pale blood drummed loudly in her ears.

'If you're positive you're all right,' she managed.

'Yeah. Can't be helped. It'll all heal over by next Sunday.' He held his hands out to her and she could see, along with the seeping blood, the thin white wire-like lines of a hundred former scars. Slowly she reached out and dipped two fingers in the blood, then raised them and drew them across her forehead and down across each cheek.

'Christ,' he said softly, then took the clean end of the rag and spit on it and gently wiped her face. She was very conscious of her bigness and leaned slightly forward so he would not have to brush against her belly. What would *their* children have been like?

Then the spell broke and he laughed self-consciously and looked around.

''Sure is a nice place you've got here,' but she was sure he didn't mean it. What would his ideal be? He was very handsome with his coarse dark hair and red-plaid lumberjacket.

'Well,' she said, with her face too open, too revealing.

'Well,' he answered, eager now to go. 'Yeah. See you around. Thanks for the use of your phone.'

She nodded and he was gone.

When Tom returned the little house was rich with smells of bread and rhubarb pie and coffee.

'Any luck?'

'Yes,' he said, 'and no. I didn't catch anything—but you did.'

'I did?' she said, genuinely puzzled.

'Yeah. One of the fishermen gave me this for you. He said you let him use the phone. It was very nice of him I must say.

And there, cleaned and filleted, presumably with the knife which had cut him so, was a beautiful bit of cod. She took it in her hands, felt the cool rasping texture of it, and wondered for an alien moment if his tongue would feel like that—cool, rough as a cat's tongue, tasting of fish.

'What did he say?' she asked, her back to the man.

'He said, "Give this to the Missus." Why?'

'Nothing. I thought he was kind of cheeky. He made me feel old.'

Later that night, on their couch before the fire, she startled him by the violence of her love-making. He felt somehow she was trying to possess him, devour him, maybe even exorcise him. And why hadn't she cooked the cod for supper? She had said that all of a sudden she didn't feel like fish. He stared at her, asleep, her full mouth slightly open, and felt the sad and immeasurable gulf between them, then sat up for a moment and pulled the curtain back, looking vainly for the reassurance of the moon behind the beaded curtain of the rain. The man shook his head. There were no answers, only questions. One could only live and accept. He turned away from his wife and dove effortlessly into a deep, cool, dreamless sleep. The rain fell on the little cabin, and on the trees and on the government wharf below, where, with persistence, it washed away all traces of the cod and the kill, except for two beer bottles, which lolled against the pilings as the two young Indians had lolled so much earlier that day. The rain fell; the baby kicked. The woman moaned a little in her sleep and moved closer to the reassuring back of the puzzle who was her husband. And still the ageless rain fell on, and Sunday night—eventually—turned into Monday morning.

BARRY CALLAGHAN

b. 1937

The Black Queen

Hughes and McCrae were fastidious men who took pride in their old colonial house, the clean simple lines and stucco walls and the painted pale blue picket fence. They were surrounded by houses converted into small warehouses, trucking yards where houses had been torn down, and along the street, a school filled with foreign children, but they didn't mind. It gave them an embattled sense of holding on to something important, a tattered remnant of good taste in an area of waste overrun by rootless olive-skinned children.

McCrae wore his hair a little too long now that he was going grey, and while Hughes with his clipped moustache seemed to be a serious man intent only on his work, which was costume design, McCrae wore Cuban heels and lacquered his nails. When they'd met ten years ago Hughes had said, 'You keep walking around like that and you'll need a body to keep you from getting poked in the eye.' McCrae did all the cooking and drove the car.

But they were not getting along these days. Hughes blamed his bursitis but they were both silently unsettled by how old they had suddenly become, how loose in the thighs, and their feet, when they were showering in the morning, seemed bonier, the toes longer, the nails yellow and hard, and what they wanted was tenderness, to be able to yield almost tearfully, full of a pity for themselves that would not be belittled or laughed at, and when they stood alone in their separate bedrooms they wanted that tenderness from each other, but when they were having their bedtime tea in the kitchen, as they had done for years using lovely green and white Limoges cups, if one touched the other's hand then suddenly they both withdrew into an unspoken, smiling aloofness, as if some line of privacy had been crossed. Neither could bear their thinning wrists and the little pouches of darkening flesh under the chin. They spoke of being with younger people and even joked slyly about bringing a young man home, but that seemed such a betrayal of everything that they had believed

305

had set them apart from others, everything they believed had kept them together, that they sulked and nettled away at each other, and though nothing had apparently changed in their lives, they were always on edge, Hughes more than McCrae.

One of their pleasures was collecting stamps, rare and mint-perfect, with no creases or smudges on the gum. Their collection, carefully mounted in a leatherbound blue book with seven little plastic windows per page, was worth several thousand dollars. They had passed many pleasant evenings together on the Directoire settee arranging the old ochre- and carmine-coloured stamps. They agreed there was something almost sensual about holding a perfectly preserved piece of the past, unsullied, as if everything didn't have to change, didn't have to end up swamped by decline and decay. They disapproved of the new stamps and dismissed them as crude and wouldn't have them in their book. The pages for the recent years remained empty and they liked that; the emptiness was their statement about themselves and their values, and Hughes, holding a stamp into the light between his tweezers, would say, 'None of that rough trade for us.'

One afternoon they went down to the philatelic shops around Adelaide and Richmond streets and saw a stamp they had been after for a long time, a large and elegant black stamp of Queen Victoria in her widow's weeds. It was rare and expensive, a dead-letter stamp from the turn of the century. They stood side by side over the glass counter-case, admiring it, their hands spread on the glass, but when McCrae, the overhead fluorescent light catching his lacquered nails, said, 'Well, I certainly would like that little black sweetheart,' the owner, who had sold stamps to them for several years, looked up and smirked, and Hughes suddenly snorted, 'You old queen, I mean why don't you just quit wearing those goddamn Cuban heels, eh? I mean why not?' He walked out leaving McCrae embarrassed and hurt and when the owner said, 'So what was wrong?' McCrae cried, 'Screw you,' and strutted out.

Through the rest of the week they were deferential around the house, offering each other every consideration, trying to avoid any squabble before Mother's Day at the end of the week when they were going to hold their annual supper for friends, three other male couples. Over the years it had always been an elegant, slightly mocking evening that often ended bitter-sweetly and left them feeling close, comforting each other.

McCrae, wearing a white linen shirt with starch in the cuffs and mother-of-pearl cuff links, worked all Sunday afternoon in the kitchen and through the window he could see the crab-apple tree in bloom and he thought how in previous years he would have begun planning to put down some jelly in the old pressed glass jars they kept in the cellar, but instead, head down, he went on stuffing and tying the pork loin roast. Then in the early evening he heard Hughes at the door, and there was laughter from the front room and someone cried out, 'What do you do with an elephant who has three balls on him . . . you don't know, silly, well you walk him and pitch to the giraffe,' and there were howls of laughter and the clinking of glasses. It had been the same every year, eight men sitting down to a fine supper with expensive wines, the table set with their best silver under the antique carved wooden candelabra.

Having prepared all the raw vegetables, the cauliflower and carrots, the avocados and finger-sized miniature corns-on-the-cob, and placed porcelain bowls of homemade dip in the centre of a pewter tray, McCrae stared at his reflection for a moment in the window over the kitchen sink and then he took a plastic slipcase out of the knives and forks drawer. The case contained the dead-letter stamp. He licked it all over and pasted it on his forehead and then slipped on the jacket of his charcoal-brown crushed velvet suit, took hold of the tray, and stepped out into the front room.

The other men, sitting in a circle around the coffee table, looked up and one of them giggled. Hughes cried, 'Oh my God.' McCrae, as if nothing was the matter, said, 'My dears, time for the crudités.' He was in his silk stocking feet, and as he passed the tray he winked at Hughes who sat staring at the black queen.

JACK HODGINS

b. 1938

By the River

But listen, she thinks, it's nearly time.

And flutters, leaf-like, at the thought. The train will rumble down the valley, stop at the little shack to discharge Styan, and move on. This will happen in half an hour and she has a mile still to walk.

Crystal Styan walking through the woods, through bush, is not pretty. She knows that she is not even a little pretty, though her face is small enough, and pale, and her eyes are not too narrow. She wears a yellow wool sweater and a long cotton skirt and boots. Her hair, tied back so the branches will not catch in it, hangs straight and almost colourless down her back. Some day, she expects, there will be a baby to play with her hair and hide in it like someone behind a waterfall.

She has left the log cabin, which sits on the edge of the river in a stand of birch, and now she follows the river bank upstream. A mile ahead, far around the bend out of sight, the railroad tracks pass along the rim of their land and a small station is built there just for them, for her and Jim Styan. It is their only way in to town, which is ten miles away and not much of a town anyway when you get there. A few stores, a tilted old hotel, a movie theatre.

Likely, Styan would have been to a movie last night. He would have stayed the night in the hotel, but first (after he had seen the lawyer and bought the few things she'd asked him for) he would pay his money and sit in the back row of the theatre and laugh loudly all the way through the movie. He always laughs at everything, even if it isn't funny, because those figures on the screen make him think of people he has known; and the thought of them exposed like this for just anyone to see embarrasses him a little and makes him want to create a lot of noise so people will know he isn't a bit like that himself.

She smiles. The first time they went to a movie together she slouched as far down in the seat as she could so no one could see she was there or had anything to do with Jim Styan.

The river flows past her almost silently. It has moved only a hundred miles from its source and has another thousand miles to go before it reaches the ocean, but already it is wide enough and fast. Right here she has more than once seen a moose wade out and then swim across to the other side and disappear into the cedar swamps. She knows something, has heard somewhere that farther downstream, miles and miles behind her, an Indian band once thought this river a hungry monster that liked to gobble up their people. They say that Coyote their god-hero dived in and subdued the monster and made it promise never to swallow people again. She once thought she'd like to study that kind of thing at a university or somewhere, if Jim Styan hadn't told her grade ten was good enough for anyone and a life on the road was more exciting.

What road? she wonders. There isn't a road within ten miles. They sold the rickety old blue pickup the same day they moved onto this place. The railroad was going to be all they'd need. There wasn't any place they cared to go that the train, even this old-fashioned milk-run outfit, couldn't take them easily and cheaply enough.

But listen, she thinks, it's nearly time.

The trail she is following swings inland to climb a small bluff and for a while she is engulfed by trees. Cedar and fir are dark and thick and damp. The green new growth on the scrub bushes has nearly filled in the narrow trail. She holds her skirt up a little so it won't be caught or ripped, then runs and nearly slides down the hill again to the river's bank. She can see in every direction for miles and there isn't a thing in sight which has anything to do with man.

'Who needs them?' Styan said, long ago.

It was with that kind of question—questions that implied an answer so obvious only a fool would think to doubt—that he talked her first out of the classroom and then right off the island of her birth and finally up here into the mountains with the river and the moose and the railroad. It was as if he had transported her in his falling-apart pickup not only across the province about as far as it was possible to go, but also backwards in time, perhaps as far as her grandmother's youth or even farther. She washes their coarse clothing in the river and depends on the whims of the seasons for her food.

'Look!' he shouted when they stood first in the clearing above the cabin. 'It's as if we're the very first ones. You and me.'

They swam in the cold river that day and even then she thought of Coyote and the monster, but he took her inside the cabin and they made love on the fir-bough bed that was to be theirs for the next five years. 'We don't need any of them,' he sang. He flopped over on his back and shouted up into the rafters. 'We'll farm it! We'll make it go. We'll make our own world!' Naked, he was as thin and pale as a celery stalk.

When they moved in he let his moustache grow long and droopy like someone in an old, brown photograph. He wore overalls which were far too big for him and started walking around as if there were a movie camera somewhere in the trees and he was being paid to act like a hillbilly instead of the city-bred boy he really was. He stuck a limp felt hat on the top of his head like someone's uncle Hiram and bought chickens.

'It's a start,' he said.

'Six chickens?' She counted again to be sure. 'We don't even have a shed for them.'

He stood with his feet wide apart and looked at her as if she were stupid. 'They'll lay their eggs in the grass.'

'That should be fun,' she said. 'A hundred and sixty acres is a good-size pen.'

'It's a start. Next spring we'll buy a cow. Who needs more?'

Yes who? They survived their first winter here, though the chickens weren't so lucky. The hens got lice and started pecking at each other. By the time Styan got around to riding in to town for something to kill the lice a few had pecked right through the skin and exposed the innards. When he came back from town they had all frozen to death in the yard.

At home, back on her father's farm in the blue mountains of the island, nothing had ever frozen to death. Her father had cared for things. She had never seen anything go so wrong there, or anyone have to suffer.

She walks carefully now, for the trail is on the very edge of the river bank and is spongy and broken away in places. The water, clear and shallow here, back-eddies into little bays where cattail and bracken grow and where water-skeeters walk on their own reflection. A beer bottle glitters where someone, perhaps a guide on the river, has thrown it—wedged between stones as if it has been there as long as they have. She keeps her face turned to the river, away from the acres and acres of forest which are theirs.

Listen, it's nearly time, she thinks. And knows that soon, from far up the river valley, she will be able to hear the throbbing of the train, coming near.

She imagines his face at the window. He is the only passenger in the coach and sits backwards, watching the land slip by, grinning in expectation or memory or both. He tells a joke to old Bill Cobb the conductor but even in his laughter does not turn his eyes from outside the train. One spot on his forehead is white where it presses against the glass. His fingers run over and over the long drooping ends of his moustache. He is wearing his hat.

Hurry, hurry, she thinks. To the train, to her feet, to him.

She wants to tell him about the skunk she spotted yesterday. She wants to tell him about the stove, which smokes too much and needs some kind of clean-out. She wants to tell him about her dream; how she dreamed he was trying to go into the river and how she pulled and hauled on his feet but he wouldn't come out. He will laugh and laugh at her when she tells him, and his laughter will make it all right and not so frightening, so that maybe she will be able to laugh at it too.

She has rounded the curve in the river and glances back, way back, at the cabin. It is dark and solid, not far from the bank. Behind the poplars the cleared fields are yellowing with the coming of fall but now in all that place there isn't a thing alive, unless she wants to count trees and insects. No people. No animals. It is scarcely different from her very first look at it. In five years their dream of livestock has been shelved again and again.

Once there was a cow. A sway-backed old Jersey.

'This time I've done it right,' he said. 'Just look at this prize.'

And stepped down off the train to show off his cow, a wide-eyed beauty that looked at her through a window of the passenger coach.

'Maybe so, but you'll need a miracle, too, to get that thing down out of there.'

A minor detail to him, who scooped her up and swung her around and kissed her hard, all in front of the old conductor and the engineer who didn't even bother to turn away. 'Farmers at last!' he shouted. 'You can't have a farm without a cow. You can't have a baby without a cow.'

She put her head inside the coach, looked square into the big brown eyes, glanced at the sawed-off horns. 'Found you somewhere, I guess,' she said to the cow. 'Turned out of someone's herd for being too old or senile or dried up.'

'An auction sale,' he said, and slapped one hand on the window glass. 'I was the only one there who was desperate. But I punched her bag and pulled her tits; she'll do. There may even be a calf or two left in her sway-backed old soul.'

'Come on, bossy,' she said. 'This is no place for you.'

But the cow had other ideas. It backed into a corner of the coach and shook its lowered head. Its eyes, steady and dull, never left Crystal Styan.

'You're home,' Styan said. 'Sorry there's no crowd here or a band playing music, but step down anyway and let's get started.'

'She's not impressed,' she said. 'She don't see any barn waiting out there either, not to mention hay or feed of any kind. She's smart enough to know a train coach is at least a roof over her head.'

The four of them climbed over the seats to get behind her and pushed her all the way down the aisle. Then, when they had shoved her down the steps, she fell on her knees on the gravel and let out a long unhappy bellow. She looked around, bellowed again, then stood up and high-tailed it down the tracks. Before Styan even thought to go after her she swung right and headed into bush.

Styan disappeared into the bush, too, hollering, and after a while the train moved on to keep its schedule. She went back down the trail and waited in the cabin until nearly dark. When she went outside again she found him on the river bank, his feet in the water, his head resting against a birch trunk.

'What the hell,' he said, and shook his head and didn't look at her.

'Maybe she'll come back,' she said.

'A bear'll get her before then, or a cougar. There's no hope of that.'

She put a hand on his shoulder but he shook it off. He'd dragged her from place to place right up this river from its mouth, looking and looking for his dream, never satisfied until he saw this piece of land. For that dream and for him she had suffered.

She smiles, though, at the memory. Because even then he was able to bounce back, resume the dream, start building new plans. She smiles, too, because she knows there will be a surprise today; there has always been a surprise. When it wasn't a cow it was a bouquet of flowers or something else. She goes through a long list in her mind of what it may be, but knows it will be none of them. Not once in her life has anything been exactly the way she imagined it. Just so much as foreseeing something was a guarantee it wouldn't happen, at least not in the exact same way.

'Hey you, Styan!' she suddenly calls out. 'Hey you, Jim Styan. Where are you?' And laughs, because the noise she makes can't possibly make any difference to the world, except for a few wild animals that might be alarmed.

She laughs again, and slaps one hand against her thigh, and shakes her head. Just give her—how many minutes now?—and she won't be alone. These woods will shudder with his laughter, his shouting, his joy. That train, that kinky little train will drop her husband off and then pass on like a stay-stitch thread pulled from a seam.

'Hey you, Styan! What you brought this time? A gold brooch? An old nanny goat?'

The river runs past silently and she imagines that it is only shoulders she is seeing, that monster heads have ducked down to glide by but are watching her from eyes grey as stone. She wants to scream out 'Hide, you crummy cheat, my Coyote's coming home!' but is afraid to tempt even something that she does not believe in. And anyway she senses—far off—the beat of the little train coming down the valley from the town.

And when it comes into sight she is there, on the platform in front of the little sagging shed, watching. She stands tilted far out over the tracks to see, but never dares—even when it is so far away—to step down onto the ties for a better look.

The boards beneath her feet are rotting and broken. Long stems of grass have grown up through the cracks and brush against her legs. A squirrel runs down the slope of the shed's roof and yatters at her until she turns and lifts her hand to frighten it into silence.

She talks to herself, sings almost to the engine's beat—'Here he comes, here he comes'—and has her smile already as wide as it can be. She smiles into the side of the locomotive sliding past and the freight car sliding past and keeps on smiling even after the coach has stopped in front of her and it is obvious that Jim Styan is not on board.

Unless of course he is hiding under one of the seats, ready to leap up, one more surprise.

But old Bill Cobb the conductor backs down the steps, dragging a gunny sack out after him. 'H'lo there, Crystal,' he says. 'He ain't aboard today either, I'm afraid.' He works the gunny sack out onto the middle of the platform. 'Herbie Stark sent this, it's potatoes mostly, and cabbages he was going to throw out of his store.'

She takes the tiniest peek inside the sack and yes, there are potatoes there and some cabbages with soft brown leaves.

The engineer steps down out of his locomotive and comes along the side of the train rolling a cigarette. 'Nice day again,' he says with barely a glance at the sky. 'You makin' out all right?'

'Hold it,' the conductor says, as if he expects the train to move off by itself. 'There's more.' He climbs back into the passenger car and drags out a cardboard box heaped with groceries. 'The church ladies said to drop this off,' he says. 'They told me make sure you get every piece of it, but I don't know how you'll ever get it down to the house through all that bush.'

'She'll manage,' the engineer says. He holds a lighted match under the ragged end of his cigarette until the loose tobacco blazes up. 'She's been doing it—how long now?—must be six months.'

The conductor pushes the cardboard box over against the sack of potatoes and stands back to wipe the sweat off his face. He glances at the engineer and they both smile a little and turn away. 'Well,' the engineer says, and heads back down the tracks and up into his locomotive.

The conductor tips his hat, says 'Sorry,' and climbs back into the empty passenger car. The train releases a long hiss and then moves slowly past her and down the tracks into the deep bush. She stands on the platform and looks after it a long while, as if a giant hand is pulling, slowly, a stay-stitching thread out of a fuzzy green cloth.

MARGARET ATWOOD

b. 1939

The Sin Eater

This is Joseph, in maroon leather bedroom slippers, flattened at the heels, scuffed at the toes, wearing also a seedy cardigan of muddy off-yellow that reeks of bargain basements, sucking at his pipe, his hair greying and stringy, his articulation as beautiful and precise and English as ever:

'In Wales,' he says, 'mostly in the rural areas, there was a personage known as the Sin Eater. When someone was dying the Sin Eater would be sent for. The people of the house would prepare a meal and place it on the coffin. They would have the coffin all ready, of course: once they'd decided you were going off, you had scarcely any choice in the matter. According to other versions, the meal would be placed on the dead person's body, which must have made for some sloppy eating, one would have thought. In any case the Sin Eater would devour this meal and would also be given a sum of money. It was believed that all the sins the dying person had accumulated during his lifetime would be removed from him and transmitted to the Sin Eater. The Sin Eater thus became absolutely bloated with other people's sins. She'd accumulate such a heavy load of them that nobody wanted to have anything to do with her; a kind of syphilitic of the soul, you might say. They'd even avoid speaking to her, except of course when it was time to summon her to another meal.'

'Her?' I say.

Joseph smiles, that lopsided grin that shows the teeth in one side of his mouth, the side not engaged with the stem of his pipe. An ironic grin, wolvish, picking up on what? What have I given away this time?

'I think of them as old women,' he says, 'though there's no reason why they shouldn't have been men, I suppose. They could be anything as long as they were willing to eat the sins. Destitute old creatures who had no other way of keeping body and soul together, wouldn't you think? A sort of geriatric spiritual whoring.'

He gazes at me, grinning away, and I remember certain stories I've heard about him, him and women. He's had three wives, to begin with. Nothing with me though, ever, though he does try to help me on with my coat a bit too lingeringly. Why should I worry? It's not as though I'm susceptible. Besides which he's at least sixty, and the cardigan is truly gross, as my sons would say.

'It was bad luck to kill one of them, though,' he says, 'and there must have been other perks. In point of fact I think Sin Eating has a lot to be said for it.'

Joseph's not one of the kind who'll wait in sensitive, indulgent silence when you've frozen on him or run out of things to say. If you won't talk to him, he'll bloody well talk to you, about the most boring things he can think of, usually. I've heard all about his flower beds and his three wives and how to raise calla lilies in your cellar; I've heard all about the cellar, too, I could give guided tours. He says he thinks it's healthy for his patients—he won't call them 'clients', no pussyfooting around, with Joseph—to know he's a human being too, and God do we know it. He'll drone on and on until you figure out that you aren't paying him so you can listen to him talk about his house plants, you're paying him so he can listen to you talk about yours.

Sometimes, though, he's really telling you something. I pick up my coffee cup, wondering whether this is one of those occasions.

'Okay,' I say, 'I'll bite. Why?'

'It's obvious,' he says, lighting his pipe again, spewing out fumes. 'First, the patients have to wait until they're dying. A true life crisis, no fakery and invention. They aren't permitted to bother you until then, until they can demonstrate that they're serious, you might say. Second, somebody gets a good square meal out of it.' He laughs ruefully. We both know that half his patients don't bother to pay him, not even the money the government pays them. Joseph has a habit of taking on people nobody else will touch with a barge pole, not because they're too sick but because they're too poor. Mothers on welfare and so on; bad credit risks, like Joseph himself. He once got fired from a loony bin for trying to institute worker control.

'And think of the time saving,' he goes on. 'A couple of hours per patient, sum total, as opposed to twice a week for years and years, with the same result in the end.'

'That's pretty cynical,' I say disapprovingly. I'm supposed to be the cynical one, but maybe he's outflanking me, to force me to give up this corner. Cynicism is a defence, according to Joseph.

'You wouldn't even have to listen to them,' he says. 'Not a blessed word. The sins are transmitted in the food.'

Suddenly he looks sad and tired.

'You're telling me I'm wasting your time?' I say.

'Not mine, my dear,' he says. 'I've got all the time in the world.'

I interpret this as condescension, the one thing above all that I can't stand. I don't throw my coffee cup at him, however. I'm not as angry as I would have been once.

We've spent a lot of time on it, this anger of mine. It was only because I found reality so unsatisfactory; that was my story. So unfinished, so sloppy, so pointless, so endless. I wanted things to make sense.

I thought Joseph would try to convince me that reality was actually fine and dandy and then try to adjust me to it, but he didn't do that. Instead he agreed with me, cheerfully and at once. Life in most ways was a big pile of shit, he said. That was axiomatic. 'Think of it as a desert island,' he said. 'You're stuck on it, now you have to decide how best to cope.'

'Until rescued?' I said.

'Forget about the rescue,' he said.

'I can't,' I said.

This conversation is taking place in Joseph's office, which is just as tatty as he is and smells of unemptied ash-trays, feet, misery, and twice-breathed air. But it's also taking place in my bedroom, on the day of the funeral. Joseph's, who didn't have all the time in the world.

'He fell out of a tree,' said Karen, notifying me. She'd come to do this in person, rather than using the phone. Joseph didn't trust phones. Most of the message in any act of communication, he said, was non-verbal.

Karen stood in my doorway, oozing tears. She was one of his too, one of us; it was through her I'd got him. By now there's a network of us, it's like recommending a hairdresser, we've passed him from hand to hand like the proverbial eye or tooth. Smart women with detachable husbands or genius-afflicted children with nervous tics, smart women with deranged lives, overjoyed to find someone who wouldn't tell us we were too smart for our own good and should all have frontal lobotomies. Smartness was an asset, Joseph maintained. We should only see what happened to the dumb ones.

'Out of a *tree*?' I said, almost screaming.

'Sixty feet, onto his head,' said Karen. She began weeping again. I wanted to shake her.

'What the bloody hell was he doing up at the top of a sixty-foot *tree*?' I said.

'Pruning it,' said Karen. 'It was in his garden. It was cutting off the light to his flower beds.'

'The old fart,' I said. I was furious with him. It was an act of desertion. What made him think he had the right to go climbing up to the top of a sixty-foot tree, risking all our lives? Did his flower beds mean more to him than we did?

'What are we going to do?' said Karen.

What am I going to do? is one question. It can always be replaced by *What am I going to wear?* For some people it's the same thing. I go through the cupboard, looking for the blackest things I can find. What I wear will be the non-verbal part of the communication. Joseph will notice. I have a horrible feeling I'll turn up at the funeral home and find they've laid him out in his awful yellow cardigan and those tacky maroon leather bedroom slippers.

I needn't have bothered with the black. It's no longer demanded. The three wives are in pastels, the first in blue, the second in mauve, the third, the current one, in beige. I know a lot about the three wives, from those off-days of mine when I didn't feel like talking.

Karen is here too, in an Indian-print dress, snivelling softly to herself. I envy her. I want to feel grief, but I can't quite believe Joseph is dead. It seems like some joke he's playing, some anecdote that's supposed to make us learn something. Fakery and invention. *All right, Joseph,* I want to call, *we have the answer, you can come out now.* But nothing happens, the closed coffin remains closed, no wisps of smoke issue from it to show there's life.

The closed coffin is the third wife's idea. She thinks it's more dignified, says the grapevine, and it probably is. The coffin is of dark wood, in good taste, no showy trim. No one has made a meal and placed it on this coffin, no one has eaten from it. No destitute old creature, gobbling down the turnips and mash and the heavy secrecies of Joesph's life along with them. I have no idea what Joseph might have had on his conscience. Nevertheless I feel this as an omission: what then have become of Joseph's sins? They hover around us, in the air, over the bowed heads, while a male relative of Joseph's, unknown to me, tells us all what a fine man he was.

After the funeral we go back to Joseph's house, to the third wife's house, for what used to be called the wake. Not any more: now it's coffee and refreshments.

The flower beds are tidy, gladioli at this time of year, already fading and a little ragged. The tree branch, the one that broke, is still on the lawn.

'I kept having the feeling he wasn't really there,' says Karen as we go up the walk.

'Really where?' I say.

'There,' says Karen. 'In the coffin.'

'For Christ's sake,' I say, 'don't start that.' I can tolerate that kind of sentimental fiction in myself, just barely, as long as I don't do it out loud. 'Dead is dead, that's what he'd say. Deal with here and now, remember?'

Karen, who'd once tried suicide, nodded and started to cry again. Joseph is an expert on people who try suicide. He's never lost one yet.

'How does he do it?' I asked Karen once. Suicide wasn't one of my addictions, so I didn't know.

'He makes it sound so *boring*,' she said.

'That can't be all,' I said.

'He makes you imagine,' she said, 'what it's like to be dead.'

There are people moving around quietly, in the living-room and in the dining-room, where the table stands, arranged by the third wife with a silver tea urn and a vase of chrysanthemums, pink and yellow. Nothing too funereal, you can hear her thinking. On the white tablecloth there are cups, plates, cookies, coffee, cakes. I don't know why funerals are supposed to make people hungry, but they do. If you can still chew you know you're alive.

Karen is beside me, stuffing down a piece of chocolate cake. On the other side is the first wife.

'I hope you aren't one of the loonies,' she says to me abruptly. I've never really met her before, she's just been pointed out to me, by Karen, at the funeral. She's wiping her fingers on a paper napkin. On her powder-blue lapel is a gold brooch in the shape of a bird's nest, complete with the eggs. It reminds me of high school: felt skirts with appliqués of cats and telephones, a world of replicas.

I ponder my reply. Does she mean *client*, or is she asking whether I am by chance genuinely out of my mind?

'No,' I say.

'Didn't think so,' says the first wife. 'You don't look like it. A lot of them were, the place was crawling with them. I was afraid there might be an *incident*. When I lived with Joseph there were always these *incidents*, phone calls at two in the morning, always killing themselves, throwing themselves all over him, you couldn't believe what went on. Some of them were *devoted* to him. If he'd told them to shoot the Pope or something, they'd have done it just like that.'

'He was very highly thought of,' I say carefully.

'You're telling *me*,' says the first wife. 'Had the idea he was God himself, some of them. Not that he minded all that much.'

The paper napkin isn't adequate, she's licking her fingers. 'Too rich,' she says. '*Hers*.' She jerks her head in the direction of the second wife, who is wispier than the first wife and is walking past us, somewhat aimlessly, in the direction of the living-room. 'You can have it, I told him finally. I just want some peace and quiet before I have to start pushing up the daisies.' Despite the richness, she helps herself to another piece of chocolate cake. '*She* had this nutty idea that we should have some of them stand up and give little testimonies about him, right at the ceremony. Are you totally out of your tree? I told her. It's your funeral, but if I was you I'd try to keep it in mind that some of the people there are going to be a whole lot saner than others. Luckily she listened to me.'

'Yes,' I say. There's chocolate icing on her cheek: I wonder if I should tell her.

'I did what I could,' she says, 'which wasn't that much, but still. I was fond of him in a way. You can't just wipe out ten years of your life. I brought the cookies,' she adds, rather smugly. 'Least I could do.'

I look down at the cookies. They're white, cut into the shapes of stars and moons and decorated with coloured sugar and little silver balls. They remind me of Christmas, of festivals and celebrations. They're the kind of cookies you make to please someone; to please a child.

I've been here long enough. I look around for the third wife, the one in charge, to say goodbye. I finally locate her, standing in an open doorway. She's crying, something she didn't do at the funeral. The first wife is beside her, holding her hand.

'I'm keeping it just like this,' says the third wife, to no one in particular. Past her shoulder I can see into the room, Joseph's study evidently. It would take a lot of strength to leave that rummage sale untouched, untidied. Not to mention the begonias withering on the sill. But for her it will take no strength at all, because Joseph is in this room, unfinished, a huge boxful of loose ends. He refuses to be packed up and put away.

'Who do you hate the most?' says Joseph. This, in the middle of a lecture he's been giving me about the proper kind of birdbath for one's garden. He knows of course that I don't have a garden.

'I have absolutely no idea,' I say.

'Then you should find out,' says Joseph. 'I myself cherish an abiding hatred for the boy who lived next door to me when I was eight.'

'Why is that?' I ask, pleased to be let off the hook.

'He picked my sunflower,' he says. 'I grew up in a slum, you know. We had an area of sorts at the front, but it was solid cinders. However I did manage to grow this one stunted little sunflower, God knows how. I used to get up early every morning just to look at it. And the little bugger picked it. Pure bloody malice. I've forgiven a lot of later transgressions but if I ran into the little sod tomorrow I'd stick a knife into him.'

I'm shocked, as Joseph intends me to be. 'He was only a child,' I say.

'So was I,' he says. 'The early ones are the hardest to forgive. Children have no charity; it has to be learned.'

Is this Joseph proving yet once more that he's a human being, or am I intended to understand something about myself? Maybe, maybe not. Sometimes Joseph's stories are parables, but sometimes they're just running off at the mouth.

In the front hall the second wife, she of the mauve wisps, ambushes me. 'He didn't fall,' she whispers.

'Pardon?' I say.

The three wives have a family resemblance—they're all blondish and vague around the edges but there's something else about this one, a glittering of the eyes. Maybe it's grief; or maybe Joseph didn't always draw a totally firm line between his personal and his professional lives. The second wife has a faint aroma of client.

'He wasn't happy,' she says. 'I could tell. We were still very close, you know.'

What she wants me to infer is that he jumped. 'He seemed all right to me,' I say.

'He was good at keeping up a front,' she says. She takes a breath, she's about to confide in me, but whatever these revelations are I don't want to hear them. I want Joseph to remain as he appeared: solid, capable, wise, and sane. I do not need his darkness.

I go back to the apartment. My sons are away for the weekend. I wonder whether I should bother making dinner just for myself. It's hardly worth it. I wander around the too-small living-room, picking things up. No longer my husband's: as befits the half-divorced, he lives elsewhere.

One of my sons has just reached the shower-and-shave phase, the other hasn't, but both of them leave a deposit every time they pass through a room. A sort of bathtub ring of objects—socks, paperback books left face-down and open in the middle, sandwiches with bites taken out of them, and, lately, cigarette butts.

Under a dirty T-shirt I discover the Hare Krishna magazine my younger son brought home a week ago. I was worried that it was a spate of adolescent religious mania, but no, he'd given them a quarter because he felt sorry for them. He was a dead-robin-burier as a child. I take the magazine into the kitchen to put it in the trash. On the front there's a picture of Krishna playing the flute, surrounded by adoring maidens. His face is bright blue, which makes me think of corpses: some things are not cross-cultural. If I read on I could find out why meat and sex are bad for you. Not such a poor idea when you think about it: no more terrified cows, no more divorces. A life of abstinence and prayer. I think of myself, standing on a street corner, ringing a bell, swathed in flowing garments. Selfless and removed, free from sin. Sin is this world, says Krishna. This world is all we have, says Joseph. It's all you have to work with. It is not too much for you. You will not be rescued.

I could walk to the corner for a hamburger or I could phone out for pizza. I decide on the pizza.

'Do you like me?' Joseph says from his armchair.

'What do you mean, do I *like* you?' I say. It's early on; I haven't given any thought to whether or not I like Joseph.

'Well, do you?' he says.

'Look,' I say. I'm speaking calmly but in fact I'm outraged. This is a demand, and Joseph is not supposed to make demands of me. There are too many demands being made of me already. That's why I'm here, isn't it? Because the demands exceed the supply. 'You're like my dentist,' I say. 'I don't think about whether or not I like my dentist. I don't *have* to like him. I'm paying him to fix my teeth. You and my dentist are the only people in the whole world that I don't *have* to *like*.'

'But if you met me under other circumstances,' Joseph persists, 'would you like me?'

'I have no idea,' I say. 'I can't imagine any other circumstances.'

This is a room at night, a night empty except for me. I'm looking at the ceiling, across which the light from a car passing outside is slowly moving. My apartment is on the first floor: I don't like heights. Before this I always lived in a house.

I've been having a dream about Joseph. Joseph was never much interested in dreams. At the beginning I used to save them up for him and tell them to him, the ones I thought were of interest, but he would always refuse to say what they meant. He'd make me tell him, instead. Being awake, according to Joseph, was more important than being asleep. He wanted me to prefer it.

Nevertheless, there was Joseph in my dream. It's the first time he's made an appearance. I think that it will please him to have made it, finally, after all those other dreams about preparations for dinner parties, always one plate short. But then I remember that he's no longer around to be told. Here it is, finally, the shape of my bereavement: Joseph is no longer around to be told. There is no one left in my life who is there only to be told.

I'm in an airport terminal. The plane's been delayed, all the planes have been delayed, perhaps there's a strike, and people are crammed in and milling around. Some of them are upset, there are children crying, some of the women are crying too, they've lost people, they push through the crowd calling out names, but elsewhere there are clumps of men and women laughing and singing, they've had the foresight to bring cases of beer with them to the airport and they're passing the bottles around. I try to get some information but there's no one at any of the ticket counters. Then I realize I've forgotten my passport. I decide to take a taxi home to get it, and by the time I make it back maybe they'll have everything straightened out.

I push towards the exit doors, but someone is waving to me across the heads of the crowd. It's Joseph. I'm not at all surprised to see him, though I do wonder about the winter overcoat he's wearing, since it's still summer. He also has a yellow muffler wound around his neck, and a hat. I've never seen him in any of these clothes before. Of course, I think, he's cold, but now he's pushed through the people, he's beside me. He's wearing a pair of heavy leather gloves and he takes the right one off to shake my hand. His own hand is bright blue, a flat tempera-paint blue, a picture-book blue. I hesitate, then I shake the hand, but he doesn't let go, he holds my hand, confidingly, like a child, smiling at me as if we haven't met for a long time.

'I'm glad you got the invitation,' he says.

Now he's leading me towards a doorway. There are fewer people now. To one side there's a stand selling orange juice. Joseph's three wives are behind the counter, all in identical costumes, white hats and frilly aprons, like waitresses of the forties. We go through the doorway; inside, people are sitting at small round tables, though there's nothing on the tables in front of them, they appear to be waiting.

I sit down at one of the tables and Joseph sits opposite me. He doesn't take off his hat or his coat, but his hands are on the table, no gloves, they're the normal colour again. There's a man standing beside us, trying to attract our attention. He's holding out a small white card covered with symbols, hands and fingers. A deaf-mute, I decide, and sure enough when I look his mouth is sewn shut. Now he's tugging at Joseph's arm, he's holding out something else, it's a large yellow flower. Joseph doesn't see him.

'Look,' I say to Joseph, but the man is already gone and one of the waitresses has come instead. I resent the interruption, I have so much to tell Joseph and there's so little time, the plane will go in a minute, in the other room I can already hear the crackle of announcements, but the woman pushes in between us, smiling officiously. It's the first wife; behind her, the other two wives stand in attendance. She sets a large plate in front of us on the table.

'Will that be all?' she says, before she retreats.

The plate is filled with cookies, children's-party cookies, white ones, cut into the shapes of moons and stars, decorated with silver balls and coloured sugar. They look too rich.

'My sins,' Joseph says. His voice sounds wistful but when I glance up he's smiling at me. Is he making a joke?

I look down at the plate again. I have a moment of panic: this is not what I ordered, it's too much for me, I might get sick. Maybe I could send it back; but I know this isn't possible.

I remember now that Joseph is dead. The plate floats up towards me, there is no table, around us is dark space. There are thousands of stars, thousands of moons, and as I reach out for one they begin to shine.

W.D.VALGARDSON
b.1939

Bloodflowers

Danny Thorson saw Mrs Poorwilly before he stepped off the freight boat onto Black Island. He couldn't have missed her. She was fat and had thick, heavy arms and legs. She stood at the front of the crowd with her hands on her hips.

'You the new teacher?' Mrs Poorwilly said.

'Yes, I'm—'

Mrs Poorwilly cut him off by waving her arm at him and saying, 'Put your things on the wheelbarrow. Mr Poorwilly will take them up to the house. Board and room is $50 a month. We're the only ones that give it. That's Mr Poorwilly.'

Mrs Poorwilly waved her hand again, indicating a small man who was standing behind an orange wheelbarrow. He had a round, red face, and his hair was so thin and blond that from ten feet away he looked bald.

Danny piled his suitcases and boxes onto the wheel-barrow. He was tired and sore from the trip to the island. The bunk had been too short. The weather had been bad. For the first three days of the trip, he hadn't been able to hold anything down except coffee.

When the wheelbarrow was full, Mr Poorwilly took his hands out of his pockets. They were twisted into two rigid pink hooks. He slipped them through two metal loops that had been nailed to the handles of the wheel-barrow, then lifted the barrow on his wrists.

At the top of the first rise, Mr Poorwilly stopped. As if to reassure Danny, he said, 'Mrs Poorwilly's a good cook. We've got fresh eggs all winter, too.'

Danny glanced back. Mrs Poorwilly was swinging cases of tinned goods onto the dock. Her grey hair blew wildly about her face.

They started off again. As there were no paths on the bare granite, Danny followed Mr Poorwilly. They walked along a ridge, dropped into a hollow. The slope they had to climb was steep, so Danny bent down, caught the front of the wheelbarrow and pulled as Mr Poorwilly pushed.

They had just reached the top when they met an elderly, wasted man who was leaning heavily on the shoulder of a young girl as he shuffled along.

Danny was so surprised by the incongruity of the pair that he stared. The girl's black hair fell to her shoulders, making a frame for her face. She looked tired, but her face was tanned and her mouth was a warm red. Her cheeks were pink from the wind. She stopped when she saw Danny.

The man with her made no attempt to greet them. His breath came in ragged gasps. His dark yellow skin was pulled so tightly over his face that the bone seemed to be pushing through. His eyes protruded and the whites had turned yellow. He gave the girl's shoulder a tug. They started up again.

When they had passed, Danny said, 'Who was that? The girl is beautiful.'

'Sick Jack and his daughter. It's his liver. Mrs Poorwilly helps Adel look after him. She says he won't see the spring. He'll be the second. How are you feeling after the trip? You look green.'

'I feel green. It was nine days in hell. The boat never quit rolling.'

'Good thing you're not going back with them, then.' Mr Poorwilly twisted his head toward the dock to indicate who he meant. 'Sunrise was red this morning. There'll be a storm before dawn tomorrow.'

Mr Poorwilly slipped his hands back into the metal loops. 'Sorry to be so slow, but the arthritis causes me trouble. Used to be able to use my hands but not anymore. It's a good thing I've got a pension from the war. Getting shot was the best thing has ever happened to me.'

Danny noticed a small, red flower growing from a crack in the rock. When he bent down to get a better look, he saw that the crack was filled with brown stems. He picked the flower and held it up. 'What is it?'

'Bloodflower,' Mr Poorwilly replied. 'Only thing that grows on the island except lichen. Shouldn't pick it. They say it brings bad luck. If you cut your finger or make your nose bleed, it'll be OK.'

Danny laughed. 'You don't believe that, do you?'

'Mrs Poorwilly says it. She knows quite a bit about these things.'

When they reached the house, Danny unloaded his belongings and put them into his bedroom. Mr Poorwilly left him and went back to the dock for the supplies Mrs Poorwilly had been unloading.

While the Poorwillys spent the day sorting and putting away their winter's supplies, Danny walked around the island. What Mr Poorwilly said was true. Nothing grew on the island except lichen and bloodflowers. Despite the cold, patches of red filled the cracks that were sheltered from the wind.

The granite of the island had been weathered smooth, but there was nowhere it was truly flat. Three-quarters of the island's shoreline fell steeply into the sea. Only in scattered places did the shoreline slope gently enough to let Danny walk down to the water. To the west the thin blue line of the coast of Labrador was just barely visible. Two fishing boats were bobbing on the ocean. There were no birds except for some large grey gulls that rose as he approached and hovered in the air until he was well past them. He would have liked to have them come down beside him so he could have touched them, but they rose on the updrafts. He reached toward them and shouted for them to come down, then laughed at himself and continued his exploring.

Except for the houses and the fish sheds, the only other buildings were the school and the chicken roost behind the Poorwillys. All the buildings were made from wood siding. Because of the rock, there were no basements. Rock foundations had been put down so the floors would be level.

Most of the houses showed little more than traces of paint. The Poorwillys' and Mary Johnson's were the only ones that had been painted recently. Danny knew the other house belonged to Mary Johnson because it had a sign with her name on it. Below her name it said, 'General store. Post office. Two-way radio.'

Danny explored until it started to get dark, then went back to the Poorwillys.

'Heard you've been looking around,' Mrs Poorwilly said. 'If you hadn't come back in another five minutes, I would have sent Mr Poorwilly to bring you back.'

'There's no danger of getting lost.' Danny was amused at her concern.

'No,' Mrs Poorwilly agreed, 'but you wouldn't want to slip and fall in the dark. You're not in a city now with a doctor down the street. You break a leg or crack your skull and your might have to wait two, three weeks for the weather to clear enough for a plane to come. You don't want to be one of the three.'

Danny felt chastised, but Mrs Poorwilly dropped the subject. She and Mr Poorwilly spent all during supper asking him about the mainland. As they talked, Mrs Poorwilly fed her husband from her plate. He sat with his hands in his lap. There were no directions given or taken about the feeding. Both Mr and Mrs Poorwilly were anxious to hear everything he had to tell them about the mainland.

When he got a chance, Danny said, 'What'd you mean "one of the three"?'

'Trouble always come in threes. Maybe you didn't notice it on the mainland because things are so complicated. On the island you can see it because it's small and you know everybody. There's just 35 houses. Somebody gets hurt, everybody knows about it. They can keep track.

Three, six, nine, but it never ends unless it's on something made up of threes.'

'You'll see before the winter is out. Last month the radio said Emily died in the sanatorium. TB. Now Sick Jack's been failing badly. He's got to be a hard yellow and he's lost all his flesh. He dies, then there'll be one more thing to end it. After that, everything will be OK.'

Mrs Poorwilly made her pronouncement with all the assuredness of an oracle. Danny started on his dessert.

'Mr Poorwilly says you think Adel's a nice bit of fluff.'

Danny had started thinking about the book on mythology he'd been reading at summer school. The statement caught him off guard. He had to collect his thoughts, then he said, 'The girl with the long dark hair? I only caught a glimpse of her, but she seemed to be very pretty.'

'When her father goes, she'll be on her own,' Mr Poorwilly said. 'She's a good girl. She works hard.'

'Does she have any education?'

'Wives with too much education can cause a lot of trouble,' Mrs Poorwilly said. 'They're never satisfied. The young fellows around here and on the coast have enough trouble without that.'

Danny tried not to show his embarrassment. 'I was thinking in terms of her getting a job on the mainland. If her spelling is good and she learned to type, she could get a government job.'

'Might be that she'll go right after her father. No use making plans until we see what the winter brings.' Mr Poorwilly turned to his wife for confirmation. 'It's happened before.'

Mrs Poorwilly nodded as she scraped the last of the pudding from the dish and fed it to her husband.

'What you want is what those people had that I was reading about. They used to ward off evil by choosing a villager to be king for a year. Then so the bad luck of the old year would be done with, they killed him in the spring.'

'They weren't Christians,' Mr Poorwilly said.

'No,' Danny replied. 'They gave their king anything he wanted. A woman, food, gifts, everything, since it was only for a year. Then when the first flowers bloomed, they killed him.'

'Must have been them Chinese,' Mr Poorwilly said.

'No. Europeans. But it was a long time ago.'

'Have you ever ridden on a train?' Mrs Poorwilly asked. 'Mr Poorwilly and I rode on a train for our honeymoon. I remember it just like yesterday.'

Mr and Mrs Poorwilly told him about their train ride until it was time to go to bed. After Danny was in bed, Mr Poorwilly stuck his head through the curtain that covered the doorway. In a low voice, he said, 'Don't go shouting at the sea gulls when you're out walking. Most of the people here haven't been anywhere and they'll think you're sort of funny.'

'OK,' Danny said. Mr Poorwilly's head disappeared.

The next day Mrs Poorwilly had everyone in the village over to meet Danny. As fast as Danny met the women and children, he forgot their names. The men were still away fishing or working on the mainland. Mr Poorwilly and Danny were the only men until Adel brought Sick Jack.

Sick Jack looked even thinner than he had the day before. The yellow of his skin seemed to have deepened. As soon as he had shaken Danny's hand, he sat down. After a few minutes, he fell into a doze and his daughter covered him with a blanket she had brought.

Mrs Poorwilly waited until Sick Jack was covered, then brought Adel over to see Danny.

'This is Adel. She'll come for coffee soon, and you can tell her about the trains and the cities. She's never been off the island.'

Adel blushed and looked at the floor. 'Certainly,' Danny said. 'I've a whole set of slides I'm going to show Mr and Mrs Poorwilly. If you wanted, you could come and see them.'

Adel mumbled her thanks and went to the side of the room. She stayed beside her father the rest of the evening, but Danny glanced at her whenever he felt no-one was looking at him.

She was wearing blue jeans and a heavy blue sweater that had been mended at the elbows and cuffs with green wool. It was too large for her so Danny assumed that it had belonged to her father or one of the other men. From what Mrs Poorwilly had said, Danny had learned that Adel and her father were given gifts of fish and second-hand clothing. When the men went fishing, they always ran an extra line for Sick Jack.

In spite of her clothing, Adel was attractive. Her hair was as black as he had remembered it and it hung in loose, natural waves. Her eyes were a dark blue. Underneath the too-large sweater, her breasts made soft, noticeable mounds.

She left before Danny had a chance to speak to her again, but he didn't mind as he knew he'd see her during the winter.

For the next two weeks, busy as he was, Danny couldn't help but notice the change in the village. The men returned at all hours, in all kinds of weather. Mostly they came two and three at a time, but now and again a man would come by himself, his open boat a lonely black dot on the horizon.

Most of the men brought little news that was cheerful. The fishing had been bad. Many of them were coming home with the absolute minimum of money that would carry them until spring. No-one said much, but they all knew that winter fishing would be necessary to keep some of the families from going hungry. In a good year, the winter fishing provided a change in diet for people sick of canned food. This year the fishing wouldn't be so casual.

By the end of September the weather had turned bitterly cold. The wind blew for days at a time. The houses rocked in the wind. Danny walked the smallest children to their homes. The few days the fishermen were able to leave the island, there were no fish. Some of the men tried to fish in spite of the weather, but most of the time they were able to do little more than clear the harbour before having to turn around.

The evening Sick Jack died, Danny had gone to bed early. The banging on the door woke him. Mr Poorwilly got up and answered the door. Danny heard the muttered talk, then Mr Poorwilly yelled the news to Mrs Poorwilly. They both dressed and left right away. Danny would have offered to go with them, but he knew that he would just be in the way so he said nothing.

Mrs Poorwilly was back for breakfast. As she stirred the porridge, she said. 'She's alone now. We washed him and dressed him and laid him out on his bed. She's a good girl. She got all his clothes out and would have helped us dress him, but I wouldn't let her. Mr Poorwilly is staying with her until some of the women come to sit by the body. If the weather holds, we'll have the funeral tomorrow.'

'Why not have the funeral while the weather stays good? It could change tomorrow.'

'Respect,' Mrs Poorwilly said. 'But it's more than that, too. I wouldn't say it to her, but it helps make sure he's dead. Once just around when I married, Mrs Milligan died. She was 70. Maybe older. They rushed because the weather was turning. They were just pushing her over the side when she groaned. The cold did it. She died for good the next week, but since then we like to make sure.'

Danny went to the funeral. The body was laid out on the bed with a shroud pulled to its shoulders. Mary Johnson sang 'The Old Rugged Cross'. Mrs Poorwilly held the Bible so Mr Poorwilly could read from it. Adel sat on a kitchen chair at the foot of the bed. She was pale and her eyes were red, but she didn't cry.

When the service was over, one of the fishermen pulled the shroud over Sick Jack's head and tied it with a string. They lifted the body onto a stretcher they had made from a tarpaulin and a pair of oars. The villagers followed them to the harbour.

They laid the body on the bottom of the boat. Three men got in. As the boat swung through the spray at the harbour's mouth, Danny saw one of the men bend and tie an anchor to the shrouded figure.

Mrs Poorwilly had coffee ready for everyone after the service. Adel sat in the middle of the kitchen. She still had a frozen look about her face, but she was willing to talk.

Sick Jack's death brought added tension to the village. One day in class while they were reading a story about a robin that had died, Mary Johnson's littlest boy said, 'My mother says somebody else is going to die. Maybe Miss Adel now that her father's gone.'

Danny had been sharp with him. 'Be quiet. This is a Grade Three lesson. You're not even supposed to be listening. Have you done your alphabet yet?'

His older sister burst out, 'That's what my mother said. She said—'

Danny cut her off. 'That's enough. We're studying literature, not mythology. Things like that are nothing but superstition.'

That night Danny asked about Adel. Mrs Poorwilly said, 'She's got a settlement coming from the mine where he used to work. It's not much. Maybe $500 or $600. Everybody'll help all they can, but she's going to have to get a man to look after her.'

During November, Danny managed to see Adel twice. The first time, she came for coffee. The second time, she came to see Danny's slides of the mainland. Danny walked her home the first time. The second time, Mrs Poorwilly said, 'That's all right, Mr Thorson. I'll walk with her. There's something I want to get from Mary Johnson's.'

Danny was annoyed. Mrs Poorwilly had been pushing him in Adel's direction from the first day he had come. Then, when he made an effort to be alone with her, she had stepped between them.

Mrs Poorwilly was back in half an hour with a package of powdered milk.

Danny said, 'I would have got that for you, Mrs Poorwilly.'

'A man shouldn't squeeze fruit unless he's planning on buying,' she replied.

Adel walked by the school a number of times when he was there. He got to talk to her, but she was skittish. He wished that she was with him in the city. There, at least, there were dark corners, alley-ways, parks, even doorsteps. On the island, you couldn't do anything without being seen.

At Christmas the villagers held a party at the school. Danny showed his slides. Afterwards they all danced while Wee Jimmy played his fiddle. Danny got to dance with Adel a good part of the night.

He knew that Mrs Poorwilly was displeased and that everyone in the village would talk about his dancing for the rest of the year, but he didn't care. Adel had her hair tied back with a red ribbon. The curve of her neck was white and smooth. Her blouse clung to her breasts and was cut low enough for him to see where the soft curves began. Each time he danced with one of the other women, Danny found himself turning to see what Adel was doing. When the party was over, he walked Adel home and kissed her goodnight. He wanted her to stay with him in the doorway, but she pulled away and went inside.

Two days before New Year's, Mrs Poorwilly's prediction came true. The fishing had remained poor, but Michael Fairweather had gone fishing in a heavy sea because he was one of those who had come back with little money. Two hundred yards from the island his boat capsized.

Danny had gone to school on the pretext of doing some work, but what he wanted was some privacy. He had been sitting at the window staring out to sea when the accident happened. He had seen the squall coming up. A violent wind whipped across the waves and behind it a white, ragged line on the water raced toward the island. Michael Fairweather was only able to turn his boat halfway round before the wind and sleet struck.

Danny saw the boat rise to the crest of a wave, then disappear, and Michael was hanging onto the keel. Danny bolted from the room, but by the time he reached the dock, Michael had disappeared.

The squall had disappeared as quickly as it had come. Within half an hour the sea was back to its normal rolling. The fishermen rowed out of the harbour and dropped metal bars lined with hooks. While one man rowed, another held the line at the back of the boat. As Danny watched, the boats crossed back and forth until it was nearly dark.

They came in without the body. Danny couldn't sleep that night. In the morning, when a group of men came to the Poorwillys, Danny answered the door before Mr Poorwilly had time to get out of his bedroom. The men had come for the loan of the Poorwillys' rooster.

Mrs Poorwilly nestled the rooster in her jacket on the way to the dock, then tied it to Mr Poorwilly's wrist with a leather thong. Mr Poorwilly stepped into the front of the skiff. The rooster hopped onto the bow. With that the other men climbed into their boats and followed Mr Poorwilly and the rooster out of the harbour.

'What are they doing?' Danny asked.

Mrs Poorwilly kept her eyes on the lead boat, but she said, 'When they cross the body, the rooster will crow.'

Danny turned and stared at the line of boats. In spite of the wind, the sun was warm. The rooster's feathers gleamed in the sun. Mr Poorwilly stood as still as a wooden figurehead. The dark green and grey boats rose and fell on the waves. Except for the hissing of the foam, there was no sound.

Danny looked away and searched the crowd for Adel. He had looked for a third time, when Mrs Poorwilly, without turning, said, 'She won't come for fear the current will have brought her father close to shore. They might bring him up.'

All morning and into the afternoon the boats crossed and recrossed the area in front of the harbour in a ragged line. No-one left the dock. The women with small babies didn't come down from their houses, but Danny could see them in their doorways.

As the day wore on, Danny became caught up in the crossing and recrossing of the boats. None of the men dragged their hooks. The only time the men in the rear of the boats moved was to change positions with the men at the oars.

When the cock crew, the sound caught Danny by surprise. The constant, unchanging motion and the hissing of the spray had drawn him into a quiet trance. It had been as if the boats and he had been there forever.

The sound was so sharp that some of the women cried out. The men with the iron bars covered with hooks threw them into the sea, and shoved the coils of rope after them. They didn't want to pass the spot where the cock crew until the hooks were on the bottom. The bars disappeared with little spurts of white foam. Danny could hear the rope rubbing against the side of the boat as it was pulled hand over hand.

'It's him,' Mrs Poorwilly said. 'God have mercy, they've got him.'

Danny turned back. It was true. Instead of a white shroud, the men were pulling a black bundle into the boat.

The funeral was bad. Marj Fairweather cried constantly and tried to keep the men from taking the body. As they started to leave, she ran to the dresser for a heavy sweater, then sat in the middle of the floor, crying and saying, 'He'll be so cold. He'll be so cold.'

In spite of Marj, the tension in the community eased after the funeral was over. People began to visit more often, and when they came they talked more and stayed longer.

Adel came frequently to the Poorwillys. When she came, she talked to the Poorwillys. but she watched Danny. She wasn't open about it, but when Danny looked at her, she let her eyes linger on him for a second before turning away. She had her colour back and looked even better than before. Most of the time, Danny managed to walk her home. Kissing her was not satisfactory because of the cold and the bulky clothes between them, but she would not invite him in and there was no privacy at the Poorwillys. In spite of the walks and goodnight kisses, she remained shy when anyone else was around.

The villagers had expected the weather and the fishing to improve. If anything, the weather became worse. Ice coated the boats. The wind blew night and day. Often, it only stopped in the hour before dawn.

Then, without warning, Marj Fairweather sent her children to the Poorwillys, emptied a gas lamp on herself and the kitchen floor, and lit a match.

This time there was no funeral. The entire village moved in a state of shock. While one of the sheds was fixed up for the children, Marj's remains were hurried to sea and dumped in the same area as her husband's.

The village drew into itself. The villagers stayed long enough to finish their business. The men quit going to the dock. Most of them pulled their boats onto the island and turned them over.

A week after the fire, Danny arrived to find his room stripped of his belongings. Mrs Poorwilly waited until he had come into the kitchen. 'Mr Poorwilly and I decided to take two of the Fairweather children. We'll take the two youngest. A fourteen-year-old can't take care of six kids.'

Danny was too stunned to say anything. Mrs Poorwilly continued. 'Some of us talked about it. We hope you don't mind, but there's nothing else to do. Besides, there's going to be no money from the mine. Adel needs your board and room worse than we do. We'll keep the Fairweather children for nothing.'

When Danny didn't reply, Mrs Poorwilly added, 'We got help moving your things. We gave Adel the rest of this month's money.'

Danny hesitated for a moment, but there was nothing to say. He went outside.

He knocked at Adel's door. She let him in. 'Mrs Poorwilly says you're to stay with me now.'

'Yes, she told me,' Danny said.

Adel showed him to his bedroom. All his clothes had been hung up and his books had been neatly piled in one corner. He sat on the edge of the bed and tried to decide what to do. He finally decided he couldn't sit in the bedroom for the next five months and went back into the kitchen.

The supper was good, but Danny was too interested in Adel to pay much attention. In the light from the oil lamp, her eyes looked darker than ever. She was wearing a sweater with a V-neck. He could see the soft hollow of her throat and the smooth skin below her breastbone. Throughout supper he told her about the mainland and tried to keep his eyes above her neck.

The next morning when he went to school, he expected to see a difference in the children's attitudes. Twice he turned around quickly. Each time the children had all been busy writing in their notebooks. There was no smirking or winking behind their hands. At noon, he said, 'In case any of you need to ask me something, there's no use your going to the Poorwillys. I'm staying at Miss Adel's now.'

The children solemnly nodded their heads. He dismissed them and went home for lunch.

Adel was at home. She blushed and said, 'The women at the sheds said I should come home early now that I've got you to look after. Since the men aren't fishing there isn't much to do.'

'That's very good of them,' Danny replied.

Danny and Adel were left completely alone. He had expected that some of the villagers would drop by, but no-one came to visit. Danny and Adel settled into a routine that was disturbed only by Danny's irritation at being close to Adel. Adel shied away from him when he brushed against her. At the end of the second week, she accepted his offer to help with the dishes. They stood side by side as they worked. Danny was so distracted by Adel's warmth and the constant movement of her body that the dishes were only half dried.

Danny put his hand on Adel's shoulder and turned her toward him. She let him pull her close. There was no place to sit or lie in the kitchen so he picked her up and carried her to the bedroom. She didn't resist when he undressed her. After he made love to her, he fell asleep. When he woke up, Adel had gone to her own bed.

Danny took Adel to bed with him every evening after that, but during the night she always slipped away to her own bedroom. At the beginning of the next week, they had their first visitor. Mrs Poorwilly stopped by to see how they were doing. They had been eating supper when she arrived. Normally, they would have been finished eating, but Adel had been late in coming from the fish sheds. The weather had improved enough for the men to go fishing. Mrs Poorwilly accepted a cup of coffee and sat and talked to them for an hour.

It was as if her coming had been a signal. After that, villagers dropped by in the evenings to talk for a little while. They nearly always brought something with them and left it on the table. Danny had wanted to protest, but he didn't know what to say that wouldn't embarrass their visitors so he said nothing.

Adel stopped going back to her own bed. Danny thought about getting married but dismissed the idea. He was comfortable with things the way they were.

The day Danny started to get sick he should have known something was wrong. He had yelled at the children for no particular reason. When Adel had come home, he had been grouchy with her. The next day his throat had been sore, but he had ignored it. By the end of the day, he was running a temperature and his knees felt like water.

Adel had been worried, but he told her not to call Mrs Poorwilly. Their things had become so mixed together that it was obvious they were using the same bedroom.

For the next few days he was too sick to protest about anything. Mrs Poorwilly came frequently to take his temperature and to see that Adel kept forcing whisky and warm broth into him. All during his sickness Danny was convinced that he was going to die. During one afternoon he was sure that he was dead and that the sheets were a shroud.

The crisis passed and he started to cough up phlegm, but he was so weak that it was an effort for him to lift his head. The day he was strong enough to sit up and eat in the kitchen, Mrs Poorwilly brought him a package of hand-rolled cigarettes.

'Nearly everyone is coming to see you tomorrow. They'll all bring something in the way of a present. It's a custom. Don't say they shouldn't or they'll think you feel their presents aren't good enough.'

Danny said that he understood.

The school children came first with hand-carved pieces of driftwood. He admired the generally shapeless carvings and after the first abortive attempt carefully avoided guessing at what they were supposed to be.

After the children left, the McFarlans came. Mr McFarlan had made a shadow box from shingle. He had scraped the shingle with broken glass until the grain stood out. Inside the box he had made a floor of lichen and pebbles. Seagulls made from clam shells sat on the lichen.

His wife stretched a piece of black cloth over the end of a fish box. On it she had glued boiled fish bones to form a picture of a boat and man.

Someone brought a tin of pears, another brought a chocolate bar. One of the men brought half a bottle of whisky.

Each visitor stayed just long enough to inquire how Danny felt, wish him well and leave a present on the table. When the last visitor had gone, Danny was exhausted. Adel helped him to bed.

He felt much better by the end of the week, but when he tried to return to work, Mrs Poorwilly said, 'Mary Johnson's doing a fine job. Not as good as you, of course, but the kids aren't suffering. If you rush back before you're ready, everybody will take it that you think she's doing a poor job. If you get sick again, she won't take over.'

Adel returned to work at the sheds, but the women sent her home. The weather had held and there was lots of fish, but they said she should be at home looking after Danny.

At first it was ideal. They had little to do except sit and talk or make love. Danny caught up on his reading. They both were happy, but by the end of March their confinement had made them both restless.

To get out of the house, Danny walked to Mrs Poorwilly's. While they were having coffee, Danny said, 'I guess everyone must have got the flu.'

'No,' Mrs Poorwilly replied, 'just some colds among the children. Adel and you making out all right?'

'Yes,' Danny said.

'Her mother was a beauty, you know. I hope you didn't mind moving, but these things happen.'

'No, I didn't mind moving.'

They sat for five minutes before Danny said, 'Could I ask you something? I wouldn't want anyone else to know.'

Mrs Poorwilly nodded her assent.

'Mary Johnson is doing such a good job that I thought I might ask her to radio for a plane. Maybe it would be a good idea for me to take Adel to the mainland for a week.'

'Any particular reason?'

'Yes. If she wants, I'll marry her.'

'Haven't you asked her?'

Danny shook his head. It had never occurred to him that she might say no.

'Wait until you ask her. The superintendent will want a reason. You'll have to tell him over the radio and everyone will know. You wouldn't want to tell him and then have her turn you down.'

Adel was standing at the window when he returned. He put his arms around her. 'You know, I think we should get married.'

Adel didn't answer.

'Don't you want to marry me?' he asked.

'Yes. I do. But I've never been off the island. You won't want to stay here always.'

'We can stay for a couple of years. We'll go a little at a time. We can start with a week on the mainland for a honeymoon. We'll go somewhere on a train.'

That evening he went to Mary Johnson's. Mary tried to raise the mainland operator, but the static was so bad that no contact could be made. Danny kept Mary at the radio for half an hour. He left when she promised to send one of the children with a message if the radio cleared.

Danny returned the next night, but the static was just as bad. Mary promised to send for him as soon as the call went through.

A week went by. The weather continued to improve. Danny checked the thermometer. The temperature was going up a degree every two days.

At the end of the week he returned to Mary's. The radio wasn't working at all. One of the tubes needed to be replaced. He left. Halfway home he decided to go back and leave a message for the plane. The radio might work just long enough for a message, but not long enough for him to be called to the set. When he came up to the house, he was sure that he heard the radio. He banged on the front door. Mary took her time coming. When she opened the door, he said, 'I heard the radio. Can you send a message right away?'

Mary replied that he must have just heard the children talking.

Danny insisted on her trying to make the call. She was annoyed, but she tried to get through. When she had tried for five minutes, Danny excused himself and left.

He walked part way home, then turned and crept back over the rock.

The windows were dark. He lay in the hollow of rock behind the house until the cold forced him to leave.

In the morning, he went to the dock to talk to fishermen. He offered to pay any one of them triple the normal fare to take him down the coast. They laughed and said they would bring him some fresh fish for supper.

When he had continued insisting that he wanted to leave, they said that a trip at this time of year was impossible. Even planes found it difficult to land along the coast. A boat could be crushed in the pack ice that was shifting up and down the shore.

Danny told Adel about the radio and the boats. She sympathized with him, but agreed with the men that it was hopeless to try and make the trip in an open boat.

'Besides,' she said, 'the freight boats will be coming in a month or so.'

True to their word, the fishermen sent a fresh fish. Danny tried to pay the boy who brought it, but he said that he had been told not to accept anything. Danny had put the money into the boy's hand. The boy had gone, but a few minutes later he returned and put the money in front of the door.

Late that afternoon, Danny walked to the dock. After looking around to see that no-one was watching, he bent down and looked at the rope that held one of the boats. He untied it, then tied it again.

He returned to the house and started gathering his heavy clothing. When Adel came into the room, she said, 'What are you going to do?'

'I'm leaving.'

'Is the plane coming?'

'I'm taking myself. I've had enough. I'm not allowed to work. You're not allowed to work. Everyone showers us with things they won't let us pay for. I try to use the radio, but it never works.' He turned to face her. 'It always worked before.'

'Sometimes it hasn't worked for weeks,' Adel replied. 'Once it was six weeks. It's the change in temperature.'

'But it works. The other night I heard it working. Then when I asked Mary Johnson to call, she said it was just the children talking.'

'Mary told me,' Adel said. 'You made her very upset. She thinks you're still not feeling well.'

'I'm feeling fine. Just fine. And I'm leaving. I don't know what's going on here, but I'm getting out. I'm going to get a plane and then I'm coming back for you.'

'You said we could leave a little at a time.'

'That was before this happened. What if something goes wrong? Three people have died. One of them died right before my eyes and I couldn't do anything about it. What if we needed a doctor? Or a policeman? What if someone took some crazy notion into his head?'

Danny took Sick Jack's nor'westers off a peg. He laid out the clothes he wanted and packed two boxes with food. He lay awake until three o'clock, then slipped outside and down to the boats.

The boats were in their usual places. He reached for the rope of the first boat. His hand closed on a heavy chain. Danny couldn't believe it. He jumped onto the boat and ran his hand around the chain. He climbed out and ran from boat to boat. Every boat was the same. He tried to break the chains loose. When they wouldn't break, he sat on the dock and beat his hands on the chains. When he had exhausted himself, he sat with his face pressed into his hands.

In the morning, Mary sent one of the boys to tell Danny that the radio had worked long enough for her to send a message. It hadn't been confirmed, but she thought it might have been heard. For the rest of the day, Danny was elated, but as the days passed and the plane did not appear, he became more and more depressed. Adel kept saying that the plane would come, but Danny doubted if it would ever come.

The weather became quite mild. Danny walked to the dock every day. The chains were still on the boats. He had spent an hour on the dock staring at the thin blue line that was the mainland and was walking back to Adel's when he noticed that the snow had melted away from some of the cracks in the granite. The cracks were crammed with closely packed leaves.

He paused to pick a leaf. *April the first*, he thought, *April the first will come and we'll be able to go*. Then, as he stared at the small green leaf in his hand, he realized that he was wrong. It was weeks later that the first freight boat came.

The rest of the day he tried to make plans for Adel and himself, but he could not concentrate. The image of thousands and thousands of bloodflowers kept spilling into his mind.

CLARK BLAISE

b. 1940

A Class of New Canadians

Norman Dyer hurried down Sherbrooke Street, collar turned against the snow. 'Superb!' he muttered, passing a basement gallery next to a French bookstore. Bleached and tanned women in furs dashed from hotel lobbies into waiting cabs. Even the neon clutter of the side streets and the honks of slithering taxis seemed remote tonight through the peaceful snow. *Superb*, he thought again, waiting for a light and backing from a slushy curb: a word reserved for wines, cigars, and delicate sauces; he was feeling superb this evening. After eighteen months in Montreal, he still found himself freshly impressed by everything he saw. He was proud of himself for having steered his life north, even for jobs that were menial by standards he could have demanded. Great just being here no matter what they paid, looking at these buildings, these faces, and hearing all the languages. He was learning to be insulted by simple bad taste, wherever he encountered it.

Since leaving graduate school and coming to Montreal, he had sampled every ethnic restaurant downtown and in the old city, plus a few Levantine places out in Outremont. He had worked on conversational French and mastered much of the local dialect, done reviews for local papers, translated French-Canadian poets for Toronto quarterlies, and tweaked his colleagues for not sympathizing enough with Quebec separatism. He attended French performances of plays he had ignored in English, and kept a small but elegant apartment near a colony of *émigré* Russians just off Park Avenue. Since coming to Montreal he'd witnessed a hold-up, watched a murder, and seen several riots. When stopped on the street for directions, he would answer in French or accented English. To live this well and travel each long academic summer, he held two jobs. He had no intention of returning to the States. In fact, he had begun to think of himself as a semi-permanent, semi-political exile.

Now, stopped again a few blocks farther, he studied the window of

Holt-Renfrew's exclusive men's shop. Incredible, he thought, the authority of simple good taste. Double-breasted chalk-striped suits he would never dare to buy. Knitted sweaters, and fifty-dollar shoes. One tanned manne-quin was decked out in a brash checkered sportscoat with a burgundy vest and dashing ascot. Not a price tag under three hundred dollars. Unlike food, drink, cinema, and literature, clothing had never really involved him. Someday, he now realized, it would. Dyer's clothes, thus far, had all been bought in a chain department store. He was a walking violation of American law, clad shoes to scarf in Egyptian cottons, Polish leathers, and woolens from the People's Republic of China.

He had no time for dinner tonight; this was Wednesday, a day of lectures at one university, and then an evening course in English as a Foreign Language at McGill, beginning at six. He would eat afterwards.

Besides the money, he had kept this second job because it flattered him. There was to Dyer something fiercely elemental, almost existential, about teaching both his language and his literature in a foreign country—like Joyce in Trieste, Isherwood and Nabokov in Berlin, Beckett in Paris. Also it was necessary for his students. It was the first time in his life that he had done something socially useful. What difference did it make that the job was beneath him, a recent Ph.D., while most of his colleagues in the evening school at McGill were idle housewives and bachelor civil servants? It didn't matter, even, that this job was a perver-sion of all the sentiments he held as a progressive young teacher. He was a god two evenings a week, sometimes suffering and fatigued, but never-theless an omniscient, benevolent god. His students were silent, ignorant, and dedicated to learning English. No discussions, no demonstrations, no dialogue.

I love them, he thought. They need me.

He entered the room, pocketed his cap and ear muffs, and dropped his briefcase on the podium. Two girls smiled good evening.

They love me, he thought, taking off his boots and hanging up his coat; I'm not like their English-speaking bosses.

I love myself, he thought with amazement even while conducting a drill on word order. I love myself for tramping down Sherbrooke Street in zero weather just to help them with noun clauses. I love myself standing behind this podium and showing Gilles Carrier and Claude Veilleux the difference between the past continuous and the simple past; or the sultry Armenian girl with the bewitching half-glasses that 'put on' is not the same as 'take on'; or telling the dashing Mr Miguel Mayor, late of Madrid, that simple futurity can be expressed in four different ways, at least.

This is what mastery is like, he thought. Being superb in one's chosen field, not merely in one's mother tongue. A respected performer in the lecture halls of the major universities, equipped by twenty years' research in the remotest libraries, and slowly giving it back to those who must have it. Dishing it out suavely, even wittily. Being a legend. Being loved and a little feared.

'Yes, Mrs David?'

A *sabra*: freckled, reddish hair, looking like a British model, speaks with a nifty British accent, and loves me.

'No,' he smiled, 'I *were* is not correct except in the present subjunctive, which you haven't studied yet.'

The first hour's bell rang. The students closed their books for the intermission. Dyer put his away, then noticed a page of his Faulkner lecture from the afternoon class. *Absalom, Absalom!* his favourite.

'Can anyone here tell me what the *impregnable citadel of his passive rectitude* means?'

'What, sir?' asked Mr Vassilopoulos, ready to copy.

'What about *the presbyterian and lugubrious effluvium of his passive vindictiveness?*' A few girls giggled. 'O.K.,' said Dyer, 'take your break.'

In the halls of McGill they broke into the usual groups. French Canadians and South Americans into two large circles, then the Greeks, Germans, Spanish, and French into smaller groups. The patterns interested Dyer. Madrid Spaniards and Parisian French always spoke English with their New World co-linguals. The Middle Europeans spoke German together, not Russian, preferring one occupier to the other. Two Israeli men went off alone. Dyer decided to join them for the break.

Not *sabras*, Dyer concluded, not like Mrs David. The shorter one, dark and wavy-haired, held his cigarette like a violin bow. The other, Mr Weinrot, was tall and pot-bellied, with a ruddy face and thick stubby fingers. Something about him suggested truck-driving, perhaps of beer, maybe in Germany. Neither one, he decided, could supply the name of a good Israeli restaurant.

'This is really hard, you know?' said Weinrot.

'Why?'

'I think it's because I'm not speaking much of English at my job.'

'French?' asked Dyer.

'French? Pah! All the time Hebrew, sometimes German, sometimes little Polish. Crazy thing, eh? How long you think they let me speak Hebrew if I'm working in America?'

'Depends on where you're working,' he said.

'Hell, I'm working for the Canadian government, what you think? Plant I work in—I'm engineer, see—makes boilers for the turbines going up North. Look. When I'm leaving Israel I go first to Italy. Right away-bamm I'm working in Italy I'm speaking Italian like a native. Passing for a native.'

'A native Jew,' said his dark-haired friend.

'Listen to him. So in Rome they think I'm from Tyrol—that's still native, eh? So I speak Russian and German and Italian like a Jew. My Hebrew is bad, I admit it, but it's a lousy language anyway. Nobody likes it. French I understand but English I'm talking like a bum. Arabic I know five dialects. Danish fluent. So what's the matter I can't learn English?'

'It'll come, don't worry,' Dyer smiled. *Don't worry, my son*; he wanted to pat him on the arm. 'Anyway, that's what makes Canada so appealing. Here they don't force you.'

'What's this *appealing*? Means nice? Look, my friend, keep it, eh? Two years in a country I don't learn the language means it isn't a country.'

'Come on,' said Dyer. 'Neither does forcing you.'

'Let me tell you a story why I come to Canada. Then you tell me if I was wrong, O.K.?'

'Certainly,' said Dyer, flattered.

In Italy, Weinrot told him, he had lost his job to a Communist union. He left Italy for Denmark and opened up an Israeli restaurant with five other friends. Then the six Israelis decided to rent a bigger apartment downtown near the restaurant. They found a perfect nine-room place for two thousand kroner a month, not bad shared six ways. Next day the landlord told them the deal was off. 'You tell me why,' Weinrot demanded.

No Jews? Dyer wondered. 'He wanted more rent,' he finally said.

'More—you kidding? More we expected. *Less* we didn't expect. A couple with eight kids is showing up after we're gone and the law in Denmark says a man has a right to a room for each kid plus a hundred kroner knocked off the rent for each kid. What you think of that? So a guy who comes in *after* us gets a nine-room place for a thousand kroner *less*. Law says no way a bachelor can get a place ahead of a family, and bachelors pay twice as much.'

Dyer waited, then asked, 'So?'

'So, I make up my mind the world is full of communismus, just like Israel. So I take out applications next day for Australia, South Africa,

U.S.A., and Canada. Canada says come right away, so I go. Should have waited for South Africa.'

'How could you?' Dyer cried. 'What's wrong with you anyway? South Africa is fascist. Australia is racist.'

The bell rang, and the Israelis, with Dyer, began walking to the room.

'What I was wondering, then,' said Mr Weinrot, ignoring Dyer's outburst, 'was if my English is good enough to be working in the United States. You're American, aren't you?'

It was a question Dyer had often avoided in Europe, but had rarely been asked in Montreal. 'Yes,' he admitted, 'your English is probably good enough for the States or South Africa, whichever one wants you first.'

He hurried ahead to the room, feeling that he had let Montreal down. He wanted to turn and shout to Weinrot and to all the others that Montreal was the greatest city on the continent, if only they knew it as well as he did. If they'd just break out of their little ghettos.

At the door, the Armenian girl with the half-glasses caught his arm. She was standing with Mrs David and Miss Parizeau, a jolly French-Canadian girl that Dyer had been thinking of asking out.

'Please, sir,' she said, looking at him over the tops of her tiny glasses, 'what I was asking earlier—*put on*—I heard on the television. A man said *You are putting me on* and everybody laughed. I think it was supposed to be funny but *put on* we learned means get dressed, no?'

'Ah—*don't put me on*,' Dyer laughed.

'I yaven't erd it neither,' said Miss Parizeau.

'To put some*body* on means to make a fool of him. To put some*thing* on is to wear it. O.K.?' He gave examples.

'Ah, now I know,' said Miss Parizeau. 'Like bullshitting somebody. Is it the same?'

'Ah, yes,' he said, smiling. French-Canadians were like children learning the language. 'Your example isn't considered polite. ''Put on'' is very common now in the States.'

'Then maybe,' said Miss Parizeau, 'we'll ave it ere in twenty years.' The Armenian giggled.

'No—I've heard it here just as often,' Dyer protested, but the girls had already entered the room.

He began the second hour with a smile which slowly soured as he thought of the Israelis. America's anti-communism was bad enough, but it was worse hearing it echoed by immigrants, by Jews, here in Montreal. Wasn't there a psychological type who chose Canada over South Africa?

Or was it just a matter of visas and slow adjustment? Did Johannesburg lose its Greeks, and Melbourne its Italians, the way Dyer's students were always leaving Montreal?

And after class when Dyer was again feeling content and thinking of approaching one of the Israelis for a restaurant tip, there came the flood of small requests: should Mrs Papadopoulos go into a more advanced course; could Mr Perez miss a week for an interview in Toronto; could Mr Giguère, who spoke English perfectly, have a harder book; Mr Coté an easier one?

Then as he packed his briefcase in the empty room, Miguel Mayor, the vain and impeccable Spaniard, came forward from the hallway.

'Sir,' he began, walking stiffly, ready to bow or salute. He wore a loud grey checkered sportscoat this evening, blue shirt, and matching ascot-handkerchief, slightly mauve. He must have shaved just before class, Dyer noticed, for two fresh daubs of antiseptic cream stood out on his jaw, just under his earlobe.

'I have been wanting to ask *you* something, as a matter of fact,' said Dyer. 'Do you know any good Spanish restaurants I might try tonight?'

'There are not any good Spanish restaurants in Montreal,' he said. He stepped closer. 'Sir?'

'What's on your mind, then?'

'Please—have you the time to look on a letter for me?'

He laid the letter on the podium.

'Look *over* a letter,' said Dyer. 'What is it for?'

'I have applied,' he began, stopping to emphasize the present perfect construction, 'for a job in Cleveland, Ohio, and I want to know if my letter will be good. Will an American, I mean—'

'Why are you going there?'

'It is a good job.'

'But Cleveland—'

'They have a blackman mayor, I have read. But the job is not in Cleveland.'

'Let me see it.'

Most honourable Sir: I humbly beg consideration for a position in your grand company . . .

'Who are you writing this to?'

'The president,' said Miguel Mayor.

I am once a student of Dr Ramiro Gutierrez of the Hydraulic Institute of Sevilla, Spain . . .

'Does the president know this Ramiro Gutierrez?'

'Oh, everybody is knowing him,' Miguel Mayor assured, 'he is the most famous expert in all Spain.'

'Did he recommend this company to you?'

'No—I have said in my letter, if you look—'

An ancient student of Dr Gutierrez, Salvador del Este, is actually a boiler expert who is being employed like supervisor is formerly a friend of mine . . .

'Is he still your friend?'

Whenever you say come to my city Miguel Mayor for talking I will be coming. I am working in Montreal since two years and am now wanting more money than I am getting here now . . .

'Well . . .' Dyer sighed.

'Sir—what I want from you is knowing in good English how to interview me by this man. The letters in Spanish are not the same to English ones, you know?'

I remain humbly at your orders . . .

'Why do you want to leave Montreal?'

'It's time for a change.'

'Have you ever been to Cleveland?'

'I am one summer in California. Very beautiful there and hot like my country. Montreal is big port like Barcelona. Everybody mixed together and having no money. It is just a place to land, no?'

'Montreal? Don't be silly.'

'I thought I come here and learn good English but where I work I get by in Spanish and French. It's hard, you know?' he smiled. Then he took a few steps back and gave his cuffs a gentle tug, exposing a set of jade cufflinks.

Dyer looked at the letter again and calculated how long he would be correcting it, then up at his student. How old is he? My age? Thirty? Is he married? Where do the Spanish live in Montreal? He looks so prosperous, so confident, like a male model off a page of *Playboy*. For an instant Dyer felt that his student was mocking him, somehow pitting his astounding confidence and wardrobe, sharp chin and matador's bearing against Dyer's command of English and mastery of the side streets, bistros, and ethnic restaurants. Mayor's letter was painful, yet he remained somehow competent. He would pass his interview, if he got one. What would he care about America, and the odiousness he'd soon be supporting? It was as though a superstructure of exploitation had been revealed, and Dyer felt himself abused by the very people he wanted so much to help. It had to end someplace.

He scratched out the second 'humbly' from the letter, then folded the sheet of foolscap. 'Get it typed right away,' he said. 'Good luck.'

'Thank you, sir,' said his student, with a bow. Dyer watched the letter disappear in the inner pocket of the checkered sportscoat. Then the folding of the cashmere scarf, the draping of the camel's hair coat about the shoulders, the easing of the fur hat down to the rims of his ears. The meticulous filling of the pigskin gloves. Mayor's patent leather galoshes glistened.

'Good evening, sir,' he said.

'*Buenas noches*,' Dyer replied.

He hurried now, back down Sherbrooke Street to his daytime office where he could deposit his books. Montreal on a winter night was still mysterious, still magical. Snow blurred the arc lights. The wind was dying. Every second car was now a taxi, crowned with an orange crescent. Slushy curbs had hardened. The window of Holt-Renfrew's was still attractive. The legless dummies invited a final stare. He stood longer than he had earlier, in front of the sporty mannequin with a burgundy waistcoat, the mauve and blue ensemble, the jade cufflinks.

Good evening, sir, he could almost hear. The ascot, the shirt, the complete outfit, had leaped off the back of Miguel Mayor. He pictured how he must have entered the store with three hundred dollars and a prepared speech, and walked out again with everything off the torso's back.

I want that.

What, sir?

That.

The coat, sir?

Yes.

Very well, sir.

And *that*.

Which, sir?

All that.

'Absurd man!' Dyer whispered. There had been a moment of fear, as though the naked body would leap from the window, and legless, chase him down Sherbrooke Street. But the moment was passing. Dyer realized now that it was comic, even touching. Miguel Mayor had simply tried too hard, too fast, and it would be good for him to stay in Montreal until he deserved those clothes, that touching vanity and confidence. With one last look at the window, he turned sharply, before the clothes could speak again.

BHARATI MUKHERJEE

b. 1940

The Lady from Lucknow

When I was four, one of the girls next door fell in love with a Hindu. Her father intercepted a love note from the boy, and beat her with his leather sandals. She died soon after. I was in the room when my mother said to our neighbour, 'The Nawab-*sahib* had no choice, but Husseina's heart just broke, poor dear.' I was an army doctor's daughter, and I pictured the dead girl's heart—a rubbery squeezable organ with auricles and ventricles—first swelling, then bursting and coating the floor with thick, slippery blood.

We lived in Lucknow at the time, where the Muslim community was large. This was just before the British took the fat, diamond-shaped subcontinent and created two nations, a big one for the Hindus and a littler one for us. My father moved us to Rawalpindi in Pakistan two months after Husseina died. We were a family of soft, voluptuous children, and my father wanted to protect us from the Hindus' shameful lust.

I have fancied myself in love many times since, but never enough for the emotions to break through tissue and muscle. Husseina's torn heart remains the standard of perfect love.

At seventeen I married a good man, the fourth son of a famous poet-cum-lawyer in Islamabad. We have a daughter, seven, and a son, four. In the Muslim communities we have lived in, we are admired. Iqbal works for IBM, and because of his work we have made homes in Lebanon, Brazil, Zambia, and France. Now we live in Atlanta, Georgia, in a wide, new house with a deck and a backyard that runs into a golf course. IBM has been generous to us. We expect to pass on this good, decent life to our children. Our children are ashamed of the dingy cities where we got our start.

Some Sunday afternoons when Iqbal isn't at a conference halfway across the world, we sit together on the deck and drink gin and tonics as we have done on Sunday afternoons in a dozen exotic cities. But here, the light is different somehow. A gold haze comes off the golf course and settles on our bodies, our new house. When the light shines right in my eyes, I pull myself out of the canvas deck chair and lean against the railing that still smells of forests. Everything in Atlanta is so new!

'Sit,' Iqbal tells me. 'You'll distract the golfers. Americans are crazy for sex, you know that.'

He half rises out of his deck chair. He lunges for my breasts in mock passion. I slip out of his reach.

At the bottom of the backyard, the golfers, caddies, and carts are too minute to be bloated with lust.

But, who knows? One false thwock! of their golfing irons, and my little heart, like a golf ball, could slice through the warm air and vanish into the jonquil-yellow beyond.

It isn't trouble that I want, though I do have a lover. He's an older man, an immunologist with the Center for Disease Control right here in town. He comes to see me when Iqbal is away at high-tech conferences in sunny, remote resorts. Just think, Beirut was once such a resort! Lately my lover comes to me on Wednesdays even if Iqbal's in town.

'I don't expect to live till ninety-five,' James teases on the phone. His father died at ninety-three in Savannah. 'But I don't want a bullet in the brain from a jealous husband right now.'

Iqbal owns no firearms. Jealousy would inflame him.

Besides, Iqbal would never come home in the middle of the day. Not even for his blood-pressure pills. The two times he forgot them last month, I had to take the bottle downtown. One does not rise through the multinational hierarchy coming home in midday, arriving late, or leaving early. Especially, he says, if you're a 'not-quite' as we are. It is up to us to set the standards.

Wives who want to be found out will be found out. Indiscretions are deliberate. The woman caught in mid-shame is a woman who wants to get out. The rest of us carry on.

James flatters me indefatigably; he makes me feel beautiful, exotic, responsive. I am a creature he has immunized of contamination. When he is with me, the world seems a happy enough place.

Then he leaves. He slips back into his tweed suit and backs out of my driveway.

I met James Beamish at a reception for foreign students on the Emory University campus. Iqbal avoids these international receptions because he thinks of them as excuses for looking back when we should be looking forward. These evenings are almost always tedious, but I like to go; just in case there's someone new and fascinating. The last two years, I've volunteered as host in the 'hospitality program'. At Thanksgiving and Christmas, two lonely foreign students are sent to our table.

That first evening at Emory we stood with name tags on lapels, white ones for students and blue ones for hosts. James was by a long table, pouring Chablis into a plastic glass. I noticed him right off. He was dressed much like the other resolute, decent men in the room. But whereas the other men wore white or blue shirts under their dark wool suits, James's shirt was bright red.

His wife was with him that evening, a stoutish woman with slender ankles and expensive shoes.

'Darling,' she said to James. 'See if you can locate our Palestinian.' Then she turned to me, and smiling, peered into my name tag.

'I'm Nafeesa Hafeez,' I helped out.

'Na-fee-sa,' she read out. 'Did I get that right?'

'Yes, perfect,' I said.

'What a musical name,' she said. 'I hope you'll be very happy here. Is this your first time abroad?'

James came over with a glass of Chablis in each hand. 'Did we draw this lovely lady? Oops, I'm sorry, you're a *host*, of course.' A mocking blue light was in his eyes. 'Just when I thought we were getting lucky, dear.'

'Darling, ours is a Palestinian. I told you that in the car. This one is obviously not Palestinian, are you, dear?' She took a bright orange notebook out of her purse and showed me a name.

I had to read it upside-down. Something Waheed. School of Dentistry.

'What are you drinking?' James asked. He kept a glass for himself and gave me the other one.

Maybe James Beamish said nothing fascinating that night, but he was attentive, even after the Beamishes' Palestinian joined us. Mrs Beamish was brave, she asked the dentist about his family and hometown. The dentist described West Beirut in detail. The shortage of bread and vegetables, the mortar poundings, the babies bleeding. I wonder when aphasia sets in. When does a dentist, even a Palestinian dentist, decide it's time to cut losses.

Then my own foreign student arrived. She was an Indian Muslim from Lucknow, a large, bold woman who this far from our common hometown claimed me as a countrywoman. India, Pakistan, she said, not letting go of my hand, what does it matter?

I'd rather have listened to James Beamish but I couldn't shut out the woman's voice. She gave us her opinions on Thanksgiving rituals. She said, 'It is very odd that the pumpkin vegetable should be used for dessert, no? We are using it as vegetable only. Chhi! Pumpkin as a sweet. The very idea is horrid.'

I promised that when she came to our house for Thanksgiving, I'd make sweetmeats out of ricotta cheese and syrup. When you live in as many countries as Iqbal has made me, you can't tell if you pity, or if you envy, the women who stayed back.

I didn't hear from James Beamish for two weeks. I thought about him. In fact I couldn't get him out of my mind. I went over the phrases and gestures, the mocking light in the eyes, but they didn't add up to much. After the first week, I called Amina and asked her to lunch. I didn't know her well but her husband worked at the Center for Disease Control. Just talking to someone connected with the Center made me feel good. I slipped his name into the small talk with Amina and her eyes popped open, 'Oh, he's famous!' she exclaimed, and I shrugged modestly. I stayed home in case he should call. I sat on the deck and in spite of the cold, pretended to read Barbara Pym novels. Lines from Donne and Urdu verses about love floated in my skull.

I wasn't sure Dr Beamish would call me. Not directly, that is. Perhaps he would play a subtler game, get his wife to invite Iqbal and me for drinks. Maybe she'd even include their Palestinian and my Indian and make an international evening out of it. It sounded plausible.

Finally James Beamish called me on a Tuesday afternoon, around four. The children were in the kitchen, and a batch of my special chocolate sludge cookies was in the oven.

'Hi,' he said, then nothing for a bit. Then he said, 'This is James Beamish from the CDC. I've been thinking of you.'

He was between meetings, he explained. Wednesday was the only flexible day in his week, his day for paperwork. Could we have lunch on Wednesday?

The cookies smelled gooey hot, not burned. My daughter had taken the cookie sheet out and put in a new one. She'd turned the cold water faucet on so she could let the water drip on a tiny rosebud burn on her arm.

I felt all the warm, familiar signs of lust and remorse. I dabbed the burn with an ice cube wrapped in paper towel and wondered if I'd have time to buy a new front-closing bra after Iqbal got home.

James and I had lunch in a Dekalb County motel lounge.

He would be sixty-five in July, but not retire till sixty-eight. Then he would live in Tonga, in Fiji, see the world, travel across Europe and North America in a Winnebago. He wouldn't be tied down. He had five daughters and two grandsons, the younger one aged four, a month older than my son. He had been in the navy during the war (*his* war), and he had liked that.

I said, ' "Goodbye, Mama, I'm off to Yokohama." ' It was silly, but it was the only war footage I could come up with, and it made him laugh.

'You're special,' he said. He touched my knee under the table. 'You've already been everywhere.'

'Not because I've wanted to.'

He squeezed my knee again, then paid with his MasterCard card.

As we were walking through the parking lot to his car (it was a Cougar or a Buick, and not German or British as I'd expected), James put his arm around my shoulders. I may have seen the world but I haven't gone through the American teenage rites of making out in parked cars and picnic grounds, so I walked briskly out of his embrace. He let his hand slide off my shoulder. The hand slid down my back. I counted three deft little pats to my bottom before he let his hand fall away.

Iqbal and I are sensual people, but secretive. The openness of James Beamish's advance surprised me.

I got in his car, wary, expectant.

'Do up the seatbelt,' he said.

He leaned into his seatbelt and kissed me lightly on the lips. I kissed him back, hard. 'You don't panic easily, do you?' he said. The mocking blue light was in his eyes again. His tongue made darting little thrusts and probes past my lips.

Yes, I do, I would have said if he'd let me.

We held hands on the drive to my house. In the driveway he parked behind my Honda. 'Shall I come in?'

I said nothing. Love and freedom drop into our lives. When we have to beg or even agree, it's already too late.

'Let's go in.' He said it very softly.

I didn't worry about the neighbours. In his grey wool slacks and tweed jacket, he looked too old, too respectable, for any sordid dalliance with a not-quite's wife.

Our house is not that different in size and shape from the ones on either side. Only the inside smells of heavy incense, and the walls are hung with rows of miniature paintings from the reign of Emperor Akbar. I took James's big wrinkled hand in mine. Adultery in my house is probably no different, no quieter, than in other houses in this neighbourhood.

Afterwards it wasn't guilt I felt (guilt comes with desire not acted), but wonder that while I'd dashed out Tuesday night and bought myself silky new underwear, James Beamish had worn an old T-shirt and lemon-pale boxer shorts. Perhaps he hadn't planned on seducing a Lucknow lady that afternoon. Adventure and freedom had come to him out of the blue, too. Or perhaps only younger men like Iqbal make a fetish of doing sit-ups and dieting and renewing their membership at the racquet club when they're on the prowl.

October through February our passion held. When we were together, I felt cherished. I only played at being helpless, hysterical, cruel. When James left, I'd spend the rest of the afternoon with a Barbara Pym novel. I kept the novels open at pages in which excellent British women recite lines from Marvell to themselves. I didn't read. I watched the golfers trudging over brown fairways instead. I let the tiny golfers—clumsy mummers—tell me stories of ambitions unfulfilled. Golf carts lurched into the golden vista. I felt safe.

In the first week of March we met in James's house for a change. His wife was in Madison to babysit a grandson while his parents flew to China for a three-week tour. It was a thrill to be in his house. I fingered the book spines, checked the colour of sheets and towels, the brand names of cereals and detergents. Jane Fonda's Workout record was on the VCR. He was a man who took exceptional care of himself, this immunologist. Real intimacy, at last. The lust of the winter months had been merely foreplay. I felt at home in his house, in spite of the albums of family photographs on the coffee table and the brutish metal vulvas sculpted by a daughter in art school and stashed in the den. James was more talkative in his own house. He showed me the photos he wanted me to see, named real lakes and mountains. His family was real, and not quite real. The daughters were hardy, outdoor types. I saw them hiking in Zermatt and bicycling through Europe. They had red cheeks and backpacks. Their faces were honest and marvellously ordinary. What would they say if they knew their father, at sixty-five, was in bed with a married woman from Lucknow? I feared and envied their jealousy more than any violence in my husband's heart.

Love on the decline is hard to tell from love on the rise. I have lived a life perched on the edge of ripeness and decay. The traveller feels at home everywhere, because she is never at home anywhere. I felt the hot red glow of blood rushing through capillaries.

His wife came back early, didn't call, caught a ride from Hartsfield International with a friend. She had been raised in Saskatchewan, and she'd remained thrifty.

We heard the car pull into the driveway, the loud 'thank yous' and 'no, I couldn'ts' and then her surprised shout, 'James? Are you ill? What're you doing home?' as she shut the front door.

We were in bed, sluggish cozy and still moist under the goosedown quilt that the daughter in Madison had sent them as a fortieth anniversary gift some years before. His clothes were on top of a long dresser; mine were on the floor, the stockings wrinkled and looking legless.

James didn't go to pieces. I had to admire that. He said, 'Get in the bathroom. Get dressed. I'll take care of this.'

I am submissive by training. To survive, the Asian wife will usually do as she is told. But this time I stayed in bed.

'How are you going to explain me away, James? Tell her I'm the new cleaning woman?' I laughed, and my laugh tinkled flirtatiously, at least to me.

'Get in the bathroom.' This was the fiercest I'd ever heard him.

'I don't think so,' I said. I jerked the quilt off my body but didn't move my legs.

So I was in bed with the quilt at my feet, and James was by the dresser buttoning his shirt when Kate Beamish stood at the door.

She didn't scream. She didn't leap for James's throat—or mine. I'd wanted passion, but Kate didn't come through. I pulled the quilt over me.

I tried insolence. 'Is your wife not the jealous kind?' I asked.

'Let's just get over this as quietly and quickly as we can, shall we?' she said. She walked to the window in her brown Wallabies. 'I don't see any unfamiliar cars, so I suppose you'll expect James to drive you home.'

'She's the jealous type,' James said. He moved towards his wife and tried to guide her out of the bedroom.

'I'm definitely the jealous kind,' Kate Beamish said. 'I might have stabbed you if I could take you seriously. But you are quite ludicrous lounging like a Goya nude on my bed.' She gave a funny little snort. I noticed straggly hairs in her nostrils and looked away.

James was running water in the bathroom sink. Only the panicky ones fall apart and call their lawyers from the bedroom.

She sat on my side of the bed. She stared at me. If that stare had made me feel secretive and loathsome, I might not have wept, later. She plucked the quilt from my breasts as an internist might, and snorted again. 'Yes,' she said, 'I don't deny a certain interest he might have had,' but she looked through my face to the pillow behind, and dropped the quilt as she stood. I was shadow without depth or colour, a shadow-temptress who would float back to a city of teeming millions when the affair with James had ended.

I had thought myself provocative and fascinating. What had begun as an adventure had become shabby and complex. I was just another involvement of a white man in a pokey little outpost, something that 'men do' and then come to their senses while the *memsahibs* drink gin and tonic and fan their faces. I didn't merit a stab wound through the heart.

It wasn't the end of the world. It was humorous, really. Still. I let James call me a cab. That half-hour wait for the cab, as Kate related tales of the grandson to her distracted husband was the most painful. It came closest to what Husseina must have felt. At least her father, the Nawab-*sahib*, had beaten her.

I have known all along that perfect love has to be fatal. I have survived on four of the five continents. I get by because I am at least moderately charming and open-minded. From time to time, James Beamish calls me. 'She's promised to file for divorce.' Or 'Let's go away for a week-end. Let's go to Bermuda. Have lunch with me this Wednesday.' Why do I hear a second voice? She has laughed at me. She has mocked my passion.

I want to say yes. I want to beg him to take me away to Hilton Head in his new, retirement Winnebago. The golden light from the vista is too yellow. Yes, *please,* let's run away, keep this new and simple.

I can hear the golf balls being thwocked home by clumsy mummers far away where my land dips. My arms are numb, my breathing loud and ugly from pressing hard against the cedar railing. The pain in my chest will not go away. I should be tasting blood in my throat by now.

RAY SMITH

b. 1941

Cape Breton is the Thought Control Centre of Canada

A Centennial Project

Why don't we go away?
Why?
Why not?
Because.
If we went away things would be different.
No. Things would be the same. Change starts inside.
No. Change can start outside.
Possibly.
Then, can we go away?
No. Perhaps. All right. It doesn't matter.

*   *   *

So you believe in Canada and you're worried about American economic domination? But you can't understand international finance? What you do know is that a landlord can give a tenant thirty days to get out, eh? And the tenant can stay longer if he has a lease, but you don't recall having signed a lease with the Americans?

So you're saying to yourself: 'What can I do? What can I do? I can't influence Bay Street . . . what can I do? . . .'

Well . . . uhhh . . . thought of blowing the Peace Bridge?

*   *   *

The Americans are loath to fight without a divine cause. Assume we provide this by electing an NDP Government, stirring ourselves up with anti-American slogans like: 'Give me liberty or give me death!' or (the most divine of all) passing legislation that is prejudicial to American money.

With their divine cause, the Americans would destroy our Armed Forces in one week. (This makes a fine game; you can play it out on a map.) Canada will have ceased to exist as a free nation. Now: *Think of the fun you'd have in the Resistance!* It's a great subject for daydreaming: Be the first kid on your block to gun down a Yankee Imperialist.

*　　*　　*

A virgin named, say, Judy, an attractive girl in her early twenties, is so curious about sexual intercourse that, despite certain misgivings, she goes to a party determined to find a man willing to do the deed. She wears an alluring but tasteful dress, has her hair done, and bescents herself with a flattering perfume.

At the party are certain men of her own age whom Judy knows and finds attractive; and certain men of her own age whom she doesn't know and finds attractive. All realize that Judy is a virgin and that she wishes to experience intercourse. Each feels he would like to help her. At the party are other girls, but they do not figure in the story, being all the same as Judy.

The party progresses pleasantly enough. The guests dance and sing and drink enough alcohol to feel light-headed, but not enough to become maudlin, violent, or unconscious. A good time is had by all.

The end of the party nears, and Judy has not yet been offered help. Desperate, she decides to make the proposal herself. In no time at all, the men are seated about her discussing the problem with her. This goes on for several hours until the men pass out and Judy walks home alone. On a dark and lonely street, she is pulled into an alleyway and raped by a stranger who leaves her with her clothes torn, her body sore and bleeding, and her eyes streaming tears.

A week later, her virginity restored in a Venus-wise bath, she goes through the same events. Judy is a happy girl, for she leads a sane, healthy, and well-balanced life.

*　　*　　*

Consider the Poles. They have built a nation which, if not great and powerful, is at least distinct.

Of course, the Poles have their own language, and they have been around for a thousand years. But they have survived despite the attentions paid them by their neighbours, the Russians and the Germans.

Analogies are never perfect, but the Poles do have what we want. Consider the Poles; consider the price they have paid and paid and paid.

*   *   *

Wit: Did you hear about the Canadian pacifist who became a Canadian nationalist?
Self: No; why did he do that?
Wit: Because he wanted to take advantage of the economical Red, White, and Blue fares.

*   *   *

Recently a friend conned me into explaining my interest in compiled fiction, an example of which you are now reading.

'Hey, that's great,' he said. 'That really sounds interesting.'

'I'm interested in it,' I replied, razoring out the distinction.

'But I hope you aren't expecting to sell any of these compilations. The publishers won't touch anything as new as that.'

'Well, that's their business, isn't it? I mean, if they figure it's not for their magazine or it's lousy or something, they reject it. It's a basic condition. If you want to demand they publish your stuff, the best and fastest way is to buy the magazine, fire the editor, and hire a yes-man.'

'I didn't mean. . . .'

'I know what you meant; but, in fact, the technique isn't new at all. I got it from Ezra Pound and he got it from some French poets. Other precedents might be Francis Bacon's essays, the Book of Proverbs . . . the whole *Bible*. . . .'

'But. . . .'

My friend babbled on. He talks a lot about writing but, so far as I know, doesn't do any.

*   *   *

You can't see up through the mist (up through the high timber where the air is clean and good) but you know the dawn is already gleaming on the snow peaks; soon it will reach down here and burn away the mist and then it will be too late. Where the hell is that bloody supply column? You hunch forward between the rock and the tree and peer into the gloom. The armoured-car escort will appear . . . there: when it gets . . . there Mackie and Joe will heave the cocktails and when the flame breaks Campbell will open up with the Bren. . . . Christ, you hope you get some arms out of this because if you don't you'll have to pack it up soon. . . . Christ, it's cold, your joints can't take much more of . . . a growl from down around the bend . . . a diesel growl. . . .

*   *   *

Do you love me?

Yes, I love you. You're my wife.

Why did you say, You're my wife?

Uhh. . . .

You said it because you think just because I'm your wife you have to love me when really it has nothing to do with it.

Perhaps. It's more complicated than that.

It's always more complicated. Why can't it be simple? You always say things are too complicated when what you really mean is you don't want to talk to me. Why can't things be simple?

They are. I love you. As simple as that. So simple there's no point talking about it.

Complicated, too, I suppose.

So complicated that to talk about it would always oversimplify it. It's the same with everything.

Then what. . . . Oh! You're impossible to talk to.

You know that isn't true.

Yes.

So. . . .

Then what is important?

Doing.

Doing what?

Heh-heh-heh. . .

Mmmmm. . . .

*   *   *

Toronto is a truly despicable city.

*   *   *

'. . . like a horse's arse!' Einar finishes. You all laugh because Einar tells a good joke and because you're all damned scared as the car flees through the prairie night. 'And what about the girl from. . . .' Suddenly the night is day . . . silence . . . then the roar . . . someone gasps, 'Did we do that?' You stop the car and stare back down the road at the towering flames . . . another flash . . . its roar . . . and again . . . thousands of barrels of oil. . . . 'Well,' says Einar, 'Now I seen the sun risin' in the west. I guess I can die happy.' Your laughter shakes some sense back into you: you'd better get the hell out of here or you'll maybe die quick. . . .

*   *   *

Two men sit on a park bench. They are just men; perhaps office workers enjoying the sunshine during their noon break. For the sake of convenience, let us call them Bill and George. They are acquainted.

Bill: Nice day.

George: Yes it is. Though the weatherman said we might get rain later.

Bill: Yeah, it looks like it.

George: It's in the air.

This chatter goes on for a while. Presently Bill remembers a bottle of whisky in his pocket.

Bill: Like a sip of rye?

George: Ummerrahhohhehh. . . .

This mumbling goes on until George, quivering through his entire frame, dies.

Bill: What a crazy guy.

Bill opens the bottle and takes a drink. He sighs with satisfaction, replaces the bottle in his pocket, takes from another pocket a revolver, and blows his brains out.

*   *   *

A distant whirr and three more flights of geese knife south through the big Manitoba sky. There was a day when you might have shot at the geese. Now you're waiting for something else to come down the wind through the sedge; there it is, the peculiar aroma of Lucky Strike tobacco and a Texas accent quietly cursing the mud. . . .

*   *   *

Well, I suppose we could move to England.

I hate England, you know I hate England. It rained and rained. . . .

Oh hell, it didn't rain that much; that was just overcast and occasional drizzle. Besides we were there in March and April.

Well, it was so dirty, God. I don't mean filth, you know, just . . . grime . . . centuries of grime on everything. . . .

But the pubs, don't forget the pubs.

Sure, I know, but who wants to spend every evening drinking beer?

Yeah, I suppose.

Perhaps we could move to the States.
Be serious.
I was only joking.

*   *   *

The Americans believe they answered all first questions in 1776; since then they've just been hammering out the practical details.

*   *   *

'Then *boom*!' cries Johnny. 'Boom and the plant got no roof anymore, eh? Ha-ha-ha!' The smoky room fills with laughter. Johnny knows no fear . . . but no nothing else either. When will they ever learn? You'll try again; your fist hits the table.'A big boom? Fine. Great. So the papers photograph it for the front page, and it's producing again the next day. But two pounds of plastic at the right place on a few essential machines and this joint won't put out a pound of steel for two years. . . .'

*   *   *

Well, then, consider one Pole. Consider Count Z. Count Z. is a Pole: *ergo,* a Polish patriot. He has his fingers into both the Defence and Foreign Affairs pies. Perhaps he is Prime Minister, perhaps an *éminence grise*. At forty he is vigorous, experienced, and intelligent.

From the window of his office, Count Z. gazes down into the bustling streets of Warsaw. Fifteen years of peace have prompted a cultural revival. In the near distance, several lines of new smoke-stacks puff their evidence of Poland's stable and bullish economy. Count Z. shades his eyes; in the far distance, the wind washes over the wheat fields which, in two months time, should become the third bumper crop in three years.

Yet Count Z. is not happy. Of course he is proud to be leading Poland to a new prosperity. But the peasants on his estate have been whispering an old saying: The Pole only buys new clothes so he'll look respectable when he commits suicide. Count Z. sighs and sits down to his work: how can I commit suicide today? (Count Z. has a subtle and self-deprecating sense of humour.)

An aide enters with the Foreign Office reports. Count Z.'s ambassadors in the Balkans say the Germans and the Russians are supplying arms and money to opposing factions in Bulgaria, Hungary, and Rumania (or whatever they were called in Count Z.'s time). The tension is moderate but unstable. Count Z. frowns.

Next the Count looks through an economic estimate sheet. Trade with Germany will increase by 12.5 per cent over the next year. This is because of a Polish-German trade agreement of two years ago. Count Z. smiles.

But next is the latest note from St Petersburg. A deadlock has been reached in talks over the disputed ten square miles of Pripet marshland. Resumption of talks is put off indefinitely. Count Z. frowns.

Another aide enters and hands Count Z. a report on Polish defences. He reads it with great interest, although he already knows what it will say: both the eastern and western defence lines are out of date and out of repair. To construct new ones would require half the capital in the country. Financially, given five years, one could be constructed. Diplomatically, however, both must be built at once so as not to risk provoking (or tempting) either the Germans or the Russians. Count Z. sighs. If he were English, he would jerry-build something. But in the holy name of St Stanislaus, how can he insult his Poland with jerry-building?

A visitor is announced: the paunchy, guffawing, monocled Baron Otto von und zu something-dorf, who was instrumental, from the German end, in working out the trade agreement. After four of his own utterly unfunny and incomprehensible jokes, the German says:

'But my dear Count Z., Poland a Defence Line in the East against the Depredations of the savage Cossack Hordes wishes to build, I understand, ja? Your friendly German Cousins—in the spirit which the Trade Agreement possible was made—the Cost of this Defence Line to share would be willing. We Germans, as you well know, *Kultur* love, and we to Civilization a Duty it consider Mankind from the Ravenings of the Bear to protect. . . .'

'Sharing only the cost?'

'Well . . . ho ho ho . . . of course, we a few Divisions to garrison . . . Transportation Arrangements . . . Security Measures would want . . . ho-ho-ho, and to a Slice of Liverwurst yourself help. . . .'

A few minutes after Baron Otto has gone, Prince Igor is announced. Prince Igor is lean and foppish. Only the most delicate efforts prevented his being recalled last year when a prostitute was found beaten to death. He speaks elaborately epigrammatic French, using the occasional Russian phrase to illustrate the quaint wisdom of the peasants.

'*Mon cher* Count Z., I have heard from Petersburg of the unfortunate breakdown in talks. Of course, love shall always exist between the Tsar and his beloved Slavic cousins. . . . The fat Prussian loves war. . . . As a token of his esteem, the magnanimous Tsar wishes his gallant Polish brothers to take immediate and indisputable possession into perpetuity of the invaluable ten square miles of Mother Russia. In addition, our mutual father wishes to build for his valiant Polish children a defence line along the Polish-German (ah, that term, it disgusts me: *c'est une mésalliance*, the union of an eagle and a pig) border. . . . But will you have a sip of vodka? . . . .'

Prince Igor returns to his villa where he finds his aides taking practice shots at the neighbour's cattle. He tells them of his subtle joke: both the pig and the eagle are interchangeable symbols of Germany and Poland.

This subtlety has not been lost on Count Z. He takes a last look at the bustling streets, the puffing smokestacks, and the waving wheat which may or may not get harvested. . . .

In the following weeks, Count Z. more and more frequently plays host to Baron Otto and Prince Igor. As politely as possible, he explains that he prefers Polish sausage to liverwurst; that vodka upsets his digestion. Baron Otto tells jokes which turn like millstones; Prince Igor weaves his *chinoiseries*. They smile till their jaws crack; they drop threatening innuendoes.

Count Z. broods. His wife and his mistress both comment on the pallor of his complexion. He will not be consoled. When he looks into the streets below his office, his eyes imagine a scene filled with arrogant, swaggering Prussians or cruel, drunken Cossacks. Tension is mounting in the Balkans: a Russian uhlan and a German dragoon have fought a duel in Sofia. The salons are hissing with rumour.

Baron Otto and Prince Igor deliver their ultimata on the same day. Accept the liverwurst and not the vodka, accept the vodka and not the liverwurst, or else. Count Z. takes a last glance out the window and sighs. At least they got the harvest in. He rejects the offers. Three weeks later he is cut down while leading a hopeless cavalry charge.

Some time later, Baron Otto and Prince Igor sit down together in what used to be Count Z.'s office. They agree that the treacherous Poles are a blot on humanity, else why did they start a war they were sure to lose (as has been proven)? Baron Otto and Prince Igor agree to divide Poland, using the line where their armies met as a basis for discussions. There will be no arguments over a few square miles here and there, for Poland is a ravaged wasteland. Of course the harvest will be seized to feed the occupying troops: the Poles are pigs, let them root in the ground for acorns if they are hungry. Prince Igor accepts some liverwurst; Baron Otto praises the vodka.

The Balkan situation is smoothed out. The Germans begin building a defence line along the eastern border of their Polish provinces; the Russians begin building a defence line along the western border of their Polish provinces. These lines will take ten years to build (the Polish slave labourers are so lazy). At that time, both the Germans and the Russians will want to test the other's line. They will go to war. The war will rage back and forth across Poland until. . . .

But let the reader construct the rest. Polish history is very simple in this way. The Poles also are simple: they love Poland.

*   *   *

Would you rather be smothered under a pillow of American greenbacks or cut open on a U.S. Marine's bayonet?

*   *   *

Curfew for civilians is long past. You sit hunched by the window listening to the laughing soldiers staggering back to their billets. *Espèce de chameaux*; they cannot take a Molson *bleu*; it is too strong for them. If you were allowed in the *tavernes*, you would show them. . . . '*Allons*,' whispers Jean-Paul. Silently, silently you slide the window up and wait as the others slip onto the roof. You follow, letting the window slide down behind you. You must hurry; already the others are onto the next roof, and creeping toward the fourth house along where the CIA is holding Marc prisoner. . . .

*   *   *

Visit/ez EXPO 67

*   *   *

Uhh . . . I guess I'd better tell you I don't like eggs fried in butter.

But . . . but. . . .

I'm sorry, but it's true.

But . . . ohh, why the hell didn't you tell me before? God, all this time I've been frying your eggs in butter and. . . .

I didn't want to hurt you.

Well, why did you tell me now? Do you want to hurt me now?

No. Of course, you might have decided all by yourself, but if I have any more eggs fried in butter, the cumulative hurt to me (and of course to you) will have been more than the single sharp hurt of telling you. Do you see?

Ohh. . . .

It took a long time to decide when was the right moment. . . .

Yes . . . yes, I see. Yes. It was the right thing to do.

I love you.
Oh! I love you.

*   *   *

During the winter, he was twenty-five; George found his work tending more and more to figure drawing. He was interested and getting good results. So, as artists will do, he set out to explore the subject more fully, spending most of his time drawing and perhaps three days a month painting this and that in a variety of styles just to keep his hand in. During the next three winters, he got together three shows of the figure drawings and each year he got better press and sales. *Canadian Art*, as it was then called, gave the third show a very good review indeed.

On the basis of these successes, George applied for and got a Canada Council grant. He used it to visit the Arctic. When he returned to Toronto, he started twelve paintings, forty-three drawings, and twenty-two prints in silkscreen, lino, and wood. He destroyed each upon completion. At last he gave up trying.

For five months he drank, slept with a variety of women, and read detective novels. A newspaper reviewer came to interview him, and George told him to go to hell.

Finally George prepared a canvas, rectangular with proportions of 2:1. On this canvas he painted the Maple Leaf flag. He hung this painting on the wall of his studio and went back to drawing nudes. Because he had already satisfied himself, at least temporarily, about figures, the drawings were quite bad. But they got him working again, which is the only way to start. After a few weeks, George found a few curiosities and set about exploring these. They led him back to painting, and since that time his work has gotten steadily better, despite the fact that his recent show received confused and confusing reviews, and one critic was angry about something.

*   *   *

'Are you sure it's the right cove?' whispers the man in the trenchcoat.

'Keep shut,' mutters Willard. Willard is being tough, but it's for the stranger's own good; he wouldn't like going ashore to the wrong reception party. Still, he's got a right to be nervous: it's an hour since you cut The *Rachel B*'s engine and no light yet. You peer through the gathering fog. If they don't show in five minutes, you'll have to take the man in the trenchcoat back to the mainland, and that'll mean coming back again and again until you see . . . the light: one long, three short . . . one long, three short. You answer: two long, two short. 'Take her in, Willard,' and the man in the trenchcoat fumbles with his suitcase while Willard dips the muffled oars into the slick black water. . . .

* * *

I have had stories rejected by a number of magazines in Canada and the U.S. No American magazine has ever kept a story longer than three weeks, and no Canadian magazine has kept one less than three months.

These stories have averaged ten pages each. That means the Canadian editors were reading just over one page a week; about two words an hour.

Do you realize that most people with the appropriate dictionary can read any language (even limiting it to our own alphabet) faster than two words an hour?

* * *

North America is a large island to the west of the continent of Cape Breton. (Pronounced: Caybrittn)

* * *

So what if you have to stay at home with the children? Lots of women in France fought in the Resistance; you can do your part too. Take the church supper tonight, for instance. All those National Guardsmen from New Jersey just got homesick; they wanted a home-cooked meal. So Mrs Parsons said to their commandant, 'Why, Colonel, we've always been friendly with your people, living so close to the border. I'm sure the Ladies Auxiliary would love to give your boys a meal. . . .' The commandant didn't object when you were chosen to make the soup, and he still doesn't know you've planned a very special soup in memory of your Bill who was shot down in front of his customs shed the day it all began. . . .

* * *

If the Americans would just read their own Constitutional documents instead of memorizing them. . . .

* * *

Do you love me?
Yes, I love you.
Ohhh!
What now, hmmm? Come here.
Oh.
What? Eh? What is it?

The . . . the way you said it. . . .

Said what?

You know, the way you said I love you.

What about it?

You know very well—you didn't mean it.

I did so . . . really.

No you didn't. You hardly looked at me and you went right back to reading your book.

I did mean it. You see . . . hell, I hate explaining. . . .

(He explains for half an hour. The burden of his thesis is that married love is different from single-people love. Thus, he loves her twenty-four hours a day, loves her in such a way that it affects his whole life, including the way he pours himself a glass of orange juice in the morning. 'It is a love beyond saying,' he explains, 'I state it in my every action, my every word, my every thought. It is like "presence" or something.' He explains that saying 'I love you' is for single people and that he prefers not to say it except at certain times when he feels for her that simple, heart-throbbing love of single people that comes to him when he watches her hip as she bends over or as she sweeps her hair from her eyes. 'At times like that I say, "I love you." ' She says she sees and he says, 'Do you see?' and she repeats, 'Yes, I see.')

I love you.

And I love you. . . . I love you.

(The question now is whether he will make love to her or go back to reading his book. This question has no answer because the scene is an amalgam of scenes, one each week since they got married a few years ago. But before they do, one little exchange remains.)

Well then, if you didn't feel like saying, 'I love you,' why did you say it?

It's better to say it even if it is a technical lie.

What an old funny you are.

Anyway, I love you.

I love you.

*   *   *

See, the way I look at it, your problem is that Joe Yank is the biggest kid on the block. Now I know you're pretty friendly with him—he being your cousin and all—but someday he's going to say, 'Johnny Canuck, my boot is dirty. Lick it.'

Now then, are you going to get down on your hands and knees and lick or are you going to say, 'Suck ice, Joe Yank'? Because if you do say,

'Suck ice,' he's going to kick you in the nuts. And either way, you're going to lick those boots. It just depends on how you want to take it.

Of course, you can always kick him first.

*   *   *

Maybe we could just stay here.

I suppose.

I mean, I like Canada, really. It's not a bad place.

It *is* home.

Perhaps, though, we could go to Montreal for a change.

Could we?

Why not? Drop your school Parisian accent and unify Canada.

Oh!

We'll have to wait till Expo's over, or we'll never get an apartment; we already have friends there. . . . I don't see why not. . . .

I love you!

Me too!

*   *   *

The internal walls of an octagonal room are covered with mirrors. In the room stands a man naked. He is an ordinary-looking man; other people would say so if they could get in to see him. They cannot get in to see him because they do not know where the entrance to the room is or, if they did, how to open it. Likewise the man does not know where the exit is or how to open it. Possibly he would not use it if he could. Likewise back again, possibly those outside would not enter if they could.

In any case, the man is ordinary looking; but at times he thinks himself surpassingly beautiful and at times surpassingly ugly. The man acts out these conflicting feelings, all the while watching himself in the mirrors. With one hand he strokes his beautiful body; with the other (it holds a whip) he lashes his ugly body. The times when he does these things are, it would seem, all times, and they run concurrently.

The situation lends itself to various interpretations. We might consider them; but let us not.

*   *   *

For Centennial Year, send President Johnson a gift: an American tourist's ear in a matchbox. Even better, don't bother with the postage.

MATT COHEN
b. 1942

The Eiffel Tower in Three Parts

1. GETTING THERE

When I was twenty-one there was something in the air. Call it sex. It used to happen then. Now, well, forget it. So I went to the Eiffel Tower instead. I walked, it's not that far, although you always think you're closer than you are. Especially if it starts to rain. Look, have you ever seen the Eiffel Tower? It's full of holes. So you go across the street to a stand where you order some *frites* to keep dry. Then it stops raining so you throw them away and you go stand in line. In front of me were 39 kids from North Carolina. Believe me, they were very unattractive. They were animals. I waited behind them for half an hour and then I got to a sign that explained how it costs more the higher you go. Excuse me, I said to myself, but I don't speak French. I mean, would you spend 128 francs on the Eiffel Tower when it was your last day in France? How about going out and getting drunk or something? I'd already been to the Louvre that day. If there was a free stairway I would have climbed it. When I was twenty-one, for my birthday, someone took me to a fancy French restaurant and I ordered a brains omelette. Of course I didn't realize what I'd ordered, the menu was in French, until the waiter brought back the plate and said: 'Who's having the brains?' I had to eat them to prove I was sophisticated.

2. BEING THERE

I come from a family of mad scientists on both sides. Fathers, uncles, grandfathers all spent their sleepless nights in search of the universal miracle. As for myself, I specialize in unemployment. To keep the coffers full, however, I sometimes take on family missions, which is how I found myself in the Charles de Gaulle airport, on the way to Geneva to straighten out a few patents.

I was sitting in a crowded airport brasserie, passing the time, when a woman talking to herself in English came to sit at my table. 'The French,' she muttered in a British accent. Then she gave me a smile.

'Would you like a drink?' I asked.

'Of course.'

Soon we were speeding downtown in a taxi.

'Amazing,' she said, 'I've been searching for you all my life. The amazing thing is that I didn't recognize you right away. To me—forgive this first impression—you were just another American tourist. You looked middle-aged, tired, too stuck-up to speak a few words to a poor English girl like myself. Then, when you offered me a drink, I was aware of a strange pounding in my ears. I thought I was having an attack of high blood pressure until I realized my heart was beginning to beat in time with yours. Darling, we were made for each other.'

To such sentiments I was helpless to reply. But before silence betrayed me, there was a loud popping sound. The driver turned around, gave us a gleaming smile, a bottle of champagne foaming at the mouth, two crystal glasses.

'From my trousseau,' she whispered. 'Please, I'd like you to meet my father.'

'Enchanted,' the father said, still smiling. 'Isn't the weather wonderful? And isn't it just like my daughter not to introduce herself? Here you are, almost in the centre of Paris, and you don't even know her name. Noreen Hammond. Noreen after her mother's mother. Hammond after me. I'm the only London taxi driver in all of Paris but that's another story. Let's talk about you.'

'My name is Keith,' I said. Don't ask me why.

'Pleased to meet you, Keith. Allow me to present my daughter, Noreen.'

'Daddy, won't you have a drink with us?'

'Never on the job, my sweet. You know that.'

Before we could finish the bottle the taxi had pulled up at the Hotel Meurice. A doorman leapt from under the awning to grapple with Noreen's trunks. I explained to him that my own suitcase had been checked through to Geneva.

'No problem, mate, it's just a wing and a hop from here. Meanwhile you can share a toothbrush with the missus, eh?'

'*Mais monsieur*,' I couldn't help saying, '*votre anglais est formidable.*'

'Nought but the best, mate. I spent three summers grading sand at Brighton. Now off you go, and don't forget to mind the gap.'

Upstairs Noreen threw off her clothes and began to gambol about the suite like a doe unchained. 'I'm feeling frisky,' she hummed, 'I feel like doing something risky.'

The telephone rang. I picked it up.

'Keith?'

'Speaking.'

'Keith, this is Noreen's dad. How are things going?'

'Pretty quiet, so far.'

'You know, Keith, Noreen is a special girl.'

'I can see that, Mr Hammond.'

'After the wedding, I hope you'll call me Roy.'

'Of course, Mr Hammond.'

'Well, Keith, I just wanted to say that if first impressions mean anything, I think you're quite a man.'

'Thank you, Mr Hammond.'

'Wedding be damned, Keith, you can start calling me Roy right now.'

'All right, Roy.'

'Goodnight, Keith. Remember, I'm trusting you.' Click.

Noreen reappeared, white fur wrapped around the rosy skin of her shoulders, new glasses of champagne in her hands. The lights were down, soft music was playing.

'Feeling tired, Keith?'

'I'm afraid so.'

'Would you like a bath?'

'I'd love a bath.'

'So would I,' Noreen said. She took my arm and led me gently into the *salle de bain*. A giant tub was filled and waiting for me, and the room echoed with the sound of pink bath bubbles exploding their strawberry scent into the damp air.

'Are you shy, Keith? Just close your eyes and make a wish.'

3. YOU CAN'T GO HOME AGAIN

It was a question of brain pollution. It was a question of the mind trying to deal with ideas, images, situations for which the mind was unsuited. Because his mind and his life were like oil and water or, more likely, vice versa. Not a personal failing, really, just a question of late-twentieth-century chaos tearing apart nineteenth-century cosmologies. It was just a matter of using the mind to analyse the question. No, not to analyse it, but to turn it round and round like a heavenly sphere.

In sum, it was a question of not knowing the question. Fortunately, he knew the answer: hard work, exercise, healthy food, less to drink. It was a question of getting back to the basics. Or at least it was a question of finding the right answer and then deciding what the question must have been. Once he had swallowed the bitter medicine, reckoned and made himself willing to pay the price—well, after that, he would stare the question in the face. Hold his spit until he saw the whites of its eyes.

Jeans, sweatshirt, thick socks. Glass of scotch, ice-cubes made from pure spring water, quadrophonic Bessie Smith.

'Okay,' he said to himself, easing into his easy chair. 'Why do I hate my life?' He picked up a newspaper. People all over the world were dying horrible deaths. His ice-cubes clinked. Bessie Smith slid an octave and a half. Through his half-open window he could hear the wind. All over the world people were crouched in caves, lying bandaged in hospitals, sitting cross legged under desert moons. They hated him, his house. They even hated his pets.

He was in the living-room, hating himself, listening to Bessie Smith while he drank scotch and smoked the remnants of a long-lost marijuana cigarette. He turned off the lights. He pulled off his socks and began to dance on the broadloom. He was talking to himself. 'Be a man. Take what's yours.' He was dancing and singing and forgetting all about the over militarized undereducated billions who quite rightfully despised him, when the light switched on to reveal Noreen standing with her hands on the hips of her white terrycloth bathrobe.

"Mind if I join the party?'

The Bloor Street promenade—WHAM WHAM WHAM—ten thousand jolts, ten thousand faces, ten thousand pairs of eyes staring aggressively into his, pushing him back into himself, bouncing him along like a rusty truck on a corrugated road.

He was sweating. He stopped in front of a restaurant. FOODWORKS, the sign declared. In the window, too, he could see his own reflection. Stocky. Fair-haired. High domed forehead. Dark sun-glasses. 'I come from a family of mad scientists,' he imagined himself saying. His lips twitched and in the window he saw his mouth hesitating between a frown and a smile. He was hungry or maybe he wanted to throw up. He wondered what would happen if he went into the restaurant.

An engine roaring. Metal tearing. A spray of glass landing on the sidewalk at his feet. He turned around. A delivery van had skidded into the lamp-post. The glass at his feet was the remains of the windshield. A woman staggered out the driver's side. Her face was a sheet of blood. She wiped a space clear in front of her eyes, looked at him, opened her mouth, screamed. 'Help me, you bastard.'

He took off his raincoat and wrapped it around her. Then, holding her to him as though they were in a thunderstorm, he hurried her into a cigarette store and asked for kleenex.

'Christ,' she was saying, 'I don't know what happened. I just lost control.' Then she asked him to come with her to the hospital because she was afraid of doctors. She was still wearing his raincoat. He didn't mind that, in fact he had been hoping the incident would finish that way—her going off in his raincoat and him feeling that for once he had found the perfect ending.

They let him ride with her in the back of the ambulance. She had to lie down in case of shock. She was still wearing his raincoat. He was sitting beside her. She was holding his hand, and he was looking at her face. He realized he had never seen the face of a woman lying on her back except in intimate circumstances. She had darkly tanned skin, bony features, angry blue eyes. 'You look like the kind of woman who drives a van for a living,' he imagined himself saying to her.

'I don't know what happened,' she said. Sitting up, a wide white bandage holding together her forehead, her sun-glasses pushed up across her dark hair, she didn't look bad. There were little scars on her cheekbones—miniature versions of the kind of scars you expect on hockey players. On her left wrist a heart was tattooed, and inside the heart was written a name he couldn't read.

'You must have spent some time in prison,' he imagined himself saying. But what an incredible thing that would be to say. What if she hadn't? What if she had? What if she was attracted to him? What if she was just frightened and wanted a cup of coffee?

They were in a restaurant. 'Thank you, Keith,' she said. 'Thanks for taking a chance on me.' She took a cigarette out of her purse and slid it between her lips. Then her mouth twisted while she searched in her pockets for a package of matches. Meanwhile the door opened. A man came in. He was big. He had forearms like tree trunks. He slid in beside the woman.

'Hey,' said the woman, 'sorry about the van.'

The big man shrugged. Now Keith saw he too had a heart tattooed inside his wrist. Inside the heart was one word: DUKE.

'Call me Duke,' Keith tried to imagine himself saying. But he couldn't.

'Hey,' Duke said. 'Call me Duke.'

Keith stood up. He wanted things to end perfectly. For example: he could go to the kitchen and ask the chef to send Duke a brains omelette. Another example: he could join the secret society and get a heart tattooed inside his left wrist. 'From now on you call me Duke,' he imagined himself announcing to Noreen.

He walked out of the restaurant. He imagined himself telling strangers the numbers of his numbered Swiss bank accounts. He imagined himself in Paris with Noreen. He imagined himself talking on the long-distance telephone with his children. He imagined himself saying that he had spent the day climbing the Eiffel Tower.

At the corner, Noreen was waiting for him in a taxi. Champagne was popping.

'Happy Birthday,' she said, 'how was your trip?'

Keith closed his eyes. 'Every day was exciting.'

SANDRA BIRDSELL

b. 1942

The Wild Plum Tree

```
Mr. Malcolm
English 100

Betty Lafreniere

                    ESSAY

              The Wild Plum Tree

    It is more than a shrub but not a tree, bark is smooth
when young. Inside, white sapwood, porous bark splits
with age and leaves
narrow tipped, fruit slightly reddish with blood
flowers showy white gracing
southern end of Manitoba and other provinces,
of no commercial value.
```

Mr Malcolm is English 100. He is also Betty's mathematics teacher, history teacher, and language arts teacher. He is straight from Jamaica and looks to pregnant wayward girls and delinquents to teach him all they know about Manitoba.

'Now surely,' he says, 'you must know more about this subject. It was your free choice.'

Betty shrugs, feigns indifference. The essay is the best she can do under the circumstances. The reference books in the classroom are *The Book of Knowledge* and *Weeds, Trees and Wildflowers in Canada*. Some of the girls have taken a bus down to the public library on William Avenue. But not her. What she doesn't know, she will make up. That's life, she tells herself.

'But you see, I asked for six pages, at least,' he says. He wears pastel colours. Pale green polyester pants, a pinkish tie against a coral-coloured shirt. She ignores him, looks out the dusty window down into the city. The rapid darting of traffic intrigues her. Where are all these people going to, coming from? And why? It seems pointless. She saw shadows in the graveyard last night. She'd sat on the radiator in her room looking out and thought, how appropriate: a graveyard in the back yard of the home for wayward girls. They were all burying things, their past, their present, the things that came out of them. And she saw shadows down there, lithe phantoms sprinting from tree to tree, leaping up from the hard granite stones. Today, several of the tombstones are toppled into the grass. The praying virgin with her blind eyes and reverent posture, hands held up in frozen supplication, lies on one side.

'Did you not understand my instructions then?' the teacher asks.

'Yes, Mr Malcolm, I understood your instructions.' She wants only to be left alone.

'Mr Jackson.'

'Yes, Mr Jackson.' His name is Malcolm P. Jackson. You have never heard the sound of a mob, he has told them. He'd sat on the desk in front of them, swinging his knees in and out, like a young child needing to urinate. I was a boy when I once heard such a mob. It was like the sound of a swarm of angry bees growing louder and louder. Let me tell you, it was not a pleasant sound. Angry people. A mob rushing along the street. I was very young but I learned quickly to be afraid of the mob.

'Well then, if you knew the instructions, why have you handed me this?' He holds up the single sheet of paper. The classroom has grown quiet. The girls stop talking to listen.

'Because I felt like it.'

Several of the girls titter. Betty has not said this for their benefit. She only needs, wants, to be left on her own. A detention is a way to accomplish this end. Mr Jackson sets the paper down, takes a piece of yellow chalk from his shirt pocket and rolls it from hand to hand.

'My dear girl. Listen. In my country, education is a privilege. Only the cleverest people go beyond grade school. Our parents made great sacrifices for us. We're grateful. With us, it is never a question, whether we feel like it or not; we do it.'

'If you're so smart,' someone says, 'then why are you here with us?'

He pretends he hasn't heard, but the muscles in his jaw contract suddenly as though he just bit into a stone.

Betty wants no part of their taunting. She wants to be away from them all, to be able to sift through all the information she has gathered, to make some order of it.

'Surely you could do better than this,' he persists. 'There must be more you could write about the wild plum tree.'

Even now, she smells the fruit of it. The tart flavour, taut skin splitting in her mouth, the slippery membrane of its meat, a piece of slime at the bottom of a quart sealer jar of home-made wine coming suddenly into her mouth like a great clot of blood. There is too much to say about the wild plum tree. The assignment has paralyzed her.

'Yes, Chocolate Drop. I'm sure there is.' She uses the girls' private name for Mr Jackson.

His nostrils flare. The room grows silent. Then laughter erupts, spills over. 'Chocolate Drop,' a girl says and then they all say, 'Chocolate Drop.'

His eyes dart about the room. Betty continues to stand before the window, toying with the frayed cord on the venetian blind. Thousands of girls have stood at this very same window and played with this cord. It's marked with their anguish, their boredom and frustrations.

'Well um,' Mr Jackson says, bouncing the chalk from palm to palm. 'Well um.' The palms of his hands are tinged pink. The skin has been worn away. It's from masturbating, flogging his meat, the girls say. He clutches at his crotch frequently in the classroom. Adjusts his testicles before he sits down on the edge of the desk to confront them.

'Who needs you, Chocolate Drop?' a girl asks.

'Well, Miss,' Mr Jackson says to Betty, 'you see what you have instigated? You may call me what you like. What can one expect from Satan's daughter?'

Betty yanks the frayed cord. It snaps free and falls to the floor. Several of the girls leave their desks. Mr Jackson turns and faces them quickly. 'Well um,' he says. 'That will be ten pages now. You seem to think she is a humorous person. Do you think ten pages is also funny?'

They groan. 'You can't make us do ten pages,' a tall girl with angry grey eyes says.

He strides to his desk, pulls open a drawer and takes out a wooden ruler. 'Ten pages, I said.' He bangs the ruler against his desk.

'Fuck off,' the tall girl says.

He walks swiftly to her and whacks her across the face with the ruler. Smiles face, all movement is suspended. A red welt rises on the girl's cheek. 'And who else wishes to express themselves in such a manner?' he asks. The girls one by one return to their desks.

'You heard her,' Betty says. 'Go fuck yourself in Jamaica and leave us alone.' A flood of tension is released suddenly. She feels the teacher's wooden ruler bounce off her shoulder blade. The girls laugh and call out their individual hate names for Mr Jackson. An eraser bounces off the wall beside his head. He backs slowly over to the classroom door and stands with one hand on the knob. His lips are flecked with spittle. 'Ten pages, you naughty spoiled children. When you can control yourselves, we will continue this class,' he says and flees.

Control yourselves. Is it lack of control then, that has brought them all to this place? The windowpane is cool against Betty's forehead as she looks down into the street. A young man cuts through the cemetery, hands plunged deep into his pockets; he walks with his shoulders hunched up, a cigarette hangs from his mouth. He glances up at the window where she stands and is gone.

```
Notes for essay on wild plum tree
Mr. Malcolm, English 100

the beginning

Suddenly you face across the street where once there was
only a coulee with bullrushes, twitch grass four feet
high, God and Indian arrowheads, a brand new house.

But first, machines squashed frogs and garter snakes and
pen once lost and never found and then ploughed them
beneath tons of landfill from a field where they also
discovered the skeletons part of which Laurence brought
to school.
(the skull)

Then, when the four-and-a-half member family move into
that new house, the dark-haired woman has a bump in front
so she is probably pregnant (being the oldest of six
teaches you to watch for those things); the beginning
ends.

through yellowing lace curtains
I have always watched
the games of others
hiding and seeking the waning sun
shadows the mourning dove's
spotted grey
bird sounds temper the shrill play
sounds
that strike my note
of sorrow
```

I have not found anything good
in tomorrow

notes   before the beginning

Leaves (somewhat hairy) of the dog mustard plant, which,
like the mother of seven, originated in Europe and was
first found in Canada at Emerson in 1922, tickle bare
legs when walking in the coulee. And their flower,
clusters of pale yellow stain white organdy, which also
scratches bare legs when walking, sitting, standing,
period. When you wander with Laurence in the coulee, he
carries your shoes and you can feel the spongy ground and
make it squeeze up between your toes and then he shows
you his hidden pool

and in the deep pool
melted snow yellows
bright all the dead grasses
pink granite stones and your face
rising and falling as feet dipped clean
drip the surface and make you wrinkle

Russian pigweed stands as high as you because you are
eight, but Laurence's head is a little above it. The
plant is like the two of you, one plant and two different
kinds of flowers, male and female.

And God is also in the coulee, moving before you. You can
feel His breath on your body, coming through the organdy
you have worn especially for Him because it is Sunday.

And Laurence, even though he does not go to any church,
is of the same plant that nods in the same breath. But
for some reason, the mother of seven doesn't think so
which is why you walk among the Russian pigweed, so she
can't see you and get angry and send you down the road to
your grandfather's house to get a lesson in the Bible.

God you were
there inside
my knees and elbows
scratched raw

```
crawling from imaginary
Indians
would take my yellow hair
make a belt or something, God
your voice
fades faster than games
of Indians don't last
forever
```

'Betty uses foul language and shows disrespect for the property of the institution,' the social worker says. She reads from the teacher's report. She wears black cat's-eyes-shaped glasses and adjusts them before she speaks again. Betty can feel her father's shyness of this woman, his eagerness to appease and have everyone agree quickly that everything will be fine so that he can go home and report to Mika with a clear conscience that he's done his best. He sits on a chair beside Betty. They face the social worker's desk beneath the window. The room is a basement room. The window is at street level and Betty watches and counts the feet of people who pass by on the sidewalk.

'If you won't adhere to the rules of this institution, what choice will we have, but to ask you to leave it?'

'Certainly, she's going to follow the rules and regulations,' Maurice says. 'There's no maybe about it.'

He plays with the brim of his hat and looks down at the floor. He's put on his suit and tie and taken the bus in from the country especially for this meeting. He's deeply embarrassed. He cannot bring himself to say the words, 'pregnant' and 'social worker'.

The woman writes something on her pad. Betty wonders if she is writing, 'Father is co-operative', or 'Supportive father'. With whom and of whom?

'What about rules regarding hitting students with rulers?' Betty asks.

'Listen here,' Maurice says, suddenly irritated. 'What makes you think you can ask that, eh? You're not in any position here to ask questions.'

'And what position am I in?'

Maurice is flustered. He twirls the hat between his thick brown fingers, clears his throat several times.

The social worker gets up quickly. 'I think the two of you need to talk alone. It's important that we reach an understanding today.' The door closes behind her. Maurice relaxes. He wipes his brow, sits up straighter and looks about the room for the first time. The walls are cement block, unpainted. There are no pictures. 'This here place is not so bad,' he says. 'I don't know what you're griping about.'

A black mongrel zig-zags across the boulevard and sidewalk. It stops and looks down into the room, sniffs and then continues on its way.

'You don't have to live here. I hate it.'

'Well now, that wasn't our doing, was it?' Maurice says. It's the closest he's come to mentioning her pregnancy. 'Anyway, it's a darn sight better than being out on the street because, believe you me, that's where you're headed if you don't shape up.'

Betty stifles the urge to laugh. Shape up. She is rapidly shaping up. She knows that her parents' number one concern is her shape. They're afraid that she might be expelled from the home and shame them with her bulging presence in the community. It's the only reason for his trip into the city. She knows she's been cut off, that she can't look to either of her parents for anything.

'It's okay,' she says. 'I'll be okay now. It's just been hard to adjust.'

Maurice brightens. He looks at her with a wide smile, his eyes uneasy though, carefully avoiding looking at her stomach. 'Adjust, absolutely. I can understand that. Certainly it takes time to get used to new situations.'

'Losing your home is a new situation all right.'

'Eh?' His hands stop in mid-air.

'I feel as though I have no home.' For one second she wants to fling herself at him, bury her face into his shoulder and hold on.

Maurice works furiously as he flicks nonexistent lint from his hat.

'Well, that's not quite so,' he says. 'You've still got a home. You're only here for a few more months, that's all. Once it's over, it's over.' He stands up and puts his hat on, adjusts the brim. 'You've learned.'

I am learning to control myself, no more fucking. 'In a few more months, I'll have my baby.' She wants him to think about this.

'On that score your mother and I agree. You can't bring the bastard home.' He takes his wallet from his pocket. 'Just in case you need something,' he says and hands her several bills. His hands are shaking. She takes the money from him. Everything is okay, taken care of, he'll tell Mika. You know, it's not easy, it takes time to adjust to these things. All she needed was a little talk and a little time. He's in a hurry, anxious to be away.

'I have to go,' she says.

The door closes behind him. She waits. She sees his feet pass by on the sidewalk along with the feet of another person, strangers passing by.

notes for the essay   Bible lessons at Opah's

Opah means Grandfather. Omah means Grandmother. (This is
for the benefit of Mr Malcolm, English 100, the Chocolate
Drop who came directly from Jamaica and wants to know
everything he can about Canada.)

The lesson for today, Opah says, is: HOW GOD LED HIS
PEOPLE OUT OF THE LAND OF EGYPT. But then he forgets and
his sky-blue eyes melt into the horizon and he speaks of
hundreds of people gathering around twenty-eight train
cars in Russia. They are coming, these people, like the
dog mustard, only a year later, to spread out across the
fields of southern Manitoba. Faith is the Victory, Faith
is the Victory, Opah hums, wiping tears from his face and
Omah comes out from the pantry wiping hands of flour onto
her apron. There is a boy in the garden, she says. When
she goes to call him in, he runs away, she explains,
worried. They still dream of thieves and Bolshevik
murderers. Laurence is waiting for the lesson to be
finished so that there will be someone to go fishing
with. He has only one friend because he is on welfare.

First you learn, Opah says, no longer can you get into
heaven free because of your parents or grandparents. When
you're twelve, you're on your own with God.

He makes you learn the ten commandments even though you
know Emily, who lives across the road, whose father is a
doctor and drives a Lincoln and with his money has built
the gingerbread house that now has a patio and one more
child added, which looks out over another row of houses
where the coulee once was, this girl, whose father's
building also destroyed an Indian burial ground, will not
hesitate to walk across the friendship and go fishing
with Laurence.

—round-leaved mallow is different from common mallow and
is a nuisance only in the prairie provinces where it
nudges aside Kentucky Blue and Shady Nook grass but that
doesn't matter because you can't really eat cultured lawn
the way you can the nutlets of round mallow an after

school treat not double bubble gum or fudgsicles but a
prairie weed that stayed behind to live in town to colour
green your teeth you forgot to brush today but ants don't
brush do they or for that matter neither do grasshoppers
they squirt tobacco—

too bad   Emily can't eat round-leaved mallow
too bad   she has to eat juicy fruit cracker jack and all
that crap
too bad   she isn't a grasshopper or an ant

I would press her lightly with my toe and scare the shit
out of her.

Emily is a stinking willie.
She is poisonous inside.
To her, fishing with Laurence is an opportunity to
practise lying. She is like a plum rotting in the grass.

I lost Laurence one summer
didn't last and he was gone
I looked: in the garden
            in the poolroom
            bowling alley
            cafe
            fair grounds
no Laurence

Look—he has waited long enough for you to go fishing.
It's your fault you learned the ten commandments.

And now, Emily wears his arrowhead around her neck. Your
arrowheads gather dust in a cigarette box in the rafters
of the icehouse while she, whose backyard has a patio
surrounded by stinking willie, wears his arrowhead
because plum wine is strong enough inside Laurence that
no longer does he care that occasionally he is on welfare
or that at ten he had lice.

The small lamp in the corner on the table spreads a pink glow in the
room. There are six girls in various stages of pregnancy dressed in
bathrobes, feet tucked up beneath them, one lies flat on her back, she is
only in her third month. 'When I get out of this place I'm going to slash
the bugger's tires, all four of them,' the girl with the angry grey eyes

says. They have been telling 'how I lost my virginity' stories. Betty listens, she has not contributed and she knows they expect her to soon. She thinks that only this tall girl has been honest.

'I used to tell my parents I was staying at a friend's house,' one of the girls says. 'They never checked, usually they never checked, that is. Then one time, wouldn't you know it, my girlfriend's father answered the phone before she could get to it? And made her tell my Dad where I was? God, I almost died. There I was, Rick was doing it to me, you get what I mean? He didn't even knock—'

'Doing what?'

'Aw, come on, you know—'

'Was it big, small, did it hurt? You've got to tell a better story than that.'

'I opened my eyes and saw my father. He just stood there staring and didn't say anything. It gave me the creeps. Like, for a minute, I didn't know what he was going to do. Then he went and waited for me in the car. When I came out he was sitting there crying. I felt like a piece of shit.'

The girls moan sympathetically. They stare at their feet, at the space in front of them. They are all getting into shape, out of control, Betty thinks. Sometimes one of their boyfriends visits and then the rest of them slouch in corners, snapping gum, dissatisfied until he leaves. Where's your boyfriend, they've asked Betty, sixty-five girls who have eaten too many sweets, superior because they have visitors, more righteous for a time, than her.

They turn to her. They wait now for her story to begin. I was fourteen. He was an old man. At first he just used his finger. I screwed sixteen men this year and have written their names down in a scribbler.

'His name is Frank,' she says. 'We're in love. He wants to marry me.'

The tall grey-eyed girl rises first and the others follow her one by one and file out of the lounge. Woolworth diamonds sparkle on their fingers. Now, at last, she can be alone.

notes for the essay   hiding and seeking

Laurence's anger moves in circles, his teeth on edge
against an unnamed foe burned off in the sound of his
motorcycle held into place by centrifugal force around
and around. His anger spent, the dust settling, he stops
moving, stands beside you and finally you are once again
behind him, your arms about his narrow leather waist

climbing the yellow fields, cutting a swathe through
black-headed cattails (fire torches, good for eating) in
the ditches beside the highway, up and down Main Street.
He doesn't speak, but only with others does he need to,
you never cared, his silence was like a lady slipper
growing beside a swampy marsh. He takes the old skull
from his saddle bag, lines it up on Main Street, takes a
run at it and shatters the old bone like pieces of
coconut shell skittering curses across a table top. Don't
do it, you think, but it's his skull, he can do what he
wants. You ride and drink until the sun is down behind
old weathered caved-in barns and he pukes plum wine,
purple and violent in the grass at your feet. He lies you
down and you are surprised at his fumbling, thought he
would know how to do it better and so you help him with
his clothing and guide him. (Was it big, was it fat or
small, did it hurt? Come on, you've got to tell a better
story than that.)

His nostril in your eye and when he turns his head you
notice: hair in his ear, dirty. Emily, Emily, he says,
not your name, but hers and his nostrils puff out warm
plum air and his mouth, not gentle, smells of sour jam as
he pins you to the earth but the worst is that after, he
pulls grass from your hair, says he's sorry and treats
you like a friend.

you are—

Listening until the sound of the engine is a distant
whine on the highway, an angry wasp, a wavering line of
sound straightening, becoming threadlike, thin, and then
it snaps and—

Betty switches off the lamp. The traffic below in the city street is a
ribbon connecting people together. The gravestones sheltered beneath
the trees seem to move in the light filtering down between the tree
branches. She hears a sharp whistle like a signal, and the figures rise up
from among the stones, gather beneath the streetlight and plan their night
errands. She watches and waits for tomorrow.

EDNA ALFORD

b. 1947

Mid-May's Eldest Child

Once off the bus Arla peeled off her bulky-knit cardigan and swung it over her shoulder, retaining only a two-finger hold on the red woollen collar. She was thinking about yesterday afternoon with David on the balcony of her apartment. Her apartment was on the west corner of the top floor of the building.

The railing on the balcony was wrought iron, spiralled white rods like screws bored into the concrete base. The base was unusually high, about two feet, so that when David laid her on the weathered boards of the inside corner and stripped her in the sun, she could not be seen. Could not be seen from across the street or by Mr and Mrs Fogle next door—as long as she was still, didn't writhe or sit up. Couldn't be heard as long as she didn't make too much noise, only whisper softly into his open mouth—as long as she withheld the sudden cry when he touched her precisely, at exactly the right moment.

The best of it was the breathing, the air clear and slightly chill, not cold but cool enough so she could feel it going down, inside and warm and out again, but quietly. The discipline was excruciating, hard and lovely, and when he fingered, she was full of water. In some ways, the balcony was a lot like Miss Moss' silly bowers, Arla thought and giggled, only no trees.

This morning the spring sun was warm again, even before seven and, along with her memory of the previous afternoon, enticed her to throw off not only the red sweater but all of her clothes, especially the clinging arnel uniform, the white nylon stockings and the duty shoes. But she remembered, wincing, today and tomorrow were work days. In fact, she had to be at work in fifteen minutes.

Even these fifteen minutes, however, appeared to Arla to stretch out long and delicious into the future. She half-walked, half-skipped toward the entrance to Maunley Park which was deserted at this hour of the morning. She often cut through the park on her way to the lodge. Here there were trees, at least—but no David, just trees.

When she reached the park gates she threw her sweater, her vinyl purse and her lunch bag on the infant grass and like a child, raced toward the naked white flag pole. Grabbing hold of it with one arm, the other swinging up and outward like a wing, she flew around and around, her light brown hair flinging itself away from her scalp, her eyes closed, her face relaxed, her lips parted to receive the mythical 'man-of-the-morning' kiss. This 'man' was not David—though she really believed she loved David and wouldn't hurt him for anything in the world. The 'man' wasn't anyone she had ever seen. Where he came from she didn't know, but he often entertained her on the long bus rides to and from the lodge.

Quickly dizzy, she let go of the pole and spun outward between a clump of lilacs and a bed of tulips and daffodils, running till she fell, then rolling over and over on the grass and coming to rest at last on her back, her arms stretched upward, reaching toward the clear young sun. She tilted her head backward. The thin lime green of new leaves floated lacy on the shiny surfaces of her eyes. She could smell lilacs and daffodils, tulips and columbine all warm between the labia of earth. And she felt playful, hopeful, knowing winter was finally over. Right then it seemed to Arla that anything was possible, probable even—that her future was as brilliant and certain as the leaves.

She fingered white blossoms like scraps of silk which had fallen to the grass from the crabapple tree directly on her right. Then she rolled over on her stomach and picked out two or three new green shoots of grass. She nibbled the sweet white ends and finally, reluctantly, looked at her watch. Three minutes to seven, it scolded; unscrupulous thief that it was, Arla thought, the watch was in no position to criticize her. But she knew she would have to hurry or she would be late for her shift, no matter how she felt about the Timex Nurse.

She rose slowly on all fours, arched her back slightly, then forced herself up onto her haunches. She patted her hair, smoothing out the bits of dry grass and twigs from the back of her head. There was no one to watch her.

She stood, started off toward the lodge, then remembering her belongings, retraced her steps. Bending down to retrieve her things, Arla noticed a moss green stain on her uniform skirt. 'Oh shit,' she said, then smiled—thinking, well at least it's not that, not yet anyway, although that's exactly what the stain reminded her of. But, she remembered with relief, today would not be altogether unpleasant. Today was the day she took Miss Moss to the barber, to get sheared as the old woman put it.

Matron Benstone had told Arla to take the old woman, which was fine with Arla. She liked Miss Moss, had taken special care of her ever since their first meeting almost two years before when Miss Moss had assessed Arla's age to be fifteen years and had said that although she found it refreshing to have a youngster on the premises, she frankly wondered if the girl could handle the job.

The reason Arla had been asked to go with her this morning while one of the matrons assumed the regular lodge duties had not been made clear. And furthermore required no explanation. Miss Moss and the matrons did not see eye to eye as she put it, and as they put it, Miss Moss was an irascible, uncompromising old witch and they would have as little to do with her as possible unless she mended her ways. Arla smiled to herself, remembering past wars between Miss Moss and the matrons. Once Arla had seen her take on both matrons at the same time. And once they had called in extra troops—a social worker from the City and Dr Jeremy, but to no avail. Miss Moss was full of spit and fire in her battles but always dignified. She was a small hawk, and neither of the matrons could match her rhetoric. She had them beat even when she lost. And they knew it.

So Arla had planned a special outing for her today. She had decided to take her to tea at one of the restaurants in the mall where the barber shop was located. Maybe they would have a bite to eat, then afterward they could walk through the park and Miss Moss could see the new flowers and they could share this remarkable spring day. And they could talk. Arla thought to herself while running up the steps to the lodge that Meredith Moss would no doubt give one of her poetry recitations with particular emphasis on the theme of 'Spring, Rebirth and Renewal—the Abundance and Beauty of Nature'. She hadn't been out of the lodge for a long time and Arla congratulated herself for thinking of the idea. It would have to be done on the sly, of course, so the matrons wouldn't get wind of it, but Miss Moss would get a kick out of that—putting one over on them. They were supposed to leave at ten o'clock.

By the time she entered the dim corridor of the lodge, flanked by rows of numbered doors, she was positively euphoric, her gait quick and rhythmic, her face radiating the stored warmth of this morning's sun. She flew past Mrs Popovich and Mrs McNaughton flinging them good mornings, hellos, like a white-robed druidic maiden throwing flowers from an inexhaustible bouquet. Mrs Popovich grimaced and Mrs Mc-Naughton sour-pursed her lips as if she had just been thrown a lemon, not a daffodil.

She proceeded to tell Mrs Popovich that someone had stolen her heating pad, her with her back so bad and all. You'd think they'd have some decency. You no sooner got something nice and poof! it was gone, stolen right out from under you. And she had her suspicions, too! There were some here who were not as god-fearing as she and Helen Popovich!

Or as self-righteous either, thought Arla. But they just hadn't been out today; they would feel better once they felt the sunshine, the lilacs, the spring. How could they help themselves?

Yet as she went about her regular early morning duties, she couldn't ignore the tedious malingering voices of some of her charges. Miss Bole refused to put on the only clean dress she had in her closet, saying the laundry woman bleached it out and how could she be expected to wear a dishrag? Mrs Emmerson regaled her with a venom-ridden tale of stolen stockings and even Mrs Warren who was generally good-natured, made accusatory allusions about the disappearance of her new bottle of Orchid Talcum Powder, as if Arla would be caught dead using it. Things—they were so preoccupied with their precious worthless belongings.

And their pains. Six of one and half-dozen of the other, thought Arla. You'd think that was all there was in the world, decay and cynicism and pain. You'd think there was no such thing as joy. Sometimes you'd think it a crime to be happy, the way they acted.

Well today, at least, she could escape. She and Miss Moss would soon be out of the lodge and into the sunshine, and she tried to think of that. In fact, it was almost time to see that Miss Moss was ready, time to call the cab. After she made the call and instructed the dispatcher to send a car at quarter to ten, she climbed the stairs and knocked at number fifteen.

'Come in, do come in Miss Pederson.' Arla was welcome in this room, had always been. When she walked in she found Miss Moss seated on a chair in front of her window, overlooking the park. She closed the book she was reading and laid it on her lap. It was a book of poetry, an anthology of the Romantic poets, she had told Arla.

This particular book seemed to be her favourite. She read from it frequently and had quoted passages of it to Arla. Meredith Moss had been a high school teacher—forty-six years at the lectern, she had told Arla more than once. And she regarded Arla as one of her students, a latecomer as it were.

Arla didn't really mind being treated this way. She enjoyed the poetry recitations and the quiet moments of well-intended philosophical instruction Miss Moss gave her. She had become very fond of Keats, Miss Moss' favourite poet—her god it seemed, and could herself now quote short passages from the most famous of his poems.

One day they had even chanted together, Miss Moss very sternly and Arla half-smiling, 'Beauty is truth, truth beauty—that is all / Ye know on earth, and all ye need to know.' And although the actual recitation had embarrassed Arla and amused her somewhat, she found herself, young as she was, in love with what she had said.

Miss Moss had been very pleased with her and had tightened her mouth around her false teeth, smacked her lips and made a small curious clucking sound, a mannerism with which she expressed both her approval and her displeasure. The two could be differentiated only by watching her eyes for sparkles or glowers.

'Good morning Miss Moss,' Arla said smiling. 'It's sure a terrific spring morning out there!'

'Yes, Miss Pederson, I *have* noticed. I have just now finished reading "The Green Linnet", by Wordsworth. Do you know it?'

Arla had taken it in her last year of high school and at that time had commiserated with her peers that it was 'dry as dust' like all the rest of the stuff, but this morning it seemed appropriate and somehow more meaningful to her and she wanted to hear it. So she said yes, it was one of her favourites. Could Miss Moss say a few lines for her.

'Yes, yes, yes, "The Green Linnet"—a beautiful piece of work, Miss Pederson—do sit on the bed if you like.' Arla sat. Miss Moss leaned back in her chair and gazed thoughtfully out her window toward the park. She began, very quietly, enunciating perfectly, giving each line its just metrical rendering.

> ' "Beneath these fruit-tree boughs that shed
> Their snow-white blossoms on my head,
> With brightest sunshine round me spread
> Of spring's unclouded weather—" '

She paused briefly, not as if remembering, but for effect, and began again.

> ' "In this sequestered nook how sweet
> To sit upon my orchard seat!
> And birds and flowers once more to greet,
> My last year's friends together." '

She stopped and in the silence which followed Arla wondered how many times she had recited the poem, how many students had ever listened. Then remembering the appointment with the barber who had said he didn't take appointments but would do so in this case (Miss Moss would have nothing to do with beauty parlours what with their fancy vanities and all that sort of malarky, she had said), and they had explained about her extraordinary age and about their limited staff, and he had relented. So Arla stood up, straightened her uniform and asked if Miss Moss was ready to leave. She was, she said. She had been dressed and waiting for well over an hour. She was always one for adequate preparation, she said.

She *was* dressed, and tastefully. She wore a crisp white long-sleeved blouse and a navy linen jumper which was not fitted but which looked smart nevertheless. Her stockings were smooth and she wore expensive navy leather oxfords. She carried a cane but used it in such a way as to suggest that it was she who made it hop about in front of her, gave it life and meaning, that the 'stick', as she called it, was dependent on her and not the other way around. She had pinned her grey hair flat behind her ears and now she flipped the wayward strands out of her eyes and muttered, 'I really don't know what he can do with this (cluck) mop, but we'll soon see, won't we.'

With that she stood and stroking the cover of her book once more, she placed it carefully in its appointed place with the other books on her dresser.

On the way downstairs and through the lower hallway of the lodge, Arla couldn't help wondering what point there was in living the way some of these people did, isolated, preoccupied with their medications and salves, their bowel movements, their tedious meals, their niggardly wardrobes, their insipid bath salts and cosmetics, their second-hand magazines and obituary sections in the morning newspaper, their gossip, and last but not least, the television set. It was on in the lounge now, at ten o'clock in the morning, loud, very loud so even the deaf could hear and the sound blared into the hall as they passed the doorway. Watching television seemed to be all they did, all some of them could do. That and wait.

'I see the fools are finished praying,' quipped Miss Moss peering through the lounge doorway. 'They never read you know,' she glowered and clucked at Arla as if to emphasize the full import of such neglect.

'I know,' said Arla. 'Some of them don't see so well no more.'

'*Anymore, anymore*! My good young woman, you must mind your speech. Discipline! That's all it takes. There is no excuse for sloppy grammar. Besides, Miss Pederson, you know very well their ignorance has nothing to do with failed sight. They *never* read. (Cluck).'

'Yes, I know,' Arla nodded though somewhat offended. She rarely made grammatical errors and this one was made half in jest. Miss Moss had not been amused.

They passed through a narrow hallway between the matrons' dining-room and front parlour. Miss Moss poked her head around the corner of the dining-room where she spied a large oak china cabinet. A flock of old and flowered teacups, formally arranged, kept watch over the musty room. 'I see they have another collection in here,' Miss Moss clucked, smiling wryly. She winked at Arla and Arla winked back.

By the time they reached the lodge veranda the cab had already pulled up to the curb at the base of the steps. Arla helped Miss Moss into the back seat of the cab, then got into the front seat with the driver. Looking back later, Arla thought this must have been her first mistake. She should have climbed into the back beside the old woman. Maybe that would have helped. But when the cabbie opened the front door for her she had responded, slipped in and crossed her legs. He climbed in behind the wheel and looked her over, focused on the cleavage of thigh at the hem of her uniform skirt. She knew he could see too much but she made no move to pull the skirt down. Instead she rested her arm on the back of the seat and said 'Rockyfoot Mall please, south entrance.' She tried to say it with professional force but her voice sounded thick, even to her.

And she took her turn, caressed the denim shoulders with her eyes, the soft dark hair on the arms and hands. The hands were broad, the fingers long and curled around the wheel. Later she couldn't remember talking to Miss Moss in the cab at all, knew she hadn't—not one word. Another mistake.

When they got out of the cab Miss Moss blinked, grew dizzy, faltered a little. With one hand, she leaned heavily on her cane and using the other hand, she sheltered her eyes from the glare of the sun. She wasn't used to so much brightness, Arla remembered. So Arla threaded her arm through the arm without the cane and began to guide the old woman saying, 'This way Miss Moss—it's not very far.' Even getting onto the curb was a laborious procedure, which surprised Arla who had hitherto thought of Miss Moss as a kind of lady metronome, her gait confident and measured, self-assured along the smooth brown linoleum of the lodge.

Although the distance to the barber's through the outdoor mall was very short, Miss Moss tired quickly, did not become animated and excited as Arla had thought she would away from the stagnant lodge air. Instead the old woman became progressively more confused and she began to wheeze. The barber shop was almost empty when they arrived. Obviously there had been no need for appointments, Arla thought.

The barber's name was Ed. She guessed he was about thirty. His skin was the colour of warm brown sand and rough. His hair was dark and long enough to fold in licentious curls around his neck. The way his hair had been styled reminded her of the pictures of the Romantic poets in Miss Moss' book.

'All right, ladies, who's it to be,' he cajoled. Arla thought it must be perfectly obvious to him from the phone call he had received and from her own duty clothes. Maybe he hoped it was her, she thought.

Miss Moss didn't move but remained standing in the shop doorway glaring with needle-like eyes at the barber. Arla nudged her forward. 'Miss Moss here wants to have her hair cut.' She found herself speaking for the old woman, something she had never before had to do with Miss Moss. 'Where would you like her to sit?'

'Right this way, ma'am,' and he waved a white linen cloth over the black leather back of the chair and with this movement seemed to fill the air with an herbal scent, Jade East, Arla thought it was. She loved the smell of Jade East, had tried to persuade David to use it but he wouldn't.

Miss Moss propped her cane against the side of the barber's chair. Arla had to help her climb onto the seat. She looked very frail, quaint, almost cute (a loathsome word to her) perched high on the chair. Her expensive leather oxfords did not reach the footrest and dangled in the air. She slowly removed the hairpins from either side of her head, shyly, as if she were performing a very personal, private act.

'And how will you have it cut, little lady?' asked the barber.

'Short,' Miss Moss responded abstractedly, 'yes, short if you please.'

That was the last intelligible word Miss Moss uttered in the barber shop until the job was finished. Arla couldn't understand it—this woman who had perfect command of the English language, whom Arla regarded as if she were the high priestess of poetry, of beautiful well-formed syllables, all of a sudden could not manage to say anything that made sense. Her speech was splintered, like the speech Arla remembered from the burnt-out old schizophrenics at the government hospital, hebaphrenics, they had called them, more shattered than split, one of the old staff had explained to her.

The old woman muttered incoherently about Prince Edward Island, her birthplace. She spoke to Ed as if he were someone else and she asked him garbled personal questions about people no one in the room knew, students from the darkest recesses of her past.

Arla watched her fidget in the chair and when Ed narrowly missed cutting her left ear lobe, Arla's efforts to calm her were useless. Ed finished the cut and flipped the linen cloth from her shoulders, brushed away the silver clippings which lay like lice on the back of the navy jumper. Then he gave her a hand mirror so she could inspect the job.

She riveted her needle eyes on the mirror and snapped, 'Sir, you are incompetent—but what can you expect—nowadays.' Arla hadn't realized how important it was for her to believe the best was in the past, *her* past, that everything was slipshod now, derelict, renegade, worthless.

Arla handed Ed a five dollar bill. He glanced at Miss Moss, then winked at Arla and Arla smiled weakly, knew that he and she were somehow, sadly, on the same side. She felt like a traitor.

Once outside, Arla automatically took Miss Moss' arm and determined to make up for her part in the conspiracy, she steered the old woman toward the restaurant two doors down—the Elite Cafe, the sign said. They would rest there, have a cup of tea and something special to eat. They would talk; things would be all right.

But things were not all right. They were the same and worse. Miss Moss wouldn't speak to her, even when Arla deliberately baited her by complimenting the food at the lodge. Ordinarily Miss Moss would have clucked and sputtered derisively, 'That—that sand!' But now she said nothing. She ignored the Boston cream pie which Arla had ordered for her remembering her say once that she favoured it above all other desserts. And she sipped sparingly at her tea, clattering the cup loudly and clumsily against the saucer each time she put it down.

Finally discouraged, Arla excused herself and called a cab. She paid the bill and they made their way slowly back to the curb at the south entrance. When they got to the curb Arla tightened her grip on the old woman's arm, said 'We're going up now, Miss Moss,' her voice amplified, as if the woman were deaf.

This time Arla told the cab driver to let them off at the corner of Maunley Park, about half a block from the lodge. Miss Moss couldn't walk far, she knew that, but Arla still harboured hope that even a few minutes resting on one of the benches beside a bed of daffodils and tulips would cheer her up, that the new spring growth would revive her, that she might still give a spring recitation.

The park was no different from the morning as Arla remembered it. If anything it was even more glorious, more opulent, more fragrant in the afternoon sun. But Miss Moss shuffled and staggered clumsily along the pebbled path. The old woman focused her eyes on the dull grey boulders lining the walkway as if she were afraid they could rise up and stone her to death if she gave them half a chance.

They passed by a circle of roses, small and blooming close to the ground. Arla's mother had called them moss roses. They were yellow and pink and red and purple, their vines and needle leaves all tangled together so that Arla couldn't tell one plant from another, couldn't trace the source of a single bloom. But they all looked soft and open-mouthed and Arla felt an urge to touch them, to run her finger round their inner lips. She was delighted. 'Look Miss Moss,' she said, 'roses! "Mid-May's eldest child, the coming musk rose"—Keats, right?' No answer. 'Miss Moss?' Still no answer. 'Let's go have a look.' Arla began to steer the old woman off the path, toward the flower bed.

'You may go yourself, Miss Pederson,' Miss Moss growled, 'but if you think this conduct is acceptable during working hours, I disagree and I'll have no part of it. I will not serve as an excuse for your irresponsible behaviour.' Then a cluck. Arla looked at her, baffled. Her eyes were full of contempt.

'No,' said Arla, confused and hurt. 'No, that's not what it is at all. I only wanted—I just wanted you to—' But the contempt on the old woman's face was solid. She could see. She gave up. What was the use?

Arla almost had to carry her back to the lodge. As for the blossoming crab-apple trees, the spirea, lilac and bridal wreath—all that had so intoxicated Arla in the early morning—Miss Moss did not hate them exactly, but she seemed to find them somehow distasteful. Once or twice she poked at a tulip or daffodil along the side of the path with her cane as she might have poked at the carcass of a dead cat. But she found no joy in them whatsoever, that was obvious to Arla. So they didn't stay, didn't rest on a bench, didn't say anything more—about poetry or anything else.

Walking back toward the lodge, Arla began to feel not so much hurt any longer, but anger toward the old woman. She felt herself withdraw, felt the old woman's power over her diminish, was relieved to find herself objective. Miss Moss was just an old woman. That's all she was.

Arla straightened her back, held her head high and looked directly at the lodge, walked with measured, confident steps, as if she were alone, as if she weren't attached to anyone, least of all linked through an old lady's arm.

From this distance, the lodge looked benign to Arla, though she knew better. But someone just walking along through the park, she thought, someone who could not see inside but who could only imagine what it was like might easily have thought that this was a fine building for housing the aged, ideal, in fact, located on the edge of the park as it was.

It sat like an aristocratic old woman, as aristocratic as anything could be in this country. But age had levied a heavy tax and if you really looked at it, you could see that the fine old three-storey building was approaching dilapidation. A long rectangular flat-roofed addition had been carelessly tacked on to the main building many years ago and was painted the same sweet cream colour as the old building.

This addition was really where all the lodgers lived, in small rooms with long narrow windows which dispassionately reflected the beautiful park back to itself and allowed only a niggardly light passage through their panes. The main building, grander and somehow retaining a part of its former dignity, was where the lodge office was located and where the matrons lived.

Arla and Miss Moss had barely reached the lodge steps when the old woman dug her fingernails into the flesh of Arla's upper arm and rasped, wheezing, 'I'm ill girl, I'm ill.' She heaved grotesquely two or three times and Arla rushed her toward the door. They managed to reach the dietary kitchen and Arla seated Miss Moss on the kitchen stool.

Her face was pale yellow, the colour of old wax. Again the woman began to heave. 'Bring the basin, for god's sake, girl, bring the basin,' she barked and the way she said it made Arla flinch.

Arla grabbed a white enamel washbasin out of one of the bottom cupboards and arrived back too late. The first eruption had already slithered from the old woman's mouth, curdled, milky, sour-reeking, onto her navy linen jumper.

Arla felt as if she were going to gag, but she held the basin in position under the woman's chin. With the next heave, Miss Moss' white dentures with the pink plastic gums clattered into the curdled mass at the bottom of the basin and Arla was sure she would be sick too, should be if she wasn't. The old woman's face was almost grey now. Her eyes, watering, avoided Arla's at all times. Her breathing was harsh, uneven. She heaved again.

This time, Arla turned her head away. Now she felt welling up within her a different kind of emesis, not only the disappointing turn of the day, but disillusionment, a disenchantment so deep it seemed to turn her inside out—a dry heave.

' "A thing of beauty is a joy forever," ' she recited to herself, her voice mocking the old woman's, her mouth twisted, her eyes glazed with anger—' "Its loveliness increases; it will never / Pass into nothingness; but still will keep / A bower quiet for us and a sleep / Full of sweet dreams and health and quiet breathing." '

KATHERINE GOVIER

b. 1948

Sociology

On the porch Ellen stood without looking behind her, like a pack horse at a crossing where she'd stopped many times before. Alec came up the steps: she heard the clinking as his hands sorted the keys from the change in his pocket. Then she heard a low, drawling voice.

'You folks stay right where you are, and this gun ain't going off. You keep right on looking at that door.'

She supposed it was time this happened. Their house was in what you called a transition area: you couldn't afford to buy there any more, but you weren't supposed to live there yet. Ellen enjoyed living there, however. She was morbidly fascinated by the differences in circumstances between themselves and the next-door neighbour who sat on his steps after dark and raised Newfoundland fishing songs to the sky. It fit with her view of the world, which was that as close as your hand were people who were not as lucky as you and therefore would like to kill you.

The man with the gun came up the stairs. He found Alec's wallet and took it. He took Ellen's purse. He asked for Alec's watch. The watch was gold with a gold band; it had been his father's, awarded for forty years' work in the factory in Quebec. Having died two months after retirement, his father had never worn it. When Alec reached 21 without a cigarette, his mother added the gold band and gave it to her only son. Wordlessly, Alec snapped it off his wrist and handed it over. Ellen groaned. Then the gunman got greedy.

'Your jewellery too,' he said. He took a handful of Ellen's hair and pulled it back to see if she was wearing earrings. She wasn't. She had only a couple of rings, her wedding band and one other, which was a pearl she'd gotten for her sixteenth birthday. Earlier that month the pearl had become tight, and she had switched it to a smaller finger. Now she pulled and got it off. The wedding ring was hopeless.

'I can't get it off,' she said to the mugger. 'My fingers are swollen because I'm pregnant.'

She looked him in the eye as she said the word pregnant. She felt she had never been in such danger; she had to enunciate the point of greatest risk. She was testing. It had been her fantasy during these last months that she would run into one of those maniacs who shot pregnant women in the belly or cut them open with a knife.

But the mugger looked back at her with a disinterested rage. Perhaps he would shoot her finger off and get the ring that way. It was still early in the evening, however, and a man was walking by only fifteen feet away, so the mugger just snarled and ran off.

Ellen and Alec attended pre-natal classes in a boys' club gymnasium in Cabbagetown. Alongside nine other pregnant women Ellen lay on the gym floor on a blanket brought from home and practised breathing patterns to prepare herself for labour. Her head on the pink and blue flowered pillowcase from their bedroom, she raised her hips and lowered them again; the water balloon that was her stomach went up and down. Then she got on hands and knees and Alec rolled tennis balls on her back as she humped it up and down like a dog trying to vomit. The idea was to make the birth natural.

They kept this up for six consecutive Thursdays. On the whole Ellen was disappointed in the classes. It was not the material so much as the other people. She'd thought their common predicament would promote instant friendship, but it had not. This was not for lack of effort on the part of the instructor, Riva, who used the word 'share' frequently. By the end they would develop a limited closeness, like that of people stuck together in a train which is liable to go off the tracks. But where they came from, where they would go afterward would not be mentioned.

Ellen tried to pin down some information. She learned that Gloria and Ted were born-agains. She divined that Miriam was at least forty and was not married to the man she came with. She explained them to Alec, who disapproved of her curiosity. The only ones she could not explain were Robert and June.

June was tall with blonde hair and moved hesitantly, but gracefully. Her eyes were cloudy blue. Sometimes the irises darted back and forth as if panicked, but Ellen did not believe she saw anything at all, not even light and shadow, because of the way she held her head. The way she held her head was the best part about her. Her carriage was like that of a large and elegant bird, her head alert and still as if she were listening for an alarm. Her seeing-eye dog lay at her feet, so devoted that he made the husband look like a redundancy. Robert was thickset, pimply, and sullen, and he watched June all the time.

June gave what the rest withheld; she laughed, she talked her fear. Ellen remembered best the day she sat on her metal stacking chair like an oracle, transparent eyelids showing the darting of sightless eyes. 'I can't believe it's me who's pregnant,' she said. 'I suppose because I've never seen myself.'

But isn't that what it's like, Ellen thought.

On the last night of class they watched a film of natural childbirth. Someone had brought popcorn, and they stared at the screen, silently passing the bucket. In the dark room Ellen could hear Robert's nasal voice very softly telling June what was being shown. 'The baby is coming out of the mother's body,' he said. Ellen and Alec both cried. Ellen thought that most of the other people in the class did too. She didn't know for sure though because when the lights went up, she didn't want to look too closely at their faces.

Riva packed the projector, and the women and their supporters made ready to leave. Swollen feet pushed back into bulging shoes, knees poked out to ten and two o'clock as legs strained to lift the immobile trunks. Stomachs first, they walked; the hard, heavy egg shapes pushing flesh away from the centre up to chest, arms, puffing the cheeks. Eyes red from strain, the ten making each other seem more grotesque than ever, the women made ready to go alone into the perilous future.

In the hospital, Ellen forgot all about her childbirth training and began screaming for an anaesthetic. The baby was two weeks late and labour was being induced with a drug. 'This baby must like you a lot,' said the doctor, turning up the dose again. 'He doesn't want to be born.' When he came, he wasn't breathing, so the nurse grabbed him and ran down the hall. 'My mother always said the cord around the neck meant they're lucky,' said Alec. Ellen lay draped in green sheets, being stitched up by the doctor. She felt robbed, raped, aching, and empty. She told Alec it was just like being mugged, and they both began to laugh.

'Tell that to Riva,' he said.

'But I don't feel bad. I feel—purified.'

'Anyone who feels purified after a mugging has a bad case,' said Alec.

In two hours they brought Alain back, cleaned up and swathed in a little white flannel blanket with a toque on his head to keep in the heat. Ellen began to think of the others in the class and how it would be for them. 'I wonder what the odds are in ten births,' she said, holding her son.

The party was at their place. There had been an RSVP on the invitation, but by the evening before, Ellen had only heard from seven of the ten couples. They were bringing potluck, and she wanted to know how many paper plates to get. She found the class list with the telephone numbers.

The first thing she discovered was that Miriam's phone had been disconnected. Ellen began to feel superstitious. The idea of losing track of one of the group, of not knowing about one of Alain's peers, startled her. She called information and found Miriam's new listing. When she reached it, it turned out she had a new baby boy, and everything was perfectly all right.

Ellen's confidence returned. She decided to call the others she hadn't heard from. The Uruguayan woman had a girl, but Ellen didn't understand any of the details because of the language problem. She hung up and dialed June. The telephone rang seven times, and no one answered.

That was odd; there was always someone home when you have a new baby. She waited until after dinner and then tried again. This time Robert answered. Ellen felt irritated by the sound of his voice; that was when she realized how much she wanted to speak with June. But she said who she was to Robert and asked if they were coming to the party.

Robert cleared a rasp from his throat. Then he sucked in air. 'I might as well be straight with you,' he said. 'We lost our baby.'

'Oh my God,' said Ellen. 'I'm so sorry. I'm so sorry to intrude.'

'We got the invitation,' he said, continuing as if she hadn't spoken, 'and we thought about coming. June wanted to, but I didn't.'

Ellen was silent. 'But anyway,' he said, 'it's kind of you to call.'

'Oh no, no I shouldn't have. I had no idea.'

'June didn't want to tell people. She wanted them just to find out,' he said, 'naturally.' Oh of course it would be natural, thought Ellen, and at whose expense? She was ready to cry with embarrassment. She was dying to know what happened too, but she couldn't ask. 'I am very sorry to intrude,' she said again, more firmly. 'It's a terrible thing.'

'Yes,' said Robert.

Then no one said anything. Robert started the conversation again with greater energy. 'But that doesn't stop me from asking about your baby.'

'We had a little boy,' Ellen said, 'and he's just fine.' She didn't tell Robert about the fright they'd had when Alain didn't breathe. It didn't seem proper to have complaints when you had a live son.

'Congratulations,' said Robert. 'Your baby will bring you a lifetime of happiness.' His tone was mean, humble but punishing. Ellen wanted to tell him that their lifetimes would never be so exclusive as he imagined, especially not now, but she didn't.

It was only as she told Alec that Ellen got mad. 'Riva knew; she could have spared me that call; why didn't she tell me?'

'Maybe sparing you wasn't her concern,' said Alec. He had not been in favour of holding this reunion. The incident only confirmed his belief that coming too close to strangers was asking for trouble. But he was sympathetic. He stood in the kitchen, holding Alain very tightly against his chest, and comforted his wife.

At noon the next day the new parents began to come up the narrow sidewalk. It was funny how nine babies looked like a mob. The oldest was three months, the youngest three weeks. Two of them had great swirls of black hair, but most were bald like Alain. One baby, born by Caesarian to the born-agains, had an angelic, calm face, but most were pinched and worried, unused to life on the outside. All through the house babies bounced on shoulders, slept on laps, sat propped in their infant seats. Now that it was all over, the parents could talk. They told birth stories about the heroism of wives, the callousness of physicians. Those whose babies slept through the night gloated over those whose babies didn't. It turned out one man was a lawyer like Alec and even had an office in the same block. One couple had a live-in already, and about half the women were going back to work.

Ellen got the sociology she wanted all along, and she was happy. Word had gone around about June, and everyone agreed it was better she hadn't come because it would have put such a damper on the party. The story was that she'd been two weeks overdue and had to go in for tests. At her second test the doctor told her the baby was dead. The worst part, all agreed, must have been having to carry the dead baby for another week. Finally June went through a difficult labour. There was nothing wrong with the baby that anyone could see.

When they told the story the women's eyes connected and their lips pressed down. It was as if a train had crashed and the person in the next seat had been crushed. They could not help but feel relief, lucky to have been missed. But with luck came fear that luck would not last, and the long, hard oval of dread that had quickened in Ellen along with her offspring was born.

Ellen wanted a picture of the babies together. They put Alain out first, in the corner of the couch, propped on his blanket. Others followed with Lila, Andrew, Evelyn, Adam, Ashley, Orin, Jackson, and William, nine prizes all in a row. Their heads bobbed down or dropped to the side; their mouths were open in round O's of astonishment. They fell asleep, leaning on their neighbour or they struck out with spastic hands and hit his face without knowing.

The parents had their cameras ready. They began to shoot pictures, laughing all the while. The line of babies was the funniest thing people had seen in ages. No one had imagined how funny it would be. The babies were startled. They looked not at each other but at the roomful of hysterical adults. One toppled, and the one next to him fell over onto him. Then the whole line began to collapse. Strange creatures with faces like cabbages and changing goblin shapes, tightly rolled in blankets or drooping into puddles of chin and stomach, they could have come from an alien star. The parents laughed, with relief at their babies' safe landing, and wonder at who they might be. The flashbulbs kept popping as the nine silly little bodies toppled and began to run together into a heap, until one of them, Evelyn, Ellen thinks it was, began to cry.

GUY VANDERHAEGHE

b.1951

Dancing Bear

The old man lay sleeping on the taut red rubber sheet as if he were some specimen mounted and pinned there to dry. His housekeeper, the widowed Mrs Hax, paused in the doorway and then walked heavily to the bedside window, where she abruptly freed the blind and sent it up, whirring and clattering.

She studied the sky. Far away , to the east, and high above the bursting green of the elms that lined the street, greasy black clouds rolled languidly, their swollen underbellies lit by the occasional shudder of lightning that popped in the distance. After each flash she counted aloud to herself until she heard the faint, muttering accompaniment of thunder. Finally satisfied, she turned away from the window to find Dieter Bethge awake and watching her cautiously from his bed.

'It's going to rain,' she said, moving about the room and grunting softly as she stooped to gather up his clothes and pile them on a chair.

'Oh?' he answered, feigning some kind of interest. He picked a flake of dried skin from his leg and lifted it tenderly to the light like a jeweller, intently examining its whorled grain and yellow translucence.

Sighing, Mrs Hax smoothed the creases of his carelessly discarded trousers with a soft, fat palm and draped them over the back of a chair. The old bugger made more work that a whole tribe of kids.

She glanced over her shoulder and saw him fingering the bit of skin between thumb and forefinger. 'Leave that be,' she said curtly. 'It's time we were up. Quit dawdling.'

He looked up, his pale blue eyes surprised. 'What?'

'Time to get up.'

'No', he said. 'Not yet.'

'It's reveille. No malingering. Won't have it,' she said, fixing an unconvincing smile on her broad face. 'Come on now, up and at 'em. We've slept long enough.'

'That rubber thing kept me awake last night,' he said plaintively.

'Every time I move it squeaks and pulls at my skin. There's no give to it.'

'Complainers' noses fall off,' Mrs Hax said absent-mindedly as she held a shirt up to her own wrinkled nose. She sniffed. It wasn't exactly fresh but she decided it would do, and tossed it back on the chair.

The old man felt his face burn with humiliation, as it did whenever he was thwarted or ignored. 'I want that damn thing off my bed!' he yelled. 'This is my bed! This is my house! Get it off!'

Mrs Hax truculently folded her arms across her large loose breasts and stared down at him. For a moment he met her gaze defiantly, but then he averted his eyes and his trembling jaw confirmed his confusion.

'I am not moved by childish tempers,' she announced. 'You haven't learned that yet?' Mrs Hax paused. 'It's about time you did. One thing about Mrs Hax,' she declared in a piping falsetto that betrayed her anger, 'is that when someone pushes her, she pushes back twice as hard. I am ruthless.' She assumed a stance that she imagined to be an illustration of ruthlessness, her flaccid arms akimbo. A burlesque of violence. 'So let me make this perfectly, crystal clear. That rubber sheet is staying on that bed until you forget your lazy, dirty habits and stop them accidents. A grown man,' she said disparagingly, shaking her head. 'I just got sick and tired of hauling one mattress off the bed to dry and hauling another one on. Just remember I'm not getting any younger either. I'm not up to heavy work like that. So if you want that rubber thing off, you try and remember not to pee the bed.'

The old man turned on his side and hid his face.

'No sulking allowed,' she said sternly. 'Breakfast is ready and I have plenty to do today. I can't keep it waiting forever.'

Dieter turned on to his back and fixed his eyes on the ceiling. Mrs Hax shook her head in exasperation. It was going to be one of those days. What went on in the old bastard's head, if anything? What made him so peculiar, so difficult at times like these?

She walked over to the bed and took him firmly by the wrist. 'Upsy-daisy!' she cried brightly, planting her feet solidly apart and jerking him upright. She skidded him to the edge of the bed, the rubber sheet whining a muffled complaint, and his hands, in startled protest and ineffectual rebellion, pawing at the front of her dress. Mrs Hax propped him upright while his head wobbled feebly from side to side and his tongue flickered angrily, darting and questing like a snake's.

'There,' she said, patting his hand, 'that's better. Now let's let bygones be bygones. A fresh start. I'll say, "Good morning, Mr Bethge!" and you answer, "Good morning, Mrs Hax!" '

He gave no sign of agreement. Mrs Hax hopefully cocked her head to one side and, like some huge, querulous bird, chirped, 'Good morning, Mr Bethge!' The old man stubbornly disregarded her, smiling sweetly and vacantly into space.

'Well,' she said, patting her dress down around her wide hips and heavy haunches, 'it's no skin off my teeth, mister.'

She stumped to the door, stopped, and looked back. The old man sat perched precariously on the edge of the bed, his white hair ruffled, tufted and crested like some angry heron. A pale shadow fell across the lower half of his face and threw his eyes into relief, so that they shone with the dull, glazed intensity of the most devout of worshippers.

Mrs Hax often saw him like this, mute and still, lost in reverie; and she liked to suppose that, somehow, he was moved by a dim apprehension of mortality and loss. Perhaps he was even overcome with memories of his wife, and felt the same vast yearning she felt for her own dead Albert.

She mustered a smile and offered it. ''Five minutes, dear,'' she said, and then closed the door softly behind her.

Bethge made no response. He was thinking—trying to pry those memories out of the soft beds into which they had so comfortably settled, sinking deeper and deeper under the weight of all the years, growing more somnolent and lazy, less easily stirred from sleep. He could no longer make his head crackle with the sudden, decisive leap of quick thought hurtling from synapse to synapse. Instead, memories had now to be pricked and prodded, and sometimes, if he was lucky, they came in revelatory flashes. Yet it was only old, old thoughts and things that came to him. Only they had any real clarity—and the sharpness to wound.

And now it was something about a bear. What?

Bethge, with a jerky, tremulous movement, swiped at the spittle on his chin with the back of his hand. In his agitation he crossed and recrossed his thin legs, the marbly, polished legs of a very old man.

Bear? He rubbed the bridge of his nose; somehow, it was important. He began to rock himself gently, his long, curving nose slicing like a scythe, back and forth, reaping the dim air of his stale little room. And as he swayed, it all began to come to him, and he began to run, swiftly, surely, silently back into time.

In the dark barn that smells of brittle straw, and sharply of horse dung, the knife is making little greedy, tearing noises. It is not sharp enough. Then he hears the hoarse, dragging whisper of steel on whetstone. Although he is afraid that the bear his father is skinning may suddenly rear to life, he climbs over the wall of the box stall and steps into the manger and crouches down. He is only five, so the manger is a nice, tight, comforting fit.

What a bear! A killer, a marauder who had left two sows tangled in their guts with single blows from his needle-sharp claws.

The smell of the bear makes him think of gun metal—oily, smoky. Each hair bristles like polished black wire, and when the sun catches the pelt it shines vividly, electrically blue.

The curved blade of the knife, now sharpened, slices through the bear's fat like butter, relentlessly peeling back the coat and exposing long, flat, pink muscles. As his father's busy, bloody hands work, Dieter feels a growing uneasiness. The strong hands tug and tear, wrestling with the heavy, inert body as if they are frantically searching for something. Like clay under a sculptor's hand, the bear begins to change. Each stroke of the knife renders him less bear-like and more like something else. Dieter senses this and crouches lower in the manger in anticipation.

His father begins to raise the skin off the back, his forearms hidden as the knife moles upward toward the neck. At last he grunts and stands. Reaches for the axe. In two sharp, snapping blows the head is severed from the trunk and the grinning mask flung into a corner. He gathers up the skin and carries it out to salt it and peg it down in the yard. Dieter hears the chickens clamouring to pick it clean.

He stares down into the pit of the shadowy stall. This is no bear. Stripped of its rich, glossy fur, naked, it is no bear. Two arms, two legs, a raw pink skin. A man. Under all that lank, black hair a man was hiding, lurking in disguise.

He feels the spiralling terror of an unwilling accomplice to murder. He begins to cry and call for his father, who suddenly appears in the doorway covered in grease and blood, a murderer.

From far away, he heard someone call him. 'Mr Bethge! Mr Bethge!' The last syllable of his name was drawn out and held like a note, so that it quivered in the air and urged him on with its stridency.

He realized he had been crying, that his eyes were filled with those unexpected tears that came so suddenly they constantly surprised and embarrassed him.

For a bear? But this wasn't all of it. There had been another bear; he was sure of it. A bear who had lived in shame and impotence.

He edged himself off the bed and painfully on to his knobbed, arthritic feet. Breakfast.

At breakfast they quarrel in the dreary, passionless manner of master and charge. He wants what she has, bacon and eggs. He tells her he hates porridge.

'Look,' Mrs Hax said, 'I can't give you bacon and eggs. Doctor's orders.'

'What doctor?'

'The doctor we saw last month. You remember.'

'No' It was true. He couldn't remember any doctor.

'Yes you do. Come on now. We took a ride downtown in a cab. Remember now?'

'No.'

'And we stopped by Woolworth's and bought a big bag of that sticky candy you like so much. Remember?'

'No.'

'That's fine,' she said irritably. 'You don't want to remember, there's nothing I can do. It doesn't matter, because you're not getting bacon and eggs.'

'I don't want porridge,' he said tiredly.

'Eat it.'

'Give me some corn flakes.'

'Look at my plate,' she said, pointing with her knife. 'I'm getting cold grease scum all over everything. Fight, fight. When do I get a moment's peace to eat?'

'I want corn flakes,' he said with a little self-satisfied tuck to the corners of his mouth.

'You can't have corn flakes,' she said. 'Corn flakes bung you up. That's why you eat hot cereal—to keep you regular. Just like stewed prunes. Now, which you want,' she asked slyly, 'Sunny Boy or stewed prunes?'

'I want corn flakes.' He smiled up happily at the ceiling.

'Like a stuck record.' She folded her hands on the table and leaned conspiratorially toward him. 'You don't even care if you eat or not, do you? You're just trying to get under my skin, aren't you?'

'I want corn flakes,' he said definitely and happily.

'I could kill that man,' she told her plate. 'Just kill him.' Then, abruptly, she asked. 'Where's your glasses? No, not there, in the other pocket. Okay, put them on. Now take a good long look at that porridge.'

The old man peered down intently into his bowl.

'That's fine. Take it easy. It's not a goddamn wishing-well. You see them little brown specks?'

He nodded.

'That's what this whole fight's about? Something as tiny as that? You know what this is. It's flax. And flax keeps you regular. So eat it.'

'I'm not eating it. What do I want with flax?' he asked quizzically.

'Sure you're crazy,' she said. 'Crazy like a fox.'

'I want some coffee.'

Mrs Hax slammed down her fork and knife, snatched up his cup, and marched to the kitchen counter. While she poured the coffee, Bethge's hand crept across the table and stole several strips of bacon from her plate. He crammed these clumsily into his mouth, leaving a grease shine on his chin.

Mrs Hax set his cup down in front of him. 'Be careful,' she said. 'Don't spill.'

Bethge giggled. In a glance, Mrs Hax took in his grease-daubed chin and her plate. 'Well, well, look at the cat who swallowed the canary. Grinning from ear-lobe to ear-lobe with a pound of feathers bristling from his trap.'

'So?' he said defiantly.

'You think I enjoy the idea of you pawing through my food?' Mrs Hax carried her plate to the garbage and scraped it with a flourish. 'Given all your dirty little habits, who's to know where your hands have been?' she asked, smiling wickedly. 'But go ahead and laugh. Because he who laughs last, laughs best. Chew this around for a bit and see how she tastes. You're not getting one single, solitary cigarette today, my friend.'

Startled, he demanded his cigarettes.

'We're singing a different tune now, aren't we?' She paused, 'N-O spells no. Put that in your pipe and smoke it.'

'You give them. They're mine.'

'Not since you set the chesterfield on fire. Not since then. Your son told me I was to give them out one at a time so's I could watch you and avoid "regrettable accidents." Thank God, there's some sense in the family. How he came by it I'm sure I don't know.'

The old man hoisted himself out of his chair. 'Don't you dare talk to me like that. I want my cigarettes—and I want them now.'

Mrs Hax crossed her arms and set her jaw. 'No.'

'You're fired!' he shouted 'Get out!' He flapped his arms awkwardly in an attempt to startle her into motion.

'Oho!' she said, rubbing her large red hands together in delight, 'fired am I? On whose say-so? Them that hires is them that fires. He who pays the piper calls the tune. And you don't do neither. Not a bit. Your son hired me, and your son pays me. I don't budge a step unless I get the word straight from the horse's mouth.'

'Get out!'

'Save your breath.'

He is beaten and he knows it. This large, stubborn woman cannot, will not, be moved.

'I want to talk to my son.'

'If you got information you feel your son should have, write him a letter.'

He knows this would never do. He would forget, she would steal the letter, conveniently forget to mail it. Justice demands immediate action. The iron is hot and fit for striking. He feels the ground beneath his feet is treacherous; he cannot become confused, or be led astray. One thing at a time. He must talk to his son.

'Get him on the telephone.'

'Your son, if you remember,' Mrs Hax said, 'got a little upset about all those long-distance phone calls—collect. And his words to me were, "Mrs Hax, I think it best if my father phone only on important matters, at your discretion." At my discretion, mind you. And my discretion informs me that this isn't one of those times. I've got a responsibility to my employer.'

'I'll phone him myself.'

'That I've got to see.'

'I will.'

'Yes, like the last time. Half the time you can't remember the city John lives in, let alone his street. The last time you tried to phone him you got the operator so balled up you would have been talking to a Chinaman in Shanghai if I hadn't stepped in and saved your bacon.'

'I'll phone. I can do it.'

'Sure you will. Where does John live?'

'I know.'

'Uh-huh, then tell me. Where does he live?'

'I know.'

'Jesus, he could be living in the basement and you wouldn't realize it.'

This makes him cry. He realizes she is right. But minutes ago he had known where his son lived. How could he have forgotten? In the sudden twistings and turnings of the conversation he has lost his way, and now he hears himself making a wretched, disgusting noise; but he cannot stop.

Mrs Hax feels she has gone too far. She goes over to him and puts an arm around his shoulders. 'Now see what's happened. You went and got yourself all upset over a silly old bowl of porridge. Doctor says you have to watch that with your blood pressure. It's no laughing matter.' She boosts him out of his chair. 'I think you better lie down on the chesterfield for a bit.'

Mrs Hax led him into the living-room and made him comfortable on the chesterfield. She wondered how an old bugger like him could make so much water: if he wasn't peeing, he was crying.

'You want a Kleenex?' she asked.

He shook his head and, ashamed, covered his face with his forearm.
'No harm in crying,' she said bleakly. 'We all do some time.'

'Leave me be.'

'I suppose it's best,' she sighed. 'I'll be in the kitchen clearing up if
you need me.'

Dieter lay on the chesterfield trying to stifle his tears. It was not an
easy job because even the sound of Mrs Hax unconcernedly clacking the
breakfast dishes reminded him of her monstrous carelessness with
everything. His plates, his feelings. He filled with anger at the notion
that he would never be nimble enough to evade her commands, or even
her wishes. That he cannot outwit her or even flee her.

The living-room gradually darkens as the low, scudding rain clouds
blot out the sun. He wishes it were a fine sunny day. The kind of day
which tricks you into believing you are young and carefree as you once
were. Like in Rumania before his family emigrated. Market days almost
always felt that way. People bathed in sun and noise, their wits honed to a
fine edge for trading and bartering. Every kind of people. The Jews with
their curling side-locks, the timid Italian tenant farmers, the Rumanians,
and people like himself, German colonists. Even a gypsy or two. Then
you had a sense of life, of living. Every good thing the earth offers or
man's hand fashions could be found there. Gaily painted wagons, piles
of potatoes with the wet clay still clinging to them; chickens, ducks and
geese; tethered pigs tugging their back legs and squealing; horses with
hooves as black and shining as basalt, and eyes as large and liquid-purple
as plums.

Nothing but a sheet of sky above and good smells below: pickled
herring and leather, paprika and the faint scent of little, hard, sweet
apples.

Innocence. Innocence. But then again, on the other hand—yes, well,
sometimes cruelty too. Right in the market.

A stranger arrived with a dancing bear once. Yes, the other bear, the
one he had forgotten. He led him by a ring through the nose. When a
crowd gathered, the man unsnapped the chain from the bear's nose and
began to play a violin. It was a sad, languorous tune. For a moment, the
bear tossed his head from side to side and snuffled in the dirt. This, for
him, was a kind of freedom.

But the man spoke to him sharply. The bear lifted his head and then
mournfully raised himself up on to his hind legs. His arms opened in a
wide, charitable manner, as if he were offering an embrace. His mouth
grinned, exposing black-speckled gums and sharp teeth. He danced,
slowly, ponderously, tiredly.

The music changed tempo. It became gay and lively. The bear began to prance unsteadily; the hot sun beat down on him. A long, glittering thread of saliva fell from his panting mouth on to the cinnamon-coloured fur of his chest.

Dieter, fascinated, tugged and pushed himself through the crowd. The bear hopped heavily from leg to leg. It was pathetic and comic. The pink tip of his penis jiggled up and down in the long hair of his loins. There was a wave of confused sniggering.

The trainer played faster and faster. The bear pirouetted wildly. He whirled and whirled, raising a small cloud of dust. The crowd began to clap. The bear spun and spun, his head lolling from side to side, his body tense with the effort of maintaining his human posture. And then he lost his balance and fell, blindly, with a bone-wrenching thump, onto his back.

The scraping of the violin bow stopped. The bear turned lazily on to his feet and bit savagely at his fleas.

'Up, Bruno!'

The bear whined and sat down. People began to laugh; some hooted and insulted the bear's master. He flourished the bear's nose lead and shouted, but the bear refused to budge. In the end, however, he could do nothing except attempt to save face; he bowed deeply, signifying an end to the performance. A few coins, a very few, bounced and bounded at his feet. He scooped them up quickly, as if he were afraid they might be reclaimed.

The audience began to disperse. Some hurried away to protect their wares. But Dieter had nothing to protect and nowhere to go, and so he stayed.

The sight of so many fleeing backs seemed to pique the bear. He got to his feet and began, once again, to dance. He mocked them. Or so it seemed. Of course, there was no music, but the bear danced much more daintily and elegantly than before, to a tune only he could perceive. And he grinned hugely, sardonically.

But the trainer reached up, caught his nose ring and yanked him down on all fours. He swore and cursed, and the bear breathed high, squeaking protests, feigning innocence.

This was unacceptable. This was rebellion. This was treason to the man who fed him, cared for him, taught him.

'Hairy bastard. Play the fool, will you,' the stranger muttered, wrenching and twisting the nose ring while the bear squealed with pain. The man punched his head, kicked him in the belly, shook him by the ears. 'Traitor. Ingrate.'

Dieter held his breath. His mind's eye had seen the bear suddenly strike, revenge himself. Yet nothing happened. Nothing; except the bear was beaten and battered, humiliated, even spat upon.

What shame he felt witnessing such an indignity, such complete indifference to the rightful pride of the bear. Such flaunting of the respect owed him for his size and his power. Couldn't the man realize what he did? Dieter wanted to shout out the secret. To warn him that appearances deceive. That a bear is a man in masquerade. Perhaps even a judge, but at the very least a brother.

But he couldn't. He ran away instead.

The house is still. He hears her footsteps, knows that she is watching him from the doorway. As always, she is judging him, calculating her words and responses, planning. Her plots deny him even the illusion of freedom. He decides he will not turn to look at her. But perhaps she knows this will be his reaction? Petulant, childish.

'I want to be left in peace.' He surprises himself. This giving voice to thought without weighing the consequences is dangerous.

But she doesn't catch it. 'What?'

'I don't chew my words twice,' he says.

She comes to the side of the chesterfield. 'Feeling better now?'

'Yes.'

'Truth?'

He nods

"Now mind, you got to be sure. I'm going down to the store. You need the bathroom?'

'No.'

'All right then. I'll just be a few minutes. That's all. You'll be okay?'

He is trying to think. All this talk, these interruptions, annoy him. He burns with impatience. 'Fine. That's fine. Good.' Suddenly, he feels happy. He can steal a little peace. He'll do it.

'I must be careful,' he tells himself aloud. How do these things slip out?

But Mrs Hax doesn't understand. 'With your blood pressure, I should say so.'

His luck, his good fortune, make him feel strong and cunning. Following her to the front door, he almost pities this fat woman. He watches her start down the street. It is lined with old and substantial homes, most of them painted modestly white, and their yards flourish tall, rough-barked elms. On this street, Mrs Hax, in her fluorescent orange rain slicker, appears ridiculous and inappropriate. Like a bird of paradise in an English garden. He waits until he loses sight of her at the first turning of the street.

He hurries to his business. His hands fumble with the chain on the front door; at last it is fastened. His excitement leaves him breathless, but he shuffles to the back door and draws the bolt. Safe. Mrs Hax is banished, exiled.

At first he thinks the noise is caused by the blood pulsing in his temples. But it fades to an insistent, whispering rush. Dieter goes to the window to look out. The rain is falling in a gleaming, thick curtain that obscures the outlines of the nearest house; striking the roadway, it throws up fine silvery plumes of spray. He decides to wait for Mrs Hax at the front door. He stands there and smells the coco matting, the dust and rubber boots. Somehow, he has forgotten they smell this way, a scent that can be peculiarly comforting when you are dry and warm, with a cold rain slashing against the windows.

And here is Mrs Hax trotting stiff-legged up the street with a shredding brown-paper bag huddled to her body. She flees up the walk, past the beaten and dripping caraganas, and around back to the kitchen door. He hears her bumping and rattling it.

Here she comes again, scurrying along, head bent purposefully, rain glancing off her plastic cap. But as she begins to climb the front steps he withdraws and hides himself in the coat closet. Her key rasps in the chamber, the spring lock snaps free. The door opens several inches but then meets the resistance of the chain, and sticks. She grumbles and curses; some fat, disembodied fingers curl through the gap and pluck at the chain. For a moment he is tempted to slam the door shut on those fingers, but he resists the impulse. The fingers are replaced by a slice of face, an eye and a mouth.

'Mr Bethge! Mr Bethge! Open up!'

Bethge stumbles out of the closet and lays his face along the door jamb, eye to eye with Mrs Hax. They stare at each other. At last she breaks the spell.

'Well, open this door,' she says irritably. 'I feel like a drowned cat.'

'Go away. You're not wanted here.'

'What!'

'Go away.'

Her one eye winks suspiciously. 'You do know who I am? This is Mrs Hax, your housekeeper. Open up.'

'I know who you are. I don't want any part of you. So go away.'

She shows him the soggy paper bag. 'I brought you a Jersey Milk.'
'Pass it through.'
Her one eye opens wide in blue disbelief. 'You open this door.'
'No.'
'It's the cigarettes, I suppose? All right, I give up. You can have your
damn cigarettes.'
'Go away.'
'I'm losing my patience,' she says, lowering her voice; 'now open this
door, you senile old fart.'
'Old fart yourself. Old fat fart.'
'You wait until I get in there. There'll be hell to pay.'
He realizes his legs are tired from standing. There is a nagging pain in
the small of his back. 'I've got to go now,' he says. 'Goodbye,' and he
closes the door in her face.
He is suddenly very light-headed and tired, but nevertheless exultant.
He decides he will have a nap. But the woman has begun to hammer at
the door.
'Stop it,' he shouts. He makes his way to his bedroom on unsteady
legs; in fact, one is trailing and he must support himself by leaning
against the wall. What is this?
The bedroom lies in half-light, but he can see the red rubber sheet. It
must go. He tugs at it and it resists him like some living thing, like a
limpet clinging to a rock. His leg crumples, his mouth falls open in
surprise as he falls. He lands loosely like a bundle of sticks, his legs and
arms splayed wide, but feels nothing but a prickling sensation in his
bladder. No pain, nothing. There are shadows everywhere in the room,
they seem to float, and hover, and quiver. He realizes the front of his
pants is wet. He tries to get up, but the strength ebbs out of his limbs and
is replaced by a sensation of dizzying heaviness. He decides he will rest a
minute and then get up.
But he doesn't. He sleeps.
Mrs Hax waited under the eaves for the rain to abate. It fell for an hour
with sodden fury, and then began to slacken into a dispirited drizzle.
When it did, she picked her way carefully through the puddles in the
garden to where the hoe lay. With it, she broke a basement window and
methodically trimmed the glass out of the frame. Then she settled herself
onto her haunches and, gasping, wriggled into the opening. She closed
her eyes, committed her injuries in advance to Bethge's head, and then
let herself drop. She landed on one leg, which buckled, and sent her
headlong against the gas furnace, which set every heat vent and duct in

the building vibrating with a deep, atonal ringing. Uninjured, she picked herself up from the floor. Her dignity bruised, her authority wounded, she began to edge her way through the basement clutter toward the stairs.

Dieter Bethge woke with a start. Some noise had broken into his dream. It had been a good and happy dream. The dancing bear had been performing for him under no compulsion, a gift freely given. It had been a perfect, graceful dance, performed without a hint of the foppishness or studied concentration that mars the dance of humans. As the bear had danced he had seemed to grow, as if fed by the pure, clear notes of the music. He had grown larger and larger, but Dieter had watched this with a feeling of great peace rather than alarm.

The sun glinted on his cinnamon fur and burnished his coat with red, winking light. And when the music stopped, the bear had opened his arms very wide in a gesture of friendship and welcome. His mouth had opened as if he were about to speak. And that was exactly what Dieter had expected all along. That the bear would confide in him the truth, and prove that under the shagginess that belied it, there was something that only Dieter had recognized.

But then something had broken the spell of the dream.

He was confused. Where was he? His hand reached out and touched something smooth and hard and resisting. He gave a startled grunt. This was wrong. His mind slipped backward and forward, easily and smoothly, from dream to the sharp, troubling present.

He tried to get up. He rose, trembling, swayed, felt the floor shift, and fell, striking his head on a chest of drawers. His mouth filled with something warm and salty. He could hear something moving in the house, and then the sound was lost in the tumult of the blood singing in his veins. His pulse beat dimly in his eyelids, his ears, his neck and fingertips.

He managed to struggle to his feet and beat his way into the roar of the shadows which slipped by like surf, and out into the hallway.

And then he saw a form in the muted light, patiently waiting. It was the bear.

'Bear?' hc asked, shuffling forward, trailing his leg.

The bear said something he did not understand. He was waiting.

Dieter lifted his arms for the expected embrace, the embrace that would fold him into the fragrant, brilliant fur; but, curiously, one arm would not rise. It dangled limply like a rag. Dieter felt something strike the side of his face—a numbing blow. His left eyelid fell like a shutter.

He tried to speak but his tongue felt swollen and could only batter noiselessly against his teeth. He felt himself fall but the bear reached out and caught him in the warm embrace he desired above all.

And so, Dieter Bethge, dead of a stroke, fell gently, gently, like a leaf, into the waiting arms of Mrs Hax.

Biographical Notes

EDNA ALFORD (b. 1947) was born in Turtleford, Saskatchewan, and now lives in Livelong, Saskatchewan. For a time she lived in Calgary, where she was one of the three founding editors of the 'little magazine' *Dandelion*. Her stories appeared in *Dandelion*, *Prism International*, *The Fiddlehead*, *The Journal of Canadian Fiction*, and were broadcast on CBC radio.

Alford's first collection of stories, *A Sleep Full of Dreams*, was published in 1981; it contains linked stories about a group of senior citizens living in a nursing home, and about young Arla, who works there. 'Mid-May's Eldest Child' is reprinted from that book. The title story of her second collection, *The Garden of Eloise Loon* (1986), first appeared in the anthology *Saskatchewan Gold*. Edna Alford was writer-in-residence at the Regina Public Library in 1985–6.

SANDRA BIRDSELL (b. 1942) grew up in rural Manitoba and now lives in Winnipeg. She began publishing her short stories in 'little magazines'—particularly those in western Canada, such as *Grain*, *Capilano Review*, *NeWest Review*, and *Prairie Fire*—and has been an active member of the Manitoba Writers' Guild for a number of years. Her first collection, *Night Travellers* (1982), consists of a series of linked stories set in the fictitious Manitoba town of Agassiz. *Ladies of the House* (1984), her second book, contains stories of rural Manitoba and others that explore the often gritty working-class life of Winnipeg.

Sandra Birdsell has written film scripts for the National Film Board, including dramatizations of her own work, and plays for Winnipeg theatres. She won a National Magazine Award for fiction, and in 1984 received the Gerald Lampert Award, administered by the League of Canadian Poets and given in alternate years for poetry and prose fiction. 'The Wild Plum Tree' is reprinted from *Night Travellers*.

CLARK BLAISE (b. 1940) was born in North Dakota of a French-Canadian father and an English-Canadian mother. In a recent book, *Resident Alien* (1986), a collection of short stories and autobiographical sketches, he wrote: 'I lived my childhood in the deep, segregated South, my adolescence in Pittsburgh, my manhood in Montreal, and have started my middle age somewhere in middle America'. Along the way, like a number of Canadian writers, he studied at the Writer's Workshop at the University of Iowa, and he has taught at several universities in the United States and at Concordia in Montreal and York University in Toronto.

Blaise's books include *A North American Education* (1973) and *Tribal Justice*

(1974), both collections of short stories; 'A Class of New Canadians' is reprinted from *A North American Education*. His novel *Lunar Attractions* (1979) won the *Books in Canada* award for the best first novel of the year, and a second novel *Lusts* was published in 1983. Blaise and his wife, the Indian-born writer Bharati Mukherjee—whose work is also represented in this book—collaborated on an unusual travel book about a visit to India, *Days and Nights in Calcutta* (1977).

GEORGE BOWERING (b. 1935) was born and raised in the Okanagan Valley in the interior of British Columbia, and became an RCAF aerial photographer after finishing high school. He then studied at the University of British Columbia and later taught at the University of Calgary and at Sir George Williams College (now Concordia University) in Montreal. At UBC Bowering became one of the editors of the 'little magazine' *Tish*, which was influenced by the Black Mountain school of contemporary American poets. He now teaches at Simon Fraser University in Vancouver.

Bowering, who has written poetry, fiction, and criticism, won a Governor General's Award for poetry in 1968 for two books, *Rocky Mountain Foot* and *The Gangs of Kosmos*. In 1980 his *Burning Water*, a novel about George Vancouver's search for the Northwest Passage, won him a Governor General's Award for fiction. He has edited short-story collections ranging from *Great Canadian Sports Stories* (1979) to the experimental *Fiction of Contemporary Canada* (1980). His many books of poetry include *Selected Poems: Particular Accidents* (1980) and a collection of long poems, *West Window* (1982). He has also written a critical study of his fellow poet Al Purdy (1970) and the lively and opinionated *The Mask in Place: Essays on Fiction in North America* (1983).

BARRY CALLAGHAN, the son of Morley Callaghan, was born in 1937 in Toronto, where he still lives, and educated at St Michael's College, University of Toronto. Since the mid-1960s he has taught contemporary literature at Atkinson College, York University. He has had a parallel and very active career in journalism as a writer and commentator on radio and television and as a contributor to such magazines as *Toronto Life* and *Saturday Night*. For a half-dozen years in the late 1960s he edited and wrote extensively for a lively, wide-ranging, and frequently controversial weekly book page in the Toronto *Telegram*. He is publisher and editor of the literary quarterly *Exile*, and under the imprint Exile Editions also publishes books, with an emphasis on imaginative literature and the visual arts.

Barry Callaghan's stories have appeared in *Saturday Night*, *Exile*, *The Ontario Review*, and frequently in the English magazine *Punch*. Notable for their literary sophistication and for the sympathy with which he writes about the gamblers, whores, gays, and other non-conformists, they have been collected in *The Black Queen Stories* (1983), from which the title story is reprinted here. Callaghan is also a poet, the author of a complex and ambitious long poem, *The Hogg Poems and Drawings* (1978), and of *As Close as We Came*, a collection that appeared in

1983. He edited an anthology of Canadian love poems in English and French, *Lords of Winter and of Love* (1983), and gathered together *The Lost and Found Stories of Morley Callaghan* (1985). He has also edited a major anthology, *Alchemists in Winter: Canadian Poetry in French and English* (1986).

MORLEY CALLAGHAN (b. 1903) was born in Toronto where he has lived most of his life. Educated at St Michael's College, University of Toronto, and in law at Osgoode Hall, he was called to the bar but never practised law. While he was a student he worked during the summers on the Toronto *Daily Star*, where he met Ernest Hemingway. Callaghan's first novel, *Strange Fugitive* (1928), and his first collection of short stories, *A Native Argosy* (1929), were both published by Scribner's in New York. In 1929 Callaghan and his wife Loretto went to Paris, where his stories had been appearing in the 'little magazines'. There he met Hemingway again, Scott Fitzgerald, James Joyce, Ford Madox Ford, and other expatriate writers and artists. He later described this period of his life in the memoir *That Summer in Paris* (1963).

After returning to Toronto, Callaghan continued to publish his novels and short stories throughout the 1930s. Novels from that period include *A Broken Journey* (1932), *Such Is My Beloved* (1934), and *More Joy in Heaven* (1937). His short stories appeared in such magazines as *The New Yorker, Atlantic Monthly*, and *Esquire*, and in a second collection, *Now That April's Here* (1936). This prolific period came to an end in the late 1930s, and during the Second World War Callaghan was chairman of the CBC radio program *Of Things to Come* and was later a regular panelist on the radio program *Now I Ask You* and a frequent guest on the TV series *Fighting Words*.

In 1951 Callaghan returned to fiction with one of his major novels, *The Loved and The Lost*, and in 1959 more than fifty of his short stories were gathered together in *Morley Callaghan's Stories*; 'Last Spring They Came Over' has been reprinted from that book. Novels that have appeared since the 1950s include *A Passion in Rome* (1961), *Close to the Sun Again* (1977), and *A Time for Judas* (1983). Two dozen stories from the 1930s and 1940s not previously published in a book have been collected in *The Lost and Found Stories of Morley Callaghan* (1985). Among the many awards Callaghan has won are a Governor General's Award for *The Loved and the Lost*, and in 1970 the Molson Prize and the Royal Bank Award.

AUSTIN CLARKE was born (in 1932) and brought up in Barbados, and moved to Canada in 1955 to study at the University of Toronto. In 1959–60 he was a reporter in Timmins and Kirkland Lake, Ontario, and then worked as a free-lance broadcaster for the CBC. He taught creative writing at Yale, Duke, and other American universities in the late 1960s and early 1970s. For a time he was general manager of the Caribbean Broadcasting Corporation in Barbados. He now lives in Toronto, where he is a vice-chairman of the Ontario Film Review Board.

Clarke's first book, *Survivors of the Crossing*, a novel about life in Barbados, appeared in 1964. Three years later he published *The Meeting Point*, the first novel in a trilogy about the lives of Caribbean immigrants in Toronto; the next two books were *Storm of Fortune* (1971) and *The Bigger Light* (1975). He has also written a political novel, *The Prime Minister* (1977), set in a developing nation, and the first volume of an autobiography, *Growing Up Stupid Under the Union Jack* (1980). Clarke's short stories, set in Barbados, Canada, and the United States, were collected in *When He Was Free and Young and He Used to Wear Silks* (1971 Canada; 1973 U.S.)—'Griff!' was included in that book—and *Nine Men Who Laughed* (1986) in the Penguin Short Fiction series.

MATT COHEN (b. 1942) was born in Kingston, Ontario, and grew up in Ottawa. He now lives in Toronto, where he has been active in the literary community as an editor of fiction for Coach House Press, in the Writers' Union of Canada, and as a reviewer and commentator on the literary scene.

Cohen began his career as a writer of fiction with an experimental novel *Korsoniloff* (1969). His second novel, *Johnny Crackle Sings* (1971), uses the Ottawa Valley as its setting. In the next few years Cohen published five ambitious novels; three of them, beginning with *The Disinherited* (1974), take place in the fictitious Eastern Ontario town of Salem. (Cohen spends some of his time on a farm he owns north of Kingston in what might be described as 'Salem' country.) In 1984 he published a historical novel, *The Spanish Doctor*. His short stories have been collected in several books, from *Columbus and the Fat Lady* (1972) to *Café Le Dog* (1983). 'The Eiffel Tower in Three Parts' is a new story that is here receiving its first publication.

ISABELLA VALANCY CRAWFORD (1850–87) was born in Dublin and came to Canada in 1858, where her father became the first doctor in Paisley, Ontario. They later moved to Lakefield and then to Peterborough, where Dr Crawford died in 1875. Isabella's only surviving sister died the next year. In the mid 1860s Dr Crawford had been tried and convicted for misappropriation of public funds while he was township treasurer in Paisley. After his death Isabella and her mother lived in poverty in Toronto until Isabella died early of heart failure.

The history of Isabella Crawford's writing is almost as depressing as the history of her family. She wrote short stories and novelettes largely for the American magazine market. Her literary reputation is based on her poems, but no reliable and complete collection of her poetry exists. Much of her poetry and fiction exists in manuscript or in magazines in the Lorne Pierce Collection of the Douglas Library at Queen's University, Kingston. A *Selected Stories of Isabella Valancy Crawford*, edited by Penny Petrone, was finally published in 1975 and a Crawford symposium was conducted at the University of Ottawa in 1977. Poets Dorothy Livesay and James Reaney have joined some modern scholars in attempting to focus attention on her work. The theme of 'Extradited', her best-known story, is betrayal.

MARIAN ENGEL (1933–85) was born in Toronto but grew up in smaller Ontario cities—Sarnia, Galt, Hamilton—and various aspects of the province later played important roles in her fiction. Educated at McMaster and McGill Universities, she studied French literature in Provence and taught for a while in Cyprus. She married, and later divorced, the writer and broadcaster Howard Engel. The first chairperson of the Writers' Union, she worked until her death towards improving the situation of her fellow writers in Canada.

Marian Engel wrote radio scripts, journalism, two books for children, and published two collections of short stories, *Inside the Easter Egg* (1975), and *The Tattooed Woman*, which appeared posthumously in 1985. Most of her fiction—the bulk of which consists of seven novels published between 1968 and 1981—reflects her life as a writer and a working mother. Her novels include *No Clouds of Glory* (later re-issued as *Sara Bastard's Notebook*); *The Honeyman Festival*; *Bear*, which achieved both a scandalous reputation and an admiring critical reception; and *The Glassy Sea* and *Lunatic Villas*.

'Anita's Dance', reprinted here, is included in The *Tattooed Woman* in the Penguin Short Fiction series.

TIMOTHY FINDLEY (b. 1930) was born and educated in Toronto. He began a career as an actor, working for the Stratford (Ontario) Shakespearean Festival in its first season in 1953, and later touring in England, Europe, and the United States as a contract player with H.M. Tennant. After returning to Canada, Findley worked in radio, television, and the theatre before making writing his major career in 1962.

His first four novels are all, in their different ways and with their varied settings, concerned with the horrors of a nightmarish society. *The Last of the Crazy People* (1967) takes place in a long, hot summer in Southern Ontario; *The Butterfly Plague* (1969) is set in Hollywood. *The Wars* (1977), set in Canada and overseas during the First World War, won a Governor General's Award, has been widely translated, and was filmed under the direction of Robin Phillips. *Famous Last Words*, a fictional work peopled with real persons, has the most experimental and filmic structure of all his novels. His latest novel is *The Telling of Lies a Mystery* (1986).

Reprinted here is the title story from *Dinner Along The Amazon*, published in 1984 in the Penguin Short Fiction series.

MAVIS GALLANT (b. 1922). Born in Montreal and educated in seventeen different public, private, and convent schools in Canada and the United States, Mavis Gallant worked briefly for the National Film Board and then on the Montreal *Standard* (a weekly newspaper that was a competitor of the *Star Weekly*; both papers are now gone). She left Montreal in 1950 and has lived in Paris ever since. She returned to Canada in 1983–4 to be writer-in-residence at the University of Toronto.

Gallant has published two novels—*Green Water, Green Sky* (1959) and *A*

Fairly Good Time (1970)—and five collections of short stories. Almost all her stories first appeared in *The New Yorker*, to which she began contributing in 1951. Her short-story collections are: *The Other Paris* (1956), *My Heart Is Broken* (1959), *The Pegnitz Junction* (1973), *From the Fifteenth District* (1979), and *Home Truths* (1981), which won a Governor General's Award. (An American edition of this collection of her Canadian stories was published in 1985 to highly favourable reviews.) Her latest collection is *Overhead in a Balloon: Stories of Paris* (1985). A selection of Gallant's stories, *The End of the World and Other Stories*, edited by Robert Weaver, was published in the New Canadian Library in 1974. 'The Ice Wagon Going Down the Street' is reprinted from *Home Truths*.

Mavis Gallant has also written much distinguished non-fiction. *The New Yorker* published (in September 1968) her two-part account of the student riots in Paris in the spring of 1968—'The Events in May: A Paris Notebook'—and a long essay that served as the introduction to *The Affair of Gabrielle Russier* (1971), about a thirty-year-old teacher of languages in Marseilles who had a love affair with a sixteen-year-old male student and later killed herself. This introduction appears in *Paris Notebooks: Essays and Reviews* (1986).

HUGH GARNER was born in 1913 in Batley, Yorkshire, and died in Toronto in 1979. In 1919 Garner's father moved his family from England to Toronto, where he soon deserted them, leaving the mother to raise four children in the Cabbagetown area of the city. Garner later described this part of Toronto as 'a sociological phenomenon, the largest Anglo-Saxon slum in North America'. His novel *Cabbagetown*, published in a badly cut paperback edition in 1950, eventually appeared in its original length in 1968.

Garner, who left school at sixteen, worked during the Depression at unskilled jobs and rode freight trains across North America. He joined the Abraham Lincoln Battalion of the International Brigade and fought for the Loyalists in the Spanish Civil War. During the Second World War he served in the Canadian Navy on convoy duty in the Atlantic. The novel *Storm Below* (1949) is based on his naval experiences. At the end of the war Hugh Garner became a full-time writer. Among his many books are the novels *The Silence on the Shore* (1962) and *The Intruders* (1976), both set in Toronto, and an autobiography, *One Damn Thing After Another* (1973). He won a Governor General's Award in 1963 for *Hugh Garner's Best Stories*. Garner also wrote three police novels—*Sin Sniper* (1970), *Death in Don Mills* (1975), and *Murder Has Your Number* (1978)—all set in Toronto.

Garner's most successful stories are realistic studies of outsiders in Canadian society. He has written about alcoholics, an itinerant evangelist, a displaced person trying to make a fresh start at the end of the Second World War by working in the tobacco fields on the north shore of Lake Erie, and a dispossessed Indian family trying to survive on the fringes of white society in Northern Ontario—in 'One, Two, Three Little Indians'.

KATHERINE GOVIER, born in Edmonton in 1948, studied at the University of Alberta. There she was encouraged as a young writer by Rudy Wiebe and Dorothy Livesay. In 1971 she received an M.A. from York University in Toronto, where she now teaches a course in creative writing. She has written articles for the Toronto *Globe & Mail*, the Toronto *Star*, *Saturday Night*, and *Toronto Life*, and has won two national journalism awards.

Govier has written two novels, *Random Descent* (1979) and *Going Through the Motions* (1982). In the late 1970s and 1980s her short stories appeared with increasing frequency in a variety of Canadian magazines; many of them, including 'Sociology', are about young urban professionals living in Toronto. Govier's first collection, *Fables of Brunswick Avenue*, was published in 1985 in the Penguin Short Fiction series.

SUSIE FRANCES HARRISON (1859–1935) was born in Toronto and educated there and in Montreal, where she developed an interest in French-Canadian culture that was to have a continuing influence on her writing. She married a professional musician and they lived in Ottawa for a few years, but after 1887 Toronto was her permanent home.

Harrison, who became well known as a professional pianist and vocalist, was principal of the Rosedale Branch of the Toronto Conservatory of Music for twenty years. An authority on French-Canadian folksongs, she was also a prolific writer of articles, essays, short stories, and poetry, and a regular contributor to newspapers and literary magazines in Canada, Britain, and the United States. Her first book, *Crowded Out and Other Sketches* (1886), was a collection of stories, some of which showed the influence of Edgar Allan Poe. She was best known in her own time as a poet, and her most ambitious poetry collection, *Pine, Rose, and Fleur de lis*, was published in 1891. French-Canadian settings appear in her two novels, *The Forest of Bourg-Marie* (1898) and the melodrama *Ringfield* (1914).

JACK HODGINS (b. 1938) was born in the Comax Valley on Vancouver Island and raised on a farm. His father was a logger and his grandfather had been a pioneer farmer. Educated at the University of British Columbia, Hodgins taught high-school English in Nanaimo, was writer-in-residence at Simon Fraser University in Vancouver and at the University of Ottawa, and now teaches creative writing at the University of Victoria, Victoria, B.C. He has published two novels and two collections of short stories. 'By the River', reprinted here, is from *Spit Delaney's Island*, a collection of stories published in 1976. That book was followed by two novels: *The Invention of the World* (1977) and *The Resurrection of Joseph Bourne* (1978). A collection of linked stories, *The Barclay Family Theatre*, appeared in 1981. Since that time, in addition to working with student writers in his various university postings, Hodgins has been writing a new novel. Most of his fiction is set on Vancouver Island in communities similar to the one in which he was born and brought up. He views those communities through the eyes of a 'magic realist', and his influences are international: William Faulkner, and Gabriel Garcia Marquez's *One Hundred Years of Solitude*.

HUGH HOOD (b. 1928) grew up in Toronto and received his Ph.D. from the University of Toronto in 1955. He taught for a few years in the United States, then joined the English department at the Université de Montréal, where he has remained since 1961.

Hood has published short stories, novels, memoirs, journalism, and sports biographies. He has produced half-a-dozen collections of short stories, including *Flying a Red Kite* (1962), whose title story is reprinted here; *Around the Mountain: Scenes from Montreal Life* (1967); *The Fruit Man, The Meat Man and The Manager* (1971); *Dark Glasses* (1976); and *August Nights* (1985). Hood's other interests include painting, film, and the theatre, and his first novel, *White Figure, White Ground* (1964), was about a painter. In 1975 he published the first of the projected twelve novels in his *New Age* series, *The Swing in the Garden*. The series, which explores Canadian society and the city of Toronto at various stages in its history, is now approaching the halfway point.

W P KINSELLA was born in 1935 in Edmonton, Alta. He worked as a civil servant, a life-insurance salesman, a cab driver, and as the manager of a pizza parlour before enrolling in the creative writing department at the University of Victoria in Victoria, B.C. Later he attended the Writer's Workshop at the University of Iowa. He taught for several years at the University of Calgary, and now lives as a full-time writer in White Rock, B.C. Kinsella has written four books of Indian stories, beginning with *Dance Me Outside* in 1977. In 1980 he published a collection of baseball stories, *Shoeless Joe Jackson Comes to Iowa*, and in 1982 a novel, *Shoeless Joe*, which won the Houghton Mifflin Literary Fellowship and the 'Books in Canada' First Novel Award. Both *Shoeless Joe* and *Dance Me Outside* have been optioned for film productions, and a second baseball novel, *The Iowa Baseball Confederacy*, was published in 1986.

In 'The Thrill of the Grass' and his other baseball stories Kinsella makes exuberant use of the traditions, myths, and present-day issues that enliven a sport that has attracted so many fiction writers in Canada and the United States. This story was broadcast on the CBC radio program 'Anthology' and the CBC stereo program 'Storyline' and later became the title story of a second collection of baseball stories, published in the Penguin Short Fiction series in 1984.

MARGARET LAURENCE (b. 1926) was born in Neepawa, Manitoba, which became the model for 'Manawaka', the prairie town in her fiction. Her parents died when she was young and she was brought up by her aunt. After graduating from United College in Winnipeg in 1947, she worked as a reporter for the Winnipeg *Citizen* and in the same year married Jack Laurence, a civil engineer. From 1950 to 1957 they lived in Africa, first in Somalia and then in Ghana just before its independence. After separating from her husband in 1962, Laurence spent ten years in England. She now lives in Lakefield, Ontario.

Laurence's African experience was fruitful for her as a writer: in 1960 she published an African novel, *This Side Jordan*; in 1962 a collection of African stories, *The Tomorrow-Tamer*; and a year later a memoir of her life in Somalia, *The Prophet's Camel Bell*. Meanwhile she was beginning her series of four Manawaka novels: *The Stone Angel* (1961), *A Jest of God* (1966), *The Fire-Dwellers* (1966), and *The Diviners* (1974). Interspersed with her fiction were several books for children and a collection of magazine articles, *Heart of a Stranger* (1976). Laurence has received many honorary degrees, literary prizes, and awards, and served as chancellor of Trent University in Peterborough, Ontario, beginning in 1980.

Many of Margaret Laurence's stories and novels have been dramatized for radio and television, and one of her children's books, *The Olden Days Coat* (1979), which was produced for television by Atlantis Films in Toronto, has been shown annually in the Christmas season. Atlantis is preparing to shoot a feature film based on *The Stone Angel*. Laurence's Manawaka stories were published in *A Bird in the House* (1970); 'The Loons' is from that collection.

STEPHEN LEACOCK (1869–1944) was born in Swanmore, England. His father failed as a farmer in South Africa and then in Kansas, and in 1876 settled his family on a farm in the Lake Simcoe area of Ontario. After failing once again, the father deserted his wife and eleven children. The third child in the family, Stephen was educated in local schools and at Upper Canada College, where he later taught for ten years. He then completed a degree in modern languages at the University of Toronto, and did graduate work in political economy at the University of Chicago under Thorstein Veblen. Leacock taught in the Department of Economics and Political Science at McGill University in Montreal, and became head of the department there.

A distinguished, sometimes controversial teacher and economist, Leacock acquired a world-wide audience as a writer and literary figure. He published almost thirty books of humour, beginning with *Literary Lapses* in 1910. *Arcadian Adventures with the Idle Rich* (1914) and *Sunshine Sketches of a Little Town* (1912) are generally considered to be his most successful works of fiction. *Sunshine Sketches*, a series of linked stories portraying life in the town of Mariposa (modelled on Orillia, Ontario), includes 'The Marine Excursion of the Knights of Pythias', reprinted here.

NORMAN LEVINE (b. 1923). In *Canada Made Me* Norman Levine has described how he grew up in the Jewish community in Ottawa's Lower Town. He served in the RCAF during the Second World War and afterwards studied at McGill University. He went to England in the late 1940s and lived there—for much of the time in St Ives, Cornwall—until his return to Canada in 1980. He now lives in Toronto. He has been a full-time writer for most of his adult life.

Levine published a collection of poetry, *The Tight-Rope Walker*, in 1950 and a war novel, *The Angled Road*, two years later. In the mid 1950s he began to work on a book that would combine autobiographical material with an investigation of Canadian society from the underside in the manner of Henry Miller and George Orwell. That book became *Canada Made Me*, published in England and the United States in 1958; but because of its disenchanted view of life in this country, there was no Canadian edition until 1979.

Levine published a second novel, *From a Seaside Town*, in 1970; but he is best known, as a writer of fiction, for his short stories. Among his collections are *One Way Ticket* (1961), *Thin Ice* (1979), and *Champagne Barn* (1984). Many of his stories have been broadcast by the CBC and the BBC, and have been translated and published throughout Europe. His translators in West Germany were the distinguished novelist Heinrich Böll and his wife.

Norman Levine's 'We All Begin in a Little Magazine', reprinted here, was originally written for broadcast on the CBC radio program *Anthology*, where many of his stories first appeared. It is included in *Champagne Barn* in the Penguin Short Fiction series.

JOYCE MARSHALL was born in 1913 in Montreal and educated at McGill University; but she has made her career as a writer, editor, and translator in Toronto. Her first novel, *Presently Tomorrow* (1946), was set in the Eastern Townships of Quebec in the early 1930s, and a second novel, *Lovers and Strangers* (1957), took place in Toronto in the late 1940s.

Among Marshall's translations are *Word from New France: The Selected Letters of Marie de l'Incarnation*, for which she wrote an important historical introduction, and *No Passport: A Discovery of Canada*, by the late Quebec travel writer Eugène Cloutier. Her translations of three books by Gabrielle Roy—*The Road Past Altamont*, *Windflower*, and *Enchanted Summer*—involved her in a close collaboration with that author; she was awarded the Canada Council Translation Prize in 1976 for her translation of *Enchanted Summer*.

Joyce Marshall's only collection of short stories, *A Private Place* (1975), brought together seven finely crafted stories written between the early 1950s and the 1970s. 'The Old Woman', reprinted here, is one of the earlier stories from that collection.

ALICE MUNRO (b. 1931) lives in Clinton in southwestern Ontario not far from Lake Huron and from another southwestern Ontario town, Wingham, where she was born and grew up. She attended the University of Western Ontario in London, and then lived for a number of years in Vancouver and Victoria, B.C., where her first husband owned a bookstore.

Munro began writing stories while she was at University. Her early stories were published in such magazines as *Chatelaine*, *The Canadian Forum*, *The Montrealer*, and *The Tamarack Review*. Her first collection, *Dance of the Happy Shades*, appeared in 1968 and won a Governor General's Award; her first novel,

Lives of Girls and Women (1971), won the Canadian Bookseller's Award in 1972. Three more collections of stories have been published: *Something I've Been Meaning to Tell You* (1974), *Who Do You Think You Are?* (1978), and *The Moons of Jupiter* (1982). *Who Do You Think You Are?* won a Governor General's Award and was a runner-up for the Booker Prize in the United Kingdom. Most of her recent stories first appeared in *The New Yorker*; one or two long stories and a memoir of her father were published in the New York literary quarterly *Grand Street*.

Several of Munro's stories have been dramatized for television; one of them, 'Boys and Girls', a production by Atlantis Films, Toronto, won an Academy Award in 1984. Her latest collection of stories is *The Progress of Love* (1986). 'The Peace of Utrecht' is reprinted from *Dance of the Happy Shades*.

BHARATI MUKHERJEE (b. 1940) was born in Calcutta, and lived in Montreal and Toronto from 1966 to 1980; she now lives in the United States. Her stay in Canada—which, she writes, 'proudly boasts of its opposition to the whole concept of cultural assimilation'—was in many ways not a happy one; in the United States, with some relief, she has discovered herself to be 'just another immigrant'.

The above quotations, which should be read in context, are from the introduction to Bharati Mukherjee's first collection of short stories, *Darkness*, published in the Penguin Short Fiction series in 1985. 'The Lady from Lucknow' is reprinted here from that book. Mukherjee is also the author of two novels, *The Tiger's Daughter* (1972) and *Wife* (1975)—both to be published in paperback by Penguin in 1987. Bharati Mukherjee is married to Clark Blaise; they were the co-authors of an unusual and attractive travel journal, *Days and Nights in Calcutta* (1977).

THOMAS RADDALL (b. 1903), whose father was an instructor in the British Army, was born while the family lived in married quarters at Hythe, England. His father was posted to Halifax in 1913, and Thomas Raddall's life has been associated with Nova Scotia ever since. He did not attend university, but served as a wireless operator on coastal stations and at sea. He then qualified as a bookkeeper, took a job with a lumber company, and soon began to write.

Raddall's many books display a wide range of interests. His historical novels include *His Majesty's Yankees* (1942), *Roger Sudden* (1944), and *Pride's Fancy* (1946). *The Nymph and the Lamp* (1950) is his major work of contemporary fiction. His non-fiction books include *Halifax, Warden of the North* (1948) and an interesting and candid autobiography, *In My Time* (1976).

Raddall began his writing career by publishing stories in *Blackwood's* and other magazines. Between 1939 and 1959 five collections of his short fiction appeared; the 1959 collection for the New Canadian Library, *At the Tide's Turn and Other Stories*, is a selection from the earlier books. 'The Wedding Gift' is an attractive example of Raddall's treatment of historical material in the short-story form.

JAMES REANEY (b. 1926) grew up on a farm near Stratford, Ontario, and now lives in London, where he has taught in the English department at the University of Western Ontario since 1960. He studied at the University of Toronto and from 1949 to 1956 taught at the University of Manitoba. As a writer of poetry, drama, fiction, and criticism—and through the magazine *Alphabet*, which he founded in 1960 and edited for ten years—he has made both the workaday and the mythic world of Southwestern Ontario the focus of his imaginative concerns.

Reaney's first book of poems, *The Red Heart* (1949), which won a Governor General's Award, was written while he was a student at the University of Toronto. *A Suit of Nettles* (1958) and *Twelve Letters to a Small Town* (1962) also won Governor General's Awards. Three other collections—*Poems* (1972), *Selected Shorter Poems* (1975), and *Selected Longer Poems* (1976)—were edited by Germaine Warkentin, whose extensive introductions provide important information about the poet.

Reaney was an established poet when he began a second career writing for the theatre. His early plays were published in *The Killdeer and Other Plays* (1962). John Hirsch staged *Colours in the Dark* at the Stratford Festival in 1967. Reaney's major dramatic work is *The Donnellys*, a trilogy about an Irish immigrant family massacred in Lucan, Ontario (not far from London), in 1880. These plays were first staged at Toronto's Tarragon Theatre between 1973 and 1975, and later toured Canada, from Vancouver to Halifax. 'The Bully', one of Reaney's few short stories, became widely known after it was broadcast in 1950, then anthologized.

MORDECAI RICHLER (b. 1931) grew up in the working-class Jewish neighbourhood around Montreal's St Urbain Street. He attended high school and briefly Sir George Williams College (now part of Concordia University) in downtown Montreal. In 1951 he went to Europe, where he spent two years, mostly in Paris; his first novel, *The Acrobats*, was published in England in 1954. Richler came back to Canada in 1952, but moved in 1959 to England, where he lived until his return to Montreal in 1972.

A prolific writer, Richler has worked in a variety of genres. His lively, abrasive journalism has been collected in several books, beginning with *Hunting Tigers Under Glass* (1968). (This book and the satirical novel *Cocksure*, also published in 1968, won a Governor General's Award for Richler.) He has edited anthologies, and is the author of a popular book for children, *Jacob Two-Two Meets the Hooded Fang* (1975). Richler has written for radio and television, the theatre, and films; his film scripts include *Life at the Top* and dramatizations of his own novels, *The Apprenticeship of Duddy Kravitz* and *Joshua Then and Now*. Since 1976 he has served on the editorial board of the Book-of-the-Month Club.

Richler has used his journalism and film scripts, at least in part, to buy time to write his novels. Notable for their wealth of character and incident, these include four major works: *Son of a Smaller Hero* (1955), *The Apprenticeship of Duddy Kravitz* (1959), *St Urbain's Horseman* (1971), and *Joshua Then and Now* (1980).

St Urbain Street, which plays a role in all these novels, is also celebrated in the short stories, including 'The Summer My Grandmother was Supposed to Die', collected in *The Street* (1969).

Sir CHARLES G.D. ROBERTS (1860–1943) was born in Douglas, New Brunswick, and educated at the University of New Brunswick. He published an important and influential poetry collection, *Orion and Other Poems*, when he was just twenty. After teaching at King's College in Windsor, Nova Scotia, for ten years, he supported himself by writing from 1897 to 1925 and lived abroad, in New York, in England, and on the Continent. He served with the British Army and then was attached to the Canadian War Records Office in London during the First World War. From 1925 until the end of his life Roberts lived in Toronto. He was knighted in 1935.

A major Canadian poet with an international reputation, Roberts also wrote romances for adult readers, edited anthologies, prepared guide books, published *A History of Canada* in 1897, and *Canada in Flanders* (1918), the third volume of Lord Beaverbrook's history of the Canadian forces in the First World War. But it was as a writer of animal stories that Roberts was most productive and most popular. 'Do Seek Their Meat from God' was his first published animal story—it appeared in *Harper's* in December 1892—and it was included in his first book of animal stories, *Earth's Enigmas: A Book of Animal and Nature Life* (1896). Almost twenty more books of animal stories appeared, the last one, *Further Animal Stories*, in 1936. These stories were remarkable for their lack of sentimentality and for being based on direct and careful observation.

LEON ROOKE was born in 1934 in North Carolina and educated there. He served in the U.S. Army in Alaska from 1958 to 1960, and taught English and creative writing in several American universities before moving to Victoria, B.C. in 1969. In 1981 he won the Canada-Australia literary prize, and in 1984–5 he was writer-in-residence at the University of Toronto. With the writer John Metcalf he edited two volumes of *The New Press Anthology*, lively anthologies of short fiction by Canadian writers.

Rooke has contributed many stories to literary magazines in Canada and the United States, and since 1968 has published almost a dozen books—both novels and short-story collections. His novels include *Fat Woman* (1980) and *Shakespeare's Dog* (1983), which won a Governor General's Award. Among his short-story collections are *The Broad Back of the Angel* (1977), *The Birth Control King of the Upper Volta* (1982), *Sing Me No Love Songs, I'll Say You No Prayers* (1984), and *A Bolt of White Cloth* (also 1984). Critics have described Rooke as a 'post-realistic' and a 'post-modernist' writer. Imaginative titles are a Leon Rooke trademark. His fiction is notable for its portraits of strong, exuberant women and often for its humour, as in 'The Woman Who Talked to Horses', reprinted here from *Sing Me No Love Songs, I'll Say You No Prayers*.

SINCLAIR ROSS was born in 1908 on a homestead near Prince Albert, Saskatchewan. After finishing high school he worked as a bank clerk, first in a succession of small towns in Saskatchewan, then in Winnipeg, and finally in Montreal until his retirement in 1968. He now lives in Vancouver.

Ross's first novel, *As For Me and My House*, attracted only modest attention when it was published in 1941, but later came to be regarded as a central work in the development of Canadian fiction. He published three later novels: *The Well* (1958), *Whir of Gold* (1970), and *Sawbones Memorial* (1974).

Beginning in 1934 Ross published almost twenty short stories, most of which first appeared in the magazine *Queen's Quarterly*. They have been reprinted in two collections: *The Lamp at Noon and Other Stories* (1968, with an introduction by Margaret Laurence) and *The Race and Other Stories* (1982). Like *As For Me and My House*, many of Ross's stories explore the grim realities of life on isolated farms and in small villages during the drought and Depression years on the Canadian prairies.

JANE RULE (b. 1931) was born in Plainfield, New Jersey, and grew up in various parts of the American mid-west and in California. She attended Mills College in California and did graduate work at University College, London. In 1956 she moved to Vancouver, and taught from time to time at the University of British Columbia. Since 1976 she has lived on Galiano Island, B.C.

Jane Rule has published four novels. Her first, *Desert of the Heart* (1964), which is set in Reno, Nevada, and explores a developing lesbian relationship, became the basis for the film *Desert Hearts*, released in 1986 to good reviews and substantial audiences in the larger cities of Canada and the United States. She has published three collections of short stories: *Themes for Diverse Instruments* (1975), *Outlander* (1981), and *Inward Passage* (1985), from which 'Slogans' has been reprinted here. Rule is also the author of *Lesbian Images* (1975)—which discusses such writers as Radclyffe Hall, Colette, and Vita Sackville West—and of a more recent essay collection, *Hot-Eyed Moderate* (1985). Best known for her writings on lesbian themes, she also deals frequently with children and family life in her fiction.

GLORIA SAWAI was born in 1932 in Minneapolis, Minnesota, but her parents moved to Saskatchewan when she was a year old, and she grew up in Saskatchewan and Alberta. A graduate of Camrose Lutheran College in Camrose, Alberta, where she now lives, she received an MFA degree in writing from the University of Montana. Her short stories have appeared in *Grain*, *NeWest Review*, *82:Best Canadian Stories*, and in an anthology of work by three Alberta writers, *3x5*. Playwrights Canada published her play *Neighbour* (1981).

DUNCAN CAMPBELL SCOTT (1862–1947) was born in Ottawa, the son of a Methodist missionary, and grew up in small towns in Ontario and Quebec. A poet and short-story writer, he is associated with Roberts, Carman, and Lampman;

all four writers were born in the early 1860s, all first published in the 1880s and 1890s, and all were romantic poets who drew their inspiration from Canadian nature. When Scott's formal education ended at seventeen, his father arranged a job interview with Sir John A. Macdonald. The boy then took a position in the Department of Indian Affairs and stayed there for fifty-two years; he was deputy superintendent from 1923 until his retirement in 1932.

A few years after Scott's appointment, Archibald Lampman joined the civil service, and it was he who encouraged Scott to write poetry. (When Lampman died in 1899 Scott became his literary executor, and in time edited four collections of his poems.) Scott's first book of poetry, *The Magic House and Other Poems* appeared in 1893, and his last book, *The Circle of Affection*, containing poems, essays, and short stories, was published the year he died.

Scott published two collections of short stories, *In the Village of Viger* (1896) and *The Witching of Elspie* (1923), both of which have influenced the development of the short story in Canada. *In the Village of Viger*—linked nostalgic tales of life in a quiet village near Montreal—was the precursor of similar collections by Leacock, Margaret Laurence, Alice Munro, Jack Hodgins, Edna Alford, Sandra Birdsell, and others.

RAY SMITH (b. 1941) was born in Cape Breton, Nova Scotia. He has lived in Toronto and in the Maritimes and since 1968 in Montreal, where he teaches English at Dawson College. The title story from his first collection of short stories, *Cape Breton is the Thought Control Centre of Canada* (1969), is reprinted here. A second book of stories, *Lord Nelson Tavern*, appeared in 1974, and *Century*, a collection of linked stories, in 1986. Ray Smith is slated to be writer-in-residence at the University of Alberta, Edmonton, in 1986–7.

AUDREY THOMAS was born in 1935 in Binghamton, N.Y., and educated at Smith College in the U.S. and St Andrews University in Scotland. She and her ex-husband immigrated to Canada in 1959, though in the mid-sixties she lived for three years in Ghana, where her husband was teaching at the time. The United States, Canada, and West Africa have all provided settings for her fiction. In recent years she has combined her own writing with periods of teaching at the University of Victoria and the University of British Columbia. In the academic year 1985–6 she was writer-in-residence at the Centre of Canadian Studies at the University of Edinburgh in the annual exchange program of Canadian and Scottish writers that is supported by the Canada Council and the Scottish Arts Council.

Thomas's first book, published in 1967, was a collection of short stories, *Ten Green Bottles*. Her other fiction includes novels (*Mrs Blood*; *Blown Figures*), two related novellas published in one volume (*Munchmeyer* and *Prospero on the Island*), and two more collections of stories, *Real Mothers* and *Two in the Bush and Other Stories*, both published in 1981.

A collection of recent stories, *Goodbye Harold, Good Luck* was published in the Penguin Short Fiction series in 1986. Volume 10, Numbers 3 & 4 of the Vancouver literary quarterly *Room of One's Own* (published in March, 1986) is an Audrey Thomas Issue that includes a substantial interview with the author, new fiction, comments by fellow writers and critics, and a select bibliography.

W.D. VALGARDSON (b. 1939) grew up in Gimli, a town in the Interlake District of Manitoba not far from Winnipeg, whose inhabitants are mostly of Icelandic descent. He was educated at United College in Winnipeg, the University of Manitoba, and the University of Iowa, where—like W.P. Kinsella and a number of other Canadian writers—he was enrolled in the university's influential Writer's Workshop. Valgardson has published three collections of short stories: *Bloodflowers* (1973), *God is Not a Fish Inspector* (1975), and *Red Dust* (1978). He is also the author of a book of poetry, *In the Gutting Shed* (1978), and a novel *Gentle Sinners*, which won the 'Books in Canada' First Novel Award for 1980. *Gentle Sinners* and several of Valgardson's short stories have been filmed for television.

Much of Valgardson's fiction deals with situations in which poverty, isolation, and random violence are commonplace. 'Bloodflowers', from his first collection of short stories, is a powerful example of his talent.

GUY VANDERHAEGHE was born in 1951 in Esterhazy, Sask. He studied history at the University of Saskatchewan, where he wrote an M.A. thesis about the novelist John Buchan. He has worked as a teacher, archivist, and researcher, and is now a full-time writer living in Saskatoon.

Vanderhaeghe began writing short stories in the late 1970s, influenced—as the critic David Staines has noted—by such prairie novelists as Margaret Laurence, Sinclair Ross, and Robert Kroetsch. Other major influences have been Alice Munro and certain writers from the American South for their treatment of small-town life. Vanderhaeghe's stories were published widely in Canadian literary magazines, and in 1980 his story 'The Watcher' won the annual contributor's prize awarded by *Canadian Fiction Magazine*. Twelve of his stories appeared in the collection *Man Descending* (1982), which won a Governor General's Award. *The Trouble with Heroes*, a second collection of stories, was published in 1983. 'The Dancing Bear' is from *Man Descending*.

HELEN WEINZWEIG (b. 1915) came to Canada from Poland at the age of nine. She attended high school in Toronto, but had to give up her schooling during the Depression to go to work as a stenographer and later as a receptionist and a salesperson. She married the musician and composer John Weinzweig in 1940. They live in Toronto. She did not publish her first novel *Passing Ceremony* until she was 57. Her second novel, *Basic Black with Pearls*, appeared in 1980 and won the City of Toronto Book Award in 1981. Both books are short novels— the longer of the two, *Basic Black with Pearls*, is only 135 pages; fantastical, perceptive, comic, and pathetic in turn, they are the work of a writer who has read widely in European and North American fiction.

Helen Weinzweig's short stories, so far uncollected, have been published in *Jewish Dialog*, *The Tamarack Review*, *Saturday Night*, *The Canadian Forum*, *The Fiddlehead*, and other magazines, and broadcast by the CBC. 'Causation', which is reprinted here, appeared in *Small Wonders: new stories by twelve distinguished Canadian writers* (1982).

RUDY WIEBE was born near Fairholme, Saskatchewan, of parents who came to Canada from the Soviet Union in 1930. He attended a Mennonite High School in Coaldale, Alberta, and the University of Alberta in Edmonton, where he now teaches English and creative writing. He has published seven novels and has edited half-a-dozen short story anthologies. Two of his novels, *Peace Shall Destroy Many* (1962) and *The Blue Mountains of China* (1970), portray the Mennonite experience in the New World. *First and Vital Candle* (1966) is about Indian and Eskimo life in the Canadian North. Both *The Temptations of Big Bear* (1973), a Governor General's Award winner, and *The Scorched-Wood People* (1977) deal with the nineteenth-century rebellions of the Indians and Métis in the Canadian Northwest.

Wiebe's stories have been collected in *Where Is the Voice Coming From?* (1974) and *The Angel of the Tar Sands and Other Stories* (1982). He has edited *Stories from Western Canada* (1972), *Stories from Pacific and Arctic Canada* (1974, with Andreas Schroeder), and *More Stories from Western Canada* (1980, with Aritha Van Herk).

ETHEL WILSON, born in Port Elizabeth, South Africa, in 1888, was orphaned at the age of ten and was sent to live with her grandmother in Vancouver. She was educated in boarding schools in England and Vancouver, and taught in the Vancouver school system from 1907 until 1920. In 1921 she married Dr Wallace Wilson, who had a distinguished medical career, including a term as president of the Canadian Medical Association. She died in Vancouver in 1980.

Ethel Wilson began writing in her fifties; her first novel, *Hetty Dorval*, was not published until 1947. Her other long fiction includes the novel *The Innocent Traveller* (1949); two novellas published in one volume as *The Equations of Love* (1952); and two further novels, *Swamp Angel* (1954) and *Love and Salt Water* (1956). The setting for most of Wilson's fiction is Canada's West Coast, as is the case with 'From Flores', which is taken from her collection *Mrs Golightly and Other Stories* (1961). Ethel Wilson's sensibility, intelligence, and unique style, as well as her ability to carve out a literary career late in life, made her an example for such younger women writers as Margaret Laurence, Jane Rule, and Alice Munro (all represented in this book).

Index of Authors